English G 21

A5
für Gymnasien

Cornelsen

English G 21 • Band A 5

Im Auftrag des Verlages herausgegeben von
Prof. Hellmut Schwarz, Mannheim
Jörg Rademacher, Ilvesheim

Erarbeitet von
Laurence Harger, Wellington, Neuseeland
Susan Abbey, Nenagh, Irland
Barbara Derkow Disselbeck, Köln
Allen J. Woppert, Berlin
sowie Claire Lamsdale, Llangybi, Wales

unter Mitarbeit von
Wolfgang Biederstädt, Köln
Joachim Blombach, Herford
Helmut Dengler, Limbach
John Eastwood, Street, England
Dr. Annette Leithner-Brauns, Dresden
Jörg Rademacher, Ilvesheim
Jennifer Seidl, München
Sabine Tudan, Erfurt
sowie Uwe Chormann, Eiselthum; Udo Wagner, Voerde;
Heike Wirant, Jena

in Zusammenarbeit mit der Englischredaktion
Dr. Christiane Kallenbach (Projektleitung);
Dr. Christian v. Raumer (verantwortlicher Redakteur);
Susanne Bennetreu (Bildredaktion); Britta Bensmann;
Christiane Bonk; Dr. Philip Devlin; Gareth Evans;
Bonnie S. Glänzer; Mara Leibowitz; Uwe Tröger;
Klaus G. Unger *sowie* Ulrike Berendt

Beratende Mitwirkung
Peter Brünker, Bad Kreuznach; Helga Estor, Darmstadt;
Katja Fabel, Freiburg; Anette Fritsch, Dillenburg;
Patrick Handschuh, Köln; Ulrich Imig, Wildeshausen;
Bernd Koch, Marburg; Thomas Neidhardt, Bielefeld;
Wolfgang Neudecker, Mannheim; Birgit Ohmsieder,
Berlin; Albert Rau, Brühl; Angela Ringel-Eichinger,
Bietigheim-Bissingen; Dr. Jana Schubert, Genf/Leipzig;
Sieglinde Spranger, Chemnitz; Marcel Sprunkel, Köln;
Harald Weißling, Mannheim; Monika Wilkening,
Wehretal

Illustrationen
Silke Bachmann, Hamburg; Roland Beier, Berlin;
Carlos Borrell, Berlin; Dylan Gibson, Pitlochry; Christian
Görke, Berlin; Graham-Cameron Illustration, UK: Eoin
Coveney; Alfred Schüssler, Frankfurt/Main

Layoutkonzept
Aksinia Raphael; Korinna Wilkes

Technische Umsetzung
Aksinia Raphael; Korinna Wilkes;
Stephan Hilleckenbach; Rainer Bachmaier

Umschlaggestaltung
Klein & Halm Grafikdesign, Berlin

www.cornelsen.de
www.EnglishG.de

Die Webseiten Dritter, deren Internetadressen in diesem Lehrwerk angegeben sind, wurden vor Drucklegung sorgfältig geprüft. Der Verlag übernimmt keine Gewähr für die Aktualität und den Inhalt dieser Seiten oder solcher, die mit ihnen verlinkt sind.

Alle Drucke dieser Auflage sind inhaltlich unverändert und können im Unterricht nebeneinander verwendet werden.

Einige der in diesem Druck verwendeten Bilder können sich von denen in vorherigen Drucken dieser Auflage unterscheiden. Der Austausch dieser Bilder war aus urheberrechtlichen Gründen notwendig, um Ihnen die Inhalte auch digital zur Verfügung stellen zu können.

© 2010 Cornelsen Verlag, Berlin
© 2018 Cornelsen Verlag GmbH, Berlin

Das Werk und seine Teile sind urheberrechtlich geschützt. Jede Nutzung in anderen als den gesetzlich zugelassenen Fällen bedarf der vorherigen schriftlichen Einwilligung des Verlages.
Hinweis zu §§ 60a, 60b UrhG: Weder das Werk noch seine Teile dürfen ohne eine solche Einwilligung an Schulen oder in Unterrichts- und Lehrmedien (§ 60b Abs. 3 UrhG) vervielfältigt, insbesondere kopiert oder eingescannt, verbreitet oder in ein Netzwerk eingestellt oder sonst öffentlich zugänglich gemacht oder wiedergegeben werden.
Dies gilt auch für Intranets von Schulen.

Druck und Bindung: Livonia Print, Riga

2. Auflage, 2. Druck 2018
broschiert
ISBN 978-3-06-031308-2
ISBN 978-3-06-032915-1 (E-Book)

1. Auflage, 4. Druck 2014
gebunden
ISBN 978-3-06-031358-7

PEFC zertifiziert
Dieses Produkt stammt aus nachhaltig bewirtschafteten Wäldern und kontrollierten Quellen.
www.pefc.de
PEFC/12-31-006

Dein Englischbuch enthält folgende Teile:

Units 1 2 3 4	die vier Kapitel des Buches
Getting ready for a test	Hier kannst du dich gezielt auf einen Test vorbereiten.
EXTRA: Text File	viele interessante Texte zum Lesen (passend zu den Units)
Skills File (SF)	Beschreibung wichtiger Lern- und Arbeitstechniken
Grammar File (GF)	Zusammenfassung der Grammatik
Vocabulary	Wörterverzeichnis zum Lernen der neuen Wörter jeder Unit
Dictionary	alphabetisches englisch-deutsches Wörterverzeichnis zum Nachschlagen

Die Units bestehen aus diesen Teilen:

Lead-in	Einstieg in das neue Thema
Part A, B, C, D	neuer Lernstoff mit vielen Aktivitäten
Practice	Übungen

In den Units findest du diese Überschriften und Symbole:

Exploring language	Hier lernst du anhand von Beispielen, neue sprachliche Strukturen zu verstehen und richtig anzuwenden.
STUDY SKILLS	Einführung in Lern- und Arbeitstechniken
Dossier	Schöne und wichtige Arbeiten kannst du in einer Mappe sammeln.
SPEAKING COURSE	Sprechkurs in vier Kapiteln mit nützlichen sprachlichen Hilfen
EVERYDAY ENGLISH	Übungen zum Bewältigen wichtiger Alltagssituationen
MEDIATION	Hier vermittelst du zwischen zwei Sprachen.
VIEWING	Aufgaben zu Filmausschnitten
Now you	Hier sprichst und schreibst du über dich selbst.
REVISION	Übungen zur Wiederholung
WORDS	Übungen zu Wortfeldern und Wortverbindungen
Extra	zusätzliche Aktivitäten und Übungen
👥 👥👥	Partnerarbeit / Gruppenarbeit
🎧 🎧	nur auf CD / auf CD und im Schülerbuch
🎥	Filmausschnitte auf DVD

Contents

Die folgenden Angebote sind nicht obligatorisch abzuarbeiten. Die Auswahl der Übungen und Übungsteile richtet sich nach den Schwerpunkten des schulinternen Curriculums.

| Australia | The road ahead | Life in the big city | Teen world |

6 Unit 1 Australia

Lead-in Blog from Oz **Part A** Australia **Part B** Two Australian teenagers **Part C** The Aboriginal people of Australia **Part D** TEXT: In the outback	**Grammatical structures** • REVISION infinitive constructions (verb + object + *to*-infinitive; after question words) • REVISION tenses • *to*-infinitives instead of relative clauses **Word fields** • weather • animals • sports • teenage life • travelling • small talk	**STUDY SKILLS** Talking about statistics Reading literature (1–3): plot, setting, atmosphere, characters **SPEAKING COURSE (1)** Having a conversation **EVERYDAY ENGLISH** Writing an e-mail **VIEWING** Rabbit-proof fence (scene from a film)

26 Extra Revision – Getting ready for a test 1

32 Unit 2 The road ahead

Lead-in Young people's plans and expectations **Part A** Personality quiz **Part B** A year abroad **Part C** The Business: A reality TV show **Part D** TEXT: How to be a teenage millionaire	**Grammatical structures** • REVISION infinitive constructions • REVISION gerunds (as subject/object of verbs; after phrases with prepositions; after prepositions) • gerund with its own subject • gerund vs. infinitive **Word fields** • personal qualities • describing people • interests • qualifications • education • hobbies, interests • work experience	**STUDY SKILLS** Writing formal letters Using a grammar Visual aids in presentations **SPEAKING COURSE (2)** Asking for, confirming, giving information **VIEWING** The interviews (scenes from a reality TV show)

50 Unit 3 Life in the big city

Lead-in A world of cities?
Part A Hong Kong: full speed ahead
Part B Johannesburg: city of contrasts
Part C Mumbai: people of the city

Grammatical structures
- REVISION participle clauses instead of relative clauses
- participles as adjectives
- participle clauses instead of adverbial clauses
- participles to provide extra information and for linking
- verbs of perception + object + present participle
- participles after verbs of rest and motion

Word fields
- cities and city life
- geography
- economy

STUDY SKILLS
Summarizing a non-fictional text
SPEAKING COURSE (3)
Giving an oral summary
EVERYDAY ENGLISH
Changing your flight
VIEWING
Hong Kong: Live it. Love it! (promotional video)

70 Extra Revision – Getting ready for a test 2

78 Unit 4 Teen world

Lead-in Teenagers – interests, activities, problems
Part A Mobile life and love
Part B Teens in trouble
Part C Get involved
Part D TEXT: The caller

Grammatical structures
- REVISION participle constructions
- REVISION future tenses
- future perfect, future progressive, simple present with future meaning
- let/make sb. do sth., have sth. done

Word fields
- you and your mobile
- teenage language
- youth culture
- agreeing and disagreeing
- growing up

STUDY SKILLS
Argumentative writing
Using an English–English dictionary
Reading literature (4): suspense
SPEAKING COURSE (4)
Having a discussion
EVERYDAY ENGLISH
Asking someone out
VIEWING
High school boot camp (scenes from a documentary)

96 Partner B
99 **Extra** Text File
  100 TF **1:** Project: The magic of Australia _____ (zu Unit 1)
  102 **TF 2** **Bilingual module** Ecosystems in Australia ____ (zu Unit 1)
  104 TF **3:** Australian signs _____ (zu Unit 1)
  105 TF **4:** The right advice? _____ (zu Unit 2)
  106 TF **5:** Going to school in England _____ (zu Unit 2)
  107 TF **6:** Mr. Wah goes to Hong Kong _____ (zu Unit 3)
  109 TF **7:** Black music, white music _____ (zu Unit 3)
  110 TF **8:** Project: Your big cities _____ (zu Unit 3)
  112 TF **9:** A lover's embrace _____ (zu Unit 3)
  113 TF **10:** Luuurve debate _____ (zu Unit 4)
  115 TF **11:** Who's guilty? _____ (zu Unit 4)
  120 **TF 12** **Bilingual module** A different kind of justice (zu Unit 4)

123 Skills File
153 Grammar File
164 Grammatical terms
167 Vocabulary
195 Dictionary (English–German)
237 Countries and continents
238 List of names
239 English sounds/The English alphabet
240 Irregular verbs
242 Classroom English
244 Acknowledgments
247 Key to *Getting ready for a test 1* and *2*
248 English-speaking countries

Unit 1 Australia

Down under in Australia

Judith in Oz

About me

I'm Judith, 15. Born & grew up in Cologne, Germany. Now live in Melbourne, Victoria, Australia. Yay! Mum's German and Dad's an Aussie, so I'm half German and half Australian. That's cool coz I speak both German and English.

- Subscribe to this blog.
- View my complete profile.
- Click here for my photos.
- Click here for my sound file to go with the photos.
- Please write to me here.

➡ LATEST:

19th November

It's getting hot now! Just back from a 'barbie' – that's a barbecue, not a dolls' party ;-) – at my friend Ella's house. There's a party nearly every weekend here coz we're too young to get into bars and clubs. Riley came too. He called me Jude, like my friends do.

➡ OLDER BLOGS:

14th October

All Aussies are sports-mad and it's catching! I used to be a couch potato and now I'm learning to surf. It's hard but so cool how the waves carry you to the beach – and you have to surf if you want to be a fair dinkum Aussie. Also, the surf instructor, Riley, is seriously gorgeous!

30th September

I know, I know – I haven't written for ages. Sorry! It's spring holiday and I've just come back from a 5-day hike in the bush. Amazing, but a bit scary too. One evening a kookaburra (the weirdest bird!) stole a sausage from my plate and the next day a snake fell out of a tree onto another girl's arm. She really freaked out!

24th July

Life is less magical now – school has started! The school year has four terms in Australia and this is Term 3. We begin at 8.30 – no worries, but then we have to stay at school until 3.15! And after that there are lots of extracurricular activities like sport, music or debates. And when that's all over, there's homework. I suppose school is going to fill my days now. :-(

22nd July

Melbourne is very beautiful and very big: pop. 3 million. My first view of the city was awesome – the Yarra River, the skyscrapers, the sea – magical.

1

09th July

Just arrived. My first night in my dad's home town in Oz – too excited to sleep so I'm beginning this blog. (I promised it to my mates and English teacher back in Cologne.) As we flew across Australia for hours, south towards Melbourne, I looked out of the window. The land seemed to go on forever. It was mainly flat and red dirt roads cut across the endless, dry outback. It looked so huge and empty and I suddenly felt very, very small – and a bit scared. When I got off the plane I got a shock. I'd left Cologne on a hot July day, but here 'down under', on the other side of the world, it was a cold winter's day.

1 Life in Australia 🎧

a) Read Judith's blog and write down five things that are new, interesting or surprising to you.

b) Now listen to Judith's sound file. What sounds can you hear?

c) 👥 Listen again and take notes on what you find out about the photos. Compare your notes with a partner's.

d) Extra 👥👥 Imagine you're in one of the photos and tell your group about it. How do you feel? What are you doing? Who are you with? What can you see, smell and hear?

e) Explain why you would/wouldn't like to go to Australia. Collect all the pros and cons in class.

f) Extra Write a comment for Judith's blog.

2 Extra Australia project

Choose one of the project topics from TF 1 on pp. 100–101. As you go through the unit, collect useful ideas, information, words and phrases for your project. (You might even do it in a blog.)

▶ Text File 1 *(pp. 100–101)* • SF Project skills *(pp. 132–133)* • WB 1–2 *(p. 2)*

Background File | AUSTRALIA

1 Australian geography
Take notes while you work.

Quick facts

Flag:

Area: 7,686,850 sq km
Population: 21.2 million
Capital: Canberra (334,000)
Largest city: Sydney (4.3 million)

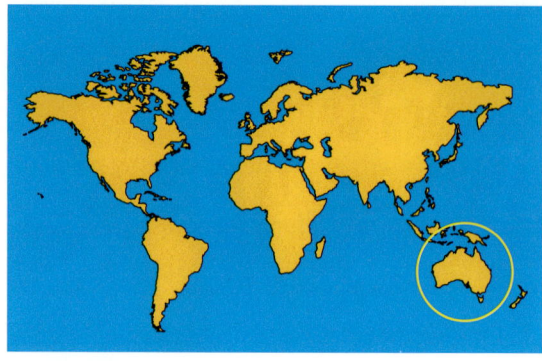

a) Look at the Australian flag. What other flag is in it? Why do you think that is? What could the stars mean?

b) Explain why Australia is often called 'Down Under'.

c) Look at the map of Australia on the front inside cover. Use the map and the Quick facts box to compare Australia and Germany (size, population, type of landscape, time zones, transport, …).

d) **Extra** Discover another interesting piece of information on the map of Australia.

2 Three aspects of Australia
Work in groups of three. Each student works on a different section – A, B or C.
Read your section and take notes on it so that you can pass on information to the others in your group.

A A short history of Australia

Over 40,000 years ago, humans first started to arrive in Australia from Asia. They spread all over the huge continent. Trade routes for stone, wood, shells and other goods crossed the country. These Aborigines changed the landscape with fire and developed the oldest rock art in the world. Their stories of the 'Dreaming' told how they thought the world was created.

Nobody knows how many Aborigines were living in Australia when the first Europeans came in the 16th century, but the figure was probably between 300,000 and 1 million. Despite that, in 1770 Captain James Cook claimed the world's largest island for Britain. In 1788 the British started a colony for convicts in what is now Sydney. Over the next 80 years, Britain brought over 160,000 convicts to Australia.

Other immigrants arrived and together with the former convicts, they started colonies in different parts of the continent. The colonies became states, and in 1901 Australia was founded and became independent.

During all this time, many Aboriginal people were killed, either by the Europeans or by the diseases the Europeans brought, until at the beginning of the 20th century there were only about 150,000 left. Today their numbers have risen again to 455,000, but they have always had to fight hard for equal rights.

In the 20th century Australia kept its close links to Britain and fought with the British in both world wars. Since the 1970s Australia has done more and more business with Asia, and large numbers of immigrants now come to Australia from Asian countries.

Be sunsmart

Australia has the highest rate of skin cancer in the world. Why is that?

- Most Australians are of European origin so their skin is fair. But Australia is much closer to the equator than Europe, so it has a different climate and the sun is stronger.
- Australians like to spend lots of time outside, at the beach, at barbecues, by the pool and doing sport.
- A suntan is seen as cool and healthy.
- Australia is not far from the Antarctic ozone hole, which means that more ultraviolet rays get through the earth's atmosphere.

Take five steps to protect yourself from the sun:

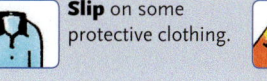

Slip on some protective clothing.

Slop on some sunscreen.

Slap on a hat.

Seek shade.

Slide on some sunglasses.

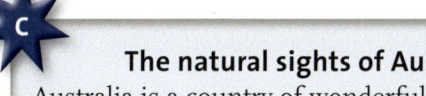

The natural sights of Australia

Australia is a country of wonderful natural sights, from rainforests to deserts, and unique wildlife like the kangaroo, koala and emu.

One of Australia's most famous natural sights is the Great Barrier Reef, the largest coral reef in the world and the only living thing on earth that can be seen from space with the naked eye. More than 2,000 km long, the reef is home to about 1,500 species of fish, 200 species of birds and 400 species of corals. Dolphins, whales, sea snakes and saltwater crocodiles can also be seen there.

Sadly, the reef is in danger. The oceans around Australia – like the rest of the world – are getting warmer and corals die if the water temperature rises by more than a few degrees. Other dangers to the reef include pollution from rivers, farms and cities on the coast, more and more tourists, the crown-of-thorns starfish and overfishing.

▶ Text File 2 *(pp. 102–103)* • Text File 3 *(p. 104)* • WB 3–5 *(pp. 3–4)*

3 Information exchange

a) Use the notes you have taken and give the others in your group the important information from your section. Try to make your talk interesting.

b) Take notes on what the others tell you. Ask questions if anything is unclear.

4 Australian facts and figures

STUDY SKILLS | Talking about statistics

A chart or table's title tells you what it is about. **Tables** show detailed figures clearly in columns. **Bar charts** are often used to compare the number or size of things. **Pie charts** help you to compare the different sections that make up the pie. Make sure you know what the figures mean – percentages or numbers. Look at them carefully and explain what they show. If possible, compare or contrast different figures, or say how they are connected.

a) *Partner A: Explain the table to your partner.*
This table shows …
Partner B: Explain the bar chart to your partner.
This bar chart compares …

b) *Look at the table and the bar chart and explain what they tell you.*
The table shows … and the bar chart gives us …
From these figures we can see …

c) *In writing, explain what the pie chart shows. Give details. Finish with a conclusion.*
The pie chart shows …
There are … main …

Table:

Country	Population (2008)
USA	304,721,000
Germany	82,400,996
UK	60,776,238
Australia	21,373,760

Bar chart:

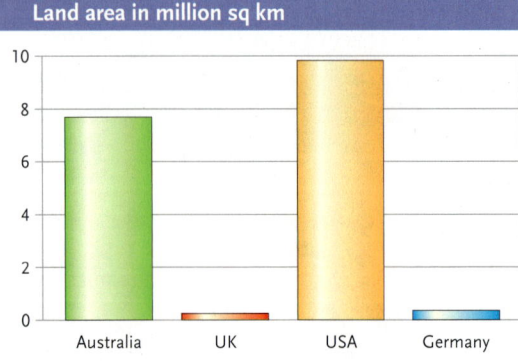

Pie chart:

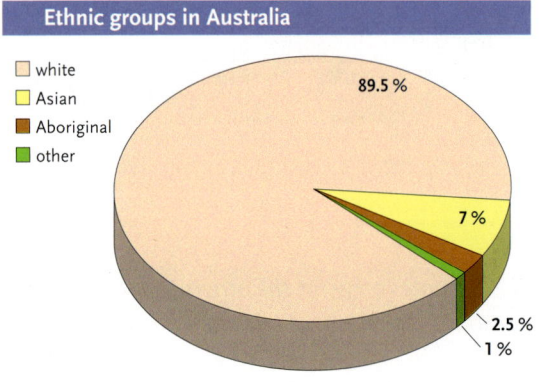

Useful language
– The (pie) chart/table is about …
– It shows the different … in/of …
– It compares the size/number of … with …
– It is divided into … sections which show …
– The figures show that …
– … has the largest/second-largest/smallest …
  … is twice/three times/… as big as …
– A huge majority/small minority is …
– They make up … % of …
– There are more than/nearly twice as many … as there are …
– You can see that … is … but/while …
– So that shows that …
– To conclude, you can say …

d) **Extra** *Look for more statistics about Australia on the internet (temperatures, fires, largest cities/rivers, sport, …). Find a chart or table and explain it to your partner.*
Present your findings to the class.

▶ SF Talking about statistics (p. 127)

Part A B C D   Practice   1

P1 WORDS Time phrases

a) Read 'A short history of Australia' on page 8. Write down all the time phrases you can find.
– over 40,000 years ago
– …

b) 👥 Read them aloud to your partner and make sure you understand what all the phrases mean. Add more time phrases you know. Many begin with words like:
after, before, on, at, in, since, for, until, while, during, …
– After we moved to Berlin …
– Before the 20th century …
– Since 2006 …
– …

c) Extra Write your 'family history'. Use as many time phrases as possible. Be careful with your tenses. You could start like this:
My family has lived in … since …
When my great-grandfather moved from … in …

P2 WORDS More than one meaning

a) 👥 Find the following words and work out together what their German translation is in this context. (Only use a dictionary if you really have to.)
Page 6: bush; cool
Page 8: close; left
Page 9: fair; spend; step

b) All these English words have at least one more German translation. Write down as many as you can.

c) Extra Choose three of the words from a) and use them to write six sentences.
I spent three hours on this report. I also spent a lot of money on books to help me write the report.
…

P3 STUDY SKILLS Talking about statistics

Write about the bar charts on the right. Explain
– what the charts are about
– what they compare
– how they are connected
– what the connection tells you

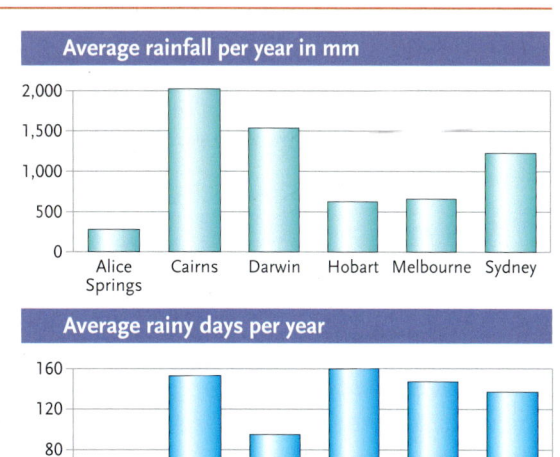

▶ WB 6–7 (pp. 4–5)

TWO AUSTRALIAN TEENAGERS

1 Jeannie – in the middle of nowhere

Read Jeannie's e-mail. Then write captions for the photos.

Hi Cath,
It was great to get your e-mail. Yes, I'd love to be your online friend, although I don't honestly think my life in western Queensland is as exciting as your life in Hong Kong.

My dad works here on a sheep station, so we live in the middle of nowhere. There are only twenty other people on the station but thousands and thousands of sheep. The nearest town is 300 miles away, so we don't have a local cinema, or doctor or even a school! But I still have school. My school is the Alice Springs School of the Air. It's cool! It comes to me through my computer. That means I don't have to sit in a classroom all day! (I can even take my laptop outside and do my work under a tree!) But I can talk to the teacher and class every day. Although Alice Springs is 800 miles away, my teachers are in a studio so I can even see them. A lot of our class have webcams, so we can see each other too. We're good friends although we only meet about three times a year at one-week courses.

You talk about your sports and hobbies – dragon boat racing, tennis and discos. Well, mine are a bit different! There's no one here at the station my age, so I have to do things on my own a lot. I ride every day – which is great. (I have my own horse, Sally.) And because we live in the middle of nowhere I'm allowed to drive a dirt bike, which is great fun.

I'm attaching some photos. Please mail again soon.
Your new online friend,
Jeannie

A

B

C

2 Now you

a) Make a table and compare your school with the School of the Air. Headings could be:
times, teacher, lessons, rooms, students, …

b) **Think:** What are the advantages and disadvantages of the School of the Air?
Pair: Compare with a partner.
Share: Discuss with another pair
– It would be boring/fun/…
– I would miss/hate/love/…
– Studying would be easier/harder because …

3 Extra Royal Flying Doctor Service

Isolated sheep stations in the outback don't have local doctors, but people can call the Royal Flying Doctor Service (RFDS). Find out more about the service and how it works.
Write a short report, illustrate it and put it in your DOSSIER.

▶ *SF Research (p. 128)*

4 Rob – sports-mad in Sydney 🎧

a) Listen to Rob. Make a list of the sports he talks about. Which ones are not on this page?

b) Listen again. What are Rob's three favourite sports? Take notes so that you can give reasons for your answer.

c) 👥 Which of the sports in your list interest you most? Why? Have you ever done any of them? Can you do them where you live?
A: I'd love to learn how to surf. It must be so exciting. But how can I? I live 600 km from the sea!
B: I'm not sure about surfing, but …

5 Now you

a) 👥 Work in groups of four. This is your topic: 'Differences between city or country life in Australia and Germany.'
On a piece of paper, write a statement or question on the topic, then pass it on clockwise. On the next piece of paper you get, write a reaction, answer the question, or write a new statement. Go on till you get your first piece of paper back. Now discuss your results. One student presents your group's results to the class.

b) **Extra** If you could visit Jeannie or Rob for a week, who would you choose? Explain why.

Part B Practice

SPEAKING COURSE Part 1

P1 SPEAKING Good to meet you (Having a conversation)

a) If you want to talk to somebody you don't know, you may have to
1. find a way to start the conversation,
2. introduce yourself,
3. ask the person questions and answer theirs,
4. ask the person for help if you need it,
5. react when you don't understand something,
6. end the conversation.

Match these things to the phrases below.

> Sorry, I didn't get that. • Sorry, can you say that again, please? • The/A … ? What's that?/What does that mean?

> Bye! • See you tomorrow.

> By the way, my name's … • How are you? • Good to meet you.

> Hi! • Excuse me, …

> Have you ever …? / Have you … yet? • What about you?

> Can you tell me …? • Do you know where … ?

b) At the beach last week, Rob met Anna, an English tourist. Listen to their conversation. Which of the phrases in a) can you hear?

c) Role play
With your partner act out a short conversation. Use the flow chart below and phrases from a).

Partner A:	Partner B:
– You want to sit down in a café.	– You're sitting alone at a table in a café.
– You'd like to see the film *Batman*, but don't know where it's on.	– You're reading a magazine with cinema tips.

- Ask if you can sit at Partner B's table.
- Answer Partner A.
- Introduce yourselves.
- Ask a few questions to get to know each other.
- Ask Partner B if he/she knows where *Batman* is on.
- Help Partner A to find out where *Batman* is on.
- Ask Partner B if he/she would like to see the film with you.
- Answer Partner A.
- End the conversation.

d) Extra Role play
In groups of three, act out a short conversation.

Situation:
The three of you are on holiday in Australia. You can't speak German. You meet in a hostel. Talk to each other about your holidays so far.

▶ SF Speaking Course (pp. 142–143) • WB 8–10 (pp. 5–6)

P2 LISTENING Learning to surf 🎧

a) When Anna got to the surf school, there were so many people there that she decided to phone them later. Listen to the conversation and complete the information below.

Easysurf – Let's go surfing!
Lessons: Beginners
Easysurf Courses
– When?   – Group size?
– How long?   – Equipment (wetsuit, surfboard)?
   – Cost?
Private Lessons

b) 👥 *Role play*
Partner B: Go to page 96.
Partner A: Use the role card below and act out the telephone conversation.

Name: Jenny
– You'd like to learn to surf.
– You've never gone surfing before.
– You're a good swimmer.
– You'd like to learn with other girls.
– You've got your own equipment.
– You want to know the price.

P3 WORDS Tricky translations

Some German words have different English translations. Find the right translations for the words in brackets and complete the sentences. If you are unsure, check in a German–English dictionary.

1 *(tragen)* When Rob goes surfing in winter he wears a wetsuit. He loves the way the waves carry him to the beach.
2 *(bringen)* … me my paper please, and then could you … this letter to the post office?
3 *(groß)* The African elephant is between 3.5 and 4 metres … and is known for its … ears.
4 *(während)* We met some nice guys … we were waiting for the train and chatted with them … our journey to Melbourne.
5 *(brauchen)* The bus from the station to the airport … about ten minutes. And it's free, so you don't … a ticket.
6 *(machen)* What are you … this evening? – Well, I have to … dinner for my family.
7 *(fahren)* My mum can't … a car, so she … her bike to work. If it rains, she … by bus.
8 *(vor)* Two weeks …, I went to see a film. I met my friends … the cinema. … the film we bought some popcorn.

P4 EVERYDAY ENGLISH WRITING Our lives (Writing an e-mail)

Look at pages 12 and 13 again. Write an e-mail to Jeannie or Rob.

– Use their names.
  Say what you find interesting or surprising about their lives.

→ I was really interested to read/hear about … • I think it's great that you can/have … • I was really jealous when I read that you …

– What else would you like to know about their lives? Ask some questions.

→ I have some questions for you. • Are you allowed to …? • What's your favourite …? • Where/When/How often do you …?

– Tell them something about your life, e.g. your school day, your favourite subject, the sports you enjoy, …

→ My life in Germany is (a bit/very) different from yours. • For example, …

– Find a good way to finish.

→ That's all from me for now. • Best wishes, … / All the best, … / Yours, …

▶ WB 11–12 (p. 7)

THE ABORIGINAL PEOPLE OF AUSTRALIA

1 The Dreaming

For Aboriginal people, Tjukurpa – the Dreaming – explains why the world exists and helps them to lead their daily lives. It is passed on in dance, song, stories and art. Here's the story of how the world began:

In the beginning the world was flat and empty. But the ancestors of all living things were asleep in the ground. One day the ancestors rose, gave birth to their children and called out their own names: I am Red Lizard, I am Mulga-tree. Then they travelled across the land and the tracks they left are the world we see today. The paths they walked along became rivers. When they put sticks into the ground, trees were formed. When they died, their bodies changed into mountains. They ate, made love, laughed, played and fought. And when they had made the whole world, the ancestors sank back into the earth.

But the Dreaming is more than stories about the past: it links the past and present and shows Aborigines how to take care of the world today.

a) What other stories about how the world was created do you know? How is the Dreaming similar or different?

b) **Extra** From what you have learned about the Dreaming, explain what attitude Aboriginal people probably have to the natural world.

2 In Uluru-Kata Tjuta National Park

Uluru at sunrise

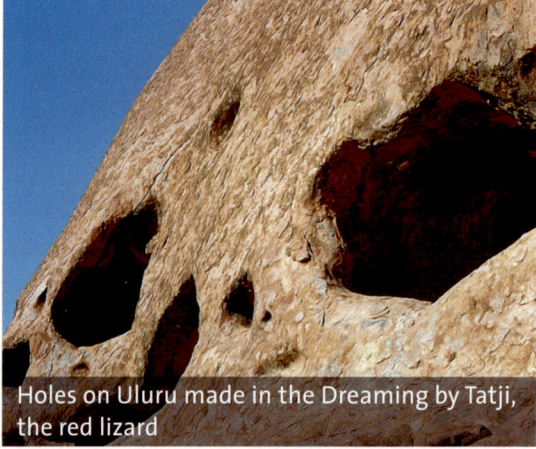
Holes on Uluru made in the Dreaming by Tatji, the red lizard

Cave painting

a) Look closely at the photos of Uluru-Kata Tjuta National Park. Explain what they tell you about the place. Think of:
climate – landscape – the Dreaming – …

b) Listen to the radio programme. What is your strongest impression? Exchange your thoughts in your group. Then write a short summary of what happens in the programme.

c) Listen again and take notes on two of the following. Then share your ideas in class.

> tourists • colours • weather • Aboriginal culture • respect • sounds/music

▶ SF Listening (p. 134)

3 The 'stolen generations'

Children were stolen for a racist ideal. Now a nation says sorry

Zita Wallace still remembers the day she was stolen from her Aboriginal family and taken to a home for orphans. The home was run by white nuns. She was seven years old.

Wallace and four other girls were tricked. One day some nuns drove up to their door. The nuns said that the girls could go shopping with them. 'They put us in the back of a truck but we never went near a shop. They took us to a home hundreds of miles away.'

At her house in Worita, 160 km from Alice Springs, Wallace spoke about her first night with the nuns. 'There were lots of children in one big room. On the floor there were hard mattresses to sleep on. I was terrified because there was no one to help us.'

She told us that she had seen terrible things and would never forget those first hours. 'There was a 4-year-old girl who just cried and cried. It was so awful that I put my head under my blanket and cried too.'

Wallace belongs to the 'stolen generations', the thousands of mixed-race children with fair skin who were taken from their families. The government wanted them to forget their Aboriginal language and traditions and to grow up like white children. 'They hit us if we spoke our language,' Wallace told us. 'And there was always cooking and cleaning to do. We only got enough education to read and write.'

The stealing of children ended after 60 years in 1970. In 1997 a government report said it was time to apologize. Now, eleven years later, Australia is finally saying sorry.

Wallace said that she didn't care about getting money from the government. 'But I can't wait to hear that word tomorrow: *sorry*.' ∎

Zita Wallace with her mother's sister Aggie

Barbara McMahon, © Guardian News & Media Ltd 2008

a) Say how you feel about what happened to Zita Wallace.

b) Summarize what the article tells you about the 'stolen generations'. Why does the headline talk of 'a racist ideal'?

c) Extra 🎧 On 12 February 2008, the Australian prime minister, Kevin Rudd, at last said sorry to the 'stolen generations'. Listen to part of his speech. Imagine Zita Wallace wrote a letter to Kevin Rudd after she heard the speech. Write the letter.

4 VIEWING Rabbit-proof fence

Rabbit-proof fence tells the true story of three Aboriginal girls who are 'stolen'. They escape and walk 1,900 miles through the outback of western Australia to get home.

a) Watch part of the film. Describe what happens.

b) What do you find out about
1 the man repairing the fence,
2 the fence,
3 the children's mother?

c) Extra Watch again. Take notes on how the acting and the music help you to understand
– the mother's feelings,
– the children's feelings.

– When the music gets louder you think ...
– The way the mother looks when the car arrives shows ...

▶ SF Taking notes (p. 135)

1 Part A B C D Practice

P1 REVISION 'Stolen generations' (Verb + object + to-infinitive)

In English, some verbs can be followed by an object + to-infinitive:
The Dreaming helps Aboriginal people to lead their daily lives.
The government wanted them to forget their traditions.

Use a verb from box A in the right tense and an infinitive from box B to complete the sentences.

A force • tell • not want (2×) • want (2×)

B to apologize • to get into • to give • to go shopping • to learn • to speak

1 Zita Wallace remembers how she was stolen. 'They **told** us **to get into** the truck.'
2 'They … us … with them. But it was a trick.'
3 'They … us … our language. They beat us if we did.'
4 'They … us … their language and the white man's way.'
5 Many Australians … their government … to the 'stolen generations' and in 2008 the government did.
6 Zita … the government … her money. Hearing them say sorry was enough for her.

P2 👥 REVISION On holiday in Australia (Question word + to-infinitive)

Partner B: Go to page 96.
a) Partner A: You're on holiday in Australia and need some help. Look at the boxes on the right and tell your partner what your problems are. Start with 'I don't know/I'm not sure …', add a question word and an infinitive construction and finish with 'Can you help? / Any ideas? / Do you know?'.

| I don't know
I'm not sure | who
where
when
how
what | be at the meeting place
bring on the tour
get to the meeting place
meet for the tour
see about the Uluru tour |

A: I don't know who to see about the Uluru tour. Can you help?
B: Yes, why don't you see the people at the tour desk?

b) Listen to Partner B and decide what to say. You can use phrases like 'Why don't you …?' or 'You should …'.

1 Ask at the tourist office.
2 Check out by 11 am.
3 Go by plane.
4 Wear a pullover. It's often a bit cold.
5 Send one to your mum.

P3 Exploring language — to-infinitives instead of relative clauses

a) Look at these two sentences from page 17.
1 On the floor there were hard mattresses to sleep on.
2 I was terrified because there was no one to help us.

You could also write them like this:
1 On the floor there were hard mattresses that we could sleep on.
2 I was terrified because there was no one who could help us.

What do we call the clauses in blue print?

b) How else could you say the following?
1 Zita wasn't the first girl to cry.
2 Your teacher is the person to ask about difficult grammar.
3 The Grammar File is the place to go to if you need answers.

▶ GF 1.3: The to-infinitive (pp. 154–155) • WB 13–14 (p. 8)

P 4 In the children's home (to-infinitives instead of relative clauses)

Here is some more of what Zita Wallace said about the children's home she was taken to. How else could you say the same thing?

1. In the children's home there were some hard mattresses that we could sleep on.
   There were some hard mattresses to sleep on.
2. There was tea we could drink and bread we could eat.
3. There was lots of work that we had to do for the nuns.
4. There were clothes we had to wash, dinners we had to cook and rooms we had to clean.
5. There was nobody who could help us.
6. We had no families who could protect us.

P 5 The Aboriginal people (to-infinitives instead of relative clauses)

Use to-infinitives and expand the notes to full sentences.

1. Aborigines – first humans who arrived in Australia
   The Aborigines were the first humans to arrive in Australia.
2. who will be the last people who live there? – nobody knows
   Nobody knows who will ...
3. Want to know more about the 'stolen generations'? *Rabbit-proof fence* is the film you should see.
   If you want to know more ...
4. Visit Uluru for more information on Aboriginal culture.
   Uluru is the place ...

Australian Aboriginal flag

P 6 MEDIATION An early morning walk at Uluru (Spoken English to German)

a) While on holiday in Australia with a friend, you think you'd like to take an early morning tour of Uluru, so you call the tour company for more information. Your friend, whose English isn't so good, has lots of questions. Listen and find out the answers. Take notes.

1. Was können wir bei dieser Tour alles sehen?
2. Wann müssen wir aufstehen?
3. Wie kommen wir da hin?
4. Sind da Leute, die uns führen?
5. Müssen wir weit laufen?
6. Wie viel kostet uns die Tour?
7. Wie können wir buchen und bezahlen?

b) Answer your friend's questions in German.

▶ WB 15–19 (pp. 9–10)

In the outback (adapted from the novel *A prayer for Blue Delaney* by Kirsty Murray)

This story is set in the outback. Before you read it, with a partner look at the photos, then use what you have already learned and make notes on what you think the atmosphere must be like in the outback. Some important new words are explained in the footnotes at the bottom of each page.

The story so far
During the 1950s Australia wanted to add to its population, so orphans were sent from the UK to children's homes there. Colm is one of these orphans. He is living in a home for boys, but the people at the home are very cruel and Colm decides to run away. He gets to know an old man, Bill, and his dog Rusty. When the police start to look for Colm, Bill offers to take him with him in Tin Annie – his old pickup truck (ute)[1] – as he travels through the Australian outback. Bill is hoping to get work on the Dog Fence, which runs from south to north-eastern Australia.

As they drove out of Ceduna, Bill said, 'I heard from an old mate that there's work on the Dog Fence. Thought I might take it. No one will follow us in that lonely[2] country.'
The Victoria Desert began to stretch out in front of them as they left town. They drove north towards the Dog Fence, through a wide, open landscape of earth and sky.

It was slow and hot travelling along the Dog Fence. The more they drove inland, the hotter the air became until Colm felt he was breathing fire. He and Rusty tried sticking their heads out the window, but it was worse than the burning heat[3] inside the car. The sandy air hurt Colm's skin and made his eyes sore. He pulled his head back inside. There was nothing to see except scrub[4] and tough little grasses in the rock and sand, and the fence stretching like a thin grey scar[5] across the landscape.

'What if we break down[6]?' asked Colm.
'Don't you worry about that. They used to do the fence on camel, but these days they use jeeps. Tin Annie here, she's part camel part jeep, so she'll be fine.'

'But what if we get lost?'
Bill smiled. 'We'll follow the fence, mate. It's more than three thousand miles long and there's no way we can lose it.'

Bill stopped next to the fence where an emu had crashed into[7] it. They both climbed out of the ute.

Bill shook his head. 'She's hit the fence very fast, this one. Looks like she broke her neck.'
In the distance another emu was running across the desert. 'See, they're so fast. They can go 30 miles an hour but they don't see the fence until they've hit it.'
Colm helped Bill as he looked for the tools he would need for the job and then climbed back into Tin Annie to wait

---

[1] pickup ['pɪkʌp], ute [juːt] (AusE) kleiner Geländewagen mit offener Ladefläche   [2] lonely ['ləʊnli] einsam   [3] heat [hiːt] Hitze
[4] scrub [skrʌb] Gebüsch, Gestrüpp   [5] scar [skɑː] Narbe   [6] (to) break down [ˌbreɪk ˈdaʊn] eine Panne haben   [7] (to) crash into sth. [kræʃ] gegen etwas fahren/laufen

while Bill repaired the fence. Later they stopped to fill in a hole made by a wombat[8]. The day dragged on[9]. They drove so slowly that Colm got tired looking at the fence. When he closed his eyes he saw the endless fence moving along in his head. Despite the flies[10] and the heat, he fell asleep[11]. When he woke up, it was to the sound of Bill repairing a fencepost[12].

Colm's shirt was wet with sweat. He went round to the back of the ute and took a long drink from the billycan[13]. The water was as warm as tea, but it was good to wet his throat. Flies buzzed around his face and although he tried to swat them away, they came back. Colm felt as if he was inside a strange and frightening[14] dream.

The days dragged on, long and boring. Colm's neck was sore from always turning his head one way to watch the fence. After a few days he took over the job of filling the wombat holes while Bill repaired the holes in the fence. They filled up the billycans at every dam or tank, and ate tins[15] of beef and vegetables until Colm felt he couldn't take another mouthful[16] of them. The nearest town was hundreds of miles away.

One morning, Rusty wasn't in camp when they woke up. Colm helped Bill to pack up the breakfast dishes, and all the time he scanned the scrub and looked for a sign of movement.

'Where is that dog?' said Bill. He put two fingers in his mouth and whistled. Nothing moved.

'I'll find her,' said Colm. He walked out into the scrub. If he closed his eyes and willed[17] it, then he should be able to feel Rusty wherever she was. He was sure she was quite close.

When he opened his eyes he saw something move in the dust. Rusty was lying under a bush: she was shaking violently.

'Bill,' called Colm. 'Bill, here, I've found her! But something's wrong! Hurry!'

Bill knelt[18] beside[19] the dog. When he touched her body, Rusty shook even more violently.

'What is it?' asked Colm.

'Snakebite[20], maybe. Then again, maybe not.'

Rusty started shaking uncontrollably, as if there was electricity running through her. Colm was cold with fear.

'What's wrong?' he cried, feeling tears in his eyes.

[8] wombat ['wɒmbæt] *Wombat (kl. Beutelsäuger)* [9] (to) drag (on) *sich hinziehen* [10] flies *Fliegen* [11] (to) fall asleep *einschlafen*
[12] fencepost ['fenspəʊst] *Zaunpfahl* [13] billycan ['bɪlikæn] *Kochtopf* [14] frightening *erschreckend* [15] tin *Dose* [16] mouthful *Bissen*
[17] (to) will sth. *etwas herbeiwünschen* [18] knelt [nelt] *kniete sich hin* [19] beside [bɪ'saɪd] *neben* [20] snakebite *Schlangenbiss*

'I think she's taken dingo bait²¹. Poison²². It might be better for her if we killed her.'

110   Colm walked beside Bill as he carried Rusty over to the ute and put her on her blanket in the back. Bill picked up the knife he used to kill rabbits.

'No! What are you doing!' Colm grabbed
115   Bill's hand. 'We have to save her.'

'Get out of my way,' said Bill. He pushed Colm away and held Rusty's head. Quickly he made cuts on the side of Rusty's ears. Blood poured²³ down.

120   'Now go and fill the billycan.' Bill pushed it at Colm and then looked for something in the food bag.

When Colm returned²⁴, Bill threw two handfuls of salt²⁵ into the water. He took Rusty
125   in his arms. 'Now I'll keep her mouth open. I want you to pour²⁶ the salty water straight down her throat.'

The salt water made Rusty throw up. When Bill put her down, she staggered²⁷ around the
130   ute, and threw up again and again. As soon as they could, they poured more water down her throat. Finally, when she'd finished, Bill carried her over to a bush and put her on her old blanket. Bill and Colm knelt beside her and
135   massaged her.

'Here, you need a break,' said Bill. 'Go get yourself a drink and sit in the car. I'll call you if I need you.'

'What are you going to do? You can't shoot
140   her, Bill. You can't.'

'I'm hoping it won't come to that.'

Colm walked back to Tin Annie, fighting back tears.

The morning grew hotter. Colm fell asleep and then, when he woke, he prayed as hard as 145 he could. He was still praying when he heard Rusty bark – a weak bark, but a bark. He ran across to where she lay.

'I prayed for her,' said Colm. 'Maybe it helped.' 150

'Maybe it did,' said Bill. 'Between your prayers and my hard work, she'll be better in no time.'

****

After several adventures Bill finds work and accommodation for the three of them with an old friend at Tara Downs, a cattle station up in the Northern Territory.

'C'mon. I've got a job to do. Can't just sit around and talk all day. A wild boar's²⁸ been 155 making trouble just south a bit. They mess with²⁹ the dams and the fences. Get in the ute and you can help.'

They drove out into the landscape where the old trees looked like burnt bones. Tin Annie 160 struggled over³⁰ the dry creek³¹ beds and Rusty put her head out the open window, watching the fine red dust fly up around the sides of the ute.

'This is the place. We'll look for the bugger³² 165 on foot from here. You stay close by me.'

---

²¹ bait [beɪt] *Köder*   ²² poison ['pɔɪzn] *Gift*   ²³ (to) pour [pɔː] *strömen*   ²⁴ (to) return [rɪ'tɜːn] *zurückkehren*   ²⁵ salt [sɔːlt] *Salz*   ²⁶ (to) pour [pɔː] *schütten*   ²⁷ (to) stagger ['stægə] *schwanken, torkeln*   ²⁸ wild boar [ˌwaɪld 'bɔː] *Wildschwein*   ²⁹ (to) mess with sth. [mes] *mit etwas herumspielen*   ³⁰ (to) struggle over ... ['strʌgl] *sich über ... kämpfen, mühen*   ³¹ creek (AusE) [kriːk] *Bach*   ³² bugger (infml, rude) ['bʌgə] *Kerl*

Colm followed Bill through the scrub. A hot, foul smell was in the air. As the smell got stronger, Rusty put her head down and walked in front, as if she was following something. She led them to what was left of a steer[33]. A cloud of flies flew up in the air.

Bill knelt down beside the dead steer. 'He's had a great time with this steer. He hasn't been gone long.'

They climbed up a nearby[34] hill and scanned the countryside. Apart from[35] a family of wallabies[36], they could see nothing.

'Damn, he heard us coming and left.'

Bill turned to walk back to the steer. There was a noise in the scrub and the black boar was on them.

Colm jumped behind a rock as the boar hit Bill and sent him flying[37]. It ran at the old man with its tusks[38], tearing his boot and ripping open his leg. Bill let out a cry of pain.

Blood poured from Bill's leg as the boar attacked again, and the old man struggled free. Rusty sank her teeth into the boar's leg, but it turned and tore her with its tusks. Rusty yelped[39] and fell.

Colm jumped out from behind the rock. He had to do something.

Bill's face was scared. 'Run, Colm, get out of here,' he shouted. 'Get help!'

Colm turned and ran down the path. He had nearly got to Tin Annie when he heard a terrible cry, more animal than human. He stopped and turned. What if Bill was killed before he could get help? What should he do? Run back to Tara Downs? Try to save Bill himself? Suddenly he realized there was only one answer and there was no time to lose.

He ran back to Bill. On the way he picked up a stick. As he came over the hill, he ran at the boar, hitting it again and again. It turned to face Colm. There was blood on its tusks.

Bill tried to pull himself away, leaving a trail of blood behind him. Colm raised the stick high and brought it down on the boar's head. The boar snorted[40], but instead of running at Colm, it turned back to Bill.

Colm threw the stick down and grabbed Bill's gun. He was shaking as he raised the gun to his shoulder. Colm knew that if he shot the animal in the back, it would only make it wild. He let out a scream, a long, loud scream. The boar turned round. For a moment it stared at him with its small black eyes. Then it lowered[41] its head and ran towards him. Colm aimed straight between the eyes.

The kickback from the gun made Colm stagger. He fell in the sand beside Rusty.

'Colm, my mate,' said Bill. He held out one bloodied hand and smiled. Then he lay back in the red dust and passed out[42].

Suddenly, everything was quiet. Blood soaked into the dry earth around Bill in a dark circle. Colm could see the bones of his leg where the boar had ripped open the flesh. He would have to stop the blood flow or Bill would bleed to death. Colm ran back to the ute and grabbed an old shirt to tie up the wound[43]. Then he took off his own shirt and tore it up for Bill's hands. When he was sure the bleeding was slower, he sat back and tried to think. He had to get help, but how? The flies were collecting. He would have to get Bill into the car.

Colm took Bill's arms and put one over each of his shoulders and then tried to pull the old man up. It was almost impossible. He'd never be able to go far like this. He laid Bill down again and ran to Tin Annie. Colm took a deep

---

33 steer [stɪə] *junger Ochse*   34 nearby [ˌnɪəˈbaɪ] *nahegelegen*   35 apart from [əˈpɑːt] *außer*   36 wallaby [ˈwɒləbi] *Wallaby (kleine Art von Känguru)*   37 (to) send sb. flying *jn. zu Boden schicken*   38 tusk [tʌsk] *Hauer (Eckzahn eines Wildschweines)*   39 (to) yelp [jelp] *aufjaulen*   40 (to) snort [snɔːt] *schnauben*   41 (to) lower [ˈləʊə] *senken*   42 (to) pass out [ˌpɑːs ˈaʊt] *ohnmächtig werden*   43 wound [wuːnd] *Wunde*

breath and turned the key. Tin Annie started. He had no idea how to drive backwards, so he moved forwards carefully, bringing the car as close to Bill as he could. Somehow he found the strength[44] to pull Bill back on his shoulders and put him into the car. Then he ran and picked Rusty up. He could just hear the dog's heartbeat and it gave him hope.

The dust flew up around the car as Colm raced along the track. Every time they hit a stone Bill cried out with pain, but at least that meant he was still alive.

When they drove across a dry creek bed, Tin Annie first struggled, then stopped. Colm tried to start her up again. But even as his foot pushed to the floor, he knew it was a mistake. The old ute died completely.

They were just at the top of the hill and he could see Tara Downs, but there was still at least a mile to go. He tried to start the car again and again, but it was no good. He would have to go on foot and leave Bill and Rusty in the car.

Colm wished the old man was conscious[45] and could tell him what to do next. Then he began the long run to Tara Downs.

Colm's heart pounded[46] and his head hurt, but the ground flew beneath him. He took the steps up to the house two at a time.

'It's Bill. An accident. He's bleeding, real bad. A boar ripped him up.'

Then Colm sank down on his knees. People appeared from nowhere. They ran, a car started up and strong arms helped Colm to his feet and took him into a bedroom. For a moment he struggled against them. 'I have to be with Bill.'

'It's all right.'

'Bill needs me,' said Colm.

'They're getting the Flying Doctor out here. We don't know if the old man will make it if we have to drive him down to the hospital in Katherine. Best to fly him to Darwin.'

Colm felt the blood drain from his face. 'He will make it. He has to make it.'

---

[44] strength [streŋθ] *Kraft, Stärke*   [45] conscious [ˈkɒnʃəs] *bei Bewusstsein*   [46] (to) pound [paʊnd] *(wild) pochen*

Working with the text

1 What do you think?
Give your opinion of the story. Say which parts were especially exciting or boring. Give reasons.

2 The plot
Divide the story into parts – look for changes of time, place, characters, or just events that start and finish. Make a flow chart like this:

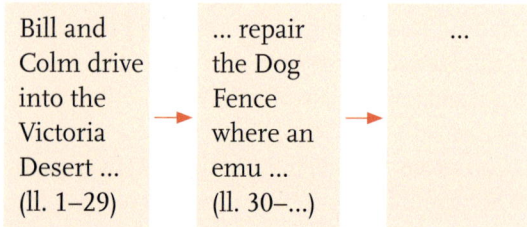

Find a part of the story where something that happens causes something else.

> **STUDY SKILLS** **Reading literature (1)**
>
> When you read literature, you'll enjoy it more and understand it better if you try to follow how the story develops (**plot**), get into the feeling of the story (**atmosphere**), and think about the **characters**.
>
> **Plot**
> The plot is the action and events that take place in a story. These events often happen because one event causes another. Stories also often use flashbacks in their plots.
>
> ▶ SF Reading literature (pp. 138–139)

3 The atmosphere

a) Look at what you wrote about the atmosphere of the outback before you read the story. How does it compare with the atmosphere of the story?

STUDY SKILLS — Reading literature (2)

Setting and atmosphere
The setting is the place and time of the story, e.g. the Australian outback in the 1950s. Atmosphere is the feeling created by the setting or by a situation in a piece of literature. This can be done through imagery: the author compares things, e.g. "the water was as warm as tea" (ll. 63–64), or creates an image with a metaphor, e.g. "the days dragged on" (l. 69).

b) Look at lines 5–20. Find out how atmosphere is created in this part of the story. Look at the adjectives. Find metaphors or comparisons.

4 The characters

a) Who are the characters in the story? Make a network of their names and describe the connections between them. What do they think of each other?

STUDY SKILLS — Reading literature (3)

Characters
The author can present the characters of a story in many ways. He or she may describe them or show the reader what they are like through their language and way of speaking, their actions, feelings, thoughts, words and their connections to other characters.

b) 👥 Choose adjectives from the box below on the right or your own adjectives and describe Bill or Colm to your partner. Give examples from the story for your choice. Listen to each other's descriptions. Do you agree? Give reasons.

> brave • clever • difficult • easy-going •
> friendly • helpful • honest • nervous • old •
> stupid • violent • young

5 Creative writing

a) Write an ending for the story.
What do you think will happen next?
– Will Bill survive?
– Will Colm try to follow Bill? Or will he go into the bush alone? Or back to the children's home?

Remember

Follow these steps of writing:
1 *Brainstorm your ideas. Make notes.*
2 *Write your text. Use linking words, adjectives and adverbs to make it more interesting.*
3 *Revise your text.*

b) **Extra** Choose one of the following:
1 Imagine you are Colm. Rewrite part of the story from your point of view, using 'I'.
2 What would you need to do if you wanted to change the story into a film? Write down ideas for a screenplay.

▶ WB 20–21 (p. 11) • **Skills Check 1** WB (pp. 12–17)

Extra Revision Getting ready for a test 1

1 WORDS Travelling

Complete the sentences with the correct words and phrases. Use the verbs in their correct forms. There are two more words/phrases than you need.

> change planes • (to) check in • city centre • departure area • flight attendant • (to) land • meal • receptionist • rucksacks • (to) take off • (to) take a taxi • ticket • ticket machines

You're flying to Australia for a wonderful holiday! At the airport, you first (1) *check in*. Then you go to the (2) … . For your flight it's gate D21.

Now you're on the plane. The flight to Australia is very long and on the way you need to eat and drink. The (3) … offers you a hot meal. There are lots of nice things on the menu today.

After you (4) … at Singapore Airport, you finally (5) … in Sydney. Of course, you hope that your (6) … arrive too! If not, you'll have to go to the lost luggage office.

So how do you travel from the airport into the (7) …? Well, the quickest and easiest way is to (8) … , but it's also the most expensive one: it costs about 50 Australian dollars. So you decide to take a train instead. The (9) … are easy to use and a (10) … to the city is only 15 Australian dollars.

Now – tired but happy – you're at your hotel. The (11) … gives you the key to your room. She also tells you about the hotel – for example, the times when you can have breakfast.

2 Judy's job (Simple present and present progressive)

a) *Judy is the flight attendant that you can see in the photo above. Finish these sentences about her job. Use the* simple present *or* the present progressive.

1 Judy's job is exciting. She often … (travel) to different countries.
2 Right now, she … (fly) to Australia.
3 A typical day for Judy starts early. She usually … (get up) at 5 o'clock. Then she … (have) her breakfast and … (drive) to the airport.
4 It is 10 o'clock now and Judy … (work). She … (bring) coffee and tea to the passengers on her plane.
5 Now it is 10 o'clock the next morning. Judy … (just / arrive) at her hotel.
6 Judy always … (stay) at a hotel when she is in another country. She … (sleep) at the hotel – then the next day she … (fly) home again.

b) *Write sentences about things that you often do and some things that you're doing right now.*
I often surf the internet. Right now, I'm chatting with my friends.

Extra Revision Getting ready for a test 1

3 Australia's most dangerous animals (Simple past and past progressive)

Read the text about Australia's most dangerous animals on the right, then complete the two stories below. Use the simple past or past progressive of the verbs in brackets.

AUSTRALIA is home to some of the world's most dangerous animals. There are snakes, spiders and sometimes sharks. The most dangerous of all, however, are crocodiles. Two or three people die every year in crocodile attacks. Here are two stories about people who were attacked.

There's a crocodile in our tent!
In January 2005, two young Australians went camping near the Pentecost River in the north of Australia. At about 2 o'clock in the morning, they (1) were sleeping (sleep) when suddenly a crocodile (2) … (come) into their tent. They (3) … (run) to their car and (4) … (climb) onto it. The next morning at 11 o'clock, they (5) …

(still / sit) on their car when some hunters (6) … (arrive) and (7) … (save) their lives.

Smile please!
In 2008, a tourist in Queensland was stupid – but lucky. He (8) … (sit) in a boat on a river when a crocodile (9) … (swim) towards the boat. The man's friend (10) … (stand) on land. 'Put your hand in the water and play with the crocodile!' he (11) … (shout). 'I'm going to take a photo.' Seconds later, the crocodile (12) … (try) to bite the man's hand. 'It was a scary moment!' he (13) … (say) afterwards.

4 WORDS It was scary! (Words that describe experiences)

a) Look at the box with adjectives. Find five pairs of adjectives that mean (almost) the same: great – …

b) Find at least eight pairs of adjectives that mean opposite things: awesome – boring; dangerous – …

c) Write about ten things you have done (or invent them). Use adjectives from the box:
1) Yesterday I played table tennis against my younger brother and lost 11–2. It was depressing!
2) …

amazing • awesome • awful • boring • cool • crazy • dangerous • depressing • different • difficult • easy • excellent • exciting • fantastic • frightening • funny • great • horrible • interesting • laughable • lovely • mad • sad • safe • scary • shocking • silly • strange • surprising • terrible • unbelievable • wonderful

5 WRITING One day last year …

a) Below is a very short story! Can you make it more interesting? Write the story again. Use some ideas from the table.

> Jake was riding his bike in the mountains. He fell off and broke his leg. He called for help on his mobile phone. Some people saved him. He went to hospital. He met Anne, a doctor. They fell in love. They got married.

When?	one day last year, last September, first, then, next, after that, finally, …
Who?	the man/woman/person/people who …
How?	quickly, slowly, suddenly, … (really) amazing/awful; (feel) wonderful/depressed, …
Linking words	that's why, however, so (that), although, when, despite, …

b) Compare your story with a partner's.

▶ SF Writing Course (pp. 144–145)

Extra Practice test Getting ready for a test 1

1 LISTENING Travelling to Australia

Listen to the announcement and conversations. While listening, answer the questions below in one to five words.
— You will hear the recordings only **once**.
— You will have 10 seconds at the end of the recordings to complete your answers.
— You now have 40 seconds to look at the task.

1 At which gate does your flight to Sydney depart? ...

2 What can you choose for dinner? *Roast chicken or* ... What drinks can you have? *(Name two.)* ... / ...

3 What is opposite the lost luggage office? ...

4 How much is the airport toll for taxis? *AU $* ...
How much is the taxi from the airport to the city all in all? *AU $* ...

5 What's your room number on the second floor? ...
When can you have breakfast tomorrow? *From* ... *to* ...

2 LISTENING Shark attack!

Listen to a radio report about a shark attack in which Jon Kerry, a young Australian, was badly hurt. The report is in two parts.
While listening, note down the correct answer:
A, B, C or D.

Part 1
– You will hear the recording only **once**.
– You will have 10 seconds at the end of the recording to complete your answers.
– You now have 15 seconds to look at the task..

1 A shark attacked a …
A diver.
B snorkeller.
C surfer.
D swimmer.

2 The attack happened near a beach in …
A New South Wales.
B South Australia.
C Western Australia.
D Queensland.

3 The shark caught Jon's …
A arm.
B leg.
C foot.
D shoulder.

4 The shark left a wound of …
A 25 cm.
B 30 cm.
C 35 cm.
D 40 cm.

[1] scar [skɑː] *Narbe*

Part 2
– Now listen very carefully. You will hear the next part of the radio report **twice**.
– You will have 15 seconds after you have heard the report for the first time and another 15 seconds after the second time to complete your answers.
– You now have 50 seconds to look at the task.

1 When Jon swam back to the beach he was …
A angry.
B depressed.
C terrified.
D tired.

2 His friends saved his life because they …
A called the sea rescue.
B chased the shark away.
C pulled him out of the water.
D took care of the injury.

3 His doctors are sure that he …
A won't be able to move for some time.
B will need future operations.
C will be fine despite a scar[1].
D won't even see a scar.

4 Experts want to …
A ask people to report shark attacks.
B calm people despite past shark attacks.
C help people to survive shark attacks.
D warn people against new shark attacks.

5 To avoid shark attacks, people should …
A not feed sharks.
B not go after sharks.
C swim with friends.
D swim in the morning.

3 LISTENING Young Australians and the internet

Listen to six students talking about the internet. While listening, match each of them with one of the statements A to G. There is one more statement than you need.
- You will hear the recording only **once**.
- You will have 5 seconds between each recording and 10 seconds at the end to complete your answers.
- You now have 30 seconds to look at the task.

A Older people know very little about the internet.
B Teenagers need to learn more about internet safety.
C You can do different activities on the web at the same time.
D People can create and define their identities on the net.
E Some teenagers waste a lot of time on the internet.
F Adults should stop warning about internet risks.
G You can have unpleasant experiences when you are online.

Student 1	Student 2	Student 3	Student 4	Student 5	Student 6

4 WRITING An online magazine for young Europeans

You often read an online magazine for young Europeans. This week, the magazine wants readers' ideas about the internet and it has a story competition. Write about 200 words on one of the topics below.

Topic 1: The internet and me
When and where do you usually use the internet? What do you do online? Which activitiy do you do most often? What are your ideas about being safe online?

Topic 2: A scary moment!
Finish this story in your own words.

> It was a Saturday afternoon in September. I was bored, so I decided to go for a bike ride. After about an hour, I was on a small road in the country ...

Self-evaluation

Check your answers to tasks 1–3 on page 247.

About the test
This test gave you the chance to try some of the kinds of tasks that you have to do one day in your exam. If you found some tasks difficult, don't worry. You've got lots of time to practise. Remember: 'Practice makes perfect!'

Listening
The first three tasks in the test were listening tasks. The following questions will help you to think about how you did. Read the questions – which answer is right for you?

1 How hard or easy was each task?

	easy	OK	quite hard	very hard
Task 1				
Task 3				
Task 4				

2 What was difficult in the tasks?
a) People spoke quickly.
b) I found the accents difficult.
c) There was a lot of information. I couldn't find the exact answers.
d) I didn't have time to write the answers to the questions.
e) There were words and phrases that I just couldn't understand.

3 How did you do the tasks?
a) I read the questions carefully first so I knew exactly what I had to listen for.
b) I looked quickly at the questions first but only read them carefully while I was listening.
c) I wrote as many answers as I could the first time I heard the text and checked them (or filled in gaps) the second time.
d) There were lots of things I couldn't understand and I panicked.

▶ SF Listening (p. 134) ·
SF How to do well in a test (pp. 150–152)

👥 Writing
The fourth task in your test was a writing task. Work with a partner. Exchange the texts you've written and read your partner's text. Copy and fill in the assessment sheet[1] below. Remember: the idea is to help your partner with your feedback!

Assessment sheet	☹	😐	☺			
Name of partner …	1	2	3	4	5	Comments
Did your partner …						
1 … write an interesting text/story?						
2 … make grammar mistakes (with a tense, plural forms, etc.)?						
3 … use interesting vocabulary or just easy words and phrases?						
4 … write longer sentences with linking words or just short sentences?						
5 … write a text that is clear and easy to understand?						

▶ SF Writing Course (pp. 144–145)

---

[1] assessment sheet *Beurteilungsbogen*

Unit 2 The road ahead

I want to spend a year at an American high school.

Forget school! I'm going to be a rock star!

1 Continue the road

How do you think the road ahead might continue for the young people above? Choose two more pictures for each of them or draw/find pictures of your own. What would the young people say about the pictures or about their future? Write speech bubbles – the box on the right might help.

do something useful • famous • find the right boy/girl • get good A-level results • get qualifications • go on all the talk shows • graduate from university • have kids • help where help is really needed • inherit a fortune • look for work as ... • make a difference • open-air rock festivals • pass exams • scientist • skills • start a career • work hard

If we want the world to be a better place, we have to do something about it.

I want to have as much fun as I can while I'm young.

2 Which road?

Which of these teenagers can you most identify with? In groups, explain your choice and why you finished their road the way you did.

3 Extra Your road

Where are you heading in life? What might the 'road ahead' hold in store for you?
Research and collect suitable vocabulary and illustrations. Then produce a poster for yourself.

▶ **Text File 4** *(p. 105)* • **WB 1** *(p. 18)*

PERSONALITY QUIZ
Where are you heading?

Want to know what sort of person you are and where that might lead you in life? Find out with this fun quiz!
(Check your score on page 98.)

1 The people you like best
- A walk around with their heads in the clouds.
- B plan their lives and know where they're going.
- C are different from one day to the next.

2 You're invited to a party. Do you
- A go and stick close to your friends?
- B go and talk to as many strangers as you can?
- C stay at home?

3 You have to stay home all weekend with no TV, phone, computer, game console or music. Which book do you choose to read?
- A Blue Eye – a beautiful love story
- B Red Eye – a magical fantasy novel
- C Neither: you read a computer mag instead.

4 You're in charge of the bag of presents at the class Christmas party. Do you give
- A the nicest presents to your friends?
- B everyone the first present that comes out of the bag?
- C the best presents to the most popular kids?

5 In the middle of the night, how often do you feel so lonely you cannot sleep?
- A Sometimes.
- B Often.
- C No idea.

6 How often do you move the furniture around in your room at home?
- A Sometimes.
- B Never.
- C When your parents tell you to do it.

7 You're researching on the internet for a project at school. Do you
- A get sidetracked and surf from website to website for hours?
- B find the information you need quickly and get back to your project?
- C forget your project and chat with friends instead?

8 You're at home when the landline phone rings. Do you
- A hurry to answer it first?
- B hope someone else will answer it?
- C not even hear it because nobody ever phones you on the landline?

9 What sort of sports do you prefer?
- A Team sports.
- B Sports like tennis, where it's one against one.
- C No sports.

10 You're home and a soap starts on TV. Do you
- A get really involved with the story and characters?
- B watch it and talk to friends on the phone at the same time?
- C turn the TV off?

11 You have an appointment this afternoon. Will you
- A be late?
- B be on time?
- C cancel the appointment?

12 What do you spend most time thinking about?
- A The future of human civilization.
- B What you're going to do at the weekend.
- C The boy/girl next door.

YOUR PERSONALITY

29–36 points
Your personal qualities:
You are a confident, energetic and flexible person.

You love an adventure. You are interested in art and you enjoy making things. You live life as it comes, but you get bored easily and you hate rules. You do not know how to sit quietly and listen, which others sometimes find annoying. You are good at starting things, but not very good at finishing them. Sometimes you try to do too many things at once and often do not have your feelings under control. You want life to be fun and exciting, don't like grey routines and would hate to give up freedom.

20–28 points
Your personal qualities:
You are a calm, friendly, helpful, and polite person.

You are a great organizer, especially of free-time activities. You are more interested in people than things, but most interested in your dreams. You love meeting new people and can talk easily to anyone you meet. You're always keen to help people to understand their problems. But sometimes you only see the world the way you'd like it to be and not as it actually is. You're very close to your family and friends. You're good at working in a team and you want to change the world.

12–19 points
Your personal qualities:
You are a reliable, organized, punctual and logical person.

You are interested in everything around you – plants, animals, technology – and you want to understand how things work. You love information and you spend a lot of time on the internet. You like people to give you clear instructions and you think rules are important. You are good at solving problems and will always come up with practical ideas. Actually, you are more interested in ideas than people and very serious about your work – perhaps too serious at times.

1 Your personality

a) *Do the quiz. Then, with a partner of your choice, take turns and guess which answers your partner has picked. Discuss the results.*
– It says that I'm/you're … but that's silly/…
– I (don't) think that's true at all.
– I think I'm/you're a … person. You're …
– …

b) *Did your results correspond 100 % with your real personality? Why do you think that is? Are magazine quizzes like this helpful? Or are they just for fun? Give reasons for your answers.*

2 Your future

Where are you heading?
You'll want to see the world before you settle down – but maybe you'll never settle down at all. But if you do, you'll travel a lot and have the wildest adventures first.

Where are you heading?
You won't let anyone force you along a particular path. You'll look inside yourself and follow your dreams, and won't mind if your family, friends and teachers disagree.

Where are you heading?
If you don't know what you want to do with your life already, you soon will. And you'll take the necessary steps to make sure you reach your goals as quickly as you can.

a) *Look at where the magazine thinks you are heading. Explain why you agree or disagree.*
– Yes, I can imagine this road ahead for me because …
– It says I'll … but I already know …
– They must be joking. I'm (not) going to …

b) **Extra** *Suggest what would be a good job for your personality type. (Use a dictionary if you need to.) Explain your choice to a partner.*

P1 WORDS Describing people

a) Look at the people in the pictures below. Pick one and write a profile of the person. What do you think they are like or their life is like? What are they going to do in the future? Try to use as many words and phrases from the boxes below as possible.

> annoying • calm • confident • energetic • flexible • friendly • good at • head in the clouds • helpful • interested in • keen on • logical • organized • polite • practical • punctual • reliable • serious about • under control

> follow his/her dreams • get qualifications (in) • get (good/bad) results (in) • get involved (in) • graduate (from) • enjoy/like/love/hate … • keep to a routine • look for work • make a difference (to) • settle down • solve problems • spend time (on) • use his/her skills • work hard

b) Read your profiles to each other. What could you add to the profile your partner wrote?

c) **Extra** Make notes on your own personal qualities, interests, future possibilities and write your profile. Remember what you did on page 35. You can put your profile in your DOSSIER.

P2 REVISION At an interview (Infinitive constructions)

a) Before an interview, James's parents gave him some tips. How did James report them? Use *wanted me to … / expected me to … / told me to …* and the infinitive.

1. Write your name clearly at the top of the personality test.
   They wanted me to write my name …
2. Be on time after lunch.
   They expected me …
3. Don't be nervous.
4. Speak clearly during the interview.
5. Listen to the questions carefully.
6. Don't eat or drink or chew gum during the interview.
7. Wear nice clothes to the interview.

b) Interviews can be scary. Sometimes you forget what to do or where to go. Put in the right infinitives after question words.

> how • what • where • who
> answer • ask • call • go (2x) • suggest • wear

Before my first interview, I didn't know *what to …* I asked my mum, but she didn't know … I finally chose a dress and took the bus.
I knew … When I was in the building, I looked around because I didn't know … for directions. The woman at the front desk knew … and told me … There was a difficult test before the interview and I didn't know … all of the questions, but I did OK.

▶ WB 2–3 (p. 19)

P3 SPEAKING Could you tell me? (Asking for, confirming, giving information) 🎧

a) Listen to the three conversations. In which one is Stella
– asking for information?   – giving information?   – confirming information?

b) Read through the phrases below and then put them under the correct heading.
Some can perhaps go under more than one heading.

ASKING FOR INFORMATION
GIVING INFORMATION
CONFIRMING INFORMATION

– Can I just confirm …?
– Do you think you could …?
– Excuse me, could you tell me …?
– Have I got that right? Do I … or do I …?

– Hello, my name is …
– I'm not quite sure about … Is it/Are they/ …?
– Is it right that …?
– Now I'd just like to tell you …
– OK, so let me put you in the picture. Now …
– Sorry, I'd just like to know …
– What else can I say? Well, I'm …
– Would you mind telling me …?

c) Compare the two sentences. Which is more polite? What makes it more polite?
Look for other phrases in your lists from b) which make sentences sound more polite.

Tell me when the next train to Victoria leaves.

Excuse me, do you think you could tell me when the next train to Victoria leaves?

Tip
When talking English to someone you don't know, you should always try to be polite. English-speakers often find Germans too direct, which makes them sound impolite.

d) Put this mixed-up conversation into the right order.

B: Yes, of course. You go back out of this building, turn right, turn right again when you get to the path next to the statue, and that leads you straight to the annex.
A: Oh, am I? I was told it was in the library. This is the library, isn't it?
A: Excuse me, could you tell me where the Newton Room is?
B: The Newton Room? Oh, I'm afraid you're in the wrong building.

A: Oh, I see. Would you mind telling me where that is?
B: Yes, this is the library, but the Newton Room is in the library annex.
B: Right. And the Newton Room is on the second floor.
A: Thanks very much.
A: OK, so I turn right out of this building and then take the path on the right next to the statue. Is that right?

e) 👥 Check your results in a group until you all agree.

f) 👥 Role play   **Partner A:** You have seen an advert for courses at a language school in the UK and phone for some more information.
Partner B: You work at the language school and try to answer your partner's questions when they phone you. Ask your teacher for your role cards. Study them and then act out the conversation together.

▶ SF Speaking Course (pp. 142–143) • WB 4–5 (pp. 20–21)

A YEAR ABROAD

1 A CV

Lukas Beyer wants to go to school in an English-speaking country for a year. His application to an exchange organization has to include a CV (British English) or résumé (American English).

CURRICULUM VITAE
Lukas Beyer

Klopstockstrasse 75B, 99096 Erfurt, Germany
Telephone: +49 (0) 361 000 8177   Mobile: +49 0178 000 4235
E-mail: lukbey30@gmx.de

Personal statement
I have always loved meeting new people and exploring new places. As English is my favourite subject at school, I am sure that spending a year at a British or American school will be a valuable experience.

I expect to improve my language skills and become a more independent person. I spent two weeks in Britain last year and now am really looking forward to getting to know the UK or the USA better and to telling people there about Germany.

Education
2004 to date	Secondary school: Heinrich-Mann-Gymnasium, Erfurt
2000–2004	Primary/Elementary school: Humboldt-Grundschule, Erfurt

Qualifications/Skills
Swimming	Gold youth swimming badge
IT skills	Good knowledge of MS Word, PowerPoint, Excel; basic knowledge of web design
Language skills	German native speaker; good written and spoken English; some French

Work experience
2008 to date	Regular job: delivering flyers by bike (1 hour per week)
May 2009	Placement: two weeks working at local IT company, organized by my school
2010 to date	Volunteer work: helping children with homework after school

Hobbies and interests
Member of school drama club; I play table tennis and basketball in after-school clubs; I enjoy reading, listening to and playing music and going to the theatre and cinema.

References
Available on request

---

a) Imagine you are applying to go to school abroad. Read through Lukas's personal statement and think about it. Then write a personal statement of your own. Make notes first and look through Lukas's CV for useful phrases.

b) **Extra** Lukas has written his CV the way they do in the UK. Compare and contrast this CV with a German CV. Consider the headings, the style, what information is missing, …

▶ SF Writing a CV (p. 148) • **Text File 5** (p. 106)

2 Writing a CV

a) *Imagine you want to spend six months at a school abroad. Use these website tips and write your CV in English. Add your personal statement from page 38.*

How to write a good CV

You want to apply for a place on an exchange programme? Or an interesting job? There will be many other candidates to choose from. So it is very important to produce a clear and effective CV.

CVs are very personal documents, different from applicant to applicant, and there is no particular 'correct' format. But these tips will help you write a good one.

1. Present your key skills, especially those the exchange organization or employer is looking for.

2. Keep it simple and do not make the pages too full. Two pages that are easy to read are better than one that is too crowded.

3. Most CVs should include:
   - Personal details: name, contact details and usually nationality. Your date of birth is not necessary.
   - Personal statement: explain what makes you suitable for the specific place or job, how it would help you develop and why you deserve to be successful in your application.
   - Education and qualifications: schools, subjects and exam results.
   - Work experience: list the jobs you have done, what you did and when, skills you used or learned there.
   - Achievements: list recent achievements (certificates, awards, etc.)
   - Extra-curricular activities: give brief information about your hobbies and interests, such as membership of and responsibilities in sport teams, clubs, organizations, etc.
   - General skills: driving licence, foreign languages and IT skills (give level, e.g. beginner, intermediate, advanced).
   - References: just write 'on request'. If employers need them they'll ask for them later.

4. Be positive. Use clear headings and language. Write short and meaningful sentences. Check your language to avoid mistakes (spelling, grammar, etc.).

5. Format: use a clear and easy-to-read font, size 9 or 10 point. The use of bold or different sizes or colours can highlight important information.

6. Let someone else check your final CV before you send it.

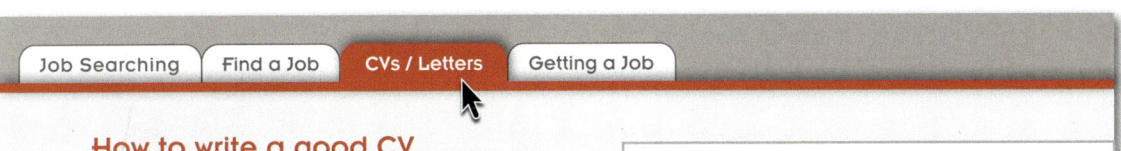

NICE TOUCH

b) *Sit in groups of four in a **correcting circle**. Pass your CV to the left. Read the CV you are given and make notes on what needs correcting (grammar, spelling, headings, layout, …). Then pass the CV and your notes to the left. Do the same again with the other CVs until you receive your own again. Use the notes from your group to correct your CV. Put it in your DOSSIER.*

3 A letter and some photos

Lukas needs to get in touch with his host family, and decides to send them a formal letter and some typical photos of his life.

My family at Christmas

Me and my mates in our band. One day we'll play Hyde Park!

Klopstockstrasse 75B
99096 Erfurt
Germany

20 February 2011

Dear Host Family

I hope you don't mind me writing before we meet. I would like to introduce myself and to say thank you for the opportunity to stay with you while I go to school in your country.

I am 15 years old and live in Erfurt, a large city in central Germany. I live with my parents and my younger sister, Julia. We have a nice flat with a big garden. My sister and I both go to the same school, which is near our flat. My parents both work. My father is an electrical engineer and my mother works in the city's housing dep…

…and I remember loving English from the very first lesson.

Before I arrive in your country, I would be very grateful if you could tell me a little about your family, the area you live in and the school I will go to.

I look forward to hearing from you soon and especially to meeting you.

Yours sincerely

Lukas Beyer

a) What features of a formal letter can you see in Lukas's letter?

b) The exchange organization gives students tips about what to write to their future host families. Imagine you are applying to go to an English-speaking country for a year. Write your letter to your host family.

c) Extra Use a **placemat** to note down the advantages and disadvantages of spending a year at a school abroad. Agree on the three most important advantages and disadvantages and write them in the middle.
Explain your opinion in a class discussion.

▶ WB 6 (p. 21)

- Give information about your personality, activities, interests, friends and goals.
- Describe what you like to do and what you have to do at home, at school, and in your community.
- Explain why you want to go to school abroad and live with a host family.
- Show your interest in *them* by asking about their activities and interests, their community and the school you will go to.
- Remember to say 'thank you' for the opportunity to live with them.

P1 STUDY SKILLS Writing a formal letter

a) Improve this covering letter for an application. What is missing at the beginning?

> Dear Ms Hall
>
> I read with interest the ad on your website about spending six months at an American high school and I would like to get a place. Here is my CV. I am 17 years old and I've just done Year 10 at my German high school.
>
> I am a friendly, helpful person and I enjoy my school work and what I do after school. I play sport (I'm in a volleyball club) and have flute lessons every week. I love music and I'd like to play in an orchestra one day. I have studied English for 6 years and my level is quite good.
>
> I can't wait to hear from you.
>
> Yours
>
> *Janine Neumann*
>
> Janine Neumann

STUDY SKILLS | Writing formal letters

1 Formal letters start with your address and usually the address of the person/organization you are writing to. Do not forget the date.
2 If you start a formal letter with the words **Dear Sir/Madam** or **To whom it may concern** (AE), you usually end it with **Yours faithfully** or **Sincerely** (AE). If you start with **Dear Mr/Ms/Mrs/Miss …**, you usually end with **Yours sincerely** or **Sincerely** (AE).
3 Avoid informal language and abbreviations such as 'ad'.

▸ SF Writing formal letters (p. 146)

c) Extra Imagine you are a couple of years older and see this advert for a summer job in Britain. Write a formal letter and apply for the job.

Ferienjob in Großbritannien?

Unsere Partnerstadt **Bangor in Wales** sucht deutschsprachige Aushilfen für die Touristen-information in diesem Sommer. Senden Sie Ihre **englischsprachigen Bewerbungsunterlagen** an:

Tourist Information Centre

Town Hall
Ffordd Deiniol
Bangor LL57 2RE
Wales

b) Replace the underlined parts with words and phrases from the box.

> advertisement • apply for •
> extra-curricular activities •
> I am a member of • I enclose •
> I have just completed •
> I look forward to hearing • I would like •
> six • Yours sincerely

P2 LISTENING Phoning about an interview

a) Listen to the phone call. How would you complete the message?

> Message for: Mr White
> Message from: Jon
> Caller's message:
> Mr … wanted to confirm — tomorrow at …
>
> Caller's contact details:
> Phone No:

b) Listen to the next call. How would you complete Jemma's notes?

> Interview time: …
> Place: … Street …
> big … building
> Ask for … at the … desk

▸ WB 7–8 (p. 22)

P3 REVISION Things your parents tell you (Gerunds as subject)

a) Use gerunds to complete the following sentences.
1. … can be dangerous.
   Riding your bike at night can be dangerous.
2. … is good for you.
3. … is bad for you.
4. … is not much fun.
5. … is great.
6. … will be really worth it.
7. … won't be very useful.
8. … can get you into trouble.
9. … makes me angry.
10. … always makes me cry.

▶ GF 2: The gerund (pp. 156–157)

b) What else can be good for you, or dangerous? Add some fun sentences of your own.
– Reading can be dangerous for your mind.
– Drinking too much water might change you into a fish!

P4 REVISION Talking about likes and dislikes (Gerunds as object)

a) Introduce yourself in writing. Write about the things you like or don't like doing and about your plans for the future. You can use the phrases below with gerunds. There are some helpful ideas in the box, but you can also add your own ideas.
– I like …   – I hate …
– I don't like …   – I enjoy …
– I don't mind …   – I prefer …
– I could imagine …
– I have never/often thought about …
– I try to avoid … – I quite fancy …

meet new people •
look after children/old people •
spend money on • learn foreign languages •
live on a farm • live abroad • work hard •
get my hands dirty • study Maths • …

b) 👥 Write six sentences about your partner. Compare your sentences with what your partner wrote.

P5 REVISION The party committee (Gerunds after prepositions)

a) Look at this information from a school notice board and complete it using prepositions from the box and the gerund of the verbs.

at (2×) • in • of (2×) • on • to

b) **Extra** Tell the Head of the Committee why you could do a good job. Say what you are good at doing, disappointed about so far, what you look forward to, what you would like to concentrate on, etc.

▶ WB 9–10 (p. 23)

- Are you tired … (sit) alone at home? YAWN
- Are you interested … (stay) at school after lessons?
- Are you good … (organize)?
- Are you keen … (get to know) new friends?
- Are you clever … (solve) problems?
- Are you sick … (go) to boring parties?
- Are you used … (work) hard?

Then join the school party committee for our next end-of-year party!

P6 STUDY SKILLS Using a grammar

a) Read this extract from a grammar. Then decide what the subjects of the gerunds in sentences 1–6 are.

1 John imagined **living** in Florida.
  John stellte sich vor, in Florida zu leben.

2 John imagined **his family living** in Florida.
  John stellte sich vor, dass seine Familie in Florida lebte.

3 John imagined **them living** in Florida.
  John stellte sich vor, dass sie in Florida lebten.

A gerund construction can be **without its own subject** (example 1), or it can have **its own subject** (examples 2 and 3). The meaning of the sentence is different in each case.

In all three examples *John* is the subject of the whole sentence. In example 1 the gerund does not have its own subject. Therefore the subject of the whole sentence is understood as the subject of the gerund *living*. In examples 2 and 3 the gerund does have its own subject. This is the 'notional subject', **the person who carries out the action** of the gerund: *family/them*. *Living* relates to these subjects (and not to *John*). In this construction a personal pronoun has the object form (example 3: *them*).

1 I can't imagine going to Australia for a year.
2 I can't imagine my best friend going to Australia for a year.
3 Jill's mum is proud of Jill going to university.
4 Jill's mum is proud of going to university.
5 I'm worried about making a mistake.
6 I'm worried about you making a mistake.

> **STUDY SKILLS Using a grammar**
>
> A grammar can help you
> – to correct or avoid mistakes,
> – to revise for a test.
> The table of contents and the index will help you to find the points you are looking for. But first you must know grammar words, like **tenses, clauses, adjectives, …**

▶ SF Using a grammar (p. 125)

P7 MEDIATION School in New Zealand

a) Partner B: Go to page 97.
Partner A: You and your partner want to spend some time at a school in New Zealand. In German, tell your partner the most important information about Wellington High School.

Wellington High School is the only state co-educational secondary school in Wellington City. We believe that learning is central and that high expectations with effective teaching produce resilient, self-directed learners.

The school has an established reputation in visual and performing arts, supported by creative technologies. Students consistently win awards in journalism, drama, computer, creative writing, jazz, film-making and a range of sports.

WHS has accepted students from around the world since the 1950s. The 80 international students at the school live with home stay families, which usually costs NZ$210 per week, but students over 18 may choose to live in the hostel or a flat.

Sports, music, drama and art are all included in the programme and international students are expected to participate in at least one activity.

WHS has seven science laboratories, photography darkrooms, seven computer laboratories, two gymnasiums, technology workshops, music and drama rooms, a recording studio, a radio station and a modern library which supports the research-based learning across the school.

All the teachers are highly qualified and experienced. They are trained to teach students for whom English is not their first language.

b) Listen to what your partner has to tell you about Onslow College.

c) In English, tell your partner which school you would prefer to go to and why.

▶ WB 11 (p. 24)

THE BUSINESS: A REALITY TV SHOW

1 Interview tips

Saturday 6.30 pm

THE BUSINESS

Rita McQueen from fashion company RMQ is the 'big boss' on this week's show. How can candidates Lucy and Mani impress Rita in their interviews and win the prize, two weeks' placement as Rita's assistant? Life coach Simon Gubbins gave them some tips.

'Big boss' Rita McQueen. Who will she choose?

Which three tips do you think are the most important? Discuss your choice with a partner.

- **Relax.** Before an interview listen to music, do yoga or breathe deeply.
- **Listen carefully** to the questions.
- **Don't talk too quickly.**
- **Smile** in the interview.
- **Be punctual.**
- **Research the company** before the interview. Show your interest in it.
- **Prepare answers** to typical interview questions like 'Can you tell us about yourself?' or 'What are your strengths and weaknesses?'.
- **Dress suitably** for the job you are applying for. Be careful with bright colours and make-up.
- **Don't talk too much.** But don't give one-word answers either.

2 VIEWING The interviews

a) Watch the interviews. Make notes about Mani and Lucy on copies of this assessment sheet.

b) Did the candidates follow Simon's advice? Watch again. Discuss. Give examples.

c) Which candidate should win? Discuss in your group. Give reasons for your choice. Then vote in class.

Assessment Sheet	☹		☺		😊	
The candidate	1	2	3	4	5	Comments
1 was relaxed and friendly				✓		smiled a lot
2 dressed suitably						
3 listened carefully						
4 talked well (not too much/too little)						
5 gave good answers						
6 was well prepared						
7 Other comments:						

d) Watch the results. Discuss Rita's decision with the help of the assessment sheet.

3 Extra Internet forum 'TV talk'

Here's what some people wrote after watching Lucy and Mani.
Write a short comment of your own for this forum.

▶ WB 12 (p. 24)

> **EJ** (1 day ago) But he was just too cheeky in the interview! Like when he said no when she asked him if he had any weaknesses. And he clearly didn't know much about Rita's business. She picked the wrong one if you ask me!
>
> **AliceW** (1 day ago) Yeah! That tie was crazy! The coach told them not to be shy – not a problem for Mani!
>
> **Max1234** (2 days ago) Did you see 'The Business' last night? I'm glad Mani won – he was cool.

P1 STUDY SKILLS Visual aids in presentations 🎥

a) Before they could become candidates for 'The Business', Mani and Lucy had to do a presentation on themselves for the programme's producers. Watch Mani and Lucy's presentations. Which did you think was better? Give reasons.

b) Read through the skills box. Then watch the presentations again. Which candidate used which visual aids? Rate how they used the visual aids from A (very good) to E (very poor).

> **STUDY SKILLS** | **Visual aids in presentations**
>
> **Why visual aids?**
> 1. Posters, transparencies and computer images show your audience the key points of your presentation. They also help you to stay organized during your presentation.
>
> **How to create visual aids**
> 2. Keep your visual aids simple and well-structured and focus on the key points.
> 3. Make your pictures BIG, **bold** and brilliant. But keep them clear.
> 4. Use a large font size and dark colours so that everybody in the room can read your visual aid.
>
> **During your presentation**
> 5. Don't talk to the visual aids, hide behind them or turn away from the audience.
> 6. Show your visual aids one by one – not all at once.

▶ SF Visual aids in presentations (p. 131)

Mani Wilson
Rita's next assistant

Lucy Shaw

c) 👥 Discuss your ratings with a partner and try to agree on them.

d) 👥👥 Do the same again in a group.

e) 👥👥 Work out and practise a presentation on one of the following:
– a great free-time activity
– the best computer game
– the best pet
– the most exciting theme park
– a wonderful book to read
– a dream holiday
– an interesting museum
– yourselves

Create visual aids to illustrate your presentation. The skills box will help. Then give your presentation to the class.

▶ WB 13–14 (p. 25)

BUSINESS

How to be a teenage millionaire

> Before you read the text, talk about these questions:
> How do teenagers usually earn money?
> Do you know anybody with their own business?

She hasn't got a rich family. She hasn't won the lottery. But at 17, Ashley Qualls, a computer geek from Detroit, is a millionaire. She's a successful businesswoman with her own company and she has bought a house for $250,000. But she's still too young to vote!

Ashley's idea was very simple. Her website, whateverlife.com, offers free designs that teenagers can use for their myspace.com pages.

Ashley, who is known as "AshBo" to her friends, has been working with websites since she was about nine years old. While other children were watching TV or playing outside, she was teaching herself HTML. She loved working with colours and designs for myspace.com layouts.

In 2004, she borrowed $8 from her mother to buy the whateverlife.com domain name. She didn't want to start a business. She just wanted a website to show her layouts to her friends.

More and more people started to visit the website and download Ashley's designs. Within a few weeks, she had 100 visitors. Then 5,000. Now her website has over 3,000 designs and gets over 7 million visitors a month. "I used to be excited when there were two people on the site and one was me!" says Ashley.

Advertisers started to get interested in advertising on her site and in September 2005 Ashley received her first cheque from the big

Ashley with some of her friends

advertising company, Value Click Media. It was for $2,700. "It was more than I made in a month," her mother says. That was just the start. The next cheque was for $5,000, the third was for $10,000.

When the first money arrived, her mother couldn't believe it. She wasn't sure if it was really possible to make money from a website. But Ashley was confident. She told her mother: "No, I really trust this. I think it's really gonna happen."

Although she was an excellent student at her high school, Ashley found it difficult to go to school and run a company. In January 2006, six months before her 16th birthday, she left school. She decided to continue studying from home so that she would have more time for the business. It was a big decision, so how did people react? "Everybody was shocked," she says. "They asked, 'Are you sure you know what you're doing?' But I had this crazy opportunity to do something different."

Most websites for teenagers are designed by adults. When you go to Ashley's site, it is clearly something that has been made by a teenager. This gives Ashley a big advantage because she understands what teenagers want. "They look at me and think, 'She's my age, she must know what I like.'"

The business now brings in as much as $70,000 a month. (The designs are still free. The money comes from advertising.) Ashley is learning how to be the 'big boss'. Her mother now works for her as a manager and she has a business adviser to help her too. She also pays some of her friends to work for her after school and at the weekend.

It's not easy to be someone's boss and their friend. Last year one of Ashley's friends was helping her, but Ashley thought she wasn't working hard enough. Ashley says that things were difficult between them for a while, but they are friends again now. Now she has a set of rules for everyone who works for her. "I tell them I need a minimum of 25 layouts a week to get paid," Ashley says. "It's just business."

Ashley had the right idea at the right time, and some people would say she was just lucky. But she clearly has a lot of ambition and determination and she works hard to make her business a success. "You have to have faith in yourself and believe in what you're doing," says Ashley. "These have been the best few years of my life, and also the most stressful … If people think running WhateverLife has always been easy, they are wrong," she explains.

Sometimes Ashley misses the normal life of a teenager. More than once she has returned to her old school, Lincoln Park High School, just for the day. "I miss the fact that I won't be graduating with my friends. They're all getting excited and it's sad to know I won't be a part of that exact moment."

And the future? Ashley hasn't got any definite plans. She wants to go to college, and she's thinking of going to design school in New York, which she calls her "dream city".

Working with the text

1 The article

a) Decide where these sub-headings should go in the article. Give line numbers.
1. A millionaire who's too young to vote
2. By a teenager for teenagers
3. Free designs for your MySpace page
4. From 100 to 7 million visitors a month
5. Hard work brings results
6. Learning to be the boss
7. Growing up too soon
8. Money from advertisers
9. No time for school
10. What next?

b) Compare results in a group and agree on where the headings should go.

c) **Extra** What else would you like to find out about Ashley? Make a list of three or four questions. Try to research the answers to the questions on the internet. Use what you find out to write a few more paragraphs for the article. Where would they best go?
▶ SF Research (p. 128)

2 The person

a) How would you describe Ashley? Use at least three adjectives from the box or others you think are better. (Look at page 36 again for ideas.) Find examples in the text to support your answer.

> ambitious • hard-working • easy-going • a geek • artistic • difficult • fun • greedy

b) Find at least four facts in the text that show the positive and negative side of Ashley's success. Present the facts in note form.

+ ASHLEY'S SUCCESS −

c) Ashley has made a lot of money from her business. But why did she start it? Explain what that has to do with her success.

d) What do you think of Ashley's story? Would you like her life? Make some notes and tell a partner what you think. Give reasons.
I'd like to … / But I wouldn't want to … because …

> study at home • earn lots of money • pay my friend/mum to work for me • be the boss • work so hard • have no time to relax • …

So to conclude, I would/wouldn't like Ashley's life. The main reasons are …

3 Your comment
Write a comment about Ashley Qualls's story for this internet forum.

Today at 13:49:17 Maria wrote:
I disagree with Chris. It wasn't luck. It was ambition, determination and hard work. The formula is: ambition + determination + ACTION = success. Remember! It is better to do one action than to think about 10 actions. Well done Ashley! She's a role model for me.

Today at 13:36:53 Chris wrote:
I don't agree. I don't think she's a role model. She's just a lucky person. We only read about her because she has lots of money. There are lots of young people who are much better role models. I'd prefer to read about young people who are trying to help other people.

Today at 13:32:38 Lea wrote:
Ashley's a role model for young people.

▶ WB 15 (p. 26) • Self-evaluation 1–2 WB (p. 27) • **Skills Check 2** WB (pp. 28–33)

4 Extra Job Day (adapted from *Speak* by Laurie Halse Anderson)

Ashley Qualls became a very successful teenage businesswoman. But what would she think of Melinda, the narrator of the passage below?

Just in case we forget that "weareheretogetagoodeducationsowecangotocollegeliveuptoourpotentialgetagoodjoblivehappilyeverafterandgotoDisneyWorld", we have a Job Day.

Like all things Hi!School, it starts with a test, a test of my desires and dreams. Do I (a) prefer to spend time with a large group of people? (b) prefer to spend time with a small group of close friends? (c) prefer to spend time with family? (d) prefer to spend time alone?

Am I (a) a helper? (b) a doer? (c) a planner? (d) a dreamer?

If I were tied to railroad tracks and the 3:15 train was ready to cut a path across my middle, would I (a) scream for help? (b) ask my little mice friends to chew through the ropes? (c) remember that my favorite jeans were in the dryer? (d) close my eyes and pretend nothing was wrong?

Two hundred questions later, I get my results. I should think about a career in (a) forestry (b) firefighting (c) communications (d) mortuary science.

Heather's results are clearer. She should be a nurse. It makes her jump up and down.

Heather: "This is the best! I know exactly what I am going to do. I'll volunteer at the hospital this summer. Why don't you do it with me? I'll study real hard in biology and go to State University and become a nurse. What a great plan!"

How could she know this? I don't know what I'm doing in the next five minutes and she has a plan for the next ten years. I'll worry about making it out of ninth grade alive. Then I'll think about a career.

a) Write out the sentence written as one word in lines 1–4 as a real sentence with separate words. What does it tell you about Melinda's opinion of Job Day?

b) Can you find other examples in the text that express Melinda's opinion of career plans and Job Day?

c) Compare Ashley's and Melinda's attitudes to a career. Discuss which phrases below go with which girl. Use the phrases and any other ideas you have and write two short character profiles. (Look back at your work on Ashley in 2 for help.)
... doesn't know how to plan ahead.
... is good at planning new projects.
... knows what she wants to do and goes for it.
... has no idea what her future will look like.
... left school when she found she was too busy.
... won't think about a career until later.

d) Have you started thinking about a career yet? If you have, tell your partner what your plans are. If not, explain why not.

Unit 3 Life in the big city

1 The cities of the world

a) Name some big cities you know. Say what you know about them, if you've visited them, why they've been in the news, films they've been in, what problems they have, what makes them exciting, ...

b) 👥 Brainstorm the pros and cons of city life.

+	–
• lots to do	• crowded
• freedom	• expensive
• ...	• ...

c) Read 'A world of cities?' and add more pros and cons to your lists.

d) 👥 Compare and agree on lists with a partner.

▶ Text File 8 (pp. 110–111)

2 Cities on the map

a) Look at the maps on p. 51 and explain what they tell you.

b) Extra Try to put these cities in order from largest to smallest. Then check to see if you are right.

> Berlin • Hong Kong • Johannesburg • Lagos • London • Los Angeles • Mexico City • Moscow • Mumbai • New York • Paris • São Paulo • Tokyo

3 👥 Three cities

This unit looks at three big cities: Hong Kong, Johannesburg and Mumbai. As you go through the unit, collect more information about the cities for your pros and cons table from 1b). Look at topics like: rich and poor, opportunities, lifestyle, crime, freedom, tradition, English, ...

A world of cities?

No one knows exactly what the world's first city was, or when it was built. But archaeologists have found some very old cities, like Uruk in southern Iraq, which was home to thousands of people 6,000 years ago. So we know that cities have been around for a very long time.

The problems ancient cities had are very similar to those of modern cities: waste disposal, clean drinking water, epidemics, traffic noise, street fights after sports events, pollution – you could see ancient Rome from a long way away because of all the smoke in the air above it.

Cities have always attracted people. Inside cities, people can exchange new ideas and enjoy more freedom and opportunity than outside. Cities mean science and progress and give people the chance to do something different with their lives.

That is what has always made cities attractive. Today, urban growth is faster than ever. In 1900 only 10 % of the world's population lived in cities. By 2007 it was 50 %. In 2050 75 % of humans will be inhabitants of cities, most of them in developing countries, and very many of these will live in slums. Even more than today, the earth will be a 'planet of slums'.

▶ WB 1 (p. 34)

The world's first city?

The world's largest city?

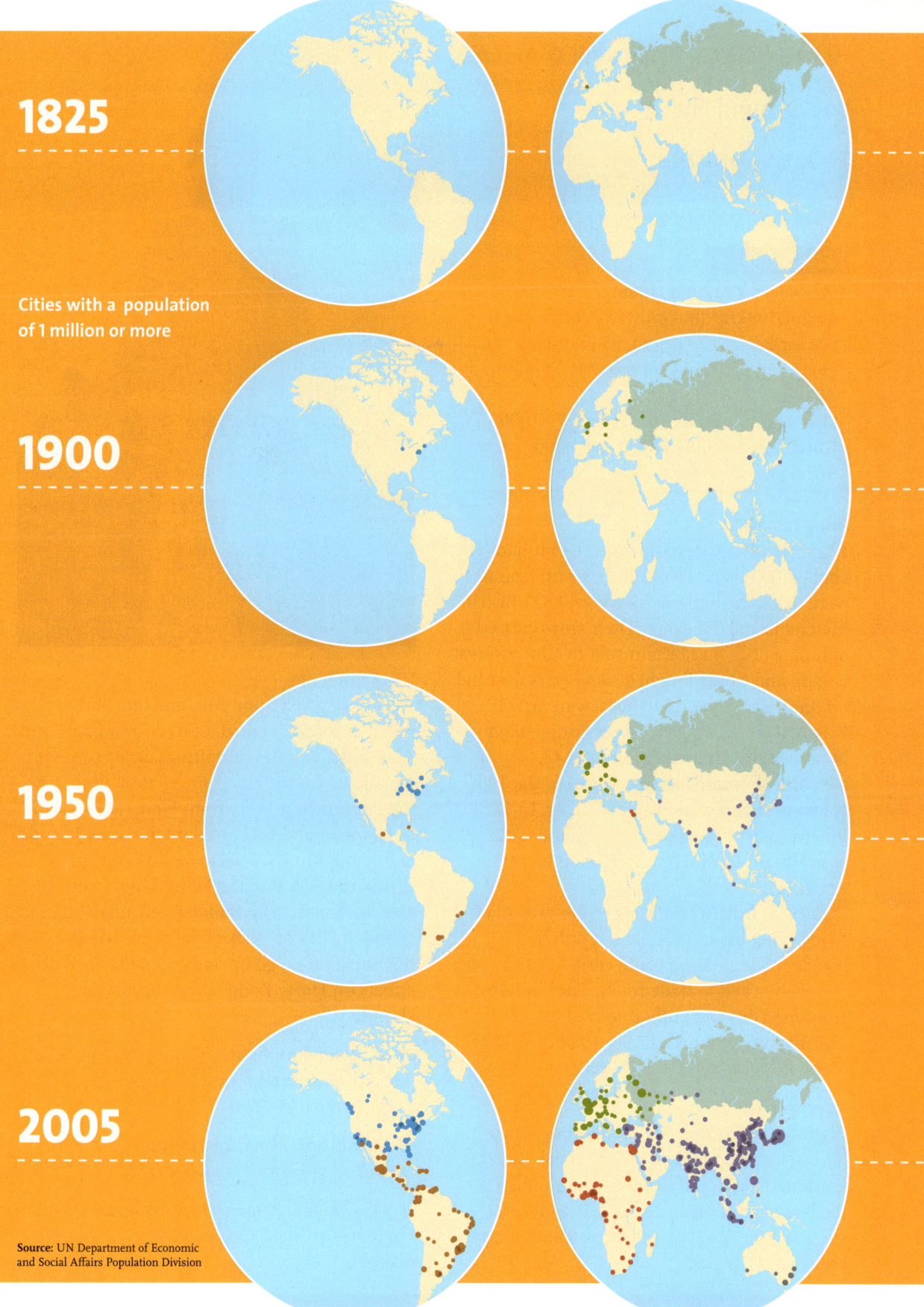

HONG KONG: FULL SPEED AHEAD

Background File

1 Asia's global city

Facts & figures
- Population: 7 million (2008)
- Area: 1,108 km² (but only 25 % urbanized)
- Life expectancy: 79 (men), 85 (women)
- Ethnic groups: 95 % Chinese, 2 % Filipino, 3 % other
- Main religions: Buddhists/Taoists 700,000, Christians 560,000, Muslims 90,000
- No. of tourists per year: 28 million

Hong Kong history
Hong Kong has been inhabited by humans for about 4,000 years. By the 18th century, pirates were using the harbour and from 1821 British merchants did the same. Their ships carried opium, a drug that Britain sold in China. Great Britain and China fought several wars over the opium trade in the mid-1800s, wars which Britain won. As a result Hong Kong Island became a British possession in 1842.

As China became less powerful in the 19th century, Britain's colony grew larger. In 1898 the two countries signed an agreement that gave Britain control of Hong Kong for 99 years.

In 1984, Britain finally agreed to give all of Hong Kong back to China, but only if the people in Hong Kong could continue to govern themselves and to trade freely. The Chinese supported this under their idea of 'one country, two systems', and in 1997 control of Hong Kong went back to China.

Hong Kong languages
English and Chinese are Hong Kong's two official languages. Most people speak the Cantonese dialect of Chinese, but English is the language of business. Hotel employees, shop and service staff and most young people speak some English.

Hong Kong now
Hong Kong is a huge port, and one of the most important centres of trade and finance in Asia and a magnet for tourists. They come to look down on the city from Victoria Peak, take the famous Star Ferry from Hong Kong Island to Kowloon and back, explore the other islands and Hong Kong's 730 km of coast, to hike, climb or watch birds in Hong Kong's countryside, to visit the Big Buddha on Lantau Island, spend the day at Disneyland or an evening at the horse races, go up and down the escalator streets on Hong Kong Island, or just go shopping.

a) What information on Hong Kong do you find most interesting? Explain why to a partner and listen to their ideas.

b) Explain how Hong Kong's history has made English an important language there.

c) **Extra** Research some more on one of the things in 'Hong Kong now'. Tell your group about it.

▶ WB 2 (p. 34)

2 VIEWING Hong Kong: Live your dream!

a) What aspects of city life would you expect to see in a film called *Hong Kong: Live your dream!*? What could the message be?
List a few ideas alone first. Then discuss all the ideas in a group. Agree on a final list in class.

b) Watch the video. Compare what it shows to your list from a). Tick the ideas that come up.

c) Watch the video again. What other aspects of city life does it show? Add them to your list.

d) Extra   Use your list and agree on what you would – and wouldn't – show in a film that advertises your hometown or area.
Present your ideas to the class.

3 Hong Kong on the move

a) Read the poem by a Hong Kong student, Brian Ng Kwok Leong. What is he trying to say about the city? How do the photos on this page illustrate the poem?

Hong Kong is
On the run
Never stops
Going.
Kinetic energy
Of people who
Never
Give up.

b) Explain what connects the poem to the video about Hong Kong that you watched.

c) Extra   Choose the name of a big city you know or would like to visit. Write an acrostic poem like the one on Hong Kong.
You can display the poems in the classroom, then put yours in your DOSSIER.

4 Hong Kong teens 🎧

We interviewed three teenagers from a school in Hong Kong. One is German-Chinese, one Chinese, and one British-Chinese.

Daniel Hanemann, 16

Terence Tang, 15

Natasha Brown, 16

a) Listen and take notes on what the teenagers say about the following topics:
– Background and family
– Languages
– School, studying and tuition
– Free time
– Friends
– Future

b) 👥 Exchange and check your notes in a group. Contrast your lifestyle with those of the teenagers. Share your ideas with the class.

c) Listen again and take notes on what you find out about:
– different areas of Hong Kong
– the languages spoken there
– the best things to do and best places to go
Which of the places or activities sound most interesting to you? Vote on the best in class.

d) Extra 'A nice place to visit, but I wouldn't want to live there.' From what you have learned about Hong Kong so far, comment on this sentence.

5 Extra High-rise Hong Kong

In his interview, Daniel mentioned the IFC mall. The International Finance Centre complex contains the mall, a hotel, offices and one of Hong Kong's largest skyscrapers, '2IFC'. It is 420 metres and 88 storeys high. Its design is simple and strong, like a huge obelisk. When lit at night, the top of its roof is a welcoming beacon above Victoria Harbour.

👥 *Find an interesting example of modern architecture from a big city. Explain what the building is used for, what is special about it, and what it expresses. Present your building to the class. Don't forget a picture.*

▶ **Text File 6** *(pp. 107–108)*

Part A B C   Practice   **3**   55

P1 WORDS Cities and city life

a) Look at the three boxes of words. What other words do you know that could be useful for talking about cities and city life? Add them to a copy of the boxes. (You might find more words on pages 50–54.)

b) Choose adjectives from the blue box that go with nouns from the grey box to make phrases, e.g.:
modern buildings, dangerous areas, …

c) Find verbs from the yellow box that go with the phrases you have found:
– *meet/see trendy people*
– *go to a huge mall, …*

d) Extra Write to an English-speaking friend about a big city you have visited. Tell them about the city. Use as many phrases from this exercise as you can.

Verbs
go • live • meet • relax • see • shop • travel • visit • work • …

Adjectives
ambitious • busy • crowded • dangerous • dirty • elegant • excellent • exciting • expensive • huge • modern • noisy • polluted • trendy • …

Nouns
– Transport: airport, traffic, tram, …
– Opportunities: concerts, discos, jobs, …
– Places: suburbs, mall, areas, …
– Buildings: museum, concert halls, stadium, …
– Problems: poverty, graffiti, pollution, …
– People: tourists, business people, inhabitants, …

P2 EVERYDAY ENGLISH SPEAKING Changing your flight 🎧

a) Michael Schulze and his mother need to change the date of their return flight from Hong Kong to Frankfurt. Listen to the conversation. Then answer the questions.

1 What's the date of the original return flight that Michael and his mother planned?
2 When do they want to return now?
3 How much will the flight change cost them?
4 Why can't they fly at 11:05 pm?
5 What are the departure and arrival times and dates of their new flight?

▶ WB 3–4 (p. 35)

b) 👥 **Role play**: Booking a flight
Partner B: Go to p. 97.
Partner A: Phone a travel agent for a return flight from Frankfurt to Hong Kong leaving 29 November. You'd like the cheapest flight but can't leave before 3 pm. You want to return on 29 December but can't leave till lunchtime.

c) 👥 You work for a travel agent. Use the information in the table to help your partner. Start by answering the phone.

29/11 – 29/12 Hong Kong Jet: EUR 730,00				
Flight	From	Dep	To	Arr
HKJ 756	FRA	13:30	BOM	01:35 + 1
HKJ 757	BOM	03:25	FRA	07:45
29/11 – 29/12 Hong Kong Jet: EUR 721,00				
HKJ 764	MUC	11:30	BOM	23:40
HKJ 765	BOM	01:30	MUC	05:50
29/11 – 29/12 Marathi Air: EUR 715,25				
Flight	From	Dep	To	Arr
MA 144	FRA	10:00	BOM	21:45
MA 191	BOM	00:50	FRA	06:05

JOHANNESBURG: CITY OF CONTRASTS

Background File

1 A world-class African city

Facts & figures

Population: 3.9 million (city)
Area: 1,644 km² (city)
Life expectancy: 50 (men), 45 (women)
Ethnic groups: 73% Black Africans, 16% Whites, 6% Coloureds, 4% Asians
Main religions: Christians 67%, no organized religion 24%, Muslims 3%, Jews 1%
No. of tourists per year: 4.5 million

Johannesburg history

In 1902, when the British and Dutch in South Africa united after the Boer War, Johannesburg was already the country's economic centre. Gold had been discovered there in 1885, which resulted in the place growing from nothing to a city of 100,000 by 1895.

However, there were no equal rights: the whites had all political and economic power. From 1948 a system of racist and oppressive laws called apartheid separated blacks and whites in all areas of life. The anti-apartheid movement fought against it for over 40 years and in the 1990s was successful. In 1994 its most famous leader, Nelson Mandela, who had spent 29 years in prison, became South Africa's first black president.

Johannesburg languages

An important event in the fight against apartheid was the Soweto Uprising in 1976. It began when black students protested against being educated in Afrikaans. For blacks, Afrikaans, the language of the Dutch colonists, was the language that represented apartheid.

Today, South Africa has eleven official languages, but English is the main language of business, government and the media.

Johannesburg now

Since the end of apartheid, Johannesburg has grown rapidly, but so has crime. That's why the rich and many businesses have moved out of the city centre to suburbs like Sandton, where security and the standard of living are high. The poorer parts of the city suffer from a high crime rate and the AIDS epidemic – 34% of people between the ages of 25 and 29 have HIV.

The 2010 World Cup brought many overseas visitors to 'Jozi'. They enjoyed the football but also the special atmosphere of a city where life is fast. They toured Soweto, visited the Apartheid Museum, had fun on the rides at Gold Reef City or relaxed in the city's many green parks.

a) Tell your partner what you find most interesting or surprising about Johannesburg.

b) Who suffered from the oppression of apartheid? What other examples of oppression have you learned about in your English classes?

c) **Extra** Research some more on one of the things in 'Johannesburg now'. Tell your group about it.

▶ WB 5 (p. 36)

2 Five reasons why I love Johannesburg 🎧

By Damaria Senne

I was recently walking along the beach in the most beautiful country imaginable where the people were welcoming and the food and shopping were great. I thought how lucky the people living there were. Yet, I wouldn't exchange it for big, noisy, crazy Johannesburg,
5   where the crime rate is high and touches us all. Here are some of the reasons why I love a city that sometimes treats its inhabitants badly:

1   The weather is beautiful. In summer, it's usually hot, with cooling thunderstorms in the afternoons or at night.
10 2   Johannesburg is a city of contrasts. If you're looking for a fast and furious lifestyle and want to play as hard as you work, this is the city for you. But it's not only a place for hard-working people. There are many quiet parts of
15 the city where you still see old people going for a walk with their dogs in the evening. Or watch kids skating on the road; the sort of place where the woman at the supermarket remembers you from when you were a child.
20 3   I love the local colour. The city centre, where it all began during the gold rush in the 1890s, is always crowded. There are people selling local crafts, fruit and vegetables on the sidewalks and in the flea markets. For the
25 fearless there is Hillbrow, a part of the city inhabited by prostitutes, drug dealers and street kids. Some of the friendliest people I've met were street kids who walked me home at night because I'd wandered there by mistake
30 when I was still new in the city. And no, they didn't mug me on the way.
    4   I love Johannesburg when the beautiful, purple jacarandas are in bloom.
    5   December is almost like one long party. Of
35 course we work, but the day is long, the weather is lovely, and we meet friends at cafés and restaurants for lunch and dinner and anything in between to relax and party. In the air, there is always a vibe that makes me want
40 to dance.

a) How does Damaria Senne feel about Johannesburg? Take notes on the positive and negative sides of life in the city.

b) 👥 Use a **placemat**. Write down the reasons why you would or would not like to visit Johannesburg.
Discuss your ideas and agree on the best reason for visiting and the best for not visiting the city. Walk around the class and look at the results of the other groups' placemats.

3 Shooting Jozi

In July 2007 one hundred people in some of the poorest townships of Johannesburg were given disposable cameras and asked to document their lives. These are some of the pictures they produced.

a) 👥 *Choose one photo and look at it closely. Then describe it to a partner.*
Discuss what your two photos tell you about people's lives in the townships of Johannesburg. Share your ideas with two other pairs.

b) *Imagine you took one of the photos. What did you want to show with your photo?*

c) **Extra** *Take a photo that illustrates an aspect of your life, e.g. at home, your journey to school, a club you go to, …*
Write a few sentences about your photo. Display your work, then put it in your DOSSIER.

▶ Text File 7 *(p. 109)*

P1 REVISION Fighting apartheid (Participle clauses instead of relative clauses)

Rewrite this draft of an article, using participle clauses instead of the underlined relative clauses.

The South African leader Nelson Mandela was the symbol of the fight against apartheid, the South African system which separated people by race. ..., *the South African system separating people by race*. He spent nearly 30 years of his life in prison.

Mandela was born in 1918. He studied law and in 1952 he opened the first law firm in South Africa which was owned by blacks. Before that, in 1944, Mandela had joined the African National Congress (ANC), an organization which fought for the freedom of black people in South Africa. Mandela soon became an ANC leader. In 1964 he was given a life sentence for his protest activities.

In the 1980s a campaign which was supported by people in South Africa and around the world to free Mandela grew. Under President F. W. de Klerk, the government freed Mandela in 1990.

Mandela became president of the ANC in 1991. He and de Klerk worked together to end apartheid. They wanted to change South Africa into a democracy that gave people of all colours equal rights. In 1993 they won the Nobel Peace Prize for their work.

In 1994 South Africa had its first free elections, elections which resulted in Mandela becoming the country's first black president. Mandela retired from active politics in 1999.

P2 WORDS During apartheid (Participles as adjectives)

a) Form compound adjectives that make sense using one word from the left and one word from the middle. Match them with a noun from the right, e.g. Afrikaans-speaking people.

Afrikaans	educated	action film
fast	looking	activist
good	loving	model
hard	moving	people
peace	speaking	professor
well	working	teacher

b) Rewrite the following sentences with some of the compound adjectives you formed in a).
1. During apartheid a white minority who spoke Afrikaans ruled South Africa.
2. Blacks who worked hard could still not enjoy the comfortable lifestyle of whites.
3. In South Africa, it was very difficult for a black person to become a lawyer with a good education like Nelson Mandela did.
4. When he became president, Mandela was still a man who loved peace.

P3 A bus tour through Soweto (Verbs of perception + object + present participle)

Look at this sentence from page 57 (ll. 15–16):
'You still **see old people going** for a walk with their dogs.'
*When you want to describe your experiences, you can use **verbs of perception** like feel, hear, see, watch, ... with an **object** and a **present participle**. During a trip to South Africa you went on a bus tour through Soweto. Describe some of the things you saw, listened to, noticed, ...*

1. see – tourists – visit the Soweto Uprising Memorial
2. listen to – guide – talk about the Uprising
3. notice – people – live in nice houses and in slums
4. watch – diners – eat good food at 'Wandies'
5. watch – man – get water from a tap in the street
6. see – children – play on a dusty road

▶ WB 6–8 (pp. 36–37)

P4 WORDS Word building (Suffixes to make adjectives)

-able	-al	-ful	-less	-y
imagin**able**	centr**al**	success**ful**	fear**less**	nois**y**

a) Copy the chart. Then use the suffixes to make adjectives from words in the box on the right. With some words, you can use more than one suffix. Use a dictionary to check.
Remember: some spelling changes may be necessary when you add a suffix.

b) Choose twelve adjectives from the chart and for each of them find two or more nouns that are often used with it:
– *a beautiful building, a beautiful day, …*
– *a dirty place, dirty clothes, …*

beauty • break • care • **centre** • cloud • colour • count • dirt • drink • dust • **fear** • help • home • hope • hunger • **imagine** • industry • job • meaning • nation • nature • **noise** • pain • pay • power • sleep • smell • **success** • tradition • trend • understand • use

c) Extra Choose five adjectives from your chart and dictate them to your partner. Take turns. Then swap what you have written and correct the words if necessary.

P5 WRITING A carjacking (Subjective versus objective report)

a) In 2007, a famous South African reggae star, Lucky Dube, was killed in a carjacking. Read the following statements by people who saw what happened.

First witness:
'I was standing in front of my house – with my wife. Everything happened so fast. There was this car, and two men came running towards it. They had guns, I could see that. They opened the door on the driver's side of the car. They shouted something. Then there were shots, two shots my wife said. I'm not sure. It was horrible. I grabbed my wife and ran inside. Man, we were scared. So I didn't really see what happened afterwards.'

Second witness:
'The carjackers came from across the street. They were fast! They opened the door on the driver's side of the car and shot the driver. Twice, I believe. But the driver wasn't dead at once. He drove away and hit some parked cars. And then he hit a tree. He must have lost control of the car by then. Poor boy – he had to see his father being shot!'

Third witness:

'I was at the street corner talking to a neighbour when I saw this car stopping at the side of the street. There was a man and a boy in the car. When the boy got out, there were two men who came running towards the car. They looked dangerous and they had guns. They didn't shoot first, but ran and opened the driver's door of the car – and then they shouted something and they fired their guns. The car drove off. And then it hit a tree. It was terrible. A lot of shouting. I think there were two shots. All this carjacking makes me sick. It's violent and so many people are killed!'

b) In groups, decide what are the objective facts and what are people's subjective opinions. Then write an objective report of the carjacking, including the important facts, but not the less important facts or the opinions.

▶ WB 9 (p. 37)

P6 I watched that film (Giving an oral summary)

a) Read the tips on how to give an oral summary. Then watch the extract from the Oscar-winning film *Tsotsi*.

b) Look at how these two students start to summarize the film for their classmates. Which one do you think is better? Give reasons.

> I watched that film on Channel X last night. At half past ten. I wasn't feeling tired at all so I decided to see what the film is like. There's this kid, a black kid and this woman, a posh lady you know, black as well, living in a wealthy part of the town. I can't remember which one. Maybe Joburg, but could be somewhere else. Anyway, she's driving a posh car, a Jaguar I think. But I'm not sure because it was raining like hell. Anyway – oh, no, before that the boy has just had a fight and then there was all this strange …

> Last night I watched a film called *Tsotsi* about a black kid from a really poor background. In this one scene, he's running away from a fight and thinking about his childhood. Then it starts raining and he's in this rich suburb and sees this posh black woman driving up in her car. She's trying to get into her house but the gate won't open. So she has to get out of her car to call for help. When the boy sees this he jumps into the car, shoots at the woman and drives …

Tip

You give an oral summary when you tell someone about something you've read, or a film or TV programme you've seen.

1. Name the main ideas or actions but leave out the details, whatever you're summarizing. Use the present tense.
2. For a written summary you have time to organize your thoughts. For an oral summary you need to think quickly.
3. The way you speak can help to get across what you want to say, e.g. through your tone of voice and the words that you stress. You might also have to answer questions from the person you are speaking to.
4. Try not to give your personal opinion.

Presley Chweneyagae stars as Tsotsi in Gavin Hood's Oscar-winning film.

c) Now watch the film extract again. Then choose a partner and continue the better summary or try your own one from the start. Your partner checks your oral summary with the points in the box above and tells you how well you did and what you could do better.

d) Extra Give each other oral summaries of a book you've read or a film you've seen, or of one scene from the film or book.

▶ SF Speaking Course (pp. 142–143) • WB 10 (p. 38)

MUMBAI: PEOPLE OF THE CITY

Background File

1 Maximum City

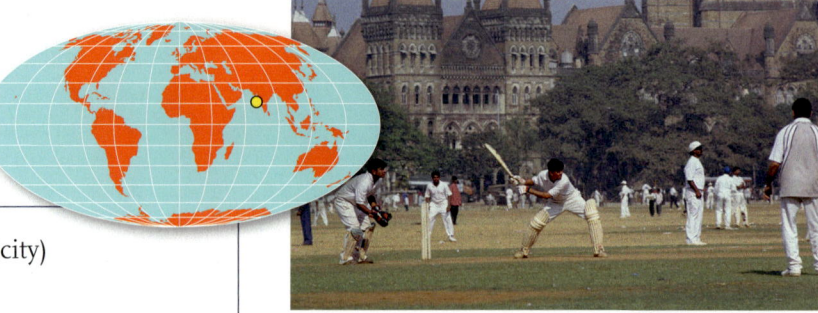

Facts & figures

Population: 13.9 million (city)
Area: 438 km^2
Life expectancy: 68
Ethnic groups: 53% Maharashtrians, 22% Gujaratis, 17% North Indians, 3% Tamils, 3% Sindhis, 2% other
Main religions: Hindus 68%, Muslims 17%, Christians 4%, Buddhists 4%
No. of tourists per year: 1 million

Mumbai history

Mumbai became a British possession in 1661 and was soon an important port for the East India Company. Bombay, as it was called then, grew steadily for nearly 200 years. Then it experienced a boom during the American Civil War (1861–1865), when it became the world's biggest cotton market.

In the 20th century Bombay was one of the centres of the fight for Indian independence from Britain. Mahatma Gandhi started the Quit India Movement in a park there. India became independent in 1947.

Now Bombay, officially called Mumbai since 1996, is the biggest, richest and fastest city in India.

Since the early 1990s Mumbai has also seen a lot of violence between Hindus and Muslims. Over 1,000 people died in riots in 1992–93 and terrorist attacks and bomb attacks since then have killed hundreds more.

Mumbai languages

Marathi is the most common language in Mumbai; the other main languages are Hindi, Gujarati and English. English is spoken by many people and is the main language of the city's office workers.

Mumbai now

Mumbai is the economic powerhouse of India, the heart of every industry from films to textiles and petrochemicals. Mumbai is:
– cricket, India's national sport,
– bhelpuri, a sweet and spicy snack on Chowpatty Beach,
– wonderful colonial buildings,
– red double-decker buses,
– a railway system carrying 2.2 billion passengers a year.

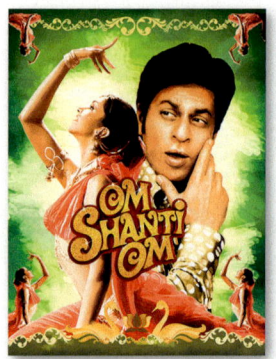

Mumbai is the glamour of Bollywood, whose films are watched by nearly a sixth of the world's population. Mumbai doesn't follow the trends, it sets them.

Mumbai is millionaires and superstars and millions living in slums.

Mumbai is endless energy – in the words of the journalist Suketu Mehta: 'Maximum City'.

a) *Compare the facts and figures for Mumbai, Johannesburg and Hong Kong with the facts and figures for Germany's largest city, Berlin (see page 65). What do you find interesting?*

b) *Explain why English is such an important language in Mumbai.*

c) **Extra** *Do some more research on one of the aspects named in 'Mumbai now'. Tell your group about it.*

▶ WB 11–13 (pp. 38–39)

2 Mumbai slums

a) Look at the two photos below and skim the report for one minute. Explain to your partner what you think it is about. Do they agree?

b) Read the report carefully. Take notes. What do you find most shocking, interesting, surprising? Tell your partner. Again, do they agree?

Mumbai is home to more than six million squatters – people who have nowhere to live so they have to occupy private or public land and build their communities there. Sanjay Gandhi Nagar is such a squatters' town.

It was Alice in Wonderland in reverse: a rabbit hole in the ceiling. That's how I entered my room in Sanjay Gandhi Nagar: having walked into my landlord's shop, I step around the guys making clothes, climb the ladder in the corner and pull myself through the opening.

Home was a bare concrete cell, perhaps 10 by 14 feet, with grey walls and two small windows. My landlord, kindly, had given me a bed, two chairs and a ceiling fan – the smallest and noisiest fan I had ever seen. I moved the bed under the fan, hoping to escape from the mosquitoes at night.

Made mostly of concrete, Sanjay Gandhi Nagar could be called an upper-class squatter community. This neighborhood of 300 families was about an hour from downtown Mumbai by train. Sanjay Gandhi Nagar had electricity. My room had no water, but the community did have water within a few feet of almost every doorway. However, the water only came on between 2:00 and 5:00 in the mornings, so when anyone needed to fill their buckets, they had to wake up in the middle of the night. I saw some of my neighbors only at 3 A.M., when we were filling our water buckets.

Sanjay Gandhi Nagar had two shared toilet blocks: ten toilets each, five for women and five for men. It sounds like a lot, but during the morning rush, you sometimes had to wait for 15 minutes or so, with your bucket of water (poor Indians don't use toilet paper).

Most people bathe outside. They sit in a large bucket, pour water over themselves,

and wash. Men bathe in their underwear; women bathe wearing saris.

I paid 1,000 rupees a month for my room: about $22. This was a fair price, but it also made my room too expensive for many squatters in Mumbai.

Abridged and adapted from Shadow cities, *by Robert Neuwirth*

c) Use a table to explain how people in Mumbai's slums manage to live with the problems they face in their everyday lives. Which problems can't they manage?

problems	can be managed	can't be managed
mosquitoes	people use a ceiling fan	…
…		

3 Mumbai homes (adapted from the novel *Koyal Dark, Mango Sweet* by Kashmira Sheth)

16-year-old Jeeta lives in Mumbai with her parents, her sisters Nimita and Mohini, and her brothers Chiraj and Vivek. She has made friends with a new girl at school, Sarina. Asked to visit by her new friend, Jeeta goes to Sarina's home on a side street off Marine Drive. After having lunch with Sarina's mother, they go to her friend's room.

It was a beautiful room, painted in the lightest blue. Besides her bed, there was a large ebony cupboard, a desk and a chair. Next to Sarina's room was her own bathroom and a balcony.

I tried to imagine a room that would have only my things: my bed, my books, my clothes, and my secrets. Mine alone. Our home was a one-bedroom apartment. All my life I'd shared a bedroom with Nimita, Mohini, Chiraj, Vivek and Mummy. Pappa slept in the living room, and many times in the middle of the night, Mummy went there too, when she thought we were asleep.

Every night we put mattresses on the floor and spread white cotton sheets on top. There were two mattresses for Mummy, Mohini and me; and Mohini and I took turns to sleep in the middle. Since Nimita couldn't see well at night, she got her own mattress and a nice corner to sleep in. Chiraj and Vivek slept on two single beds. After Nimita got married, Mummy slept in Nimita's corner and Mohini and I got our own mattress, which made Mohini and me happy. No more sleeping on the crack!

"Let's go out on the balcony," Sarina said. I followed.

From the balcony I could almost touch one of the palm trees. Looking up, I saw some small coconuts. They were hanging down like green balloons. Sarina's room didn't face the ocean, but from the left side of the balcony I could see a little of it. It didn't matter. The wind brought the scent of the ocean to us. "Only yesterday, after the first rain of the monsoon, did we turn off the air-conditioning. It feels good to open all the windows and doors and smell the earth, doesn't it?"

"We don't have AC," I said, watching the horizon with my eyes.

Marine Drive, Mumbai

She put her hand on my shoulder. "In Mumbai you really don't need it anyway. It never gets so hot here. For a few years, we were in New Delhi and it got so hot there that I wished I was a water buffalo sitting in a muddy pond. If you ever live there, make sure you have one."

"A pond or a buffalo?"

She laughed. "No. I meant an air-conditioner."

"Oh!" I said. "We're not rich. We only have one apartment in Mumbai. I could never imagine having a place in two cities. You know, I've never lived anywhere except Mumbai and I don't think I ever will."

"Why not? We're not rich either. We get this apartment to live in because Pappa is a judge. In Delhi we also had a nice place to live in, but we didn't own that place either. Pappa jokes that one day before he retires we'll have to find a place of our own to live in. Mummy and Pappa say that they never imagined they'd live in such a fancy place. So you see, you never know. You might live in Delhi or somewhere else."

"You mean, get married to someone who's not from Mumbai?"

"Get married! I wasn't thinking about that. What if you go somewhere to study or work?"

I stared at her.

The thought of me going far away to study or work was completely new to me. In my house the conversations were always about getting someone married. First it was Nimita, now it was Mohini, and I knew that as soon as Mohini was married, Mummy would start thinking about me.

a) Compare what you find out about the homes of Jeeta and Sarina. What extra information does this give you about the people of Mumbai?

b) What idea of Sarina's surprises Jeeta so much? Explain what this tells you about their two families.

c) Extra Write about something that surprised you when you first went to a friend's home.
▶ Text File 9 *(p. 112)*

Berlin

Facts & figures
Population: 3.4 million
Area: 892 km²
Life expectancy: 76 (men), 82 (women)
Ethnic groups: 87% German, 4% Turkish, 6% Other European, 4% Other
Main religions: No organized religion 60%, Christians 32%, Muslims 6%, Jews 0.4%
No. of tourists per year: 6 million

Brandenburger Tor

Hackesche Höfe

P1 Exploring language | Participle clauses

a) Look at these sentences:
Asked to visit by her new friend, Jeeta goes to Sarina's home.
Looking up, I saw some small coconuts.
Asked to visit by her new friend and *Looking up* are participle clauses. They are used instead of adverbial clauses with **when**:
When she is asked by her new friend to visit her, Jeeta goes to Sarina's home.
When I looked up, I saw some small coconuts.

b) Here are some more sentences with participle clauses. Can you rewrite them? (Where would you use the conjunction **when**, where would you use **because**? Where could you use **when** OR **because**?)
1 Arriving in Mumbai, I started to look for a room.
2 Feeling tired, I went up to my room.
3 Worried about the mosquitoes, I moved the bed under the fan.

c) Can you rewrite the following sentences? (Think about which action happened first.)
1 Having filled our buckets, we stayed and talked for a few minutes.
2 Having gone back to my landlord's shop, I climbed the ladder to my room.

d) Translate the sentences in b) and c) into German.

e) How could you translate the following sentences into German? Which linking words would you use – 'und' or 'indem' or 'wobei' or ...?
1 Using a ladder, I was able to pull myself through the opening in the ceiling.
2 I stood in the queue, waiting to fill my bucket with water.

▶ GF 3.4–3.5: Participle clauses (pp. 159–161)

P2 Work and school in Mumbai (Participle clauses)

a) Shorten the sentences. Use present participle clauses.
1 Most inhabitants of Mumbai begin their day early because they want to do a lot before it gets too hot.
   Most inhabitants of Mumbai ..., wanting ....
2 After they have got onto the crowded trains, commuters hang out of the doors.
3 When they arrive at their destinations, they hurry to work.
4 In the evening they hurry onto the trains because they hope to get a seat.
5 After they have worked hard all day, many commuters sleep on their journey home.

b) Decide if you need a **present** or a **past** participle clause and shorten the following sentences.
1 After she moved to Mumbai, Sarina went to Majiraj School.
2 The other girls talked about her because they were surprised by her arrival.
3 When she was given a seat next to the new girl, Jeeta decided to be nice to her.
4 When she sat down next to Sarina, she gave her a big smile.
5 As they liked each other a lot, they soon became great friends.

▶ WB 14 (p. 40)

P3 The day begins in Mumbai (Participle clauses)

*Shorten the following sentences. Use **present** and **past** participle clauses.*
1 Beggars sit on the busy streets <u>and hold out their hands for money</u>.
   Beggars sit on the busy streets, holding ...
2 They sit there all day <u>and are burned brown by the hot sun</u>.
3 Thousands of cars and mopeds move into the city <u>and add their heat to that of the sun</u>.
4 People walk through the markets <u>and enjoy all the sights and smells</u>.
5 Tourists enjoy an expensive breakfast <u>while they look forward to a day of sightseeing</u>.
6 Children in uniform walk to school <u>and are carried along by the crowds in the street</u>.

P4 Extra Jeeta's visit (Participle clauses with conjunctions)

Sometimes you need a conjunction in front of a participle clause to make clear exactly what you mean. Compare:

1 Having lunch with his girlfriend's parents, Tom fell asleep.

2 After having lunch with his girlfriend's parents, Tom fell asleep.

Shorten the following sentences. Use participle clauses with conjunctions.
1 After they had lunch with Sarina's mother, they went to Sarina's room.
2 Before she left, Jeeta looked at her friend's photos of the USA.
3 Jeeta thought she would like to go to America, if she was given the chance.
4 Although she was interested in hearing about the USA, her sister could not imagine living there.
5 The two sisters argued while they cooked.

▶ *GF 3.6: Participle clauses (p. 161)*

P5 Mumbai travel guide (Participle clauses)

Try to improve the travel guide information by rewriting and linking sentences. Use participle clauses for the underlined parts.
Mumbai, earlier known as Bombay, is ...

Mumbai, <u>which was earlier known as Bombay</u>, is the largest city in India and the capital of Maharashtra state. The city has a population of nearly 21 million, a figure <u>which makes it one of the largest cities in the world</u>. It is also home to India's largest slums.

Mumbai is one of the most important cities in India <u>because it is the financial and business capital of the country</u>. Mumbai is also the home of Bollywood and at the centre of the largest film industry in the world.

Mumbai is a magnet for people from all over India and the world. They come for many reasons. It might be a 14-year-old <u>who has run away</u> to become a film star. Or a 30-year-old who has come here to earn money and support a family in a village. Or a business person <u>who has been attracted by an exciting new job</u>. All these people come to the city <u>because they are dreaming of a better future</u>.

What is it about Mumbai that fascinates them? What is it about this city that they never want to leave again? <u>When you arrive for the first time</u>, you may not immediately know – but stay for a while <u>and explore the city by day and by night</u> and you will find out.

▶ *WB 15–16 (pp. 40–41)*

P6 A Mumbai street

Read these two descriptions of a Mumbai street scene. Which uses more participle clauses? What does that tell you about participle clauses in English?

> You know, there are lots of people. It's really crowded and they're selling all sorts of stuff, fruit and vegetables, at the side of the road. The traffic is slow because there are so many people on the street, the cars can't really get through.

> The shadows are long in the busy Mumbai street, showing that the sun is going down. Two tall trees rise into a milky blue sky, giving shade to the people selling fruit and vegetables by the side of the road. A man sitting in a blue car wonders when the traffic will start to move again, but there is little chance of that.

P7 MEDIATION Travel advice

Maria and Marcel are planning a trip to India and want to visit Mumbai. They've only got an English-language travel guide, which Maria has been reading. Marcel wants to know what it says about a few topics. Read the travel guide extracts. Try to understand as much as you can without a dictionary but use one for key words if you have to. How could Maria summarize the extracts in easy German for Marcel?

> Ich glaube, in Asien muss man immer aufpassen, dass man nichts Falsches sagt, oder?

> Mumbai ist doch riesig. Wie kommt man in der Stadt herum?

> Und wie sicher ist die Stadt für Touristen?

> Steht da auch drin, wie man einigermaßen gesund bleibt?

▶ WB 17–18 (pp. 41–42)

Etiquette
Despite its cosmopolitan outlook, Mumbai is still governed by strict social mores, most of them linked to religion. Immodest dress – i.e. anything that exposes the thighs or shoulders – meets with universal disapproval, though shorts and T-shirts are gaining popularity among the middle classes. Public displays of affection may also cause frowns.
 Shaking hands – always with the right hand – is the standard greeting between men in Mumbai. Like most Asians, Mumbaikers prefer to avoid confrontation. Public arguments in particular are considered very bad form. If you take bargaining too seriously, everyone will lose face.

Getting around
To get from A to B with the minimum of fuss, flag down a cab. The only reason to use other forms of transport is a) for fun, and b) during morning and afternoon rush hour when the traffic is gridlocked.
 In this book the nearest train station is noted after the 🚆 in each listing. You may have to walk or take a taxi or autorickshaw to reach your destination.

Emergencies
Crime is not a major problem for visitors to Mumbai, though petty theft and scams are reasonably common. Pickpockets can be a problem on public transport and at crowded tourist attractions – keep an eye on your valuables! As in any big city, women should avoid walking around alone late at night. Intercommunal violence is a problem in Mumbai – avoid demonstrations and other potential flashpoints.

Precautions
Avoid drinking or brushing your teeth with tap water, peel or wash fruit, clean your hands regularly and only eat street food that you see prepared freshly in front of you. Fruit juices prepared with water or ice are particularly risky, as are salads, though the *bhelpuri* (Mumbai-style salad) served at Chowpatty Beach is usually safe. Bottled purified water is available everywhere – dispose of plastic bottles responsibly. Be alert to dehydration, sunstroke, heat exhaustion and prickly heat.

P8 STUDY SKILLS Summarizing a non-fictional text

a) Read the following text carefully. Then, on a piece of paper, make notes on the main points and on the important details.

b) Write your summary. You need not follow the chronological order, but make sure you use your own words.

c) Revise your summary. Are your sentences linked logically?

d) Now swap your summary with a partner and check your partner's summary. Give each other some useful tips on how to improve the text.

▶ SF Summary writing (p. 149)

> **STUDY SKILLS** | **Summarizing a non-fictional text**
>
> A summary of a non-fictional text presents its main ideas in a shorter form for someone who did not read the original. Begin by either marking a copy of the text or by making notes. You can use the following method:
> Divide a piece of paper into two columns. On the left, write the **main points**; on the right, write down a few **important details**, explanations or key phrases to go with the main points.
> Write your summary from your notes.

Slumdog Millionaire: Changing film-making in India

by Paul MacInnes, Mumbai, 4 June 2009

Abridged and adapted from The Guardian

Mumbai has many slums but the one that Danny Boyle's Oscar-winning movie has made famous is Dharavi. Tourist companies now run daily tours through the sprawling district. Like watching the movie itself, it is a strangely optimistic experience; a few hours in Dharavi – with all its colours, industry and life – feels not like watching other people's poverty, but rather like being forced to think about your own laziness.

Dharavi is now on the map, and it seems unlikely that the effect of *Slumdog Millionaire* on the country where it was set will end there. In fact, it could be said that the film is changing the very face of Indian movie-making.

Slumdog Millionaire has been a huge success in India, taking more than $6m at the country's box offices since its release earlier this year. And the hype is still continuing, which is partly because of the film's eight-Oscar success, allowing national newspapers to trumpet that, at last, the Indians were coming.

But as Priyanka Sinha, editor of the magazine Screen explains, there were other reasons too. 'People liked the movie, they liked the optimism,' she says. 'The story was very Indian, it was very Bollywood, because Bollywood always has these impossible plots, these happy endings. We're great suckers for the happy endings, we Indians. We love to see the hero win, get the girl he loves, all of that.'

For Indian audiences then, while the format of the film is not unusual, the subject matter is. Loveleen Tandan, who was *Slumdog*'s co-director, says, 'People who live in our slums are hardly ever represented in the movies. It's good that everyone has been exposed to this reality.'

Then there's what might be called the Slumdog style of shooting, which was 'completely different from that of Indian cinema,' says Cyrus Bharucha, a professor at a film school in Mumbai. 'Indian films are still very old-fashioned in their photography. They would never have shot the slum sequences with a small handheld camera as Danny Boyle did. And they don't even know how to keep the action moving because of all the bloody songs that interrupt it.'

Ah, the bloody songs. As Sinha points out, there has been this crazy tradition in India of going to the cinema, not to have your worldview challenged but to be entertained.

Slumdog appears to have found its audience by entertaining them – everyone I spoke to in Mumbai, whether they agreed with the film or not, said that they liked it – but its success has also been part of a trend away from Bollywood's simple potboilers and towards what western audiences might know as good old arthouse cinema.

Tandan says that she and her colleagues have been trying to make more 'gritty' movies for years, only to hear a 'no' from the Bollywood studios. Now, she says, 'You simply mention the word "slumdog" and suddenly they listen.'

▶ WB 19 (pp. 43)

Extra Revision Getting ready for a test 2

1 WORDS Free-time activities

What do you do in your free time? Are you sporty? Is your hobby running? Or do you like reading a good book?

a) Work with a partner. How many free-time activities can you add to the list below?

> riding • drawing and painting •
> listening to music • playing a musical
> instrument • watching TV or DVDs •
> playing basketball • playing football •
> cycling • using a computer •
> reading books or magazines • relaxing •
> meeting friends • …

b) Look at your list and put the activities into groups.

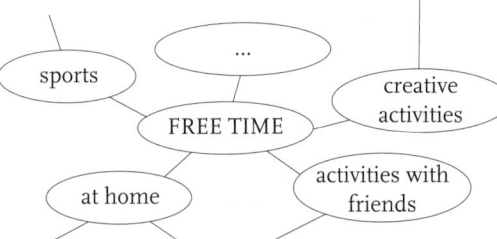

c) Talk about all your free-time activities. Tell each other why you like/don't like doing them.
A: I often go riding. I love horses and I think it's great to be with them every day.
B: Well, I don't agree. I think it's too much work. But I enjoy listening to music …

2 WORDS Talking about films

You see this film review on a movie website. Find the missing words and phrases to complete the text. Put the verbs into their correct forms

> (to) act • actor • award • (to) be based on •
> (to) be into • (to) come out • (to) end • main
> character • (to) tell the story

Take the Lead ● ● ● ● ● ○
'**Ballroom dancing meets New York's gangs**'
The film *Take the Lead* (1) *tells the story* of Pierre Dulaine, a ballroom dance teacher, who goes to work in one of New York's most difficult inner city schools full of problem kids. *Take the Lead* is actually (2) … true events, and Pierre Dulaine is, in fact, a real person. He still works with American teenagers around the USA and has become quite famous since the film (3) …

The star of the film is the Spanish American (4) … Antonio Banderas. He plays the (5) …, Pierre Dulaine. When Dulaine first arrives in the school, the kids all think he is crazy. They (6) … hip hop, not classical dance. However, after Dulaine shows them a tango with another professional dancer, the kids start to get interested. The film (7) … when they all take part in a national ballroom competition.

The kids are all 'normal' American teenagers and had never (8)… before. But they are all great natural acting talents and some of them are amazing hip hop dancers.

In 2006, *Take the Lead* won an (9) … for 'Best Teen Movie'.

Extra Revision Getting ready for a test 2

3 I'd love to be a movie star (Conditional sentences type 2)

Finish these sentences about being a famous movie star. All the sentences are conditional sentences type 2.

1 If a famous director *chose* (choose) me for one of his films, *I'd / would be* (be) famous too.
2 I … (go) to Hollywood if I … (become) a famous actor.
3 I … (not live) here if I … (be) rich.
4 If I … (act) in a movie, all my friends … (come) to see me.
5 If I … (have) lots of money, I … (buy) a yacht.
6 If I … (play) a part in a movie, I … (meet) famous actors every day on the film set.
7 But the problem is, if I … (be) a movie star, I … (not see) my family very often.
8 Perhaps I … (not be) so happy if I … (be) a film star!

4 SPEAKING Having a conversation

Talk to your partner for about two minutes about something that interests you – films, magazines, music, what you did last weekend, the town where you live, … The phrases below will help you.

starting a conversation	Hello. / Hi. / My name's … / What's your name? / …
likes and dislikes	I like / don't like … / What about you? / And you? / …
showing interest	Really? / Oh, that's interesting! / Sounds great! / Wow! / …
agreeing and disagreeing	Yes, me too. / That's right! / Oh, I don't. / Sorry, I don't agree. / …
asking questions	So when did you …? / Why …? / How long …? / Where …? / Sorry, can you say that again please? / …
ending the conversation	See you soon. / Bye!

5 WORDS Tom and Kate (Words that describe feelings)

a) *Complete these sentences with words or phrases from the box on the right.*

1 Tom and Kate have been together for a month now and they … still … each other.
2 Kate was … when Tom asked her if she'd like to date him. She thought he liked Laura.
3 Tom wasn't nervous on their first date. He is usually very …
4 But last week, when Kate left his MP3 player on the bus, he was very … with her.
5 Sometimes Kate is … when Tom tries to be funny – his jokes are very strange!
6 First she didn't want to meet Tom's parents as she always feels a bit … with new people.

angry • be afraid • be mad about sb./sth. • bored • confused • cool • different • excited • great • happy • independent • jealous • lonely • (to) look forward to sth. • nervous • proud • relaxed • responsible (for) • sad • safe • scared • silly • strange • surprised • terrible • tired • shy

7 When Kate met her old boyfriend Pete at a party, Tom was a bit … – until he saw that she wasn't interested in Pete any more.
8 They're … the summer holidays this year: they're going to Canada for three weeks!

b) *Write six sentences like these with words you haven't used in a).*

1 READING Dev Patel

Read the text from an online British movie magazine. Then tick the correct answer (A, B, C or D).

Meet Dev Patel, teenage movie star

Slumdog Millionaire, described as the 'feel-good film of the decade', won eight Oscars in 2009 and rocketed the young British actor Dev Patel to international stardom. The film tells the story of 17-year-old Jamal from the slums of Mumbai (he is a 'slumdog' in the local slang), who appears on the Indian TV show *Who wants to be a millionaire?* and wins the top prize – as well as finding the girl he loves.

WHEN the then 17-year-old Dev Patel arrived in Mumbai to film *Slumdog Millionaire*, it was only his second visit to India. Indeed, learning the Mumbai accent was, he says, one of his hardest tasks. Nor was he a famous actor. He had enjoyed drama at school, and had played a small role in a British TV series, but he had no formal theatrical training and was certainly not well-known. So how did he end up getting the part of Jamal and how did he find the experience of suddenly becoming a superstar?

Dev was born the son of Indian immigrants near London in 1990. His dad is a computer technician, his mum a carer[1].

He attended a 'typical' English secondary school. Growing up, his early interests included martial arts, first karate then later tae-kwon-do, and he was good enough at both to represent England at the Youth Olympics. However, it was a part in a school play that led him to discover that his greatest love was to be acting. This was something that his parents wanted to encourage, and when Mrs Patel came across a small advertisement in a newspaper, she gave it to Dev. A British TV company was looking for fresh young people for a new series, called *Skins*, about a group of multicultural teenage friends. Dev got one of the parts. He was 14.

Three years later, the successful British film director Danny Boyle was planning *Slumdog Millionaire* and had a problem with the main character, Jamal. India has a booming film industry ('Bollywood') and there was no lack of actors. But none looked as if they had grown up in a slum – they were all too good-looking. It was Boyle's daughter, a long-time *Skins* fan, who suggested Dev. It took five auditions[2] before he was finally chosen. 'I was crying at the end because I didn't think I'd get the part,' he says.

For the young man from London, actually filming the movie was like a dream: working with a famous director, surrounded by famous Bollywood actors, playing opposite the beautiful young woman who is Jamal's girlfriend in the film. 'I grew up five years in those five months,' is how he sums it up.

Another amazing experience for Dev was to get to know the real slumdogs of Mumbai. It was above all their attitude to life that he noticed. 'Don't tell them we're poor,' they told him. 'Tell them we're happy. We aren't poor because we're happy.'

[1] carer ['kɛərə] *(Alten-)Pfleger/in* [2] audition [ɔː'dɪʃn] *Sprechprobe*

1 What role does Dev Patel play? Someone who …
A likes TV shows.
B moves to the Mumbai slums.
C wins a lot of money.
D wins an Oscar.

2 What was very difficult for Dev?
A Acting in a very poor environment.
B Dealing with his fame.
C Learning new pronunciation.
D Travelling to Mumbai.

3 What was Dev good at before he started acting at school?
A English
B Music
C Science
D Sports

4 What did his parents do when Dev found out that he liked acting? They …
A helped him find his first job.
B paid for acting lessons.
C printed an advert for him.
D wrote a letter to a TV company.

5 Why didn't the director Danny Boyle choose an Indian actor?
A Bollywood actors didn't want the role.
B Bollywood actors are too beautiful.
C Boyle's daughter didn't like Bollywood actors.
D There are very few good Bollywood actors.

6 How did Dev feel when he finally got the role?
A Anxious
B Funny
C Nervous
D Surprised

7 Why does Dev say that he grew up five years while filming? Because …
A filming was a lot of hard work.
B he fell in love with his partner.
C he worked with international stars.
D making the film took very long.

8 How does Dev feel about the people living in the Mumbai slums? He …
A admires them.
B avoids them.
C feels sorry for them.
D supports them.

2 READING Choosing a book

These American high school students are in their English literature class. They have to choose a book to read in order to present it to the class.

Look at the profiles of the five students and the seven book summaries below. Who will choose which book?

Answer: Student A – Book …

Student A : Conrad
Conrad doesn't really enjoy reading short stories or novels. He reads magazines, however, because he loves sport. He is also interested in music and skateboarding.

Student B : Brittany
Brittany has her own blog where she writes her thoughts. She is fascinated by young people, their loves and fears, their relationships, and their problems.

Student C : Jeanette
Jeanette loves reading stories. For her, a 'good book' is one where the characters have lots of real-life adventures. She doesn't like fantasy or horror stories.

Student D : John Paul
John Paul is interested in football but the thing he likes best is computer games. He particularly loves fantasy games where 'anything is possible'.

Student E : Ricki
Ricki's family came to the US from Puerto Rico. Now, as a teenager, he is interested in politics and wants to help people from ethnic minorities.

BOOK SUMMARIES

Fiction
1 **Dark Universe**   Three teenage friends fall through a 'time hole' and find themselves in a parallel world where amazing and fantastic things happen. Can they survive – and will they ever return to their old lives?
2 **Something**   Something is 'out there'. Waiting. Watching. Looking for you! VERY scary!
3 **Lola and the Detective Agency**   When Lola and her friends find out about a crime, nobody believes them. They have to set up their own detective agency to catch the criminals. Lots of action right up to the last page!

Non-fiction
4 **Voices from the Fields**   Fascinating interviews with migrant workers from Mexico who talk about their lives in the fields of California where they pick fruit.
5 **Strategies for Teens**   Being a teenager is not always easy but this book is full of great advice about families, boy/girlfriends and many other aspects of teen life.
6 **The Journey West**   The book uses diaries, letters and old photos to tell the fascinating story of the long journeys to the West in America's history.
7 **Babe**   Babe Ruth was probably the greatest baseball player who has ever lived. This biography tells the true story of his life. Wonderful descriptions of exciting games!

Extra Practice Test Getting ready for a test 2   75

3 MEDIATION A note to your friend

Your American friend is staying with you in Germany at the moment. Your friend would like to know about some interesting things to do. Read the brochure below and write a short note in English to your friend. Give the main points about the tours. Use the example on the right to help you.

> Hi!
> Hope you slept well. You wanted to know about some interesting things to do while I'm at school. I found out about some guided cycle tours that sound great. Here are the main points:
> –
> –

Erleben Sie die Stadt per Rad

Fahrrad-Stadtrundfahrten

Fahrrad-Rundfahrten durch die Stadt – für Gruppen von 10–15 Personen – begleitet von erfahrenen Stadtführern

Sehen Sie unsere Stadt und ihre Attraktionen vom Fahrrad aus. Wir machen Halt an interessanten Punkten. Dort werden Sie Informationen über die Geschichte der Stadt und touristische Highlights erhalten.

Dauer
Unsere abwechslungsreiche Tour führt durchs Stadtzentrum und verschiedene Stadtteile und dauert ca. 120 Minuten, in denen wir etwa 12 km zurücklegen.

Abfahrt
März–September
täglich 10:00 und 14:00 Uhr.

Treffpunkt ist vor dem Informationszentrum neben der Liebfrauenkirche im Stadtzentrum (bei schlechtem Wetter im Informationszentrum).

Preise
€ 29,– pro Person inkl. Fahrradmiete (bei angemeldeten Gruppen mit mehr als 25 Teilnehmern € 22,50 pro Person)

4 SPEAKING Talking about a picture

a) Look at the two photographs. Compare and contrast them.
– What is similar?
– What is different?
– Which situation would you prefer and why?

b) Talk about your sports activities (what, when, where, how often, why …).

5 SPEAKING Planning a visit to the cinema

You and your friend want to go to the cinema together. Discuss what films are on and agree on which you want to see.

These ideas may help you:
– What kind of films are there?
– What may each film be about?
– Ticket price?
– Day/time?
– Personal preferences? Why? …

Casino Royale
Mon -- Tue -- Thu
6 pm -- 8:30 pm
£ 7.50

Lord of the Rings
Monday till Friday
6 pm -- 8:30 pm
£ 7.00

Star Wars II
Tue -- Sat
6 pm -- 10:30 pm
£ 9.50

Meet Dave
Tue -- Wed -- Fri
7 pm -- 9:30 pm
£ 7.50

Romeo + Juliet
Saturday and Sunday
3:30 pm -- 6 pm --
8:45 pm   £ 6.50

Self-evaluation

Check your answers to tasks 1 and 2 on page 247.

About the test

This second test gave you the chance again to try some of the kinds of tasks that you will do one day in your exam. This time, the tasks tested your reading, mediation and speaking skills. If you found some tasks difficult, don't worry. You've got lots of time to practise. Remember: 'Practice makes perfect!'

Reading

Task 1 and task 2 in the test were reading tasks. The following three questions will help you to think about how you did. Read the questions – which answer is right for you?

1 How hard or easy was each task?

	easy	OK	quite hard	very hard
Task 1				
Task 2				

2 What was difficult in the tasks?
a) The texts were quite long and complicated.
b) There were words and phrases that I just couldn't understand.
c) There was a lot of information. I couldn't find the exact answers.
d) The tasks weren't like the tasks that we do in class.

3 How did you do the tasks?
a) I always read the questions carefully so that I knew what to look for in the texts.
b) I tried to understand the main ideas of the text first. That helped me to guess words that I wasn't sure about.
c) If there was a question that I wasn't sure about, I left it out and came back to it later.
d) I scanned the text when I looked for a special piece of information.
e) I checked my answers at the end to make sure I hadn't made a 'silly' mistake.

▶ *SF Reading Course (pp. 136–137)*

▶ *SF How to do well in a test (pp. 150–152)*

Speaking

1 Copy and fill in the assessment sheet[1] below about your partner's presentation in the fourth task (Talking about a picture).

Assessment sheet	☹	😐	☺			
Name of partner …	1	2	3	4	5	Comments
Did your partner …						
1 … speak clearly and loudly enough?						
2 … find enough to say?						
3 … answer all the questions?						
4 … have problems finding the right words?						
5 … make grammar or vocabulary mistakes?						

2 Now look at the checklist on the right and talk about how well you did in the fifth task, the dialogue about a visit to the cinema.

– We listened to each other.
– We only gave short answers.
– We showed interest in each other.
– There was a good flow in our dialogue.[2]

▶ *SF Speaking Course (pp. 142–143)*

---

[1] assessment sheet *Beurteilungsbogen*   [2] There was a good flow in our dialogue. *Unser Gespräch verlief flüssig.*

Teen world

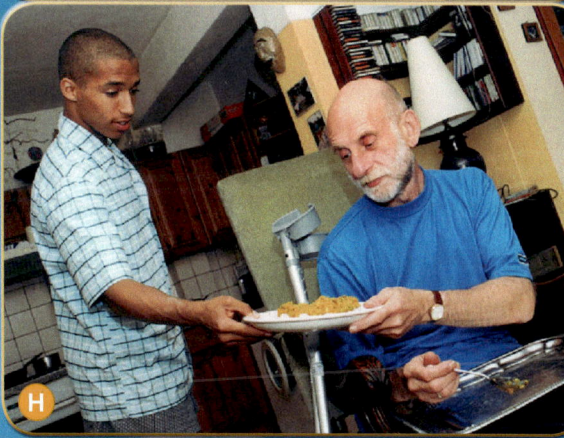

1 Teenagers

a) Look at the pictures for a few minutes. Then choose one for each of the topics in the list below. Note down your reasons for your choices.

TEENAGERS HELP OUT
TEENAGERS IN LOVE
TEENAGERS IN TOUCH
TEENAGERS IN TROUBLE

b) Discuss your choices in a group. Can you agree on the best picture for each topic? Which of the pictures could be from the area you live in?

c) Listen and match the extracts (1–9) to the pictures (A–I).

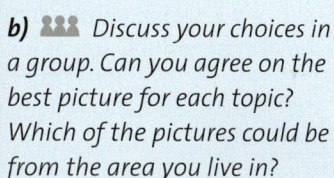

2 Stories

a) Write a story of 50–100 words from the point of view of one of the people in the pictures. You might want to listen again before you begin. The story could take place before or after what you hear.

b) Extra Read your story to your group and listen to theirs. Can the listeners say which picture the story is linked with? You can put your story in your DOSSIER.

▶ WB 1 (p. 44)

MOBILE LIFE AND LOVE

1 Mobile behaviour

teen connection – the online mag that keeps teenagers in touch

Home | mobile life | competition time | downloads | contact

Thanks to everyone who texted us their answers to our MOBILE LIFE questionnaire. Here are the results:

1. Is it OK to send a text message while you're talking to somebody?
   sure! 43%   no way! 51%   dunno. 6%

2. Is it OK to talk on a mobile in a café or restaurant?
   sure! 74%   no way! 19%   dunno. 7%

3. Is it OK to send or receive text messages during lessons at school?
   sure! 50%   no way! 42%   dunno. 8%

4. Would you secretly film someone or take a photo of them with your mobile?
   sure! 14%   no way! 71%   dunno. 15%

5. Would you let your parents look at the texts and pictures on your mobile?
   sure! 20%   no way! 68%   dunno. 12%

6. Is it a good idea to ask someone out on a date by text message?
   sure! 55%   no way! 32%   dunno. 13%

7. Would you end a relationship by text message?
   sure! 42%   no way! 42%   dunno. 16%

8. Do you feel unwanted if a whole day goes by and your mobile phone doesn't ring?
   sure! 34%   no way! 46%   dunno. 20%

We had so many comments in our questionnaire forum on the role mobiles and social networking sites play in relationships. Here are some highlights. Click here to see all the forum comments. (We're closing the forum next week, so send your comment soon!)

Sometimes I wish I didn't have a mobile. My boyfriend is always texting and phoning me to check up on me, like where I am and who I'm with. I never have any time for myself. Does he own me or what? *goodgirl*

My girlfriend has just chucked me. Did she tell me in person? Or phone me? Or even text me? No way! When I checked her Facebook status it said 'Relationship: Single'. That sucks! *jayjay95*

I have NEVER changed my Facebook status – it has always been 'single', even when I had a girlfriend. I think it's better this way, until you are VERY serious, because people talk and it can ruin your chances with other girls. *jonny-b-good*

My boyfriend cheated on me. The other girl looked up his Facebook status. When she saw I was his 'official' Facebook girlfriend, she contacted me. We're going to make his life hell. *cute_as_keira*

Facebook is a website. It's not the real world. Stop freaking out about it. Then one day you'll have a real relationship in real life! *coolconcrete*

a) Note down your own answers to the Teen Connection questionnaire on a piece of paper. At the top just write BOY or GIRL, not your name.

b) With a partner, compare all your answers.
A: How did you answer question 1/2/…? I …
B: Oh, I had the same answer as you. / My answer was different. I …
A: I think it's OK to … I've done it once/a few times/often. What about you?
B: I agree/don't agree. I've never …

c) Extra Do a survey on the class's answers. How does your class compare with the readers of Teen Connection? Is there a difference between boys and girls?

d) Read the forum comments and say who
1 has contacted her boyfriend's other girlfriend,
2 has just found out his girlfriend has ended their relationship,
3 is worried her boyfriend is behaving like a spy,
4 thinks giving your relationship status on a social networking site is stupid,
5 wants to stay open for new relationships.

e) Choose one of the forum comments and write your own reaction to it. Give your opinion on it: do you agree or disagree with it? Do you understand the writer? Do you feel sorry for them or angry about them?

2   Are you on the internet?

a) Divide the class into two groups, A and B. Group A students: Think of arguments why people should put personal information about themselves (text, photos, …) on the internet. Write them down.

Group B students: Think of arguments why people should not put personal information about themselves (text, photos, …) on the internet. Write them down.

b) Exchange your arguments in a **double circle** – Group A students on the inside, Group B on the outside. Change partners when your teacher tells you.

3 Extra Text message love

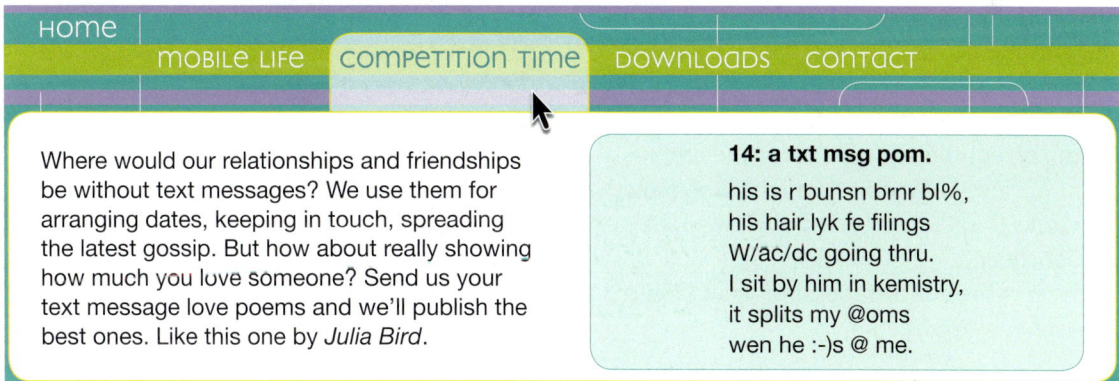

a) List the ways the magazine says text messages play a role in relationships and friendships. In what other ways do text messages play a role in your social life? Add to the list.

b) Write your own text message poem.

Translation:
14: a text message poem
his eyes are bunsen burner blue,
his hair like iron filings
with ac/dc going through.
I sit by him in chemistry,
it splits my atoms
when he smiles at me

▶ **Text File 10** *(pp. 113–114)* • WB 2 *(p. 44)*

P1 STUDY SKILLS Argumentative writing

a) Structuring your text
Imagine you have to discuss the topic 'Students should not be allowed to take mobiles to school' in a written English test. Brainstorm your ideas. Then use an outline to order your text.

"Yes, Jason, you may go to the lavatory, but next time just raise your hand."

Your outline should include
– arguments for and against,
– examples, support for the arguments, perhaps including statistics,
– your personal opinion.

▶ SF Outlining (p. 129)

STUDY SKILLS | Argumentative writing

An outline can help you to structure your text before you start writing.
1 Introduction
2 First point of view
   2.1 First argument
   2.2 Second argument
   2.3 …
3 Opposite point of view
   3.1 First argument
   3.2 …
4 Conclusion
   4.1 Summing up
   4.2 Personal opinion

▶ SF Argumentative writing (p. 147)

---

b) Presenting the arguments
1 Introduction
First introduce the topic. Start with a personal experience or a general question.
2 The first point of view
Present one point of view. It's often better to start with the view you disagree with. Explain the arguments and give examples to support them.
3 The opposite point of view
Then present the arguments for the other point of view. Begin this part with a sentence that links it to the first point of view.
4 Conclusion
Sum up with your own point of view. Don't present new arguments.

Which other arguments and examples could you add? Where?

c) Discuss the following in writing:
'Students should rate their schools on the internet.'
Brainstorm arguments first, then outline your text. The phrases on the right and the text in b) might help.

▶ WB 3 (p. 45)

MOBILE PHONES AT SCHOOL

Nearly all students have mobiles. But should they be allowed to take them to school?

Some people say that students really need their mobiles at school. They might have to call their parents after school, for example when they miss the bus. Or parents might want to contact their children because …

However, other people disagree. One common reason is because they think students might use them to get help from outside with a test. Another argument against mobiles is …

After looking at both sides, I think there are more disadvantages than advantages for having mobiles at school. That's why they should not be allowed there. In my opinion, it's just unfair when some students use them to do better in a test. That has happened at my school. Added to that …

Added to that • After looking at both sides • However • In my opinion • Other people disagree. • So … • Some people say • That's why … • To sum up, …

P2 REVISION Boys meet girls (Talking about the future)

These are the most important future forms in English (look at GF 4, p. 162, for more details):

Making plans	*going to*-future	We're going to make his life hell.
Making predictions	*will*-future	Then one day you'll have a real relationship.
Talking about arrangements	present progressive	We're closing the forum next week.

a) Complete the sentences with a future form of the verb in brackets. Sometimes more than one form is possible.

1. She … probably … (find) me boring.
   She'll probably find me boring.
2. She's coming over here. I … (talk) to her.
3. What … you … (do) tomorrow night?
4. I think she … (go out) with me – well, perhaps.
5. Look at the clouds. It … (rain). I … (take) you home on my moped.
6. I … (meet) her at the cinema at eight.
7. I shouldn't look at her so much. She and her friends … (laugh) at me.
8. Have you seen the latest James Bond film? I'm sure you … (like) it.
9. She … (get) the next bus into town. I … (meet) her at the bus station.

b) Extra Match the sentences from a) to one of the boys below. Explain your decisions.

Peter
He is very self-confident. When he wants to date a girl he always has a plan and knows how to persuade her.

Tom
He is quite shy. He often wonders what to say to a girl and is never sure what will happen, but sometimes he can be very spontaneous.

P3 EVERYDAY ENGLISH Role play: Asking someone out

Partner B: Go to page 98.
Partner A: You want to ask Partner B out on a date. You'd like to go to the cinema and then to a party at a friend's house. You have never talked much to each other before and you are unsure about your partner's feelings. Try to persuade him/her to go out with you. Be as nice as you can. The words and phrases in the box will help you to get the conversation started and to say something nice.

Hey, <name>, I was wondering … • How about … • Have you seen … • I'd like to ask … • Have you got any plans for … • Guess what, … • Would you like to … • Let's go … • It's going to be a really fun party. • You'll love it. • There's a really good film on at … • Or we could go to … • It would be so cool if you … • I don't fancy going with anyone else … • I'll come and pick you up. • I'll take you home. • We'll have a really great time, I promise.

▶ WB 4–6 (pp. 45–46)

TEENS IN TROUBLE

1 ▼

'ASBO has helped me'

By Jeremy Armstrong

Shane Preston, from Darlington in the north-east of England, was a trouble-maker who kicked footballs against his neighbours' houses and cars, caused trouble at school, rode motorbikes on pavements and attacked other teenagers. Then the courts hit him with a four-year anti-social behaviour order (ASBO).

At just 14 he was banned from some areas of his hometown. He was not allowed to leave home between 9 pm and 7 am, and the police sent photos of him to hundreds of houses in the area.

It was tough – but the surprising thing is that it has worked. Now 17, Shane has volunteered with the YMCA and helped to build a children's play area. Hoping for a career in the construction industry, he has started training as a builder. His course finishes soon and he'll be looking for work then.

Shane believes the ASBO has helped him to straighten up his life. 'I've grown up, I think, and the ASBO has helped me. It will have kept me out of trouble for four years when it finishes. It was embarrassing when pictures of me appeared around town. I used to hang out with other kids in front of the shops. But I've got different friends now. And in the end it's got nothing to do with others, it's up to me.'

Young Brits on their way to an ASBO?

ASBOs: What for?
ASBOs can be given to punish behaviour like
- spraying/writing graffiti
- using racist language
- making too much noise late at night
- being drunk in the streets
- smoking or drinking under age
- dealing drugs
- violence
- vandalism

Every year thousands of people are given an ASBO. But many people think they don't work.

ASBOs: What happens?
Anti-social behaviour orders are given by courts. An ASBO tells you what you are not allowed to do, like
- go out at night
- go to particular places in your area
- go into particular shops, bars or cinemas
- carry particular things with you, like spray cans or alcohol
- meet more than one or two other people in public

If you break your ASBO, you can go to prison.

---

a) Read the article and say
– what Shane did wrong and how he was punished
– why Shane thinks the ASBO was good for him
– how his life has changed since he got the ASBO
– what Shane thought was the worst thing about the ASBO

b) What do you think was the worst thing about Shane's ASBO?
Do you think ASBOs would be a good idea in your city/area? Why? Why not?

▶ Text File 11 *(pp. 115–119)* • Text File 12 *(pp. 120–122)*

2 Now you

a) *What kind of anti-social behaviour happens where you live? Look at the list under 'ASBOs: What for?' in the article for ideas.*

b) *What happens in your area/school to teenagers who cause trouble? Contrast this with the punishments listed in 'ASBOs: What happens?'.*

3 Teenagers on the streets

a) *Brainstorm arguments for and against:*
'15-year-olds should not be allowed on the streets between 9 pm and 6 am.'
Note down your ideas on cards.

b) *Arrange your class for a fishbowl discussion. Four students sit on chairs in the middle and discuss the pros and cons of the statement. When other students want to take part, they stand behind the chair of a person they support and give their own opinion, agree, disagree, ask a question, etc.*

4 VIEWING High school boot camp

High school boot camp is a film about the 'Eagle Academy', a military-style school in Florida. Teenagers in trouble volunteer to go there for six months – no one makes them go. Here is what one of them, Dave Murray, said before he went to the camp:

> Right now I'm screwing up, erm, not listening to no one. What I expect to get out of this camp is to get bigger, stronger and straighten up my life.

a) *What do you think might happen at a boot camp? Collect ideas in a group.*

b) *Watch Part 1 of the DVD about the teenagers' first day at the camp. How do you feel about what happens there? Is it different from what you expected?*
– It's really shocking/funny/stupid/scary/…
– I think the boys were really scared/shocked/
  …
  The drill instructors are loud/crazy/scary/…
– …

c) *Watch Part 1 again. Take notes on as many things that happen as you can. Collect your notes in your group.*
Everyone chooses one thing from the notes and explains why they think it happens.

d) *Watch Part 2 of the DVD about the teenagers' final day at the camp. Do they feel good or bad about their time there? Give as many of their reasons as you can.*

e) *Look back at what Dave Murray said before he went to the boot camp. Do you think boot camps really help people like him to straighten up? Give reasons. Here are some key phrases to help:*

> discipline doesn't … • obey rules •
> forget later • get fit • learn discipline •
> think for yourself

f) **Extra** *Hang two poster-size pieces of paper on the classroom wall. At the top of one write:*
We NEED boot camps in Germany because …
At the top of the other write:
We DON'T NEED boot camps in Germany because …
Each student then adds an opinion to one of the posters.

▶ WB 7 (p. 46)

P1 SPEAKING Boot camps (Having a discussion)

a) Collect as many arguments for and against boot camps as you can. (Look back at your work from page 85.)

FOR	AGAINST
– boot camps help people to learn discipline	– kids soon forget about the boot camp and get in trouble again
– ...	– ...

b) Match the phrases in the box to the steps of a discussion that are shown on the right.

... because ... • Could you say that again? • First, .../Second, ... • For example ... • I agree (with you). • I don't think you can say ... • I see what you mean but ... • I think/I feel ... • In my opinion ... • No, that's not right. • Sorry, I don't agree with you. • Sorry, but I don't understand what you mean. • That's a good point. • That's why ... • Yes/Yeah, but ... • You're right.

> **Remember**
> Try to be polite in a discussion. Don't interrupt other speakers unless they will not let you speak. Then interrupt politely:
> 'Excuse me, but could I say something now?'
> 'Could I just interrupt for a moment, please?'

c) Listen to a discussion about boot camps. Which of the phrases from b) can you hear?

d) **Extra** Use your arguments from a) and the phrases from b) to continue the discussion you've just heard. Make sure at least one of you argues FOR and one AGAINST.

e) In your group, choose one of the statements on the right as a topic for a discussion. Decide alone what your point of view is, think of arguments to support your point of view and note them down. Then have a short discussion on the topic.

Steps of a discussion

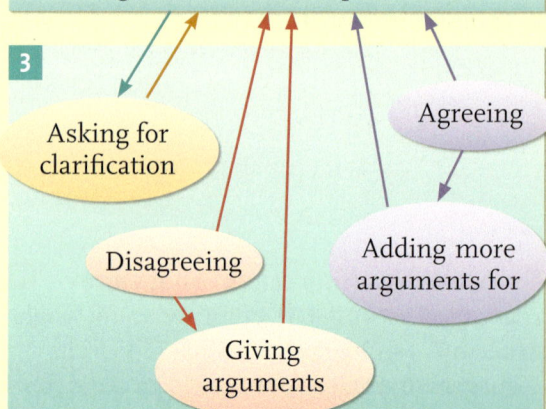

1. Expressing an opinion
2. Giving reasons and examples
3. Asking for clarification / Agreeing / Disagreeing / Adding more arguments for / Giving arguments
4. Giving more reasons and examples

– 'We should ban violent computer games.'
– 'Teenagers should not be allowed to drive a car.'

▶ SF Speaking Course (pp. 142–143) • WB 8 (p. 47)

Part A **B** C D Practice **4** 87

P2 WORDS Anti-social behaviour, crime and the law

Complete each sentence with three phrases from the box on the right, using the correct form of the verbs. Give reasons for your answers.
1 I think it's anti-social to ...
2 It should be illegal for young people to ...
3 Young people who ... should go to prison.
4 What worries me in my area are people who ...

> attack someone • be in a gang • break the law • bully other students • cause trouble • drink alcohol • obey stupid rules • get drunk • hang out in shopping malls • harass old people • kill someone • make lots of noise • sell drugs • smoke on planes or buses • spray graffiti • steal things from shops • take drugs • use racist language

P3 REVISION Boot camps banned (Participle clauses instead of other subordinate clauses)

Shorten the report by using participle clauses instead of the underlined subordinate clauses.

Boot camps banned in Florida

This Wednesday, June 1, a law was passed in Florida <u>which bans boot camps</u> *banning boot camps*.
After they learned that their son had died in a boot camp, the family of 14-year-old Martin Lee Anderson wanted action, as they hoped to prevent this from happening again.
Martin's death has been the subject of much discussion. Was he killed by drill instructors when he was forced to continue an exercise after he had collapsed?
The new law replaces boot camps with so-called STAR academies. As they are not allowed to use too much force, these new academies are more about education and aftercare. After they had had a private meeting with Governor Bush, the Anderson family spoke to the public. They said if boot camps had been banned earlier, Martin would still be alive.

P4 The bus leaves at ... (Simple present with future meaning)

Use the pictures, the words and phrases to make statements about when things will happen. Use the simple present with future meaning. For example:
The Tampa bus leaves Miami at 1 pm.

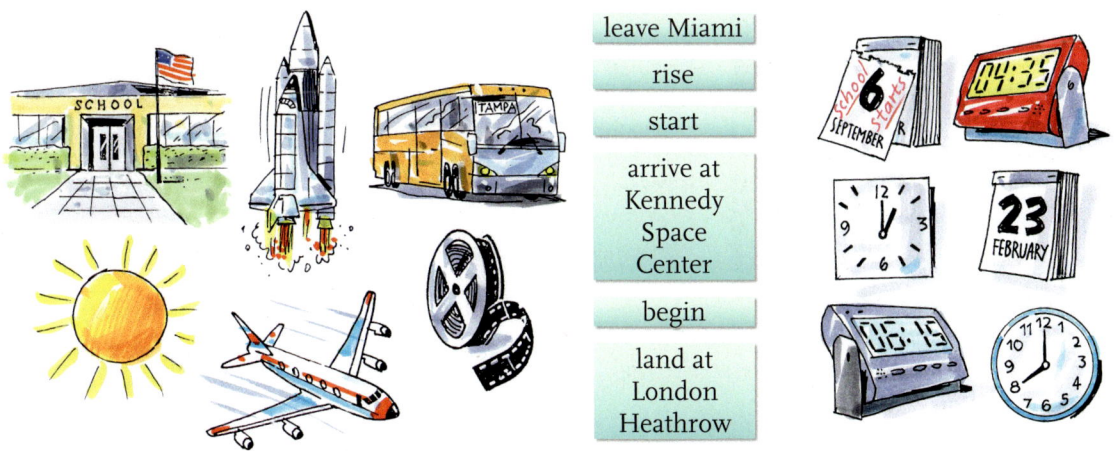

leave Miami
rise
start
arrive at Kennedy Space Center
begin
land at London Heathrow

▶ GF9: Talking about the future (pp. 162–163) • WB 9 (p. 48)

GET INVOLVED

1 Club blogs

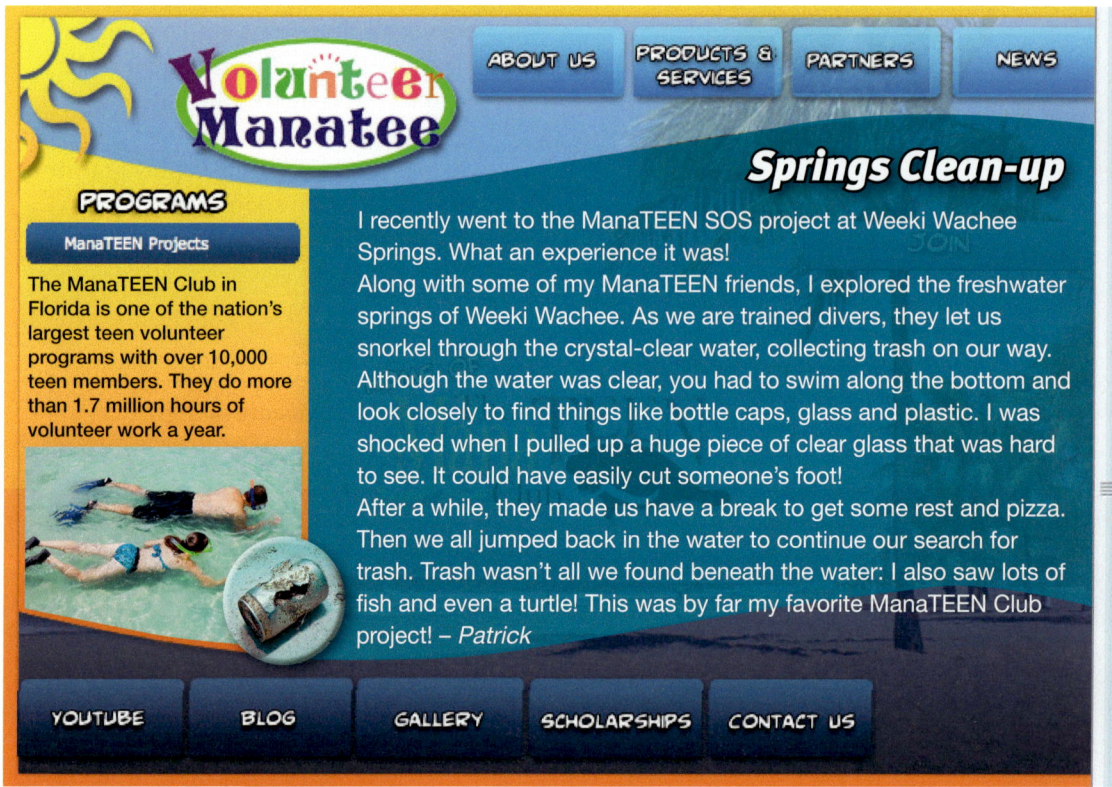

Springs Clean-up

I recently went to the ManaTEEN SOS project at Weeki Wachee Springs. What an experience it was!
Along with some of my ManaTEEN friends, I explored the freshwater springs of Weeki Wachee. As we are trained divers, they let us snorkel through the crystal-clear water, collecting trash on our way. Although the water was clear, you had to swim along the bottom and look closely to find things like bottle caps, glass and plastic. I was shocked when I pulled up a huge piece of clear glass that was hard to see. It could have easily cut someone's foot!
After a while, they made us have a break to get some rest and pizza. Then we all jumped back in the water to continue our search for trash. Trash wasn't all we found beneath the water: I also saw lots of fish and even a turtle! This was by far my favorite ManaTEEN Club project! – *Patrick*

The ManaTEEN Club in Florida is one of the nation's largest teen volunteer programs with over 10,000 teen members. They do more than 1.7 million hours of volunteer work a year.

••• Hickory Soup Kitchen

This summer we haven't spent our time hanging out by the pool: we've been raising money for the Hickory Soup Kitchen, so others would have something to eat.
   We both like helping and wanted to get more involved. We announced what we were doing at our church and lots of people have donated. During vacation Bible school, all the kids had a competition to see who could bring in the most money, so a lot of coins and dollar bills have been donated.
   Altogether we've raised $427 and collected 400 pounds of food too, which we gave to the soup kitchen as we received it. Then we went to the store today and bought 45 pounds of beef, 36 cans of green beans and 30 bottles of ketchup. We're having the food delivered to the soup kitchen tomorrow. – *Alex & Andrew*

a) Describe what kind of community service the American students did.
Find reasons they give for their volunteering. Why do they think it's a good idea?

b) Can you name any organizations in your area that help to clean up the environment or give food to people in need?

2 Community service, US-style

Volunteering for community service is an important tradition in the US, where the state sometimes does not provide enough social services. Many young people get involved because they want to – but others do community service because their schools, churches or parents make them. They think it will be good for the young people, as this website shows:

Community Service

Students at Fountain Valley School of Colorado are required to do Community Service (C.S.). When they do C.S. they learn how important it is to give to others. Each student must do a minimum of 10 hours of C.S. every year. More hours are encouraged.
Many students get involved in projects which they organize on their own but FVS teachers and interested parents offer many other opportunities such as reading and playing with younger children, helping in the El Paso County Park, building and repairing trails, giving to food and blood banks, and serving at local soup kitchens.

a) Describe the system of community service at Fountain Valley School.

b) Students at FVS have to *volunteer and do community service*. Can it really be called volunteering if your school makes you do it?

c) Do you think it would be a good idea to have this system at your school? Why/Why not?

d) **Extra** Who do you know who needs help from people doing community service? Say who helps them, how, and why.

3 Now you

a) Have you ever volunteered for community service? What did you do and why? If you haven't volunteered, explain which sort of community service you would/wouldn't like doing.

b) What kind of service would help your town/area most? Use a **placemat** to find the best ideas in your group. Explain how you could help.

▶ WB 10 (p. 49)

P1 Jobs and privileges (let/make somebody do something)

The verbs *let* and *make* can be followed by an object + infinitive without to.
Compare:

They	let	us	have a break.	[jemandem erlauben, etwas zu tun]
	let +	object +	infinitive without to	
They	made	us	have a break.	[jemanden zwingen/veranlassen, etwas zu tun]
	make +	object +	infinitive without to	

a) Teenagers have jobs and privileges at home. One of you is Jessica, the other Jacob. What can you tell each other about your home life? Use let or make + object + infinitive. Example:
Clean the bathroom/twice a week. *My parents make me clean the bathroom twice a week.*

Jessica
– feed the cat / every day
– watch TV / two hours a day
– talk to my grandmother / once a month
– write Christmas cards / every year
– tidy up my room / every Saturday
– do a paper round to earn some money / every week
– talk to my friends on my mobile / every day

Jacob
– walk the dog / twice a day
– play computer games / one hour every day
– eat pizza / once a month
– watch the Champions League / whenever it's on
– ride my bike to school / every day
– study hard for school / every day
– look after my little brother / at the weekends

b) **Extra** Who do you think has life easier at home – Jacob or Jessica? Discuss with a partner.

c) Tell your partner about your jobs and privileges at home.

P2 Why do it yourself? (have something done)

Have + object + past participle shows that someone is doing something for us and that we're not doing it ourselves.
Compare:
We delivered the food to the soup kitchen. [We did it ourselves.]
We had the food delivered to the soup kitchen. [We arranged for someone else to do it for us.]
Look at the pictures. Did the people do it themselves or have it done?
The woman repaired her moped herself, but the man …

▶ WB 11–12 (pp. 49–50)

P3 READING Soup kitchen (Understanding adverts)

a) Which advert attracts your attention more? Try to say why.

b) What are the adverts trying to make you do?

c) 👥 Describe one of the adverts to your partner and listen to their description of the other.

d) 👥 Describe the differences between the adverts. How do they get across their message? Explain how language, layout, colour, illustration, etc. play a part.

P4 MEDIATION Volunteering in Germany

You're thinking of doing community service for a year (Freiwilliges Soziales Jahr). You've found some information online. Explain in an e-mail to an American friend
– what sort of jobs you can do,
– where you can do your community service,
– how it will help you in the future.

Ein Beitrag für sich und die Gesellschaft

Aus freien Stücken anderen helfen. Behinderte Menschen im Alltag unterstützen. Im Naturschutzpark Nistkästen anbringen und Fußwege sauberhalten. Im Jugendklub eine Disco organisieren oder einen Musik-Workshop vorbereiten. Mit alten Menschen mal einen Spaziergang unternehmen. In Russland in einem Kinderheim arbeiten. Im Sportverein Kids das Dribbeln beibringen. Sportspiele im Schulhort organisieren. Oder auf der Open-Air-Bühne mit Kindern Griffe auf der Rockgitarre üben – das und vieles mehr ist möglich im Freiwilligen Sozialen Jahr (FSJ) – oder im Freiwilligen Ökologischen Jahr (FÖJ). Dem freiwilligen Engagement sind keine Grenzen gesetzt und auch im Ausland gibt es zahlreiche Möglichkeiten.

Wer sich dafür entscheidet, zwischen Schule und Ausbildung einen Freiwilligendienst zu absolvieren, bekommt oft mehr als nur eine berufliche Orientierung. Erste Fachkenntnisse und die erworbenen sozialen Kompetenzen machen junge Menschen fit für den Berufseinstieg und erhöhen ihre Beschäftigungschancen. Zugleich tut es gut, sich für andere einzusetzen und Verantwortung zu übernehmen. Manch einer sammelt dabei die ersten Auslandserfahrungen. Von dem Engagement profitieren also beide Seiten: die jungen Freiwilligen und die Gesellschaft.

Quelle: Bundesministerium für Familie, Senioren, Frauen und Jugend

▶ WB 13–15 (pp. 50–51)

The caller by Robert D. San Souci (abridged and adapted)

What would happen if you lost your mobile phone? Or if it was stolen? Think about what would happen. Then look at the pictures in the following story. Who do you think 'the caller' in the story might be? Some new words are translated in the footnotes at the bottom of each page.

It was hot at Aunt Margaret's funeral. Lindsay Walters had to stand in the hot sun, sweating in her ugly[1], black dress, while the minister prayed.

Lindsay was angry because she should be at Missy's, helping her best friend get ready for a party.

A cell phone rang. Lindsay knew from the ringtone that it was her father's. He went red in the face. At least she knew enough to turn hers off at a funeral. Her father pulled his phone out and shut off the signal but looked quickly at the caller's number. He checked his watch.

At the end of the funeral, Lindsay went behind a tree, took out her own cell phone, and dialed Missy's number. It was busy. Probably her friend was making plans with Noelle or Candice for the party. She made a face at the phone, turned, and bumped into[2] her father, who was talking into his phone.

She went back to her mother, who introduced her to some boring old ladies. She had to nod and look sad as they talked about her aunt. When her father returned, Lindsay asked, "Can we go now?"

"I just have to make one more call," her father said. He moved off again.

When the last old lady and the minister had gone, Lindsay said to her mother, "Please, please, please make Daddy get off the phone so we can go!"

"Stop whining," her mother said. But she waved impatiently[3] at Lindsay's father. She ordered Lindsay and her brothers, Darren and David, to the car, then marched over to where Mr. Walters was still talking on the phone. She made him end his call. Now both of them were angry. Mr. Walters put his cell phone into his coat[4] pocket. "All right, let's get this show on the road[5]," he said.

Some people from the funeral had stopped by the house. Lindsay's sad-looking parents and their guests drank coffee and talked about how nice Aunt Margaret had been.

"As long as you didn't make her angry," said Mr. Walters with a laugh. "I remember as a kid she could be terrible if she thought someone had been rude or was lying[6] or cruel." Lindsay knew what he was talking about. Lindsay thought of her aunt in heaven, terrorizing the angels for not being holy enough.

But the guests finally left. Lindsay ran to her room to change so that her father could drive her to Missy's party. When she was ready she took out Aunt Margaret's gold ring with real diamonds[7]. She had always loved it, and Aunt Margaret had promised it to her just before she died. Her mother told her to only wear the ring at special times. Well, showing off to Missy and Noelle and Candice and the others was special!

Her cell phone rang.

There was some strange static, then a lot of whispering, sounding like a crowd. Finally a tired, dry, old voice said, "Lindsay, darling[8], this is Aunt Margaret."

"Right! Nice try, Missy, guys – see you in a few minutes." Lindsay hung up and put her phone into her party bag. Putting her ring in her jeans pocket so her parents wouldn't see, she ran down the stairs two at a time.

"Where's Dad? He's supposed to drive me to Missy's."

"He's in the car looking for his cell phone," her mother said. "It fell out of his pocket."

Lindsay helped her father search[9] the car, but the phone was gone. He was in a bad mood[10]. She was glad she was spending the night at Missy's after the party.

At Missy's party, all the girls were jealous of the real diamonds on Lindsay's finger. She forgot about their phone joke.

---

[1] ugly ['ʌgli] *hässlich* [2] (to) bump into sb. *jn. anstoßen* [3] impatient [ɪmˈpeɪʃənt] *ungeduldig* [4] coat [kəʊt] *(AE) Jackett*
[5] Let's get the show on the road. *(infml) Fangen wir an.* [6] (to) lie [laɪ] *lügen* [7] diamond [ˈdaɪəmənd] *Diamant*
[8] darling [ˈdɑːlɪŋ] *Liebling, Schatz* [9] (to) search sth. [sɜːtʃ] *etwas durchsuchen* [10] (to) be in a bad mood [muːd] *schlechte Laune haben*

"I hated to go to that smelly old folks' home," Lindsay told them. "I just pretended[11] I wanted to go, because I wanted this ring."

Her cell phone rang and she answered it.

Lots of static, more whispers, the same dry voice saying, "Lindsay, this is Aunt Margaret. I must talk to you."

Clearly it wasn't her friends trying to trick her. That meant it had to be Darren and David. She whispered to her friends, "It's my creepy[12] brothers pretending to be my aunt's ghost[13]."

The others rolled their eyes.

"Is it *really* you, Aunt Margaret?" asked Lindsay, trying to sound little-girl scared.

"Yes. I just wanted to hear your voice again. You were my favorite. You loved me best."

Lindsay held up the ring as she talked. "Well, it was really your ring I loved. I hated going to that place where you stayed. And all that stuff you told me about when you were young was so boring. So thanks for the ring and goodbye, *Aunt Margaret!*" Lindsay ended the call.

She pushed *69 and saw that her brothers were calling from her father's cell phone.

"They're using my dad's phone that he lost. They must have found it in the car. They are going to get so *busted*[14] for this when I get home."

When the party ended and the other girls left after dinner, Missy's parents said they were going to visit neighbors. As soon as they were gone, the girls went upstairs to Missy's room to call their friends. Lying at opposite ends of Missy's bed, they chatted into their cell phones.

Lindsay was just going to dial her boyfriend of the week when her phone rang.

"Lindsay, I am very disappointed in you." The same voice. "I don't think you deserve my ring. I'm coming to get it back."

"Get real!" Lindsay ended the call. It had come from her father's cell phone. She dialed the number but the phone just rang and rang. She hung up and dialed her home. Her mother answered.

"Mom," she said, "Darren and David found Dad's phone. They've been using it to call and bug[15] me. They just did it again."

"That's not possible," said her mother. "They've been watching TV for the past hour. And your father is sure he dropped his phone at the funeral this afternoon." Now her mother sounded worried. "Perhaps it's a crank caller."

"The calls are coming from Dad's cell phone," Lindsay explained. "But –"

There was some loud static. The phone went dead. Missy looked up as her phone went dead too. The lights in the house dimmed[16], then went out. "Blackout[17]," said Missy. All the other houses in the neighborhood were dark.

"I don't think that would shut off our phones," said Lindsay.

"Well, it did," said Missy. "Anyway[18], I was bored. This is cool. We can tell ghost stories."

"I don't want to," said Lindsay, wishing she were home and not in a house without lights.

"Chicken[19]!" her friend said.

There was a knock downstairs at the front door. Thump. Thump. Thump.

Missy got up to answer it.

"Don't!" cried Lindsay. She couldn't say why she was frightened, but she was.

"You are so stupid," said Missy. "My folks forgot their keys or something. Probably the doorbell doesn't work in the blackout."

"Please, don't go!"

---

[11] (to) pretend [prɪˈtend] *so tun, als ob* [12] creepy [ˈkriːpi] *nervig* [13] ghost [ɡəʊst] *Gespenst, Geist* [14] (to) bust sb. [bʌst] *(infml) etwa: jn. zur Schnecke machen* [15] (to) bug [bʌɡ] *nerven* [16] (to) dim [dɪm] *schwächer werden* [17] blackout [ˈblækaʊt] *Stromausfall* [18] Anyway, … [ˈeniweɪ] *Aber egal, … / Wie dem auch sei, …* [19] chicken [ˈtʃɪkɪn] *(infml) Feigling*

"Stay here if you're so scared," said Missy, shaking her head. "What a wuss!" She left.

Lindsay closed the bedroom door and locked it. She heard the front door open and close a moment later. She thought she heard a soft sound like something falling. Then quiet.

Her cell phone rang.

She grabbed it, hoping it was her mother.

"Lindsay, I've come for my ring, you unhappy child. I'm at the bottom of the stairs right now. Let's play that game I played when you were a little girl. The one your father told me not to play, because it frightened you so? But you loved it – you loved being scared. Don't you like being scared anymore?"

"Missy? Is this a trick? This isn't funny."

But Missy's phone was still on the bed where she had left it.

"One step, two – I'm coming for you," said the voice on the phone.

Thump, thump on the stairs.

"Three steps, four – better lock the door. Five steps, six – say your prayers quick."

If the phone was working, Lindsay thought, she could call for help. She hung up and dialed home. It was answered on the third ring.

"Seven steps, eight – not long to wait," said her mother's voice.

She hung up and dialed 911.

"Nine steps, ten – we're near the end," said a man's voice.

She hung up and threw the phone onto the bed beside Missy's.

"Eleven, twelve, and one step more – too late for you, I'm at the door!" It was Aunt Margaret's angry voice.

Someone knocked loudly.

THUMP! THUMP! THUMP!

"Go away! Leave me alone! I didn't mean what I said!" Lindsay started to cry.

"Gotcha![20]" cried Missy through the door. "You're crying! This is better than telling ghost stories! Wait till Noelle and Candice hear I made you cry. You and that stupid ring you think is so cool."

Angry at how she'd been tricked, Lindsay wiped away her tears and opened the door.

"I never want to talk to you again!" she shouted.

But it wasn't Missy holding Lindsay's father's phone in a muddy hand as the lights came on.

Working with the text

1 The story

a) When you have read the short story once, finish these sentences:
1 Lindsay gets a diamond ring from …
2 Before Lindsay goes to Missy's house, she …
3 Lindsay doesn't believe that the caller …
4 At Missy's house, Lindsay gets another call …
5 While Lindsay is speaking to her mum …
6 When everything is dark, …
7 Missy wants to … but Lindsay …
8 When Lindsay opens the door, …

b) Whose 'muddy hand' do you think it is at the end of the story?

---

20 Gotcha! ['gɒtʃə] (= I've got you!) Hab dich! Reingelegt!

2 Working with words

STUDY SKILLS — Using an English–English dictionary

You use an English–English dictionary to find out the **different meanings** of English words.
The **entries** also show you in which **contexts** and **collocations** the words can be used. They give you **synonyms** and **antonyms**. They also have information on **pronunciation** and **spelling** in **British** and **American English**.

▶ SF Using an English–English dictionary (p. 125)

a) Use an English–English dictionary.
– Find two different meanings of the verb *(to) whine*. Which one is used in l. 33?
– Which part of speech (noun, adjective, verb, etc.) is *crank* (l. 140)?
– Find several collocations for *holy* (l. 52).
– How else could you say *What a wuss!* (l. 165)?

b) Find all words and phrases in the semantic field phones/phone calls. Check their meanings in the dictionary. Are they used in BE or AE?

3 An exciting story?

STUDY SKILLS — Reading literature (4)

Suspense
Writers can make a story exciting by creating suspense. How? They can make something unexpected happen. They can end a story, or part of it, in the middle of an exciting event. They can offer explanations for events and then show why they can't be right. They might use noises, rhythm, repetition. They can leave the reader 'hanging over a cliff' at the climax of a story.

▶ SF Reading literature (pp. 138–139)

a) Look for examples of how the author of "The caller" creates suspense and makes it rise and fall. For instance, look at lines 66–67:
'Lindsay, darling, this is Aunt Margaret.'

b) Where does the story reach a climax?

4 Lindsay's character

a) Read lines 15–20, 60–62, 68–69 and 81–83 again. What do they tell you about Lindsay's character? Describe what is important to her in her relationship to Missy and the other girls.

b) How does Lindsay feel about her aunt? Find a quotation from the story that shows this well. Compare your idea with a partner's. Who has the better quotation?

c) Discuss a freeze frame for the following part of the story:
'She had to nod and look sad as they talked about her aunt.' (ll. 23–25)
Try to imagine the scene. Where are the people standing/sitting? What might Lindsay be thinking/hoping/feeling at the moment?
Then act the freeze frame for the class.
Take a photo of your freeze frame for your DOSSIER.

d) Extra Choose another part of the story and discuss and act a freeze frame for it. Can the other groups guess which part of the story it is?

e) Extra Does the story have a moral or a message? If you think it has, what is it? How is it connected to Lindsay's character?

5 Extra Beyond the story

a) Do you like scary stories like "The caller" or scary films? Can you say why?

b) Write a script for a three-minute film based on this story.

▶ WB 16 (p. 52) • Self-evaluation 3–4 WB (p. 53)

Unit 1 Part B

P2 LISTENING Learning to surf

b) *Role play:*
Use the role card on the right and act out the telephone conversation.

> **Name:** Matt
> – You work at the surf school.
> – You answer the phone.
> – You have to find out
>   – if the caller has gone surfing before.
>   – if she can swim.
>   – if she has her own equipment.
> – You offer the EasySurf course.
> – You can also offer the Surf Girl course, which is like EasySurf but only for girls. It costs 85 dollars for two hours.

Unit 1 Part C

P2 On holiday in Australia (Question word + *to*-infinitive)

a) *Listen to Partner A and decide what to say. You can use phrases like 'Why don't you …?' or 'You should …'.*
1. A bottle of water, a hat and some sunscreen.
2. Be there by 5:30 am.
3. Just take the lift.
4. Meet in front of the hotel.
5. See the people at the tour desk.

b) *Partner B: You're on holiday in Australia and need some help. Look at the boxes below and tell your partner what your problems are. Start with 'I don't know/I'm not sure …', add a question word and an infinitive construction and finish with 'Can you help? / Any ideas? / Do you know?'.*

I don't know	who	ask about plane tickets
	where	check out of the hotel
	when	get from here to Sydney
I'm not sure	how	send a postcard to
	what	wear on the plane

B: I don't know how to get from here to Sydney.
A: I think you should go by plane.

Unit 2 Part B

P7 MEDIATION School in New Zealand

a) Partner B: You and your partner want to spend some time at a school in New Zealand. Listen to what your partner has to tell you about Wellington High School.

b) In German, tell your partner the most important information about Onslow College.

c) In English, tell your partner which school you would prefer to go to and why.

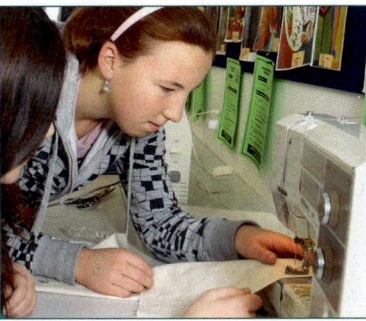

- Onslow College is a co-educational state school with about 1150 students and is situated 10 minutes north of central Wellington, the capital of New Zealand.
- It is driven by a sense of community rather than conformity. Our challenge is to enable students to develop their potential through high quality education in a cooperative, friendly, stimulating and well-disciplined environment.
- Onslow has a long tradition of welcoming international students and has run cultural exchanges for many years. Some international students live with their families who work for their country's embassy. Over 10% of all our students are from non-English-speaking backgrounds.
- Academic subjects available for international students include Computer Studies, Drama, Music, Art Design, Photography and Economics as well as Spanish, Japanese, German, Maori and Chinese.
- In their English course, international students are also taught the necessary study skills to function effectively in their classes including time management, exam preparation, note-taking, setting goals and vocabulary learning.
- Sports include skiing, basketball, tennis, badminton, rowing, rugby, table tennis and soccer. Students can learn clarinet, drums, flute, guitar, keyboards, recorder, saxophone, trombone, trumpet or voice. The school has bands, chamber ensembles, a jazz band, a choir and an orchestra.
- The school arranges accommodation with a host family ($220 per week) and provides training and support for the host parents, who are contacted and visited regularly.

Unit 3 Part A

P2 EVERYDAY ENGLISH Changing your flight

b) **Role play:** Booking a flight
You work for a travel agent. Use the information in the table to help your partner. Start by answering the phone.

c) Phone a travel agent for a return flight from Germany to Mumbai leaving 29 November. You'd prefer to fly from Frankfurt but could fly from Munich. You'd like to be back as early as possible on 29 December and would really like the cheapest flight.

29/11 – 29/12 Go Pacific: EUR 768,09				
Flight	From	Dep	To	Arr
GP 288	FRA	13:50	HKG	07:50 + 1
GP 282	FRA	18:50	HKG	13:35 + 1
GP 285	HKG	23:05	FRA	05:15 + 1
GP 289	HKG	23:50	FRA	05:25 + 1
29/11 – 29/12 Hong Kong Jet: EUR 781,00				
Flight	From	Dep	To	Arr
HKJ 738	FRA	17:40	HKG	11:25 + 1
HKJ 739	HKJ	13:30	FRA	18:45

B   Partner B

Unit 4   Part A

P3 EVERYDAY ENGLISH   Role play: Asking someone out

Partner B: Partner A wants to ask you out on a date. You aren't sure yet whether you like the idea or not. While you talk to your partner, you have to make a decision. Try to be nice and polite – you don't want to hurt your partner's feelings.
You must either agree to go out with your partner or explain that you don't think it's a good idea. The words and phrases in the two boxes will help you to say what you want and to be nice and polite about it.

That sounds like a great idea. • Sounds good. • Why not? • That will be so much fun. • Yeah, I'd like that. • I'm really looking forward to … • Yes, thank you. • Cool, I'd love to. • I'm flattered.

I need some time to think about this. • I'm not sure. • I'll have to ask my parents. • I have to be home by … • Sorry, I'm not allowed to. • You're a nice guy/girl, but … • I'm sorry but … • It's very sweet of you, but … • I'm afraid I can't. • I'll give you a call, OK?

2   Part A B C D

PERSONALITY QUIZ   RESULTS CHECKER

Score points as follows:

1. A 2 B 1 C 3
2. A 1 B 2 C 3
3. A 3 B 2 C 1
4. A 3 B 2 C 1
5. A 2 B 1 C 3
6. A 2 B 1 C 3
7. A 2 B 1 C 3
8. A 1 B 2 C 3
9. A 2 B 3 C 1
10. A 1 B 2 C 3
11. A 2 B 1 C 3
12. A 1 B 2 C 3

Text File

TF 1–12		Inhalt	Seite
Unit 1	TF 1	*Project:* The magic of Australia	100–101
Unit 1	TF 2	*Bilingual module* Ecosystems in Australia	102–103
Unit 1	TF 3	Australian signs	104
Unit 2	TF 4	The right advice?	105
Unit 2	TF 5	Going to school in England	106
Unit 3	TF 6	Mr. Wah goes to Hong Kong	107–108
Unit 3	TF 7	Black music, white music	109
Unit 3	TF 8	*Project:* Your big cities	110–111
Unit 3	TF 9	A lover's embrace	112
Unit 4	TF 10	Luuurve debate	113–114
Unit 4	TF 11	Who's guilty?	115–119
Unit 4	TF 12	*Bilingual module* A different kind of justice	120–122

TF 1 Project: The magic of Australia

Australia is the world's smallest continent and the only continent occupied by just one country. A small continent, but a huge country. Doing a project about different aspects of the place may help you to understand more about the magic of Australia.

a) Divide the class into groups. Each group works on one of the topics here or another topic of their choice. Some students might like to work alone.

b) Work on the project. Groups can give different tasks to different students.

c) Present your project to the class. Use appropriate visual aids (transparencies, handouts, computer presentation, ...).

d) Listen to or look at the other groups' presentations and evaluate them.

▸ SF Visual aids in presentations (p. 131) •
SF Project skills (pp. 132–133)

Topic 1 The geography Australia

Australia is a huge place and has lots of different landscapes, from desert to rainforest to coral reefs. You could do your project on one of these landscapes, on the island of Tasmania, or on an important city. Where are they located? Find out what these places are like, who or what lives there, how they survive, what the places are famous for, what visitors can do there. You might even like to plan a trip to Oz.

The Great Barrier Reef

A famous Sydney landmark

Topic 2 Culture and art in Australia

Australia is not just a place of natural wonders. Humans have lived there for at least 40,000 years and human culture always involves[1] the production of art, music, dance, literature. Find out about the culture and art of Australia: you could look at ancient Aboriginal rock art or modern Aboriginal painting, the Australian popular music scene, movies or the theatre. Or about great Australian literature from Dreamtime stories to modern novelists and poets. How about performing an Australian song, poem or dance?

An Aborigine dot painting

---

[1] (to) involve sth. [ɪnˈvɒlv] mit etwas zu tun haben

Topic 3 The animals of Australia

Everyone has heard of the kangaroo, and everybody loves koalas. But Australia has lots of other fascinating animals. You might want to research which ones can only be found in Australia. Which ones are dangerous? Are any of them threatened? Why are rabbits such a problem? Check out your local zoo for animals from Oz.

A platypus

A Tasmanian Devil

A salt-water crocodile, or 'salty'

Topic 4 The first people of Australia

Perhaps you'd like to learn more about the Aboriginal people of Australia: How do they live in modern Australia – are their lives different from those of white Australians? What can you find out about their beliefs and legends or their art and music? Perhaps you can find a Dreamtime story and act it out.

People at an Aboriginal settlement in the Northern Territory

Topic 5 Dry Australia

Australia is the world's driest inhabited continent. Find out what that means for the environment and the people who live in it. How are Australians touched by drought[2] and bushfires? What effects will climate change have on the country? Find out about water restrictions in Sydney or Adelaide and try to live according to them for a day or so.

An Australian bushfire

---

[2] drought [draʊt] *Dürre*

Bilingual module – Biology

TF 2 Ecosystems[1] in Australia

1 Food chains[2]

Plants and animals need energy, which they get from food. Plants make their own food by photosynthesis, so they are called **producers**. Animals must get their food by eating plants or other animals, so they are called **consumers**.

Complete the food chain in Diagram A. Use the words in the box.

> insects • crocodiles • plants • frogs

Diagram A: A food chain

Producer ⟶ Primary consumer ⟶ Secondary consumer ⟶ Tertiary consumer[3]
.... are eaten by .... are eaten by .... are eaten by ....

2 Food webs

a) A food web consists of many connected food chains, like those shown in the food web below. Find six food chains in the food web an write them down, e.g. grass > kangaroo > dingo
How many different kinds of food do the different animals eat?

Diagram B: A food web

a ⟶ b a is eaten by b

b) What will happen if the population of one part of the food web in Diagram B increases or decreases?

| If the population of | snakes kangaroos ... | increases, decreases, | then the population of | frogs dingoes ... | will increase. will decrease. |

BIOLOGY SKILLS Talking about food webs

If the population of one part of a food web changes, the populations of other parts of the food web will also change. Some animals will eat more of another animal or plant. Some animals will not have enough food and they will die.

---

[1] ecosystem [ˈiːkəʊsɪstəm] Ökosystem [2] food chain [ˈfuːd tʃeɪn] Nahrungskette [3] primary/secondary/tertiary consumer [ˈpraɪməri kənˌsjuːmə, ˈsekəndri, ˈtɜːʃəri] Primär-/Sekundär-/Tertiärkonsument [4] (to) increase [ɪnˈkriːs] anwachsen, zunehmen [5] (to) decrease [dɪˈkriːs] zurückgehen, abnehmen, sinken

3 An ecosystem in disorder[1]

a) Look at the photos, the map and the fast facts box. Describe what they show.

TOADZILLA!

27 March 2007

A toad as big as a small dog was found in Australia this week. The cane toad was 20 cm long – twice as big as most cane toads.

In 1935, farmers in Queensland brought 102 cane toads to Australia because they had problems with insects in their fields. They wanted the cane toads to eat the insects.

Unfortunately that was a really bad idea! Today there are about 200 million cane toads and native Australian animals are in danger.

The government is now asking people to hunt cane toads and kill them.

So, why is the situation so bad for the native animals of Australia?

The main reason is the fact that cane toads are poisonous. Animals (like crocodiles, snakes, lizards and birds) that try to eat the cane toad, or its eggs, die from the poison.

Also cane toads eat anything that moves, including native snakes, frogs, lizards and birds.

Scientists are searching for a way to control the cane toad population in Australia ... before it's too late.

Fast facts: Cane Toads

From: South America
Scientific name: Bufo marinus
Size: About 100 to 150 mm long
What do they eat? Almost anything, including cat and dog food, insects, lizards, frogs and small snakes
What are they eaten by? Snakes, lizards, crocodiles, birds
Reproduction: Cane toads have about 8,000 to 25,000 eggs twice a year. It is estimated that about 0.5% survive to become adult toads.

Where cane toads are found (1935, 2007)

b) Find out how cane toads came to Australia, why they are such a serious problem now, and what the Australian government wants people to do about them.

c) Look at Diagram B on page 102 again. What will happen if the cane toad arrives in this place?

d) The article says that scientists are looking for a way to control the cane toad population. Do you think that it would be a good idea to bring a new animal to Australia that could eat the cane toad? Why/Why not?
I think it might make the situation better/worse because ...

Activate your English
– The photo/map/fast facts box shows/gives information about ...
– It says that .../It shows ...
– This is a photo/map of ...
– In 1935 cane toads were found in ...
   In 2007 they were found in ...

4 Introduced species

Write about another introduced species and its effects, e.g. the rabbit in Australia, the raccoon in Germany, the kudzu vine in the USA or the red-eared terrapin in Britain. Say where the species came from and how/why it was introduced. Include a fast facts box, a map and/or a diagram.

---

[1] in disorder [dɪsˈɔːdə] *in Unordnung; (funktions)gestört* [2] toad [təʊd] *Kröte*

TF 3 Australian signs

1 Signs talk

a) Work in groups of five. Each person describes one of the signs 1–5. You might need to look up words you don't know in a dictionary.

b) Discuss where you would expect to find each of the signs, what they mean and what they tell you about Australia.

2 Funny signs

a) What is the message of the sign below?

b) Draw a sign of your own – it can be serious or funny. Swap signs with a partner. Explain what you think your partner's sign is trying to say.

TF 4 The right advice? 🎧

a) The following four poems and a song all give advice on life in some way. Read them and choose the one which you feel is most relevant to your life. Write a few sentences that explain the 'message' of the poem.

b) 👥 Find a partner who has chosen the same poem. Compare your explanations of the message.

c) 👥 Now get together with a partner who has chosen a different poem. Explain the message of your poem to them and listen to their explanation. Tell them why you find your poem relevant.

From Breathe (2 AM)
Anna Nalick

'Cause you can't jump the track, we're like cars
   on a cable[1]
And life's like an hourglass[2], glued to the table
No one can find the rewind button, girl.
So cradle your head in your hands
And breathe … just breathe,
Oh breathe, just breathe

Dreams
Langston Hughes

Hold fast to dreams
For if dreams die
Life is a broken-winged bird
That cannot fly

Hold fast to dreams
For when dreams go
Life is a barren[3] field
Frozen with snow.

Somewhere in the sky
Leo Aylen

Somewhere
In the sky,
There's a door painted blue,
With a big brass knocker seven feet high.
If you can find it,
Knock, and go through –
That is, if you dare.
You'll see behind it
The secrets of the universe piled on a chair
Like a tangle of wool[4].
A voice will declare
'You have seven centuries in which to
   unwind[5] it.
But whatever
You do,
You must never,
Ever,
Lose your temper and pull.'

I meant to do my work today
Richard LeGallienne

I meant to do[6] my work today –
But a brown bird sang in the apple tree,
And a butterfly flitted across the field,
And all the leaves were calling me.

And the wind went sighing over the land
Tossing[7] the grasses to and fro[8],
And a rainbow held out its shining hand –
So what could I do but laugh and go?

---

[1] car on a cable ['keɪbl] *(gezogene) Straßenbahn*   [2] hourglass ['aʊəglɑːs] *Stundenglas, Sanduhr*   [3] barren ['bærən] *unfruchtbar, öde*
[4] wool [wʊl] *Wolle*   [5] (to) unwind [ˌʌn'waɪnd] *(etwas Verheddertes) mühsam aufdrehen*   [6] (to) mean to do sth. [miːn] *vorhaben, etwas zu tun*
[7] (to) toss [tɒs] *werfen*   [8] to and fro [frəʊ] *hin und her*

TF 5 **Going to school in England**

Just imagine you've gone back in time and you're growing up and going to school again, but this time in England. How will your life be different?

1 Your years of fun and play at nursery school[1] won't be as easy and they'll come to an end more quickly in England. You have to start primary school in the term after your fifth birthday – there are three school terms in England: from September to Christmas, from January to Easter, after Easter to July. Some parents send their children to primary school earlier, so perhaps you'll only be four when you start your six years there!

2 In this new life, you'll move to secondary school from Year 7. If your parents are wealthy, they might send you to an independent school. These are private schools and you have to pay to go there. Seven per cent of school students in England go to independent schools. The most traditional ones are called public schools. Some independent schools are also boarding schools[2], so you might have to live and sleep there during term. But unless you're a wizard[3], you won't go to Hogwarts.

3 So your mum and dad aren't rich? You'll end up in an ordinary state comprehensive school[4]. They offer a general education to students of all abilities. What will you learn there? Well, all students have to do the subjects on the National Curriculum[5]. Many subjects are similar[6] to those in Germany, but there is Citizenship[7] in Years 7–11, Design & Technology in Years 7–9 and Work-related Learning in Years 10–11.

4 How will you find out how you're doing? Your teachers will assess you and there are exams in Year 9 and national GCSE exams in Year 11 (you might do GCSEs in some subjects in Year 10).

5 At the end of Year 11 you could leave school. Or go to a College of Further Education. But if you stay at school for years 12 & 13, known as the Sixth Form, or go to a Sixth Form College, you'll study four or five subjects and take AS exams in year 12 and then do A2 exams in three subjects in Year 13. AS and A2 together make up A-levels. With good A-level results, you might be able to get a place at a university.

Describe the main similarities and differences between the German and the English school systems. You might like to draw a diagram to help you.

---

[1] nursery school ['nɜːsəri] *(BE) Kindergarten*   [2] boarding school ['bɔːdɪŋ] *Internat*   [3] wizard ['wɪzəd] *Zauberer, Zauberin*
[4] comprehensive school [ˌkɒmprɪ'hensɪv] *Gesamtschule*   [5] curriculum [kə'rɪkjələm] *Lehrplan*   [6] similar ['sɪmələ] *ähnlich*
[7] Citizenship ['sɪtɪzənʃɪp] *Staatsbürgerkunde*

TF 6 Mr. Wah goes to Hong Kong (abridged and adapted from "The ferry" by Jess Row)

Have you ever been in a situation where you felt like an outsider? If so, describe the situation.

This is what it's like to be a freak, Marcel thinks. He walks across the empty arrivals hall, pleased to be standing after a sixteen-hour flight, and the woman in the pale green uniform at the passport desk lifts her head and stares at him, openmouthed, as if he has just flown down from the air. Her lips form a single syllable: Wah. It's like a chorus: the stewardesses, the kids in tracksuits, the old women in traditional jackets look at him and say it immediately, involuntarily. That's me, he says to himself, folding back the cover of his new passport, looking around for the signs to the baggage claim. I'm Mr. Wah.

Hello? A hand touches his arm; he turns around. A young Chinese woman with silver hair gives him a nervous half-smile, giggles, and covers her mouth. Excuse me, I wonder if you please sign autograph[1]? She gives him an open magazine, a picture of a basketball player, surrounded by Chinese writing.

But that's not me.

She looks confused. Sorry? she says. Not you?

No, he says. That's Alonzo Mourning. You basketball player?

No, he says. I mean, sure. I play basketball. But I'm a lawyer.

Oh, she says. OK. But she stays there with the magazine, waiting.

So that's why I can't sign this, right? You don't want my autograph, do you?

Sorry, she says. Don't understand.

You don't – for God's sake, he thinks, make the woman happy. OK, he says. Give me the pen.

Peace, he signs, *Marcel Thomas.* But he writes the words close together, and thinks, she'll never know the difference.

Hong Kong is like no place he has ever imagined. Green hills rising out of a steel-colored sea. Rows of identical white apartment blocks that seem to grow from low-hanging clouds, like mushrooms after rain. When he steps outside the airport the air sticks to his skin, and he feels a little sick, his joints[2] like rubber, a bad taste in his mouth. He'd give anything for a shower. Thirteen thousand

[1] autograph [ˈɔːtəɡrɑːf] *Autogramm* [2] joint [dʒɔɪnt] *Gelenk*

miles, he thinks, staring at the handrails on the escalator, the green glass walls of the taxi stand, as if looking for evidence¹ of that fact, some basis for comparison. Thirteen thousand miles from San Francisco. This. And this. And me.

He falls asleep on the long ride into the city, lying across the backseat with his head on his bag. When the taxi stops suddenly his eyes open and he sits up carefully. The car is surrounded by people rushing past, bumping against the window, and he hears a muffled roar: voices, horns and music.

What is it? he says. Is it a riot?

Yih ging lai dou ah, the driver says. Causeway Bay. Excelsior Hotel. OK?

When he steps out into the street, he finds himself staring down at a sea of black-haired heads, none higher than his chest. People moving in every direction, holding on to shopping bags and mobile phones and children; no one looks up at him here. A van turns the corner fast, and they scatter² out of the way; *like ants,* he thinks, *like cockroaches,* and feels ashamed. He makes his way across the street, holding his bags shoulder-high, as if crossing a river. Without quite knowing why, he holds his breath until the hotel's doors close behind him, and then releases³ it with a gasp.

There's no place like it on earth, Wallace Ford tells him later that evening, on the outdoor patio at the American Club, twenty-two stories⁴ above Central. From his seat Marcel can see the shining columns of office buildings crowded close together, and between them, the dark shadow of Victoria Peak. The glow of the city turns the sky a dirty orange. It's like another world, he thinks, as if Hong Kong were one of those cities in science fiction movies, where everyone lives far above the

ground. It wouldn't surprise him to see a spaceship passing silently among the skyscrapers, or a white robot coming out to serve them drinks.

You take New York, Ford says. San Francisco. L.A. Chicago. Even London and Paris – none of it compares to this. The Chinese were living in cities before anybody else on the planet. They've got it figured out⁵. It's not always pretty – or at least we don't think so. But it works.

1 A freak?
Explain why Marcel thinks 'This is what it's like to be a freak.' Why do people in Hong Kong who see Marcel behave as they do? Support your ideas with quotes from the story.

2 Impressions of Hong Kong
a) Take notes on Marcel's impressions of Hong Kong under these headings:
Landscape   Climate
People   City of the future

b) Give examples of the imagery the author uses to create the atmosphere of Hong Kong.

c) Imagine Marcel writes a postcard or email home with his impressions of Hong Kong. What will he write?

---

¹ evidence [ˈevɪdəns] *Beweis*   ² (to) scatter [ˈskætə] *sich zerstreuen, auseinandergehen*   ³ (to) release one's breath [rɪˈliːs] *ausatmen*
⁴ story [ˈstɔːri] *(AE) Stockwerk*   ⁵ (to) have got sth. figured out [ˌfɪɡəd_ˈaʊt] *etwas verstehen*

TF 7 Black music, white music 🎧

One of South Africa's best-loved musicians is Johnny Clegg, who was born in England in 1953 and moved with his family to Johannesburg at the age of nine. When he was 13 or 14 he began to learn to play the guitar. Through this interest he met Charlie Mzila, a Zulu cleaner who played street music near Clegg's home.

Johnny began to go secretly into the townships and migrant workers' hostels with Charlie to play guitar and learn traditional Zulu dancing. However, the apartheid laws meant it was illegal for Johnny to play with black musicians or move around the black areas of Johannesburg, and he was arrested more than once. During this period he developed a reputation[1] as a good Zulu guitarist.

This reputation reached the ears of Sipho Mchunu, a migrant Zulu worker who had come to Johannesburg in 1969. He wanted to meet this young white boy who could dance like an African and play Zulu street music. When they did meet, they immediately became friends. Johnny was 16 and Sipho 18. Together they wrote songs that mixed Zulu rhythms and English and African lyrics. Most had a strong element of protest.

They formed a group, *Juluka*, which means *sweat* in English, but as a mixed-race group they were often the targets of racists and the police. Their music was banned or censored and they could only play in a few places, like churches and university halls.

In 1976 Johnny and Sipho had their first hit song called "Woza Friday". In late 1979 their first album *Universal Men* was released. Other

Savuka with Johnny Clegg (centre)

albums followed and Juluka toured the world with great success until they split in 1985. Sipho went back to the farm in Zululand where he was born.

Johnny went on to form another crossover[2] band, *Savuka* ('We have risen'), which mixed African music with Celtic folk music and international rock sounds. Savuka became an even bigger success for Johnny, but he did not forget Sipho. Johnny helped Sipho to produce his own solo album in 1989 and in 1996 they reformed Juluka and released a new CD, *Crocodile Love*.

Johnny Clegg still works with Sipho Mchunu. At the same time, he has continued his very successful solo career and the 'white Zulu' from Johannesburg plays his fusion of black and white music to large audiences all over the world.

Journey's end (Emalonjeni)
Juluka (Johnny Clegg & Sipho Mchunu)
...
I don't know where you are
My eyes are fixed upon your star
I know that at the journey's end
I will see your face again
Indlela 'yasidedela
(The way is now clear for us)
Sihamb' emalonjeni
(we begin our long journey)

---

a) Read 'Black music, white music' and note down what it tells you about apartheid and the city of Johannesburg. Explain what effect this had on Johnny Clegg.

b) 👥 Discuss the names of Johnny Clegg's two groups, Juluka and Savuka. Comment on them to the class.

c) Listen to the Juluka song "Journey's end (Emalonjeni)". Would you play it to a friend? Why/why not?

d) **Extra** Choose a musician you like a lot. Research and write a short presentation on them. Or find out more about Johnny Clegg and present your new information.

---

[1] reputation [ˌrepjʊˈteɪʃn] *Ruf* [2] crossover [ˈkrɒsəʊvə] *Cross-over-, unterschiedliche Musikstile verbindend*

TF 8 Project: Your big cities

Which big cities of the world do you find most fascinating? Modern cities? Ancient cities you've learned about in history? Cities you've already visited or cities you'd love to see one day? These pages will help you to do a project on a big city of your choice.

a) Find other students who would like to work on the same cities as you. The suggestions below might help. You could also work alone.

b) Work on the project, dividing the tasks between you if you're in a group.

c) Present your project to the class. Use appropriate visual aids (transparencies, handouts, computer presentation, …).

d) Listen to or look at the other groups' presentations and evaluate them.

▶ SF Project skills (pp. 132–133)

Suggestion 1: Your favourite big city

Which big cities have you visited? Which is your favourite? Is it somewhere in your own country, like Hamburg or Berlin? Or somewhere you've been on holiday, like Rome or Paris? Maybe it's a city where you have relatives, like Istanbul or Moscow. What do you like most about the city? What are the best sights to see? Or would you like to do a project on a city you have always wanted to go to?

Catch a boat in Hamburg.

Get spicy in Istanbul.

Skateboard Paris.

Suggestion 2: Ancient cities

The oldest cities were probably not terribly big, but some cities in ancient times did grow very large. Why did people start to live in cities, and when? Which ancient cities grew very large and why? Which ancient cities are still big cities today? Which are just ruins or have disappeared as history passed them by? Was Ur in Iraq the first big city with more than 100,000 inhabitants? Or was it Jinxu in China? Was Rome the first city that passed the 1 million mark? Or was it Alexandria in Egypt with its famous lighthouse?

The pharos – ancient Alexandria's lighthouse

Ancient Rome might have looked like this.

Suggestion 3: Music cities

In the United States, Nashville is the home of country music while New Orleans has a reputation for the blues and Chicago for jazz. Detroit is famous for Motown's soul and New York and L.A. have led the hip hop revolution. But cities in many other parts of the world are also closely connected with music. In South America that music is dance music: there's Buenos Aires and its tango, and at Rio de Janeiro's famous carnival, samba is king. Music from the films of Bollywood has spread from Mumbai all over the world. Berlin and techno go together – the famous Love Parade started there.

What city is the home of your favourite music?

Dance to the music – Berlin.

Dance to the music – Buenos Aires.

Suggestion 4: English-speaking cities

During the last five years, your English book has taken you to lots of big cities where English is the main language: Bristol, London, New York, Toronto, Los Angeles, Atlanta, San Francisco, Sydney, Hong Kong. What is special about these places? What else would you like to find out about them? How old are they? When did they grow to be big cities? What are their most famous sights? What are their hidden treasures? How would you have fun?

Atlanta has the world's largest aquarium.

A short ferry ride takes you to the Toronto Islands.

TF 9 A lover's embrace[1] (abridged and adapted from *Mumbai* by Suketu Mehta)

The manager of Bombay's railway system was recently asked when the system would improve so that it could carry its five million daily passengers in comfort. 'Not in my lifetime,' he answered. Certainly, if you take the train into Bombay, you find out about the temperature of the human body as it curls around you on all sides and adjusts itself to every curve of your own. A lover's embrace was never so close.

One morning I took the rush hour train to Jogeshwari. There were so many passengers I could only get halfway into the carriage[2]. As the train got faster, I hung on to the top of the open door. I feared I would be pushed out, but someone said: 'Don't worry, if they push you out they also pull you in.'

Asad Bin Saif is a scholar of the slums, moving tirelessly among the sewers[3], cataloguing the riots, seeing first-hand the slow destruction[4] of the city. Asad, of all people, has seen people at their worst. I asked him if he felt pessimistic about the human race.

'Not at all,' he replied. 'Look at the hands from the trains.'

If you are late for work in Bombay, and reach the station just as the train is leaving, you can run up to the crowded compartments[5] and you will find many hands stretching out to grab you on board, unfolding outward from the train like petals. As you run beside the train you will be picked up, and some tiny space will be made for your feet in the open doorway. The rest is up to you; you will probably have to hang on to the door frame with your fingers, being careful not to lean out too far. But consider what has happened: having stood like this for hours, your fellow[6] passengers, already packed tighter than cattle, their shirts wet with sweat, can still feel with you, know that your boss might shout at you or cut your pay if you miss this train. They make space where none exists to take one more person with them. And at the moment of contact, they do not know if the hand that is reaching for theirs belongs to a Hindu or Muslim or Christian or Brahmin or untouchable or whether you were born in this city or arrived only this morning or whether you're from Bombay or Mumbai or New York. All they know is that you're trying to get to the city of gold, and that's enough. Come on board, they say. We'll adjust.

a) Which problems of life in Mumbai does "A lover's embrace" mention?

b) Read lines 54–63 again and explain what they tell you about Mumbai society.

c) Why isn't Asad Bin Saif pessimistic about the human race? Summarize the main message of the text in a few sentences.

d) Describe an example of something from your own area that connects people from different ethnic or religious groups.

---

[1] embrace [ɪmˈbreɪs] *Umarmung* [2] carriage [ˈkærɪdʒ] *Wagen* [3] sewer [ˈsuːə] *Abwasserkanal* [4] destruction [dɪˈstrʌkʃn] *Zerstörung*
[5] compartment [kəmˈpɑːtmənt] *Abteil* [6] fellow [ˈfeləʊ] *Mit-*

TF 10 Luuurve debate (adapted from *Don't call me Ishmael* by Michael Gerard Bauer)

Ishmael, Orazio ('the Razz') and Scobie are in the debating team of their school. They go to a workshop to learn more about debating. But is Ishmael's mind on the talk?

The day of the debating workshop at Moorfield High School was the day I first saw Kelly Faulkner. Not that she noticed me, of course. I was just one of the thirty or so students taking the workshop. But I noticed her, and Orazio Zorzotto also noticed me noticing her.

"Hey, Leseur, stick your tongue back in – you're starting to dribble."

It was the lunch break. Orazio and I were waiting outside a classroom for Scobie, the captain of our team. He was still talking to one of the workshop presenters inside.

"What?"

"Come on, you can't fool the Razz. You've been perving at[1] that weird chick in the red T-shirt all day," he said and nodded at a group of girls sitting under a tree.

"What? I wasn't perving at anyone."

"If you say so."

"And she's not weird," I added, perhaps a little too quickly.

"Woo … Sorry, I didn't mean to say anything bad about your girlfriend."

"Girlfriend! What are you talking about?"

"Look, don't get me wrong. I don't blame you. She is *kinda* cute in a … weird sort of way. It's just, she's not my type, you know?"

I didn't really know, but I guessed Razza's type would be someone like Britney Spears or Paris Hilton. You know, the sex-goddess-next-door type.

"You should go and chat her up."

Oh yes, that'll happen. What a terrific idea. I could just go over and say, "Excuse me. My name is Ishmael Leseur … Yes, I agree, it is an interesting name … Anyway, I thought you might be dying to leave all your friends and join a complete stranger in a conversation. Or, on the other hand, you and your friends might prefer just to stare at me, like I'm a three-headed zombie, before you laugh and point at me and call me things like 'complete loser,' and 'absolute dork'."

"Look, Razza, I don't know what you're talking about. I haven't been *looking* at anyone, I don't want to *talk* to anyone, and I'm not *interested* in anyone, okay?"

"Really? Then how about telling me the four steps of good debating."

"What?"

"The four steps of good debating. Go on – we just had a talk on them."

"What's that got to do with anything?"

"Well, it's just that the speaker-dude in there told us those steps about a zillion times *and* put them up on the overhead projector. So unless your mind was on some babe in a red T-shirt during the whole talk, you'd have to remember them, wouldn't you? So, come on, lover-boy, I'm waiting."

"This is stupid. I don't have to do this!"

"*Can't* do it, you mean. Look, I'll make it easy for you: just give us a couple of the steps – they don't even have to be in the right order. How about one, then? Oh my god. Don't tell me you can't even remember one? This is worse than I thought! Quick, help me get this arrow from your heart before it's too late!"

Suddenly Razza had both hands on my chest and was pulling at my shirt. "Arrrgh! Curse you, Cupid!"

"Back off!" I said. "I bet you can't even remember them yourself."

Razza froze immediately and then told me the steps, like a robot. "First: say what the other team said. Second: say why they are wrong. Third: say what your team says. Fourth: say why you are right."

"So I wasn't listening. So what?" I said quietly. "What does that prove[2]?"

"It proves to *me*, Ishmael, my man, that when you should have been learning about good debating, you were in fact" – and here he leaned close to my ear and whispered – "logged on to the website of luuurve!"

---

[1] (to) perve at sb./sth. [pɜːv] *jn./etwas anglotzen* [2] (to) prove [pruːv] *beweisen*

"You're mad," I said and pushed him away. "You realize that, don't you? They shouldn't let people like you into the community with normal people."

Razza stuck out his jaw and spoke to an empty bench³ in front of him. "Ladies and gentlemen, *chair*⁴, I give to you the four steps of good debating. One: my love-struck colleague, Ishmael, said that I was mad. Two: my lover-boy friend is wrong, because he is not a doctor and so cannot make such a diagnosis. Three: I say my teammate is accusing me of being mad to cover the fact that he is totally in love with a certain red T-shirt-wearing girl but doesn't want to admit it. And four: I am right, because if anyone can make such a diagnosis, it is I, because I am the Razzman, and the Razzman is the doctor of luuurve!"

I looked at the smiling face before me. I wanted to kill him ... slowly.

"I pretty much think that's game, set and match⁵ to me, Ishmael, old pal. And just in time. Here comes our leader."

Finally some sense.

"Herr Scobie, I am sorry to report that I no longer think Comrade Leseur here can be a member of our team. He hasn't taken any notes and I have discovered to my horror that he doesn't even know the four steps of good debating. I'm sorry, but his mind is just not on the job. What on earth do you think is wrong with him, Herr Scobmeister?"

Scobie looked at me, then turned to Razza. At last, he was going to put Razza in his place.

"He was probably staring at that girl in the red T-shirt all morning?"

Razza put both arms into the air and threw his head back. "Whoo, hooo! Yes! The Scobster slam-dunks it! You da man, Scobie baby. You–da–*man*!"

Orazio Zorzotto danced around me, pushed me in the back, messed up my hair. When I look back, I realize that I should have killed him then, while I had the chance. When the jury⁶ heard all the evidence, they would probably have only given me a few hours' community service.

1 The main point
Read the extract, take notes and then write a summary of it together. Partner A starts and writes a sentence, then Partner B adds a second sentence, and so on. Write no more than eight sentences.

2 The characters
Which of the following characters would you most like to meet? And which would you not like to meet? Explain why.
Ishmael – Orazio – Scobie – Kelly

3 What's so funny?
What is the funniest part of the extract for you? Can you explain why?

4 The language
a) *The story has many examples of the sort of informal language young people often use. Look at the following. How could you say them in more formal/normal English? You might need to use a dictionary.*

1. ll. 14–15: You've been perving at that weird chick ...
2. l. 26: She is kinda cute ...
3. l. 32: You should go and chat her up.
4. ll. 36–37: I thought you might be dying to leave all your friends ...
5. l. 43: ... absolute dork.
6. l. 54: ... the speaker-dude ...
7. l. 55: ... a zillion times ...
8. l. 85: ... logged on to the website of luuurve!
9. ll. 124–125: The Scobster slam-dunks it!
10. l. 125: You da man, Scobie baby.

b) *What effect does this use of informal language have on the reader?*

---

³ bench [bentʃ] Bank (zum Sitzen) • ⁴ chair Herr Vorsitzender, Frau Vorsitzende • ⁵ game, set and match *(im Tennis)* Spiel, Satz und Sieg •
⁶ the jury ['dʒʊəri] die Geschworenen

TF 11 Who's guilty[1]? (abridged and adapted from *Just* by Ali Smith)

Cast
Dead body — Townsperson 1
Victoria — Townsperson 2
Albert — Mrs Wright

A body is lying on the ground in the middle of the stage. It's dead. It has an umbrella sticking out of its back. Stage left is a big green pot plant. Stage right is a bus stop with a bench next to it.
5 *Victoria enters and stands at the bus stop for a minute. She looks at the pot plant, frowns. She gets out a map book and looks at it, as if she's not sure where she is. She looks at the bench and thinks about sitting on it, decides not to. Then she*
10 *senses[2] something behind her, turns around and sees the body.*

Victoria Oh my – oh my God.
She goes over to take a look. She stands over the body and looks all around for what can have
15 *happened. She shakes her head. She looks at the body from head to feet without touching it. She looks disgusted[3], but then looks at the handle of the umbrella. She looks around, as if to check that no one can see, then leans forward as if she is*
20 *going to touch the handle. Just as she leans forward, Albert enters from the back. He's dressed as a policeman. As Victoria gets closer with her arm, just about to touch, Albert comes forward.*

Albert Oh my God! Oh my God, what have you done?
Victoria No, it wasn't me. I was just –
Albert What have you done here?
Victoria But that's just what I'm trying to tell you. I didn't – I was just standing at the bus stop.
Albert What happened?
Victoria Like I say, just standing at the bus stop, thinking about, well it sounds a bit strange maybe, but I was thinking about apples. And I got this creepy[4] feeling at the back of my neck, and I turned, and I saw this, him, just, well, lying here, like that, and I said 'Oh my God,' exactly like you just did, and I came over.
Albert Did you have a big argument?
Victoria Who with?
Albert *(points at the body)* Was it, like, a lovers' tiff[5]?
Jack No, no, I just told you, I don't know him –

---
[1] guilty ['gɪlti] *schuldig*   [2] (to) sense sb./sth. *etwas/jn. spüren*   [3] disgusted *angewidert*   [4] creepy (infml) *unheimlich*   [5] tiff *Streit*

	Albert	You *don't know* him?
	Victoria	No.
50	Albert	Oh my God. You didn't even know him. I mean, I could have understood it if you'd argued. A crime of fashion, that's OK.
	Victoria	A crime of what?
55	Albert	People get very upset when there's fashion. And rightly so.
	Victoria	Eh, I think you might not mean –
	Albert	I'm the type of person who can forgive things done in the name of fashion.
60	Victoria	You mean passion[6].
	Albert	That's what I said.
	Victoria	You said fashion.
	Albert	No I didn't. You're twisting my words.
65	Victoria	No I'm not.
	Albert	And you killed this man in old blood.
	Victoria	In what?
70	Albert	I saw you.
	Victoria	But you didn't. You didn't see what you think you saw. Like you didn't say what you think you said.
	Albert	Yes I did. I *instinctly* saw you.
75	Victoria	You keep saying things wrong.
	Albert	No I don't.
	Victoria	You don't mean instinctly. You mean distinctly[7].
	Albert	That's what I said.
80	Victoria	No it isn't.
	Albert	Don't argue with me. It was one of the most distinctly things I've ever seen in my life. You stabbed that man with that umbrella.
85	Victoria	Well, if that's what you saw you must be totally blindly as a fuckingly batly[8].
	Albert	It makes me shiver to be anywhere near someone so old-blooded.
90	Victoria	It's cold-blooded. Cold-blooded.
	Albert	It's quite exciting. You're under arrest.
	Victoria	Look. I can explain. I was just reaching forward.
95		In that way you do. Like for *Excalibur*.
	Albert	The film?
	Victoria	No, I mean, yes, it is, but I mean it's like Excalibur the sword.
100	Albert	There's a sword as well as a film?

Victoria looks at him like she can't believe he doesn't know the story.

	Albert	I just didn't know there was both a film and a sword called Exc... that word. And that's not my fault, is it? 105 Not as if I had the chance to know and turned it down and said no, I simply don't *want* to know that it's a sword and a film. Not as if someone said to me, Albert, do you 110 want to know all the things that ... that word ... can mean, and I said, no thank you, I do not wish to know.
115	Victoria	What are you talking about?
	Albert	The film. And the sword. Both with that name. See, I know there's a sword now too. I'm a quick learner.
120	Victoria	So.
	Albert	So.
	Victoria	Where were we again?
	Albert	Uh, you know. The sword.
	Victoria	Yes. Right. Sword in the stone.
125	Albert	In the what?
	Victoria	You know. Excalibur. For fuck sake.
	Albert	Oh, so there's a stone now as well called it, is there?
	Victoria	Called what?
130	Albert	Ex... cammimur.
	Victoria	What?
	Albert	You know. That word.

Enter the two Townspeople from stage left at the front, walking across the stage. They speak their lines in chorus. Victoria and Albert turn and watch them. 135

	Townspeople	Here's the lovely pot plant. Ooh, it's looking very clean! Someone's done its leaves again. 140 D'you think with Mr Sheen[9]?

---

[6] passion ['pæʃn] *Leidenschaft*   [7] distinct *deutlich*   [8] blind as a bat „*blind wie ein Maulwurf*"   [9] Mr Sheen *Markenname eines Reinigungsmittels*

		Ooh they're very shiny.

                         Ooh they're very shiny.
                         Mr Sheen brings out the green.
                         D'you think a real Mr Sheen
145   exists?
                         I often wonder.
                         D'you think the rain'll hold off?
                         Weather said thunder.
                         Ooh, here's the bus stop.
150   Let's wait for the bus.
                         Ooh, we're first in the queue.
                         Great!
                         No one here but us.
     Townspeople stand at the bus stop and wait.
155 Victoria   Am I imagining it, or are they
                         speaking in rhyme?
     Albert   Don't try and change the subject.
     Victoria   Not very good rhyme either.
     Townspeople hear this and are angry. They turn to
160 *look at Victoria.*
     Townspeople
                         Ooh! Look! A body!
                         Ooh, I say[10]!
                         That's not something you expect to
165   See every day.
                         Ooh! He's been stabbed!
                         Ooh! It's *The Bill*!
                         Ooh, look at her.
                         She looks really evil!
170 Victoria   I do not!
     Townspeople
                         Ooh! Look at the murder weapon!
                         You'd think she might have hid it.
                         You'd think she might have tried.
175   Look at her. Evil. She definitely did
                         it.
     Victoria   I did not.
     Townspeople
                         Ooh, that's that policeman
180   That gets his words wrong.
                         I knew his mother.
     They nod darkly at this to each other.
     Townsperson 1 taps his or her head twice.
     Townsperson 1
185   Do you recognise that evil-looking
                         one?
     Townspeople
                         She's not from round here, is she?

                         No.
                         Do you recognise that fella?   190
                         No. Me neither. Well, if it rains
                         We can always borrow his
                         umbrella.
     They laugh really loudly then stop and look at
     their watches.   195
     Townspeople
                         Ooh, look at the time!
                         I think we've missed the bus.
                         Ooh well, let's walk home.
                         A walk'll be good for us.   200
     Townspeople go off, stage right. Victoria and
     Albert watch them go, then go back to their
     argument.
     Victoria   Where were we again?
     Albert   I was arresting you for murder.   205
     Victoria   Yes. See, I thought for a minute
                         that this, all this, this sticking up in
                         the air like this, was like a kind of
                         grotesque Excalibur.
     Albert   I know. It's a sword, and a film and   210
                         a stone.
     Victoria   Well, it's not a stone, it's *in* the
                         stone.
     Albert   I know! I know!
     He clearly doesn't.   215
     Victoria   So you know the story of Excalibur,
                         then?
     Albert   Oh, so it's not just a sword and
                         a stone and a film, now it's a story
                         too, is it?   220
     Victoria   Well, yes.
     Albert   Are you deliberately trying to
                         infuse me?
     Victoria   *(takes a deep breath)* 'The story of
                         Excalibur, *you* know.   225
     Albert   I know, I know – I know it really
                         well, actually, don't go thinking
                         I don't ... just remind me of the
                         beginning of it again.
     Victoria   You know, first it's stuck in the   230
                         stone and only the rightful[11] king
                         can take it out, and all the strong
                         people try and pull it out and they
                         can't, then, a little weak guy comes
                         along and because he's the rightful   235

---

[10] I say! (BE infml, old-fashioned) *Meine Güte!* [11] rightful *rechtmäßig*

		king it just slides out of the stone in his hand and he's King Arthur. As if the sword is waiting for him and him alone!
240	Albert	*(nodding, echoing her just after she's spoken, as if he knows, though he doesn't)* Him and him alone …
	Victoria	And then the lake, and the hand coming out of it, and someone
245		throws it into the lake, I can't remember who, and an arm comes out of the lake and catches it, the Lady of the Lake, and it disappears for ever under the water till the
250		rightful king comes to claim it again.
	Albert	Anyway, you're still under arrest.
	Victoria	No, listen, because I was reaching forward when you saw me, because
255		I just wondered, for a moment, just a moment, what it would be like to … unlikely, I know. But the point is, I never actually held it. I never actually touched it. When
260		you look for fingerprints on it, they won't be my fingerprints.
	Albert	That's 'cause I saw you wiping them off.
	Victoria	You did *not*!
265	Albert	I know what I saw.
	Victoria	But you don't. You so clearly don't.
	Albert	Don't you tell me what I know and what I don't know.
	Victoria	Yeah, I know. You saw me
270		'instinctly'.
	Albert	Are you making fun of me?
	Victoria	Show me exactly what you think you saw. You came round the corner, there, and you *distinctly* saw
275		me do *what* exactly?
		Enter Mrs Wright at the back. She carries a handbag and is blindfolded.
	Albert	*(miming what he saw)* I *distinctally* saw you let go of the handle of the
280		murder weapon, and you letting go of the handle was distinctally immediately after you'd distinctally
		run at the victim even though he was a total stranger to you, who you didn't even know enough to
285		have had an argument of fashion with. And then you stabbed him in the back with it. And then you carefully wiped your fingerprints off the handle of the murder
290		weapon.
	Victoria	But I *didn't*.
	Mrs Wright	*(coming blindly forward)* Oh my God. What have you people done?
	Albert	Begging your pardon, ma'am, but
295		as usual it wasn't me.
	Victoria	It wasn't me either. And what do you mean, as usual?
	Mrs Wright	I saw it. I saw all of you.
	Victoria	But you're blindfolded.
300	Mrs Wright	I am blindfolded to prevent me from being biased[12] about what I see. And I heard you *(to Victoria)* with your hand raised in that
305		violent way. I heard you with your hand on the – the murder weapon. And *(to Albert)* I heard you watching like an accomplice.
	Victoria	No. I was just waiting for a bus. I was thinking about apples. I'm
310		an apple-farmer – well, I used to be.
	Mrs Wright	Objection[13]. Irrelevant.
	Victoria	Up to last year I had my own applefarm. Orange Pippin.
315		Ashmead's Kernel. Discovery. Worcester. Charles Ross. Russett. Gascoyne's Scarlet. And apples from all over the world. Ida Red. Jonathan. McIntosh. Northern Spy.
320		And those are just a few. Over the last year or so my life has changed completely. Anyway, enough about me. The point is – I was at the bus
325		stop and I happened[14] to see the body, and I came over to have a look because I couldn't believe my eyes, and then, weirdly, the

---

[12] biased ['baɪəst] *voreingenommen* [13] objection *Einspruch* [14] (to) happen to do sth. *zufällig etwas tun*

		handle of it looked a bit like it might be Excalibur –
330	Albert	*(to himself)* Excalibur.
	Victoria	– so I just put my hand out – like this, and then out of nowhere this person here accused *me* of *murder*.
335	Albert	Because I know the truth.
	Victoria	I know the truth too!
	Mrs Wright	Neither of you knows the truth. Only I know the true truth. You are both guilty. My mind's eye sees everything. You *(pointing wildly, blindly, at nobody)* are Ida the Red. And you *(pointing wildly in the opposite direction)* are Jonathan McIntosh. You are both northern spies.
340		
345		

Enter Townspeople again, same as before, stage left, crossing the stage, speaking, as before. Mrs Wright lifts her blindfold a little, to see them and nod hello, and to check for herself who Albert is.

	Townspeople	
350		Here's the lovely pot plant.
		Ooh, see how much bigger it's got!
		Look! Someone's written graffiti on a leaf.
355		Disgusting! Whoever did it should be shot.
		Protesters are worse than hooligans.
		Off with their heads!
360		Ooh, look at him with the umbrella stuck in him.
		Still there. Still dead!
		Ooh, look. It's Mrs Wright. It'll be all right now.
365		And there's that policeman who gets his words wrong.
		And there's that evil cow.

At this, Victoria stares them down. They look away.

	Mrs Wright	Now, where were we? Oh, I know. Guilty! Guilty! Guilty!
370		

1 👥 Twenty questions

Before you perform the play, discuss the following questions in your group.

1. Where is the action taking place?
2. Who are the characters?
3. Why are they here?
4. Who is the dead person?
5. Who is the murderer?
6. What problem does the policeman have with words?
7. What things does he say he saw, things that never really happened?
8. How does Victoria react to this?
9. Why do King Arthur and Excalibur come up?
10. Who are the Townspeople and why don't they have a name?
11. Why do they speak together? Why do they speak in rhyme?
12. Why do the townspeople know the policeman and Mrs Wright?
13. Why is Mrs Wright blindfolded?
14. Why does she lift her blindfold once?
15. Why does Mrs Wright call Victoria Ida the Red? And the policeman Jonathan McIntosh?
16. Is anyone really waiting for the bus?
17. What is the purpose of the pot plant?
18. What is going to happen next?
19. Would you call the play realistic or absurd? Funny or exciting?
20. Who's guilty?

2 The next scene

Write another short scene for the play. How will the characters react to Mrs Wright's decision that Victoria is guilty? Make sure all the characters have something to say.

TF 12 A different kind of justice[1]

1 Crime in England and Wales: some facts and figures

a) Look at the chart and describe what it shows.

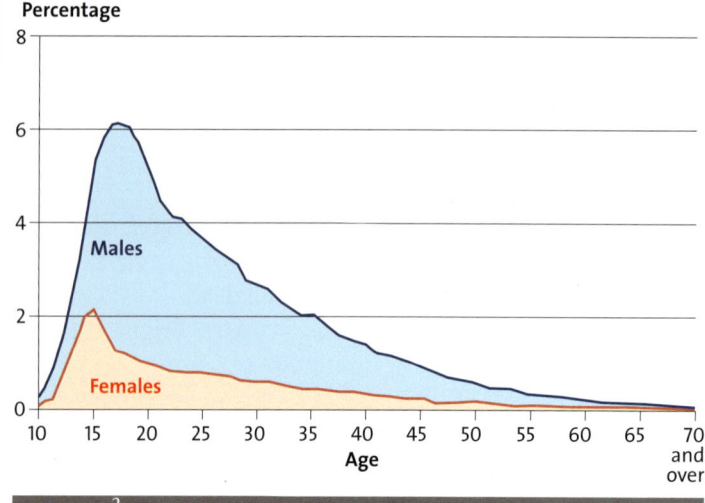

Offenders[2] as a percentage of the population: by age, 2006, England and Wales

Activate your English
– The chart shows us …
– From the chart we can see that …
– It gives us the figures/percentages/numbers/… for …
– With the facts and figures we can compare …
– They show that more/fewer … than …
– The percentage of … is/rises/drops … between (the age of) … and …

b) Discuss the other facts and figures with your partner.

- In **2006**, **1.42** million offenders were found guilty[3] of crimes or were warned in England and Wales.
- **80 per cent** of these offenders were male.
- **7** per cent were aged under 18.
- In June **2006** there were **10,230** young offenders aged **15–20** in prison.
- **Four** out of every **10** young offenders commit another crime in their first year after leaving prison.

2 Bus attack (Part 1)

Now read this case study of two young offenders in England.

Over a period of time two boys had been throwing stones at the Number 67 bus as it went past Gateway School. The bus wasn't hit but some passengers were frightened[4].
5   One day a stone came through the bus window next to the seat of 71-year-old Margaret Wilson. Mrs Wilson was shocked and had a mild heart attack.
    The bus driver, Phil Saunders, stopped the
10 bus and called an ambulance. Mrs Wilson was taken to hospital.
    Mr Saunders had never experienced anything like this in his fifteen years as a bus driver and was shaken up by the attack. His
15 bus company contacted the police.

---

[1] justice ['dʒʌstɪs] *Gerechtigkeit*   [2] offender [ə'fendə] *Straftäter/in*   [3] (to) find sb. guilty ['gɪlti] *jn. schuldig sprechen, für schuldig befinden*
[4] frightened ['fraɪtənd] *verängstigt*

Sergeant Brian Yates, a police officer who works with schools, went to Gateway School. He held an assembly¹ in which he told the students about the attack and asked them to put a note in a box if they knew who the stone-throwers were.

The notes in the box named two 15-year-old boys, Luke and Reece. After Sergeant Yates spoke to them, Luke and Reece admitted² that they were guilty.

a) Match the sentence halves correctly.
1 Two boys sometimes threw stones
2 One day a stone
3 It shocked
4 She had
5 She was taken
6 A police officer held
7 He asked students to write notes
8 Two boys, Luke and Reece,

a) a mild heart attack.
b) an assembly at Gateway School.
c) an old lady.
d) at the Number 67 bus.
e) if they knew who the stone-throwers were.
f) to hospital.
g) went through the bus window.
h) were named.

b) Why do you think Luke and Reece threw stones at the bus? Collect ideas in class.
fed up with school, to look big³, …

c) What do you think will happen next?

Luke and Reece will | go to court
 | get an ASBO
 | …

d) **Extra** 👥 What would happen to them if they were students at your school? Discuss.
see the head teacher, have to apologize, …

"Here's my report Dad.
I got an A, an S, a B and an O."

3 Bus attack (Part 2)

Sergeant Yates didn't want Luke and Reece to be prosecuted⁴ and get a criminal record⁵. He said the boys were still young and they had never been in trouble with the police before. So he suggested a restorative justice conference⁶ where the two boys would meet the people they had harmed⁷ face to face.

Next, Yates visited the boys' families. Luke lived with his grandparents. They were terribly upset by the case, especially by what had happened to the victim, Margaret Wilson.

At first Luke and Reece were not sorry about what they had done – only about

---

¹ assembly [əˈsembli] *Versammlung*   ² (to) admit [ədˈmɪt] *zugeben*   ³ (to) look big *groß tun, sich wichtig machen*   ⁴ prosecuted [ˈprɒsɪkjuːtɪd] *strafrechtlich verfolgt*   ⁵ criminal record [ˌkrɪmɪnl ˈrekɔːd] *Vorstrafe*   ⁶ restorative justice conference [rɪˌstɔːrətɪv ˈdʒʌstɪs ˌkɒnfərəns] *ein außergerichtliches Treffen von Täter/in, Opfer und Vermittler/in mit dem Ziel des Täter-Opfer-Ausgleichs*   ⁷ (to) harm [hɑːm] *schaden, schädigen*

getting caught. So Brian Yates and some teachers at the school spent a lot of time with them before the conference. They wanted to help them understand what harm they had done.

At the conference, Luke and Reece sat face to face with people from the police and the bus company. And with the bus driver and Mrs Wilson's daughter.

The conference had a very big effect on Luke and Reece.

'I'm sure Mum would be sad to see how upset the boys are,' Mrs Wilson's daughter told the conference. 'And she'll be happy to hear that they've promised to make up for[1] what they've done.'

In the end, the agreement was that Luke and Reece would go to the bus company every Saturday for six months to clean the buses. And they did. Their families reported that it had changed their behaviour.

But Luke and Reece still didn't understand why other students had 'grassed'[2] on them. So Sergeant Yates arranged another assembly at school. Here, a number of children explained why they had named Luke and Reece. They said it had given Gateway School a bad reputation[3] and that someone could have been badly hurt.

Luke and Reece were respected more at school for cleaning the buses. The other students thought it showed they were sorry. The two boys felt they had made up for what they had done and this made a big difference to them.

a) Were you surprised by what happened in the case after the boys had thrown stones at the bus? Why (not)?

b) Give a short summary of the case.

Activate your English
– This is a case study of a crime in …
– The crime was committed by …
– They admitted they were …
– The victim of the crime was …
– The boys were not prosecuted …
– They went to a restorative justice conference.
– They made up for their crime by …

4 👥 **Discussing the case**

Discuss the case in your group. The following questions might help you. Present your ideas to the class.
– Should the bus company or the victim have prosecuted Luke and Reece? Why/Why not?
– Was the restorative justice conference a good idea in their case? Give reasons.
– Do you think the agreement at the conference was fair? Or would some time in prison or an ASBO have been better? Explain your opinion.
– Was it right of other students to 'grass on' Luke and Reece? Give reasons.

▶ SF Having a discussion (p. 143)

| **SOCIAL STUDY SKILLS** | **Case study** |

You usually look at a case from the outside. Then think about:
– **the people**: who was involved in the case and what did they do?
– **the people**: what happened exactly?
– the possible **solutions** and the **consequences** (e.g. for the offenders)
– what you can **learn from** the case.

You can also try to look at the case from the **inside**. Consider:
– how the people who were involved might have felt.
– what you would have done in their position.

---

[1] (to) make up for sth. *etwas wieder gutmachen* [2] (to) grass on sb. [grɑːs] *(infml) jn. verpfeifen* [3] a bad reputation [ˌrepjuˈteɪʃn] *ein schlechter Ruf, ein schlechtes Ansehen*

Skills File

Skills File – Inhalt

Seite

STUDY AND LANGUAGE SKILLS
REVISION	Using a bilingual dictionary	124
REVISION	Using an English–English dictionary	125
Using a grammar		125
REVISION	Learning words	126
REVISION	Describing pictures	126
Talking about statistics		127
REVISION	Research	128
REVISION	Outlining	129
REVISION	Giving a presentation	130
REVISION	Handouts	130
Visual aids in presentations		131
Project skills		132–133

LISTENING AND READING SKILLS
REVISION	Listening	134
REVISION	Taking notes	135
REVISION	Marking up a text	135
REVISION	READING COURSE	136–137
	Working out the meaning of words	136
	Skimming and scanning	136
	Finding the main ideas of a text	136
	Careful reading	137
	Text types: fiction and non-fiction	137
Reading literature		138–139

MEDIATION SKILLS
REVISION	Mediation	140

SPEAKING AND WRITING SKILLS
REVISION	Paraphrasing	141
REVISION	Brainstorming	141
SPEAKING COURSE Zusammenfassung		142–143
	Having a conversation	142
	Asking for, confirming, giving information	142
	Giving an oral summary	143
	Having a discussion	143
REVISION	WRITING COURSE	144–145
	Writing better sentences	144
	Using paragraphs	144
	Linking paragraphs	145
	Correcting your text	145

Seite

Writing different types of text — 146–149
    REVISION Writing a report — 146
    REVISION Writing a letter to a magazine — 146
    Writing formal letters — 146
    Argumentative writing — 147
    Writing a CV — 148
    REVISION Summary writing — 149

EXAM SKILLS
    REVISION How to do well in a test — 150–152

Im **Skills File** findest du Hinweise zu Arbeits- und Lerntechniken. Was du in den Skills-Kästen der Units gelernt hast, wird hier näher erläutert.

Was du bereits aus Band 4 von English G 21 kennst, ist mit **REVISION** gekennzeichnet, z. B.
– **REVISION Describing pictures**, Seite 126
– **REVISION Giving a presentation**, Seite 130.

Viele neue Hinweise helfen dir bei der Arbeit mit Hör- und Lesetexten, beim Sprechen, beim Schreiben von eigenen Texten und beim Lernen von Methoden.

STUDY AND LANGUAGE SKILLS

SF REVISION Using a bilingual dictionary

Wann brauche ich ein zweisprachiges Wörterbuch?

Du verstehst einen Text nicht, weil er zu viele Wörter enthält, die dir unbekannt sind, und die Worterschließungstechniken (▶ *Working out the meaning of words, p. 136*) helfen dir nicht weiter?

Du sollst einen Text auf Englisch schreiben, und dir fehlt das eine oder andere Wort, um deine Ideen auszudrücken? Du willst z. B. über die Ankunft eines Einwanderers in einem neuen Land schreiben und kennst das Wort für „Grenze" nicht? Dann hilft dir ein zweisprachiges Wörterbuch.

Wie benutze ich ein zweisprachiges Wörterbuch?

- Die **Leitwörter** *(running heads)* oben auf der Seite helfen dir, schneller zu finden, was du suchst. Auf der linken Seite steht das erste Stichwort, auf der rechten Seite das letzte Stichwort der Doppelseite.
- **drehen** ist das **Stichwort** *(headword)*. Stichwörter sind alphabetisch geordnet: **d** vor **e**, **da** vor **de** und **dre** vor **dri** usw.
- Die *kursiv* gedruckten Hinweise helfen dir, die für deinen Text passende Bedeutung zu finden.
- Die **Ziffern** 1, 2 usw. zeigen, dass ein Stichwort mehrere ganz verschiedene Bedeutungen hat.
- **Beispielsätze** und **Redewendungen** sind dem Stichwort zugeordnet. In den Beispielsätzen und Redewendungen ersetzt eine **Tilde** (~) das Stichwort.
- Im englisch-deutschen Teil der meisten Wörterbücher findest du außerdem Hinweise auf **unregelmäßige** Verbformen, auf die **Steigerungsformen der Adjektive** und Ähnliches.
- Die **Lautschrift** gibt Auskunft darüber, wie das Wort ausgesprochen und betont wird.
- Bei kniffligen Wörtern gibt es in vielen Wörterbüchern **Info-Boxes**, in denen dir mehr Hilfen und Hinweise gegeben werden.

Dr.
Dr. (*Abk. für* **Doktor**) Dr., Doctor
Drache dragon
Drachen *Papierdrachen* kite; *Fluggerät* hang glider
Drehbuch screenplay, script
drehen 1 *Verb mit Obj; Film* shoot*; *Zigarette* roll **2**: **sich ~** turn; *schnell* spin*; **sich ~ um** *übertragen* be* about
Drehkreuz turnstile; **Drehorgel** barrel organ ['ɔːɡən]; **Drehort** location; **Drehstuhl** swivel chair; **Drehtür** revolving door
Drehung turn; *um eine Achse* rotation
Drehzahl (number of) revolutions *Pl od.* revs *Pl*
Drehzahlmesser rev counter
drei three
Drei three; *Note etwa* C; **ich habe eine ~ geschrieben** I got a C
dreidimensional 1 *Adj* three-dimensional **2** *Adv*: **etwas ~ darstellen** depict sth. three-dimensionally; **Dreieck** triangle ['traɪæŋɡl]; **dreieckig** triangular [traɪˈæŋɡjʊlə]

bringen
bring (**herbringen**; **mitbringen**) wird nur verwendet, wenn jemand oder etwas zum Ort des Sprechers oder Hörers gebracht wird:

Schön, dass du zu meiner Party ko... | I'm glad you can come to my party. Can you bring a salad or something?

take (**weg-, hinbringen; mitnehmen**) wird verwendet, wenn jemand oder etwas woanders hingebracht oder mitgenommen wird:

Kannst du morgen deinen Bruder zur Schule bringen? | Can you take your brother to school tomorrow?

Also: Lies immer erst den **gesamten Wörterbucheintrag**, bevor du dich für eine bestimmte Übersetzung entscheidest. Nimm nicht einfach die erste Übersetzung, die dir angeboten wird.

Wenn du unsicher bist, ob du die richtige Übersetzung gefunden hast, schau dir den Eintrag zu dieser Übersetzung an. Wenn du z. B. überprüfen willst, ob „spin" im zweiten Satz unten die richtige Übersetzung für „drehen" ist, such einen Eintrag unter „spin" und lies ihn dir durch.

„drehen"=?

She's a good dancer, she loves to ... round and round as fast as she can.

Lots of Hollywood stars come to Berlin to ... their films here.

Skills File

SF REVISION Using an English–English dictionary

Wenn du englische Texte liest oder selbst einen englischen Text schreibst, kannst du ein einsprachiges englisches Wörterbuch zur Hilfe nehmen. Hier findest du mehr über ein englisches Wort heraus als in einem zweisprachigen Wörterbuch:

– Das einsprachige Wörterbuch erklärt die **Bedeutung** eines englischen Wortes **auf Englisch**. Manche Wörter haben mehrere Bedeutungen. Lies alle Einträge und Beispielsätze genau und vergleiche sie mit deinem englischen Text, um die richtige Bedeutung herauszufinden.

– Das Wörterbuch hilft dir auch, die passende **Verbindung mit anderen Wörtern** zu finden, z.B. zu Verben, Präpositionen oder in bestimmten Wendungen. Das ist besonders nützlich, wenn du selbst einen englischen Text schreiben willst und nach den richtigen Wörtern suchst.

> **deadly** ['dedli] *adj*
> **1** *able or likely to kill people* {= lethal}: This is no longer a deadly disease.
> **deadly to** The HSN virus is deadly to chickens.
> **a deadly weapon** The new generation of biological weapons is more deadly than ever.
> **2** (*only before noun*) {= complete}: **deadly silence** There was deadly silence after his speech.
> **a deadly secret** Don't tell anyone – this is a deadly secret.
> **in deadly earnest** *completely serious*: Don't you laugh – I am in deadly earnest!
> **3** (*informal*) *very boring*: Many TV programmes are pretty deadly!
> **4** *always able to achieve something*: The new Chelsea striker is said to be a deadly goal scorer.

SF Using a grammar ▶ Unit 2 (p. 43)

Vielleicht hast du beim Schreiben oder Korrigieren deiner Klassenarbeiten schon einmal bemerkt, dass du immer die gleichen Fehler machst. Um diese Fehler zu vermeiden, kannst du ein Grammatikbuch zu Hilfe nehmen, das dir bei der Verwendung bestimmter grammatischer Strukturen helfen kann. In einem zweiten Schritt kannst du mit einer Grammatik auch an der Verbesserung deines Stils arbeiten, wenn es z.B. um die Verwendung von Partizipien in formalen Texten geht.

Schritt 1: Lege eine individuelle Fehlerstatistik an, d.h. notiere dir aus den Korrekturen deiner Klassenarbeiten die Fehlersorten *Wortschatz, Grammatik, Satzbau, Stil, …*
Schritt 2: Suche dir aus dem Bereich, in dem am häufigsten Fehler auftreten, einen Schwerpunkt heraus, z.B. *Grammatik ▶ tenses*.
Schritt 3: Suche im Inhaltsverzeichnis deiner Grammatik die betreffenden Kapitel heraus und lies sie dir nochmals gründlich durch. Vergleiche sie mit den Fehlern, die du in deinen Klassenarbeiten machst.
Schritt 4: Schreib dir einige wenige Mustersätze und Merkregeln zu diesen grammatischen Strukturen auf einen Merkzettel. Vor der nächsten Klassenarbeit solltest du ihn dir nochmals anschauen.

Clause elements	20	17-20
The verb		
Summary	23	21
Modal auxiliaries	23	22-48
Be, have and do	36	49-57
The short forms of the auxiliaries	40	58-60
Full verbs	42	61-71
Summary: the tenses of the full verbs	50	72-73
The tenses of the full verbs	54	74-94
Simple present	54	74-75
Present progressive	56	76-77
Simple present and present progressive in contrast	57	78
Present perfect (simple form)	58	79-80
Present perfect progressive	60	81-82

He goes to school every day.
he, she it, ein -s muss mit!!!

SF REVISION Learning words

Worauf solltest du beim Lernen und Wiederholen von Vokabeln achten?

– Lerne neue und wiederhole alte Vokabeln regelmäßig – am besten jeden Tag 5–10 Minuten. Lerne immer 7–10 Vokabeln auf einmal.

– Lerne mit jemandem zusammen. Fragt euch gegenseitig ab.

– Schreib die neuen Wörter auch auf und überprüfe die Schreibweise mithilfe des *Dictionary* oder *Vocabulary*.

Wie kannst du Wörter besser behalten?

– Sammle **Gegensatzpaare**, z. B. alive – dead, majority – minority, find – lose.

– Sammle Wörter mit **gleicher Bedeutung**, z. B. (to) train – (to) practise.

– Sammle Wörter in **Wortfamilien**, z. B. (to) dance, dance, dancer, dancing lessons, shop, shopper, shopping, shopping list, shop assistant, …

– Sammle und ordne Wörter in **Wortnetzen** *(networks)*.

SF REVISION Describing pictures

Wie kann ich Bilder beschreiben?

Wo?

– Um zu sagen, wo genau auf dem Bild etwas Bestimmtes dargestellt ist, verwende
at the top/bottom • in the foreground/background • in the middle • on the left/right • behind • between • in front of • next to • under

– Um zu beschreiben, was die Personen auf dem Bild tun, verwende das **present progressive**.
The girl is riding her horse.

Wie kann ich beschreiben, was die abgebildeten Personen fühlen?

Oft sollst du dich in eine Person auf einem Foto hineinversetzen und beschreiben, was sie fühlt oder denkt. Schau dir das Foto genau an und nimm dir Zeit, dir die Situation vorzustellen. Beim Formulieren helfen dir *phrases* wie:
Maybe the woman/man in the photo feels … / is thinking about … •
I think he/she might want to …

Skills File

SF Talking about statistics ▶ Unit 1 (p. 10)

Welche Arten von Diagrammen gibt es?

Diagramme bilden statistische Vergleiche zwischen mindestens zwei Sachverhalten grafisch ab. Die **Überschrift** des Diagramms ist sehr wichtig, denn sie gibt bereits genaue Informationen darüber, worum es bei der betreffenden Abbildung geht. Die **Darstellungsform** richtet sich häufig danach, ob man Zahlen oder Prozentsätze miteinander vergleichen will:
- *Bar chart* (**Säulendiagramm**): Anzahl oder Größe von zwei oder mehr Dingen
- *Pie chart* (**Kreis-/Tortendiagramm**): prozentuale Verteilung
- *Table* (**Tabelle**): Vergleich unterschiedlicher Daten anhand von Zahlen und Prozentsätzen
- *Line graph* (**Kurvendiagramm**): Entwicklung im Verhältnis unterschiedlicher Größen

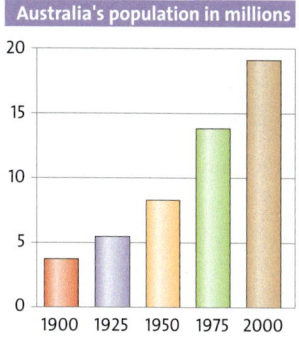

Wie beschreibe ich ein Diagramm?

Um ein Diagramm zu beschreiben, solltest du folgende Fragen beantworten:
- What is the graph/chart about?
  The bar/pie chart is about ... / It deals with ... / It is taken from ...
- What does the graph/chart/table refer to/compare?
  The pie chart compares the size/number of ... / It shows the different ... in ... / It is divided into ... slices which show ... / The graph/chart/table shows the relation between ... and ... / The table compares the population in terms of / with regard to ...
- What does the chart tell you? What information does it give you?
  ... has the largest/second largest/... / ... is twice/three times/... as big as ... / A huge majority/small minority is ... / ... per cent are ... / There are more than/ nearly twice as many ... as there are ...

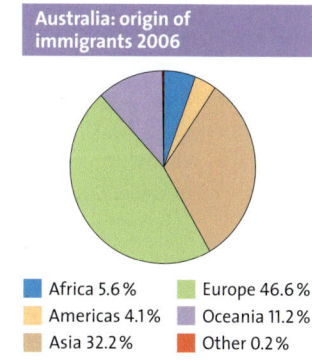

Manchmal kann es hilfreich sein, wenn du auch noch Aussagen über den Zeitraum der Statistik und/oder die Form der Darstellung machst:
It covers a period of ... months/years. / It shows a development of three months/ years from 2002 to 2005. / The vertical / horizontal line shows / represents... / The figures are expressed as a percentage of the total population / total number of ...

Country	Population (2008)
USA	304,721,000
Germany	82,400,996
UK	60,776,238
Australia	21,373,760

Achte bei der Beschreibung von Diagrammen auf die **Zeitformen** des Englischen:
- Benutze das *simple past*, wenn du dich auf einen Zeitpunkt in der Vergangenheit beziehst: **The rainfall was 2207 mm in Cairns in 2008.**
- Das *simple present* verwendest du bei allgemeingültigen Aussagen (**The average rainfall in Cairns is 1992 mm per year**) oder wenn du deine Schlussfolgerungen wiedergibst.
- Benutze das *present perfect*, wenn du dich auf einen Zeitraum beziehst, der von der Vergangenheit bis heute reicht: **Three millions Asians have come to Australia since 2000.**

Wenn du dich auf die Zahlen bzw. Größen eines Diagramms beziehst, dann verwende **amount** für nicht zählbare Nomen: **A large amount of meat/rain/ food/...** Für zählbare Nomen benutzt du das englische Wort **number**: **The number of immigrants/Asians/people/...**

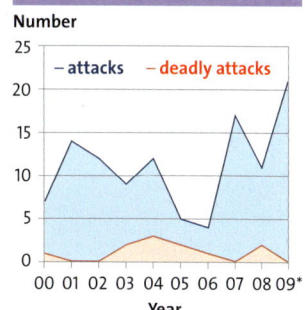

SF REVISION   Research

Material sammeln (recherchieren)

Wenn du über ein Thema etwas schreiben oder einen Vortrag halten sollst, suchst du zuerst Informationen in Büchern oder in Zeitschriften, im Internet und in anderen Quellen. Verwende möglichst englischsprachige Quellen.

Damit du die Übersicht behältst, solltest du das Gefundene in einem Ordner sammeln und von vornherein sortieren. Orientiere dich dafür an der Gliederung bzw. *outline*, die du für deinen Text oder deine Präsentation vorbereitet hast (▶ *Outlining, p. 129*). Du kannst deine Materialien auch danach ordnen, ob es sich um sachliche Informationen, also Tatsachen, oder um persönliche Meinungen handelt.

Wichtiges herausschreiben (exzerpieren)

Sichte das Material und entscheide, welche Informationen du tatsächlich verwenden möchtest. Du kannst die betreffenden Passagen markieren (▶ *Marking up a text, p. 135*), herausschreiben oder auch ausschneiden und in fortlaufender Reihenfolge auf DIN-A4-Blätter kleben. Vergiss die Quellenangabe nicht. Deine eigenen Gedanken fügst du in Stichpunkten an den entsprechenden Stellen hinzu. Wenn du eine Präsentation vorbereitest, kannst du am Rand notieren, welche Medien du jeweils einsetzen möchtest.

Aus Materialien, die du im Internet gefunden und in elektronischen Ordnern gesammelt hast, überträgst du die wichtigen Informationen mit „Kopieren" und „Einfügen" in ein neues Dokument, wo du sie dann bearbeiten (also kürzen, ergänzen, umschreiben usw.) kannst.

Zitieren, umschreiben, Quellen angeben

Formuliere deinen Text oder deine Präsentation mit deinen eigenen Worten – schreibe nicht einfach aus deinen Quellen ab. Wenn du deine Argumentation einmal mit einer Expertenaussage unterstützen oder deinen Text mit einem Auszug aus einem Buch, einem Interview o. Ä. interessanter und abwechslungsreicher gestalten möchtest, markiere solche Zitate durch Anführungszeichen und gib Autor und Quelle einschließlich Seitenzahl an (bei Internetquellen die Webadresse und das Datum des Aufrufs). Das gilt auch dann, wenn du eine fremde Aussage mit eigenen Worten umschreibst. Gib auch bei einer Abbildung den Fundort an.

Kündige in deiner mündlichen Präsentation deine Zitate an und erkläre schwierige Wörter. Schaffe logische Übergänge zu deinen eigenen Argumenten.

Aber denk daran: Lange Zitate können deine Leser oder Zuhörer auch ermüden und erwecken leicht den Eindruck, dass du selbst nur wenig zu sagen hast. In der Kürze liegt die Würze!

http://www.shootingjozi.net/assets/images/gallery/142.jpg (17 April, 2010)

SF REVISION Outlining

Wenn du zu einem komplexen Thema einen Text schreiben oder eine Präsentation vorbereiten sollst, sammelst du zunächst Informationen und Unterlagen (▶ *Research, p. 128*). Eine zuvor erstellte Gliederung (*outline*) hilft dir dabei, denn so weißt du von vornherein genau, was du suchst. Und auch beim Ordnen deines Materials solltest du dich gleich an einer *outline* orientieren.

Outlines werden in Stichpunkten oder kurzen Sätzen verfasst. Schreibe dir zunächst deine Hauptpunkte auf. Bestimme dann Unterthemen und überlege dir, mit welchen Beispielen und Erläuterungen du deine Gedanken dazu unterstützen möchtest. Wenn du eine Mindmap erstellt hast, kannst du sie für deine Gliederung verwenden.

Achte auf eine logische Reihenfolge deiner Gedanken. Sie sollen sich in deiner *outline* widerspiegeln. Beim Gliedern kannst du verschiedene Möglichkeiten der Aufzählung (Zahlen, Groß- und Kleinbuchstaben, ...) nutzen. Mach dir einen Vermerk, z. B. am Rand des Blattes, welche Zitate, Statistiken, Bilder, Medienbeiträge usw. du an welcher Stelle einsetzen möchtest.

Die *outline* dient dir als Vorlage für deinen Text bzw. als Ausgangspunkt für deine Präsentation. Darüber hinaus kannst du sie dazu verwenden, deinen Lesern oder Zuhörern einen Überblick über dein Thema zu geben, indem du sie deinem Text oder deiner Präsentation voranstellst, z. B. bei einem mündlichen Vortrag auf einer Folie.

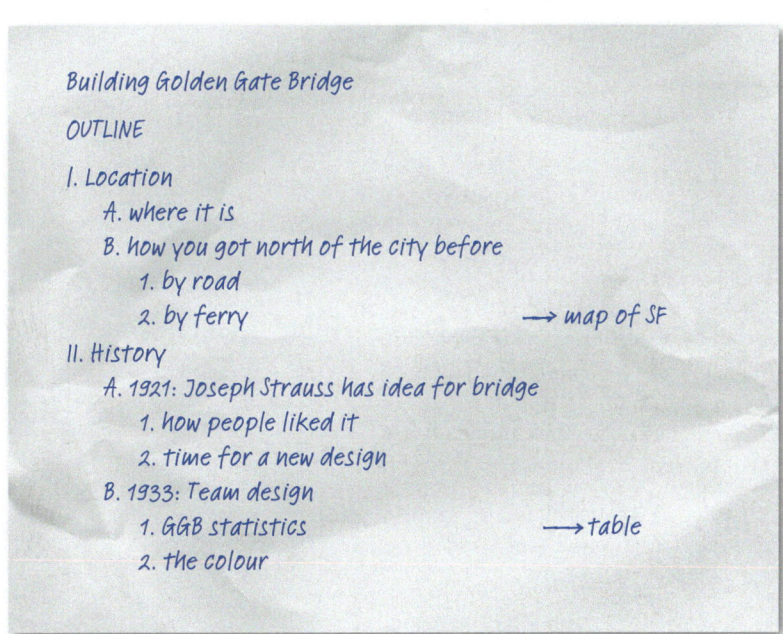

Merke dir also:
- Eine Gliederung (*outline*) hilft dir beim Recherchieren und beim Ordnen deines Materials.
- Bestimme zuerst die Hauptpunkte, dann die Unterthemen.

SF REVISION Giving a presentation

Wie mache ich eine gute Präsentation?

Vorbereitung
- Ordne deine Gedanken und notiere sie, z. B. auf nummerierten Karteikarten oder als Mindmap.
- Bereite ein Poster, eine Folie oder ein Handout
  (▶ Handouts, siehe unten) vor. Schreib groß und für alle gut lesbar.
- Übe deine Präsentation zu Hause vor einem Spiegel.
  Sprich laut, deutlich und langsam, mach Pausen.
  Reicht die Zeit?

Durchführung
- Bevor du beginnst, bereite deine Medien vor und sortiere deine Vortragskarten.
- Warte, bis es ruhig ist. Schau die Zuhörer an.
- Erkläre zu Anfang, worüber du sprechen wirst.
- Lies nicht von deinen Karten ab, sondern sprich frei.
- Schreibe die Gliederung sowie unbekannten Wortschatz und Eigennamen an die Tafel.

Schluss
- Sag, dass du fertig bist.
- Frag die Zuhörer, ob sie Fragen haben.
- Bedanke dich fürs Zuhören.

> My presentation is about …
> First, I'd like to talk about …
> Second, …

> This picture/photo/ … shows …

> That's the end of my presentation. Thank you for listening. Have you got any questions?

SF REVISION Handouts

Ein Handout enthält die wichtigsten Informationen einer Präsentation. Manchmal bietet es auch zusätzliche Informationen an, z. B. in Form von Statistiken, Quellenangaben oder Illustrationen.
Ein Handout kannst du vor, während oder nach deiner Präsentation austeilen:
- vor oder während der Präsentation, damit die Zuhörer die Gliederung deines Vortrags verstehen und ihm besser folgen können;
- nach der Präsentation, damit die Zuhörer später noch einmal nachlesen und sich besser an die Präsentation erinnern können.

Strukturiere dein Handout klar und übersichtlich, z. B. durch eine Überschrift, deinen Namen, das Datum, durch Teilüberschriften, Beispiele, tabellarische oder grafische Übersichten.

Du kannst in ganzen Sätzen schreiben, z. B. bei einer Zusammenfassung, oder in Stichpunkten.

Wenn du Abbildungen verwendest, gib ihnen eine Bildunterschrift und vergiss nicht die Quellenangabe. Mit Symbolen kannst du dein Handout übersichtlicher gestalten und die wesentlichen Informationen hervorheben.

Lass ausreichend Platz für die Notizen der Zuhörer, z. B. durch einen breiten Rand an der Seite oder im unteren Teil des Blattes.

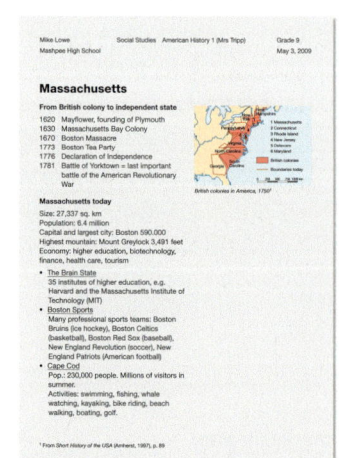

SF Visual aids in presentations ▶ Unit 2 (p. 45)

Um die Ergebnisse deiner Arbeit besser anschaulich zu machen, kannst du verschiedene Präsentationsmedien verwenden. Sie helfen dir außerdem, deine Präsentation gut strukturiert vorzutragen, und erleichtern deinen Zuhörern das Verständnis.

Es gibt sehr **unterschiedliche visuelle Präsentationsformen**. Poster, Overhead-Folien und Computerpräsentationen sind die am häufigsten verwendeten, aber auch eine Zeichnung an der Tafel kann sehr anschaulich sein.

Bei visuellen Hilfsmitteln musst du einige wesentliche Aspekte beachten, damit sie erfolgreich eingesetzt werden können:

1. Verwende je nach Form des Hilfsmittels eine **Schriftgröße**, die von allen überall im Klassenraum gelesen werden kann. Was man nicht lesen kann, hilft nicht! Überprüfe vor deiner Präsentation die Lesbarkeit von verschiedenen Stellen im Klassenzimmer aus.

2. Deine Folien, Poster usw. sollten eine **klare Struktur** haben. Benutze Fettdruck oder Großbuchstaben, um besonders wichtige Dinge hervorzuheben. Auch Symbole wie zum Beispiel Pfeile und Aufzählungszeichen helfen dabei.

3. **Vermeide zu viele Informationen auf einmal.** Eine Idee pro Folie reicht bei einer elektronischen Präsentation vollkommen. Vermeide, wenn möglich, längere zusammenhängende Texte. Halte nur die Hauptaspekte deines Vortrags fest.

4. **Bilder, Illustrationen und Grafiken** unterstützen das Gesagte und die Anschaulichkeit deines Vortrags. Auch hier gilt: auf die Größe achten!

5. Die einzelnen Visualisierungen brauchen einen **klaren Ablaufplan**, d.h. sie sollen deinen Vortrag begleiten. Verwende sie deshalb nacheinander und gib deinen Zuhörern die Möglichkeit, sie parallel zu deinem Vortrag lange genug wahrzunehmen.

6. Vermeide es, während der Präsentation selbst auf deine visuellen Hilfsmittel zu schauen bzw. dich hinter einem Poster oder einem Handout zu verstecken. Halte zu jeder Zeit den **Blickkontakt** mit deinen Zuhörern aufrecht.

7. Dein Körper ist ein wichtiger Teil der Visualisierung. Achte auf deine **Körpersprache**. Bleibe deinem Publikum zugewandt, halte Augenkontakt, stehe sicher vor der Gruppe und halte deine Hände oberhalb der Gürtellinie. Verstecke dich nicht hinter einem Skript. Auch ein Lächeln kann sehr überzeugend sein!

SF Project skills ▸ Unit 1 (p. 7)

Organisation ist (fast) alles

Bei einer Projektarbeit, die du mit anderen gemeinsam durchführst, kommt es darauf an, dass du dich und deine Arbeit sehr gut organisierst und die einzelnen Phasen eines Projektes berücksichtigst. Meistens findet die Bearbeitung eines Projektauftrags innerhalb einer gewissen Zeitspanne statt, während parallel dazu der Unterricht weitergeht. Oft findet also ein Großteil der Arbeit außerhalb des Unterrichts statt – ein guter Grund, um nochmals auf die einzelnen Schritte einer Projektarbeit zu schauen, die dir helfen sollen, zur verabredeten *deadline* dein fertiges Produkt abgeben zu können.

Projektarbeit Schritt für Schritt

Schritt 1: Entscheide dich für dein Thema
Zuerst musst du dir darüber klar werden, welches Thema dich interessieren könnte. Zu welchem Thema weißt du vielleicht schon etwas, sodass du auf diesem Wissen aufbauen kannst?

Schritt 2: Finde deine Projektpartner
Nun musst du Mitschülerinnen und Mitschüler finden, die dein Thema ebenfalls interessant finden. Bei einer Projektarbeit kommt es auch darauf an, dass sich Menschen mit unterschiedlichen Talenten in einer Gruppe finden: Wer kennt sich gut mit dem Internet aus, wer kann zeichnen, wer schreiben, ...?

Schritt 3: Tauscht eure Ideen aus
Was weiß eure Gruppe schon über das gewählte Thema? Wie soll eure Arbeit aussehen? Sammelt alle Ideen und Anregungen – vielleicht in Form einer *placemat* oder Mindmap? Vergesst nicht, euch auch auf die Form eures Handlungsproduktes, dem Ergebnis eurer Projektarbeit, zu einigen. Das kann zum Beispiel ein Poster, ein Text, ein Booklet oder eine Präsentation sein.

Schritt 4: Plant eure Arbeit
Wer übernimmt welche Aufgabe? Setzt euch einen realistischen Zeitrahmen und überprüft regelmäßig euren Arbeitsstand.

Schritt 5: Recherchiert Material
Für euer Produkt braucht ihr Informationen, Material, Bilder und vieles mehr. Stellt sicher, dass jeder etwas beiträgt.
▸ *Research, p. 128*

Schritt 6: Seid effizient
Haltet euch nicht zu lange an Materialien und Ideen auf, die euch nicht zum Ziel führen. Bei der Auswahl helfen euch unter anderem die Lesetechniken *skimming* und *scanning*.
▸ *Skimming and scanning, p. 136*

Schritt 7: Schreibt eine Outline
Wenn ihr ausreichend Material zusammengetragen habt, dann ordnet es anhand einer Outline an.
▸ *Outlining, p. 129*

Schritt 8: Beginnt mit der Herstellung eures Produktes
Beginnt recht zügig, die einzelnen Teile eures Produktes zusammenzufügen. Text, Bilder, aber auch Poster oder elektronische Präsentationen brauchen viel Zeit. Zeigt euch regelmäßig den Stand eurer Arbeiten, um mögliche Fehler frühzeitig zu bemerken.

Schritt 9: Kontrolliert gemeinsam das Produkt
Bevor ihr fertig seid, müsst ihr einen letzten Durchgang der Fehlersuche und -korrektur durchführen. Auch an Stil und Layout kann man jetzt noch Verbesserungen vornehmen.

Schritt 10: Präsentiert eure Ergebnisse
Wenn ihr eure Ergebnisse in einer Präsentation vorstellen wollt, müsst ihr diese gut vorbereiten. Denkt an eine aussagekräftige Visualisierung und ein Handout.
▶ *Giving a presentation, p. 130*
▶ *Handouts, p. 130*
▶ *Visual aids in presentations, p. 131*

Schritt 11 (fakultativ): Beurteile deine eigene Arbeit
Denke zum Schluss an dein nächstes Projekt und beurteile daraufhin nochmals das gerade durchgeführte. Was ist euch gut gelungen? Worauf müsst ihr das nächste Mal stärker achten?

Schritt 12: Genießt die Ergebnisse
Ihr habt ganz selbstständig eine Aufgabe gemeistert und seid sicherlich zu tollen Ergebnissen gekommen. Genießt die Produkte der anderen Gruppen, lasst euch Zeit beim Anschauen und lobt eure Mitschülerinnen und Mitschüler für die Dinge, die ihnen besonders gut gelungen sind!

LISTENING AND READING SKILLS

SF REVISION   Listening

Vor dem Hören

- Frag dich, was du schon über das Thema weißt.
- Nutze Überschriften oder Bilder um zu erahnen, was dich z.B. bei einer Geschichte erwarten könnte.
- Lies dir die Aufgaben auf deinem Aufgabenblatt genau durch und überlege, auf welche Informationen du dich konzentrieren musst.
- Bereite dich darauf vor, Notizen zu machen. Leg z.B. eine Tabelle oder Liste an.

Während des Hörens

Listening for gist:
Konzentriere dich beim ersten Hören auf allgemeine Informationen, z.B. die Personen (unterschiedliche Stimmen), das Thema, die Umgebung (Geräusche), die Atmosphäre (die Sprechweise der Leute).

Listening for detail:
- Mach dir noch einmal bewusst, worauf du genau achten willst (Hörauftrag), besonders bei Durchsagen (*announcements*), die du vielleicht nur einmal hören kannst.
- Gerate nicht in Panik, wenn du meinst, du hättest gerade etwas Wichtiges verpasst. Konzentriere dich auf die nächste wichtige Information.
- Lass dich nicht von anderen Einzelheiten oder Geräuschen ablenken.
- Mach nur kurze Notizen, z.B. Anfangsbuchstaben, Symbole oder Stichworte.
- Manche Signalwörter machen es dir leichter, den Hörtext zu verstehen.
  Aufzählung: **and**, **another**, **too**
  Gegensatz: **although**, **but**
  Grund, Folge: **because**, **so**, **so that**
  Vergleich: **larger/older/... than**, **as ... as**, **more**, **most**
  Reihenfolge: **before**, **after**, **then**, **next**, **later**, **when**, **at last**, **at the same time**
- Auch andere Details wie z.B. die Stimme, der Akzent oder der Tonfall des Sprechers oder der Sprecherin können dir helfen, Informationen über seine oder ihre Gefühle, Herkunft usw. zu bekommen.
- Unterteile Telefonnummern beim Aufschreiben: 0171 572 42 589.

Nach dem Hören

- Vervollständige deine Notizen sofort.
- Wenn du den Text ein zweites Mal hören kannst, konzentriere dich auf das, was du beim ersten Mal nicht genau verstanden hast.
- Schau dir noch einmal die Aufgabenstellung an. Sollst du die gehörten Informationen nutzen, um einen neuen Text zu schreiben? Dann achte auf die richtige Textform: Bericht, Beschreibung, ...

SF REVISION Taking notes

Worum geht es beim Notizen machen?

Wenn du beim Lesen oder Zuhören Notizen machst, kannst du dich später besser daran erinnern, wenn du etwas vortragen, nacherzählen oder einen Bericht schreiben sollst.

Wie mache ich Notizen?

In Texten oder Gesprächen gibt es immer wichtige und unwichtige Wörter. Die wichtigen Wörter werden **Schlüsselwörter** *(key words)* genannt und nur die solltest du notieren. Meist sind das Substantive und Verben, manchmal auch Adjektive oder Zahlen.

Deine Notizen sollten knapp sein:
- Verwende Ziffern (z. B. „7" statt „seven").
- Verwende Symbole und Abkürzungen, z. B. ✔ (für Ja) und + (für und) oder GB für Great Britain, K für Katrina.
  Du kannst auch eigene Symbole erfinden.
- Verwende **not** oder ✗ statt „doesn't" oder „don't".

SF REVISION Marking up a text

Wann sollte ich einen Text markieren?

Du hast einen Text mit vielen Fakten vor dir liegen und sollst später über bestimmte Dinge berichten. Dann wird es dir helfen, die für dich wichtigen Informationen im Text zu markieren.

Wie gehe ich am besten vor?

Lies den Text und markiere nur die für dein Thema wichtigen Informationen. Nicht jeder Satz enthält Informationen, die für deine Aufgabe wichtig sind, und oft reicht es aus, nur ein oder zwei Wörter in einem Satz zu markieren.
– Du kannst wichtige Wörter einkreisen.
– Du kannst sie unterstreichen.
– Du kannst sie mit einem Textmarker hervorheben.

ABER:
Markiere nur auf Fotokopien von Texten oder in deinen eigenen Büchern.

Sydney Opera House
The Sydney Opera House is one of the most famous buildings in the world. It houses the large Concert Hall (2,678 seats), the Opera Theatre (1,507 seats), other smaller theatres and a place for open-air events.

Sydney Opera House
The Sydney Opera House is one of the most famous buildings in the world. It houses the large Concert Hall (2,678 seats), the Opera Theatre (1,507 seats), other smaller theatres and a place for open-air events.

Sydney Opera House
The Sydney Opera House is one of the most famous buildings in the world. It houses the large Concert Hall (2,678 seats), the Opera Theatre (1,507 seats), other smaller theatres and a place for open-air events.

REVISION Reading course – Zusammenfassung

Working out the meaning of words

Das Nachschlagen unbekannter Wörter im Wörterbuch kostet Zeit und nimmt auf Dauer den Spaß am Lesen. Oft geht es auch ohne Wörterbuch:

1. Bilder und Zeichen erklären und ergänzen oft Dinge aus dem Text. Schau sie dir deshalb vor und nach dem Lesen genau an.

2. Manche Wörter erklären sich aus dem Textzusammenhang, z.B. *When we reached the station, Judy bought our tickets.*

3. Zu manchen englischen Wörtern fallen dir vielleicht deutsche, französische oder lateinische Wörter ein, die ähnlich geschrieben oder ausgesprochen werden, z.B. **excellent**, **millionaire**, **nation**, **reality**.

4. Es gibt neue Wörter, in denen du bekannte Teile entdeckst, z.B. **friendliness**, **helpless**, **understandable**, **gardener**, **tea bag**, **waiting room**.

Skimming and scanning

Beim **Skimming** überfliegst du einen Text schnell, um dir einen **Überblick** zu verschaffen. Du willst dabei herausfinden, worum es in dem Text geht. Achte dabei auf
– die **Überschrift**,
– die **Zwischenüberschriften** und hervorgehobene Wörter oder Sätze,
– die **Bilder** und **Bildunterschriften**,
– den **ersten Satz** und den **letzten Satz** jedes Absatzes,
– **Grafiken**, **Statistiken** und die **Quelle** des Textes.

Beim **Scanning** suchst du nach **bestimmten Informationen**. Dazu suchst du den Text nach Schlüsselwörtern (*key words*) ab und liest nur dort genauer, wo du sie findest. Geh dabei so vor:

Schritt 1: Denk an die Schlüsselwörter und geh mit deinen Augen oder dem Finger schnell durch den Text, in breiten Schlingen wie bei einem „S" oder „Z" oder von oben nach unten wie bei einem „U". Die gesuchten Wörter werden dir sofort „ins Auge springen".

Schritt 2: Wenn das gesuchte Wort nicht im Text vorkommt, überlege dir andere, themenverwandte Wörter (z.B. **lesson** → **school**, **subject**) und suche nach diesen.

Finding the main ideas of a text

Zeitungsartikel, Berichte oder Kommentare verstehst du besser, wenn du ihre wesentlichen Aussagen erkennst und dir klar machst, wie sie zusammenhängen. Die wichtigsten Aussagen findest du so:

1. Jeder Text hat ein Thema mit mindestens einer Hauptaussage, z.B.: *Drinking soda is one of the worst things you can do to your health.*
   Diese Hauptaussage findest du oft im **ersten Absatz**.

2. Die Hauptaussage wird in der Regel durch weitere Aussagen bzw. Gedanken unterstützt, z. B.: *Experts agree that sugary soft drinks and fast food are the main reasons why so many American teenagers are fat.*

3. Diese weiteren Aussagen bzw. Gedanken werden oft durch Beispiele und Begründungen ergänzt, z. B.: *About 7% of the calories that they take in come from soft drinks alone.*

Careful reading

Schwierige Texte musst du besonders sorgfältig und konzentriert lesen, damit du alle darin enthaltenen Informationen und Gedanken verstehst.

1. Lies den Text genau. Welches sind seine wesentlichen Aussagen? (▶ *Finding the main ideas of a text, pp. 136–137*)

2. Manchmal musst du dir die Antwort auf eine Frage aus einzelnen Informationen erschließen, die du an verschiedenen Stellen im Text findest. Nimm zum Beispiel den Text auf S. 17: Warum ist in der Überschrift von einem „racist ideal" die Rede? Für die Antwort musst du mehrere Aussagen aus dem Text zusammentragen:

<u>FACTS</u>: • Zita Wallace and thousands of other mixed-race children with fair skin were taken from their Aboriginal families. • The government wanted them to forget their Aboriginal traditions and grow up like white children. • The children were hit if they spoke their own language. • They had to work all the time and didn't get any real education.
<u>CONCLUSION</u>: The government thought that Aboriginal culture had no value. The mixed-race children were forced to grow up among white people, but at the same time they were discriminated against.

Text types: fiction and non-fiction

Wenn du einen Text liest, ist es sinnvoll sich klar zu machen, ob er von einer vom Autor erdachten Welt handelt (*fictional text,* deutsch: Dichtung) oder sich mit der Wirklichkeit auseinandersetzt (*non-fictional text,* deutsch: Sachtext).

Fiktionale Texte sind z. B. Kurzgeschichten und Romane. Der Autor wählt Figuren (*characters*) aus und erzählt von ihren Gefühlen und Handlungen, von deren Motiven und Hintergründen. Die Handlungen finden in einem oder mehreren Handlungsrahmen statt, z. B. an einem Ort, zu einer bestimmten Zeit und unter bestimmten Umständen (*setting*). Die Ereignisse können aus verschiedenen Perspektiven erzählt werden (*point of view*). Oft verwendet der Autor für seine Geschichte eine anschauliche Sprache, z. B. ausschmückende Adjektive, Metaphern, Vergleiche, direkte Rede oder er lässt den Leser an den Gedanken seiner Figuren oder des Erzählers teilhaben.

Nicht-fiktionale Texte sind z. B. Berichte in Zeitungen, wissenschaftliche Artikel, Aufsätze oder Kommentare. Hier informiert der Autor über ein Thema der realen Welt oder nimmt Stellung dazu.

Es gibt auch Texte, die eine **Mischform** aus beiden Textarten sind.

SF Reading literature ▶ Unit 1 (pp. 24–25), Unit 4 (p. 95)

Sachtexte und literarische Texte

Wenn du englische Texte liest, können dies Sachtexte oder literarische Texte sein. **Sachtexte** – z.B. Zeitungsberichte oder Reden – wollen vorwiegend informieren oder zu etwas auffordern. **Literarische Texte**, die oft in einer besonderen Form oder Sprache verfasst sind, zeigen eine Welt oder Umgebung, die der Autor oder die Autorin erdacht hat. Im Englischen nennt man diese Texte auch *fiction*, weil sie von einer erdachten oder erfundenen (englisch: *fictional*) Welt handeln, im Gegensatz zu *non-fiction*, die sich mit der wirklichen Welt auseinandersetzt.

Alles, was du bereits über das Lesen von Texten im Allgemeinen gelernt hast (▶ *Reading course, pp. 136–137*), wird dir auch beim Lesen von Literatur helfen. Markiere deshalb, wenn es dir möglich ist, auch in einem literarischen Text Dinge, die dir auffallen und die du wichtig findest.

Literarische Gattungen und ihre Merkmale

Grundsätzlich unterscheidet man drei **Arten von literarischen Texten** bzw. literarischen Gattungen (*genre*): Gedichte (Lyrik = *poetry*), Erzähltexte (Epik = *fiction*; damit wird der Begriff *fiction* im Englischen auch in einem etwas anderen, engeren Sinne gebraucht) und Dramen (Dramatik = *drama*).

Du erkennst sie meist schon an ihrer äußeren Form. In der Regel
– bestehen Gedichte aus gebundener Sprache, d.h. aus Verszeilen und Strophen,
– haben Erzähltexte fortlaufenden Text,
– ist ein Drama in Monologen und Dialogen als direkte Rede gesetzt.

Du kannst Literatur natürlich einfach zum Vergnügen lesen, zum Beispiel, weil dir die Geschichte, ein bestimmtes Thema oder die dargestellten Personen interessant, spannend oder unterhaltend erscheinen. Zum besseren Verständnis kann es aber beitragen, wenn du etwas über formale, stilistische oder technische Besonderheiten des Textes weißt. Bemerkst du diese beim Lesen, kannst du dir überlegen, warum der Autor oder die Autorin wohl ausgerechnet diese Mittel einsetzt und welcher Eindruck oder welches Gefühl bei dir dadurch während des Lesens entsteht.

Solche Besonderheiten sind beispielsweise
– in einem Erzähltext die Entwicklung der Handlung (*plot*), die Beschreibung der Figuren (*characters*) und des Schauplatzes (*setting*) und die dadurch geschaffene Atmosphäre (*atmosphere*) oder der Aufbau von Spannung (*suspense*),
– bei einem Gedicht die äußere Aufteilung in Strophen (*stanzas*), die Verwendung von Reim (*rhyme*) und Rhythmus (*rhythm*) oder eine auffällig bildhafte Sprache (*images*, z.B. *metaphors*)
– und bei einem Drama die Art und Weise, wie die Handlung in Dialogen (*dialogues*) und Monologen (*monologues*) sichtbar gemacht wird.

Es kommt auch vor, dass du Texte – vor allem literarische Texte – nicht nur verstehen, sondern umsetzen musst, indem du sie darstellst oder sprichst, eigene kleine Formen von Literatur verfasst, sie um- oder weiterschreibst. Gerade dann ist es wichtig, dass du dir über die Besonderheiten des zugrundeliegenden Textes im Klaren bist.

Dreams
Hold fast to dreams
For if dreams **die**
Life is a broken-winged bird
That cannot **fly**
Hold fast to dreams
For when dreams **go**
Life is a barren field
Frozen with **snow**.

Langston Hughes

Gedichte können Reime und Metaphern enthalten.

It was as **slow and hot** travelling along the Dog Fence. The more they drove inland, the hotter the air became until Colm felt **he was breathing fire**. He and Rusty tried sticking their heads out of the window, but it was worse than the burning heat inside the car.

From A Prayer for Blue Delaney *by Kirsty Murray*

In Erzähltexten wird der Schauplatz (*setting*) häufig durch bildhafte Adjektive und Metaphern beschrieben.

Über literarische Texte sprechen

Wenn du über Texte schreiben oder sprechen musst, sind folgende Formulierungen hilfreich:

The story/novel/play/poem/song is about …
The story is set in …
The text tells the story of …
The author uses a …

The main character/hero/heroine is …
He/she comes across as a strong/weak/aggressive/brave/… person.
You can see this in line …

I liked it/didn't like it when …
I found the ending/story/characters interesting/funny/confusing …
The words and expressions in the text create an exciting/thrilling/… atmosphere.
The text made me feel happy/sad/angry/…

The poem consists of … verses/stanzas, each with … lines.
The lines of the poem (don't) rhyme.
Every other line rhymes.
I think the … is a metaphor/symbol for …
With it the author wants to express …

In the dialogue between … and … there is a lot of emotion/tension/anger …
The action takes place during …
The stage directions are (not) very detailled.

Victoria **Show me exactly** what you think you saw. You came round the corner, there, and you *distinctly* saw me do *what* exactly?
Enter Mrs Wright at the back. She carries a handbag and is blindfolded.
Albert *(miming what he saw)* I *distinctally* saw you let go of the handle of the murder weapon, and you letting go of the handle was distinctally immediately after you'd distinctally run at the victim even though he was a total stranger to you, who you didn't even know enough to have had an argument of fashion with. And then you stabbed him in the back with it. And then you carefully wiped your fingerprints off the handle of the murder weapon.
Victoria But *I didn't*.
Mrs Wright *(coming blindly forward)* Oh my God. What have you people done?

From Just by Ali Smith

In einem Drama ergeben sich sowohl aus den Dialogen als auch als den Bühnenanweisungen (*stage directions*) Handlungsanweisungen für die Darsteller.

MEDIATION SKILLS

SF REVISION Mediation

REVISION Wann muss ich zwischen zwei Sprachen vermitteln?

Manchmal musst du zwischen zwei Sprachen vermitteln. Das nennt man **mediation**.

1. Du gibst englische Informationen auf Deutsch weiter:
   Du fährst z.B. mit deiner Familie in die USA und deine Eltern oder Geschwister wollen wissen, was jemand in einem Café gesagt hat oder was an einer Informationstafel steht.

2. Du gibst deutsche Informationen auf Englisch weiter:
   Vielleicht ist bei dir zu Hause eine Austauschschülerin aus den USA oder Dänemark zu Gast, die kein Deutsch spricht und Hilfe braucht.

3. In schriftlichen Prüfungen musst du manchmal in einem englischen Text gezielt nach Informationen suchen und diese auf Deutsch wiedergeben. Oder du sollst Informationen aus einem deutschen Text auf Englisch wiedergeben.

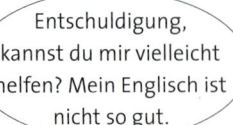

Entschuldigung, kannst du mir vielleicht helfen? Mein Englisch ist nicht so gut.

Worauf muss ich bei *mediation* achten?

– Übersetze nicht alles wörtlich, sondern gib den Sinn wieder.
– Gib nur das Wesentliche weiter, lass Unwichtiges weg.
– Verwende kurze und einfache Sätze.
– Wenn du ein Wort nicht kennst, umschreibe es oder ersetze es durch ein anderes Wort.

You can go by train from Sydney to Perth. Trains go twice a week. The next train leaves Sydney on Saturday at 3 in the afternoon and arrives in Perth on Tuesday at 9 in the morning.

Was kann ich tun, wenn ich ein wichtiges Wort nicht kenne?

Vielleicht findest du es manchmal schwer, mündliche Aussagen oder schriftliche Textvorlagen in die andere Sprache zu übertragen, z.B. weil
– dein Wortschatz nicht ausreicht,
– dir bekannte Wörter „im Stress" nicht einfallen,
– spezielle Fachbegriffe auftauchen.

Wir können mit dem Zug fahren, das dauert von Samstagnachmittag bis Dienstag früh.

Manche Wörter kannst du umschreiben, z.B. mithilfe von Relativsätzen wie:
It's somebody/a person who …
It's something that you use to …
It's an animal that …
It's a place that/where …

▶ *Paraphrasing, p. 141*

Was hältst du davon, wenn wir einen Hubschrauberrundflug machen würden? Frag doch mal, wo man so was machen kann?

Excuse me, we'd like to do a tour around Uluru with … something that you can fly with.

… a helicopter …

SPEAKING AND WRITING SKILLS

SF REVISION Paraphrasing

Worum geht es beim Paraphrasing?

„Paraphrasing" bedeutet, etwas mit anderen Worten zu erklären. Das ist hilfreich, wenn dir ein bestimmtes Wort nicht einfällt oder wenn dein Gegenüber dich nicht verstanden hat. Paraphrasing ist auch besonders nützlich für **mediation** (▶ *Mediation, p. 140*).

Wie gehe ich beim Paraphrasing vor?

– Man kann mit einem Ausdruck umschreiben, der dieselbe Bedeutung hat:
 'To wonder' is the same as 'to ask yourself'.
 Oder man sagt das Gegenteil:
 'Alive' is the opposite of 'dead'.
– Manchmal braucht man mehrere Wörter, z.B. wenn man etwas beschreibt oder erklären will, wie man etwas verwendet. Dabei verwendet man ein allgemeines Wort (**general word**) und nennt weitere Eigenschaften:
 A skyscraper is a very tall building.
– Oder du umschreibst das Wort mit **... is/are like ...**
 A lodge is like a small house or cabin. You find it in the country.
– Du kannst auch einen Relativsatz (**relative clause**) verwenden:
 She is someone who looks after small children. – Ah, she's a nanny!
 A ticket office is a shop where you can buy tickets for shows and concerts.

SF REVISION Brainstorming

Was ist Brainstorming und wofür ist es gut?

Bei vielen Aufgaben ist es nützlich, wenn du im ersten Schritt möglichst viele Ideen zum Thema sammelst. Beim Sammeln und beim Auswerten der Ideen helfen dir die folgenden Techniken.

Drei verschiedene Brainstorming-Techniken

Technik 1: Making a list
Schreib die Ideen so auf, wie sie dir einfallen, und zwar für jede Idee eine neue Zeile. Lies im zweiten Schritt alle deine Ideen durch. Überlege, welche Ideen davon für dein Thema sinnvoll sind und nummeriere sie nach Nützlichkeit.

Technik 2: Making a mind map
Leg eine Mindmap an. Überlege dafür, welche Oberbegriffe zu deinem Thema passen. Verwende unterschiedliche Farben für jeden Oberbegriff. Ergänze jede Idee, die zu einem Oberbegriff passt, auf einem Nebenast. Nimm dafür nur wichtige Schlüsselwörter. Du kannst statt Wörtern auch Symbole verwenden und Bilder ergänzen.

Technik 3: The 5 Ws
Schreib die Fragewörter **Who? What? When? Where? Why?** in eine Tabelle. Die Ideen, die dir zu der jeweiligen Frage kommen, werden darunter geschrieben.

6. watch DVDs
3. swimming pool
 no jobs for parents
 parents not at home
1. sleep late – every morning
 hang out
2. no homework
5. disco/party with friends
 watch TV
4. see friends cinema

SPEAKING COURSE – Zusammenfassung

Having a conversation ▶ *Unit 1 (p. 14)*

Ein Gespräch beginnen

Ein Gespräch auf Englisch zu beginnen ist einfacher, als du vielleicht denkst. Es gibt immer mehrere Möglichkeiten:

– **Wenn du etwas erfragen willst** (z.B. den Weg oder die Uhrzeit) **oder um Hilfe bitten möchtest:**
  Excuse me, do you know ... • Excuse me, can you tell me ... • Excuse me, do you know where... • Could you help me, please?
– **Wenn du jemanden begrüßen möchtest oder kennen lernst:**
  Hi! • Hello! • Good morning. • (bei Erwachsenen) Good afternoon.
  Oft kann man das Gespräch dann mit einer allgemeinen Bemerkung weiterführen: Great day today! • Nice concert, isn't it? • ...
  Oft hört man zur Begrüßung auch How are you? oder How do you do? Das sind einfache Begrüßungsformeln, auf die keine ausführliche Antwort erwartet wird. Am besten sagst du einfach Fine, thanks. How about you?
– **Wenn du jemanden wiedertriffst:**
  Hi, ..., how are things? • Hi, how is it going? • How are you? • Hi, good to see/meet you.

Fantastic concert, isn't it?

Ein Gespräch führen

Für den weiteren Verlauf des Gesprächs sind diese Wendungen nützlich:
– **Sich vorstellen:** By the way, my name's ... • I'm ...
– **Sich kennen lernen:** Have you ... before? • Have you ever ...? • What about you?
– **Sich bedanken/auf Dank reagieren:** Thanks! • Thanks for your help. • You're welcome.
– **Sich verabschieden:** See you tomorrow/next week. • Bye!

Und wenn du einmal etwas nicht verstanden hast, kannst du nachfragen:
Sorry, I didn't get that. • Sorry, can you say that again, please?

Asking for, confirming, giving information ▶ *Unit 2 (p. 37)*

Ein Gespräch ist mehr als nur der Austausch von Informationen; es kommt auch auf einen höflichen und angenehmen Ton an. Das gilt natürlich auch für Gespräche auf Englisch. Diese Wendungen können hilfreich sein:
– **Asking for information:** Oft beginnt man eine Anfrage oder Auskunft mit
  Excuse me... • Excuse me, could you tell me, ... • Would you mind telling me ... • Sorry, I'd just like to know ... • I'm not quite sure about ... • Is it/Are they ...? • Is it right that ...? • Can I just ask ... • Excuse me, I've just got a question ... • Excuse me, do you think you could ...?
– **Confirming information:** Wenn du nachfragen oder sicher gehen möchtest, dass du etwas richtig verstanden hast, kannst du das z.B. so tun: Can I just confirm ...? • Is it right that ...? • Have I got that right ...? • ..., (is that) right? • Could you just say that again, please? Auch question tags drücken den Wunsch nach Bestätigung aus: This is the library, isn't it?
Denke auch daran, dich für die erhaltenen Informationen freundlich zu bedanken.

– **Giving information:** Auch wenn du selbst eine Auskunft erteilst, versuche freundlich und höflich zu sein, z.B. mit einer kurzen Einleitung:
Sure. • Of course, no problem. • Well, just a second. • Give me a minute to think about it.
Wenn du nicht weiter helfen kannst, drückst du dein Bedauern aus:
Oh, I'm sorry, I don't know. • Sorry, I'm afraid I can't help you.

Giving an oral summary ▶ Unit 3 (p. 61)

Wenn du etwas, was du gehört, gesehen oder gelesen hast, für jemanden anderen zusammenfassen willst, tust du dies oft spontan. Du hast also nicht lange Zeit zum Überlegen und solltest auch nicht zu lange reden.
– Gib **nur das Wesentliche** des Inhalts wieder. Du brauchst dich nicht unbedingt an die chronologische Reihenfolge der Handlung zu halten:
I watched that film … last night. • Yesterday I read that web article about … • I've recently come across that ad/article about … • I've just read that story about …
– Verwende das **Präsens** zum Nacherzählen:
There's this kid … In this one scene he's running away from … then it starts raining … and he's trying … so she has to get out of the car …
– **Halte deine Meinung** zu dem betreffenden Film, Buch usw. **zurück**. Natürlich kannst du durch die Art und Weise, wie du erzählst, indirekt deinen Eindruck wiedergeben, z.B. durch den Ton deiner Stimme, deine Körpersprache und deine Wortwahl.

Having a discussion ▶ Unit 4 (p. 86)

Seine Meinung sagen und erklären

– **Expressing an opinion:** In einer Diskussion ist es gut, wenn du möglichst klar und deutlich sagst, was du zu einer bestimmten Frage denkst:
I think … • I feel … • In my opinion …
– **Giving reasons and examples:** Es ist aber noch wichtiger, dass du Beispiele und Argumente nennst, die deine Meinung unterstützen – schließlich willst du deine Gesprächspartner ja überzeugen: because … • First … / Second … • For example … • Let me explain … • That's why …

Auf andere reagieren

– **Asking for clarification:** Manchmal ist es notwendig nachzuhaken:
Could you say that again? • Sorry, but I don't understand what you mean.
– **Agreeing with someone:** Die Meinung eines anderen unterstützt du mit
I agree (with you/…). • That's a good point. • You're right.
– **Disagreeing with someone:** Oft widerspricht man nicht direkt, sondern leitet seine Reaktion z.B. mit Sorry, … ein. Zeig immer Respekt für die Meinung anderer.
I don't think you can say … • I see what you mean but … • No, that's not right. • Sorry, I don't agree with you. • Yes, but …, • Well, I don't think you can say that … • Ah, come on, …

▶ *Classroom English (pp. 242–243)*

REVISION Writing course – Zusammenfassung

The steps of writing

1. Brainstorming – Ideen sammeln und ordnen (▶ *Brainstorming, p. 141*)

2. Schreiben. Dabei achte darauf,
   - deine Sätze zu verbinden und auszubauen (*Writing better sentences*),
   - deinen Text gut zu strukturieren (*Using paragraphs*),
   - bei einem Bericht die 5 Ws abzudecken (▶ *Writing a report, p. 146*),
   - bei einem Leserbrief an eine Zeitschrift eine höfliche Anrede und Schlussformel zu verwenden (▶ *Writing a letter to a magazine, p. 146*).

3. Deinen Text inhaltlich und sprachlich überprüfen (*Correcting your text*)

Writing better sentences

Linking words verbinden Sätze und machen sie interessanter. Verwende z. B.
- **Time phrases** wie **at 7 o'clock**, **every morning**, **in the afternoons**, **a few minutes later**, **suddenly**, **then**, **next …**,
- **Konjunktionen** wie **although**, **and**, **because**, **but**, **so … that**, **that**, **when**, **while**,
- **Relativpronomen** wie **who**, **which** und **that**.

Auch mit **Adjektiven** und **Adverbien** kannst du deine Sätze verbessern.
- **Adjektive** bestimmen Personen, Orte, Gegenstände oder Erlebnisse genauer und machen sie ebenfalls interessanter:
  The man looked into the room. → **The young man looked into the empty room.**
- Mit **Adverbien** kannst du beschreiben, wie jemand etwas macht:
  The young man looked nervously into the empty room.

Using paragraphs

Structuring a text

Einen Text versteht man viel besser, wenn er in Absätze gegliedert ist:
- eine Einleitung (**beginning**) – hier schreibst du, worum es geht;
- einen Hauptteil (**middle**) – hier schreibst du mehr über dein Thema,
- einen Schluss (**end**) – hier bringst du den Text zu einem interessanten Ende.

Am Anfang eines Absatzes sind kurze, einleitende Sätze (**topic sentences**) gut, die den Lesern sofort sagen, worum es geht, z. B.
- Orte: **My trip to … was fantastic. / … is famous for … / … is a great place.**
- Personen: **… is great/funny/interesting/clever/…**
- Aktivitäten: **… is great fun. / Lots of people … every day.**

Wie kann ich meine Absätze interessant gestalten?

- Beginne mit einem interessanten Einstiegssatz:
  Guess what happened to me today! / Did I tell you that …?
- Fang für jeden neuen Aspekt einen neuen Absatz an.
- Beende deinen Text mit einer Zusammenfassung oder etwas Persönlichem.

Linking ideas

Damit sich dein Text flüssig liest und beim Leser Interesse weckt, solltest du auf gute Übergänge von einem Absatz zum nächsten achten. Die folgenden Formulierungen kannst du verwenden
- um zu zeigen, wie dein Text aufgebaut ist:
  In the article, the writer describes how … Firstly, he states that … Secondly, …
  Then he goes on to say that … Another point he makes is that … Finally, …
- um etwas zu begründen:
  Because of / As a result of the growing population, …
  … had been in trouble with the police, so …
- um zwei oder mehr Gedanken einander gegenüberzustellen:
  Although one could say that …, I believe …
  While most people would …, the Prime Minister has said …
  Serious scientists all say that … However/But some politicians …
- um Beispiele zu geben:
  This is true in a number of cases, for example / for instance / e.g. …
- um Ergebnisse und Folgen zu erklären:
  As a consequence, / All in all, one can say that …
  To sum up, I would like to say …

Correcting your text

Lies jeden Text, den du geschrieben hast, mehrmals durch
- um zu sehen, ob er vollständig und gut verständlich ist,
- um ihn auf Fehler zu überprüfen, z. B. **Rechtschreibfehler** *(spelling mistakes)* und **Grammatikfehler** *(grammar mistakes)*.

Spelling mistakes

Beachte folgende Regeln:
- Manche Wörter haben Buchstaben, die man nicht spricht, aber schreibt, z. B. talk, climb.
- Manchmal ändert sich die Schreibweise, wenn ein Wort eine Endung erhält, z. B. take → taking, terrible → terribly, lucky → luckily, try → tries (aber stay → stays), run → running, drop → dropped.
- Beim Plural tritt manchmal noch ein -e zum -s, z. B. church → churches.

Grammar mistakes

Diese Tipps helfen dir, typische Fehler zu vermeiden:
- Im **simple present** wird in der 3. Person Singular **-s** angehängt: she knows
- **Unregelmäßige Verben**: Manche Verben bilden die Formen des *simple past* und des Partizip Perfekt *(past participle)* unregelmäßig. Die unregelmäßigen Formen musst du lernen. Die Liste steht auf S. 240–241.
  go – went – gone; buy – bought – bought
- **Verneinung**: Im *simple present* werden Vollverben mit don't/doesn't verneint, im *simple past* mit didn't.
- **Satzstellung**: Im Englischen gilt immer (auch im Nebensatz):
  a) subject – verb – object (SVO):   … when I saw my brother.
                                      … als ich meinen Bruder sah.
  b) Orts- vor Zeitangabe: I bought a nice book in the city yesterday.

Writing different types of text

SF REVISION Writing a report – organizing ideas

Hierauf kommt es bei einem Bericht an:
- Gib dem Leser eine **schnelle Orientierung**, was passiert ist.
- Beginne mit **wichtigen Informationen** und gib erst dann Detailinformationen.
- Gib Antwort auf die **5 Ws**: **Who? What? When? Where? Why?** und manchmal auch auf **How?**.
- Verwende das *simple past*.

SF REVISION Writing a letter to a magazine

Wenn du auf einen Zeitschriftenartikel reagieren und einen Leserbrief schreiben möchtest,
- beginne deinen Brief mit **Dear + (Name der Zeitschrift/des Autors des Artikels)**,
- lege deine Meinung dar und begründe sie (**I would like to comment on …, I agree/disagree with …, I think …, That is why …, For example, …**),
- beende deinen Brief mit **Yours sincerely** oder **Yours**.

SF Writing formal letters ▶ Unit 2 (p. 41)

Bei Briefen unterscheidet man zwischen privaten Briefen (*informal letters*) und Geschäftsbriefen (*formal letters*). Da du mit Geschäftsbriefen ein Anliegen bei einer Behörde, einer Firma oder einer Organisation verfolgst, sollten sie knapp, präzise, objektiv, aber trotzdem höflich formuliert sein (*KISS rule: Keep it short and simple*).

① Schreibe deine Adresse (ohne Namen) und das Datum in die rechte obere Ecke. Verwende keine typisch deutschen Buchstaben wie z.B. ß, ä, ö oder ü.
② Die Anschrift steht links.
③ Die Anrede lautet *Dear Sir or Madam*. Wenn du den Namen des Adressaten kennst, beginne deinen Brief mit *Dear Mr/Mrs/Ms …*
④ Verwende Langformen (*I am, I would like* statt *I'm, I'd like* usw.), vermeide unnötige Abkürzungen.
⑤ Nenne zu Beginn den Grund deines Briefes.
⑥ Bedanke dich bei Bitten und Anfragen im Voraus (*I look forward to hearing from you. Thank you.*).
⑦ Beende den Brief mit *Yours faithfully*, wenn du den Adressaten nicht kennst. Hast du den Adressaten am Anfang des Briefes mit Namen angeredet, dann schreibe *Yours sincerely*. (Im amerikanischen Englisch heißt es dagegen in beiden Fällen *Sincerely*.)
⑧ Unterschreibe den Brief und tippe zusätzlich deinen Namen.

① Schillerstr. 17
    37067 Goettingen
    Germany

② Jane Hall   4 May 2010
   Meadows Home Farm Shop
   Harston
   Cambridge CB22 4BE
   Great Britain

③ Dear Ms Hall

⑤ ④ I am writing to you about the advertisement from April 21st in the Cambridge Weekly News. I would love to ④ work for you at Meadows Home Farm this summer.

I am 16 years old and I have a good level of English but would like to improve my speaking skills. I am hard-working, friendly and a fast learner. At home I look after two horses so farm work is not new to me. I have also worked in a sports shop so I have experience in serving people and working in a team. My hobbies are horse riding, playing volley ball and hiking. Please find my CV with this letter.

Thank you for your time. I look forward to hearing from ⑥ you.

⑦ Yours sincerely
   Tamara Wille
⑧ Tamara Wille

SF Argumentative writing ▸ *Unit 4 (p. 82)*

„Schriftliche Diskussion"

Argumentative writing ist ähnlich der deutschen Erörterung die **schriftliche Diskussion eines Gedankens oder eines Themas**. Dabei müssen Argumente, Beispiele und Belege zu einer logisch aufgebauten Struktur zusammengefügt werden.

Oft verlangt die Aufgabenstellung von dir, dass du **Argumente für und gegen etwas** findest (z.B. *"Students should wear school uniforms." Discuss.*). Manchmal musst du auch eine Problemstellung oder eine Frage mit Argumenten belegen (häufig als W-Frage formuliert, z.B. *What should young people do in their free time?*). In beiden Fällen sollst du – in der Regel am Ende deines Textes – auch deine **eigene Meinung** äußern. Bemühe dich aber dennoch um einen **objektiven Stil**. Formulierungen wie *That's total nonsense* oder *I think it's very stupid* sind völlig fehl am Platz!

Wie gehe ich vor?

Vorbereitung:
- Lies die Aufgabenstellung sorgfältig, achte besonders auf die Arbeitsanweisungen oder „Operatoren" (▸ *How to do well in a test: Aufgabenstellungen verstehen, p. 151*) und entscheide, um welche Art von *argumentative writing* es sich handelt.
- Werde dir über deine eigene Meinung zum Thema klar.
- Sammle Ideen, Argumente, Belege und Beispiele (▸ *Brainstorming, p. 141*) und ordne sie, z.B. in einer Mindmap.
- Fertige eine Gliederung (▸ *Outlining, p. 129*).

Verfassen des Textes:
- Wie fast jeder Text ist auch das Ergebnis deines *argumentative writing* grundsätzlich in drei Hauptabschnitte gegliedert: Mit der Einleitung führst du zum Thema hin und weckst das Interesse deiner Leser, im Hauptteil entwickelst du deine Argumente (dies kann auch in mehreren Absätzen geschehen), mit dem Schluss fasst du zusammen und präsentierst deine Meinung oder auch einen Kompromiss.
- Verbinde die einzelnen Teile gut miteinander (z.B. mit **on the one hand, on the other hand, first/second/third, however, additionally, moreover, contrary to that**) und belege und begründe die jeweiligen Argumente (**that's why, because, a reason for it is**).
- Im Schlussteil (**all in all, to come to a conclusion, I would like to finish by saying**) solltest du keine neuen Argumente mehr anführen.

Überprüfen des Geschriebenen:
- Wie immer beim schriftlichen Arbeiten solltest du deinen Text am Ende überprüfen und korrigieren (▸ *Correcting your text, p. 145*). In Zweifelsfällen hilft dir ein Wörterbuch (▸ *Using a bilingual dictionary, p. 124, Using an English–English dictionary, p. 125*).

Mindmap: **Mobile phones in school?**
- PROS: student might miss bus; parents might need to call
- CONS: student might cheat in test

Introduction	Most students have mobiles. Should they be allowed in school?
Main body	Pros: student might miss bus parents might need to call … Cons: student might cheat in test …
Conclusion	More disadvantages than advantages → Should not be allowed

SF Writing a CV ▸ Unit 2 (p. 38)

Das Leben auf einen Blick

Dein Lebenslauf ist eine **klar gegliederte Zusammenfassung** deiner persönlichen Daten, Fähigkeiten und Erfahrungen und gibt Auskunft über die wichtigen Stationen deines Lebens. Da der Adressat sich schnell informieren will, ist es wichtig, dass der Lebenslauf fehlerfrei und übersichtlich, d.h. in der Regel in tabellarischer Form, erstellt worden ist.

Wie sollte ein Lebenslauf aussehen?

Weil Lebensläufe ganz persönliche, individuelle Dokumente sind, unterscheiden sie sich inhaltlich natürlich stark voneinander. Dennoch gelten bestimmte **inhaltliche und formale Regeln** – für englische Lebensläufe manchmal andere als für deutsche:

- Der Lebenslauf muss Namen, Kontaktdaten (Adresse, Telefonnummer, ggf. E-Mail-Adresse) und Nationalität enthalten. Das Geburtsdatum oder Auskünfte zur Familie sind nicht unbedingt notwendig.
- Die Lebensstationen sollten zeitlich lückenlos dargestellt werden. Sie können chronologisch (also beginnend mit den frühesten Daten) oder umgekehrt chronologisch (beginnend mit der Gegenwart) angeordnet sein.
- Die Daten und Informationen werden nach unterschiedlichen Aspekten gegliedert, z.B. *Education* (welche Schulen hast du wann besucht?), *Qualification/Skills* (welche besonderen Fähigkeiten hast du?), *Work experience* (wo hast du schon gearbeitet?), *Achievements* (hast du vielleicht eine Auszeichnung erhalten, einen Preis gewonnen oder etwas Besonderes erreicht?), *Hobbies and interests*, *References* (schriftliche Beurteilungen, Empfehlungsschreiben).
- Empfehlungsschreiben musst du, außer wenn es ausdrücklich verlangt wird, nicht sofort zur Verfügung stellen, sondern kannst sie auf Nachfrage zusenden.
- Im Englischen kann der Lebenslauf z.B. zusätzlich zu den nüchternen Daten und Fakten auch einige persönliche Ausführungen enthalten. In einem solchen *personal statement* kannst du einige deiner persönlichen Vorzüge hervorheben und erläutern, warum du die betreffende Position oder diesen bestimmten Arbeitsplatz anstrebst. Übertreibe es aber nicht – also nicht: *I am a very clever and intelligent person*, sondern etwas bescheidener (und leichter zu belegen): *I have always been quite successful at school*.
- In der Regel musst du einem englischen Lebenslauf kein Bild beifügen. Auch unterschreiben musst du ihn nicht.

SF REVISION Summary writing

Wenn du einen Lese- oder Hörtext oder einen Filmausschnitt zusammenfassen möchtest, schreibst du eine *summary*. Dabei gehst du folgendermaßen vor:

1. Lies dir den Text noch mindestens einmal genau durch (bzw. hör ihn dir ein weiteres Mal an oder sieh dir den Filmausschnitt noch einmal an). Bei einem Lesetext markierst du wichtige Passagen oder machst am Rand des Textes kurze Anmerkungen. Auch bei Hörtexten und Filmausschnitten machst du dir Notizen (▶ *Listening, p. 134*).

2. Wenn es sich um einen geschriebenen Text handelt, lies ihn jetzt ein weiteres Mal, Satz für Satz. Wenn du mit einer Kopie arbeitest, unterstreiche die Passagen im Text, die dir Antwort auf die **5 Ws** geben:
   - **Who?**   Who does … / Who is the … about?
   - **What?** What happens? / What does he/she do?
   - **When?** When does it take place?
   - **Where?** Where does it happen?
   - **Why?**   Why does he/she act in this way?

   Zusätzlich zum Unterstreichen kannst du alle Sätze, Satzteile und Wortgruppen einklammern, die *nicht* zu den wesentlichen Gedanken des Autors gehören. Dazu gehören auch Beispiele, Vergleiche, symbolhafte Ausdrücke, Zitate, direkte Rede, ausschmückende Adjektive und andere Textteile, die der Beschreibung dienen.

3. Notiere dir alles, was du nicht eingeklammert hast, in Stichpunkten auf einem separaten Blatt Papier. Überprüfe noch einmal, ob du wirklich alle unnötigen Textstellen weggelassen hast.

4. Alternativ kannst du deine Notizen auch so anfertigen: Teile ein Blatt Papier in zwei Spalten ein. Notiere die Hauptaussagen des Textes auf der linken Seite. Suche dann zu diesen Aussagen Beispiele, Erläuterungen, Zitate, Zahlenund Fakten. Entscheide, welche du für besonders wichtig hälst, und notiere sie auf der rechten Seite deines Arbeitsblatts, neben den Hauptaussagen.

5. Nun schreibe mit deinen eigenen Worten einen neuen Text im *simple present* (auch wenn du eine Geschichte zusammenfasst, die in der Vergangenheit spielt). Bringe die Informationen in eine logische Reihenfolge. So kannst du anfangen:
   The story is about … • The text describes … • The article shows … • In the story we get to know …
   Im Hauptteil solltest du die wichtigsten Ereignisse einer Geschichte oder die Hauptpunkte eines Artikels wiedergeben. Verwende dafür deine Notizen zu den 5 Ws. Schreib den Text nicht ab, sondern verwende deine eigenen Worte.

6. Überprüfe deinen Entwurf noch einmal. Enthält dein Text wirklich die wichtigsten Gedanken, Ereignisse, Ideen aus dem Original? Achte auch auf sprachliche Fehler, besonders auf
   – die Rechtschreibung,
   – die Verwendung des *simple present*,
   – die Wortstellung,
   – logische Übergänge zwischen den Sätzen durch *linking words* (*and, therefore, that's why, but, because* …).

7. Bringe den korrigierten Entwurf in eine Reinschrift.

EXAM SKILLS

SF REVISION   How to do well in a test

▶ *Getting ready for a test (pp. 26–31, 70–77)*

Countdown zum Testerfolg

Ein Test ist angekündigt? Kein Grund zur Panik. Wichtig ist, dass du weißt, worauf du dich vorbereiten musst. Im Zweifelsfall frag deine Lehrerin oder deinen Lehrer. Der Countdown kann beginnen!

Eine Woche vor dem Test

1. Lies noch einmal die **Texte** der zuletzt durchgenommenen Unit (A-Section und Text, eventuell auch das Background File). Fasse mündlich oder schriftlich zusammen, worum es ging.

2. Wiederhole den **Wortschatz** der Unit mit Hilfe des *Vocabulary* oder des *Wordmaster*. Schreibe dir die Wörter und Wortverbindungen, die du immer wieder vergisst, auf ein Blatt Papier. Eine Mindmap oder ein Wortfeld helfen beim Behalten.

3. Geh auch noch mal die neue **Grammatik** durch. Aufgaben zur Selbstüberprüfung und zum Üben findest du im *Practice*-Teil, auf der Seite „How am I doing?", im *Grammar File* (S. 153–166), in deinem *Workbook* und im *e-Workbook*.

Zwei Tage vor dem Test

1. Wiederhole den **Wortschatz**. Manche Wörter sitzen noch nicht? Schreibe einen kurzen Text, in dem du sie verwendest.

2. Lies die **Texte** ein weiteres Mal.

3. Erkläre einem Freund oder einer Freundin die neue **Grammatik**. Das klappt nicht richtig? Dann lies nochmal im *Grammar File* nach.

Am Abend vor dem Test

1. Entspanne dich. Du kannst lesen, dich in die Badewanne legen, Musik hören, fernsehen, …

2. Geh zur gewohnten Zeit ins Bett.

Am Morgen des Tests

1. Steh rechtzeitig auf, damit du nicht hetzen musst.

2. Lies irgendetwas „zum Aufwärmen", aber schau nicht mehr in dein Schülerbuch.

Während des Tests

1. Denk daran: Du hast dich gut vorbereitet. Es gibt keinen Grund, nervös zu sein.

2. Konzentriere dich auf den Test, lass dich nicht ablenken.

3. Lies dir die Aufgaben genau durch. Dann löse zuerst die Aufgaben, die dir einfach scheinen. Wende dich erst danach den schwereren Aufgaben zu.

4. Aufgaben, die du bearbeitet hast, hakst du ab. So siehst du, wie du vorankommst, und behältst den Überblick.

5. Schau ab und zu auf die Uhr. Du solltest dir für den Schluss noch etwas Zeit einplanen, um deine Antworten noch einmal durchzulesen und wenn nötig zu korrigieren.

Aufgabenstellungen verstehen

Bevor du anfängst, die Aufgaben zu bearbeiten, vergewissere dich, dass du genau weißt, was du tun sollst. Lies die Aufgabe Wort für Wort langsam und gründlich und von Anfang bis Ende durch. Du kannst besonders wichtige Teile der Aufgabenstellung unterstreichen und die Aufgabe, wenn nötig, für dich in einzelne Schritte unterteilen.

Den folgenden Arbeitsanweisungen begegnest du häufig:

Add	Verbinde eine Information oder einen Sachverhalt mit einer/einem anderen auf die geforderte Art und Weise.
Choose	Wähle zwischen verschiedenen Möglichkeiten die passende Information aus.
Comment	Kommentiere einen Sachverhalt durch die Darstellung deiner eigenen Meinung dazu. Begründe und erläutere sie möglichst genau.
Compare	Vergleiche Dinge, Wörter oder Sachverhalte, indem du prüfst, ob und auf welche Weise sie gleiche oder verschiedene Eigenschaften, Aussehen, Bedeutungen oder Funktionen haben.
Complete	Ergänze eine Information, indem du sie an dem dafür vorgesehenen Platz einträgst und damit z. B. einen Satz sinnvoll beendest.
Describe	Beschreibe ein Objekt oder eine Person, d.h. stelle dar, wie sie aussehen, wie das Objekt funktioniert oder die Personen handeln. Vermeide eigene Wertungen wie z. B. „beautiful", „useful" oder „great".
Discuss	Diskutiere ein Thema, eine Behauptung oder eine Aussage. Untersuche möglichst viele Seiten davon, z. B. Vor- und Nachteile, und stelle diese geordnet dar.
Explain	Erkläre einen Sachverhalt, d. h. gib wesentliche Fakten über ihn und erläutere, wie sie logisch zusammenhängen.
Fill in	Trage die geforderten Informationen in den dafür vorgesehenen Platz ein, z. B. in eine Lücke oder eine Tabelle.
List	Schreibe einzelne oder mehrere Informationen übersichtlich und geordnet auf, z. B. in einer Reihe, Tabelle oder einem anderen Verzeichnis.
Listen	Höre dir einen Text, einzelne Informationen oder Sachverhalte an.
Match	Ordne die angegebenen Informationen einander zu, wie es die Aufgabe erfordert. Finde z. B. Satzanfänge und passende Satzenden und füge sie zusammen.
Use	Verwende eine Tatsache, ein Wort usw. so, wie es in der Aufgabe gefordert wird.
Write a …	Schreibe etwas in einem geforderten Textformat auf, z. B. deinen Kommentar zu etwas oder eine Geschichte.

Ein besonderer Aufgabentyp sind **Multiple-choice-Fragen**. Tipps für den Umgang mit solchen Aufgaben findest du im folgenden Abschnitt. ▶▶

Worauf sollte ich bei Multiple-choice-Aufgaben achten?

- Lies die Frage oder den Satz sehr genau durch.
- Bevor du dir die Lösungsangebote anschaust, deck sie mit Papier ab. Überleg dir, was die richtige Antwort sein könnte. Wenn das dann auch als eine Lösungsmöglichkeit angeboten wird, ist es meistens richtig.
- Lies immer alle vorgegebenen Lösungen, bevor du dich entscheidest.
- Achte darauf, dass du nur eine der Antworten ankreuzt – es sei denn, dass in der Aufgabenstellung ausdrücklich gesagt wird, dass mehrere Antworten richtig sein können.
- Mach erst alle Aufgaben so gut du kannst. Lass keine Aufgabe aus, aber geh zum Schluss zu den Fragen zurück, bei denen du unsicher bist.
- Wenn das alles nichts hilft, such nicht mehr nach der richtigen Antwort, sondern nach den falschen Antworten. Weil drei Antwortmöglichkeiten falsch sein müssen, kannst du erschließen, dass die vierte Antwort richtig ist. Hier ist ein Beispiel. Stell dir vor, du hörst folgenden Dialog:

Boy — *Wow, that was great, Dad. Thanks. Can we do it again next weekend?*
Dad — *Sure, Greg – if the weather's nice. But let's find an easier tour then – I'm a bit tired.*

Dazu wird dir diese Multiple-choice-Aufgabe gestellt:

1. Greg and his dad have just
   A   been swimming.
   B   been to a fitness club.
   C   seen a movie.
   D   been on a bike ride.

Greg und sein Vater müssen etwas im Freien gemacht haben, denn Gregs Dad spricht über das Wetter. Also sind die Antworten B und C falsch. Man schwimmt keine Touren, also ist A auch falsch. Daher muss D die richtige Antwort sein.

Grammar File

Grammar File – Inhalt

			Seite
Unit 1	GF 1	**The *to*-infinitive** Der Infinitiv mit *to*	**154**
		1.1 REVISION **Verb + object + *to*-infinitive** Verb + Objekt + *to*-Infinitiv	154
		1.2 REVISION **Question word + *to*-infinitive** Fragewort + *to*-Infinitiv	154
		1.3 **The *to*-infinitive instead of a relative clause** Der *to*-Infinitiv anstelle eines Relativsatzes	154
Unit 2	GF 2	**The gerund** Das Gerundium	**156**
		2.1 REVISION **The gerund as subject and object** Das Gerundium als Subjekt und als Objekt	156
		2.2 REVISION **The gerund after prepositions** Das Gerundium nach Präpositionen	157
		2.3 Additional information **The gerund with 'its own subject'** Das Gerundium mit „eigenem Subjekt"	157
Unit 3	GF 3	**Participles** Partizipien	**158**
		3.1 REVISION **Participle forms** Formen des Partizips	158
		3.2 REVISION **Participle clauses instead of relative clauses** Partizipialsätze anstelle von Relativsätzen	158
		3.3 **The present participle after certain verbs** Das Partizip Präsens nach bestimmten Verben	158
		3.4 **Participle clauses instead of adverbial clauses** Partizipialsätze anstelle von adverbialen Nebensätzen	159
		3.5 **Participle clauses giving additional information** Partizipialsätze zur Angabe von Zusatzinformationen	160
		3.6 Extra **Participle clauses with conjunctions** Partizipialsätze mit Konjunktionen	161
Unit 4	GF 4	**Talking about the future** Über die Zukunft sprechen	**162**
Grammatical terms (Grammatische Fachbegriffe)			**164**
Lösungen der Grammar-File-Aufgaben			**166**

> **In English: The *to*-infinitive**
>
> The *to*-infinitive is used
> – after *ask, cause, expect, force, help, tell, want, would like*
> – after a question word, instead of a subordinate clause

In English-Abschnitte enthalten kurze Zusammenfassungen der wichtigsten grammatischen Regeln auf Englisch.

> **Additional information**
>
> We **stood** <u>watching</u> the street artists.
> Wir standen da und sahen den Straßenkünstlern zu.

So gekennzeichnete Abschnitte enthalten Grammatik, die du nicht selbst zu verwenden brauchst.
Du solltest aber verstehen, was dort erklärt wird, damit du keine Schwierigkeiten mit Texten hast, in denen diese Grammatik vorkommt.

> Verwende *to*-Infinitive, um die folgenden Sätze
> 1 The first guest **who arrived** at the bar
> 2 When I needed help with my new com
> 3 The person **who you should talk to** ab

▸ *Unit 1: P 3–5 (pp. 18–19)*

Bei den **Can you …?**-Tafeln findest du kleine Aufgaben zur Selbstkontrolle.
(Deine Lösungen kannst du auf S. 166 überprüfen.)

Hinweise wie ▸ *Unit 1: P 3–5 (pp. 18–19)* geben an, welche Übungen zum behandelten Thema gehören – hier: Übungen 3–5 auf den Seiten 18 und 19.

GF 1 The *to*-infinitive   Der Infinitiv mit *to*

1.1 REVISION Verb + object + *to*-infinitive

Kim **helped** me to write my French essay.
Kim half mir, meinen französischen Aufsatz zu schreiben.

Sharon **asked** me not to use her photo.
Sharon bat mich, ihr Foto nicht zu verwenden.

They **told** us to get into the truck.
Sie sagten, dass wir in den LKW einsteigen sollten.

The government **wanted** them to forget their traditions.
... wollte, dass sie ihre Traditionen vergessen.

Wallace **would like** the government to apologize.
... möchte, dass sich die Regierung entschuldigt.

▶ Unit 1: P 1 (p. 18)

Verb + Objekt + *to*-Infinitiv

◀ Nach bestimmten Verben kann ein **Objekt + *to*-Infinitiv** stehen, z. B. *ask/help/force/teach sb. (not) to do sth*.

Nach den entsprechenden deutschen Verben steht meist ein Infinitiv mit „zu":
jn. bitten/jm. helfen/..., etwas (nicht) zu tun.

◀ Auch nach den Verben *cause, expect, tell, want, would like, would love* kann ein **Objekt + *to*-Infinitiv** stehen.

❗ Nach den entsprechenden deutschen Verben steht ein Nebensatz mit „dass". Auf die englischen Verben darf jedoch <u>kein</u> *that*-Satz folgen:
Wir **wollen**, dass du uns hilfst.   We **want** you to help us.
          Nicht: We want ~~that you help~~ us.

1.2 REVISION Question word + *to*-infinitive

We **don't know** what to do.
(... what we should/could do)
Wir wissen nicht, was wir tun sollen/könnten.

Let's **ask** someone how to get to the bus station.
..., wie wir zum Busbahnhof kommen (können).

They **wondered** whether to go or to stay.
..., ob sie gehen oder bleiben sollten.

I'm **not sure** which direction to take.
..., welche Richtung ich nehmen soll/muss.

▶ Unit 1: P 2 (p. 18)

Fragewort + *to*-Infinitiv

Der *to*-Infinitiv steht oft nach einem **Fragewort** (*what, who, when, where, how* usw.) sowie nach *whether* („ob"). Er entspricht meist einem Nebensatz mit modalem Hilfsverb (*can, could, might, must, should*).

Die Kombination aus Fragewort und *to*-Infinitiv steht oft nach den Verben *ask, explain, find out, know, show, tell, wonder* und nach *I'm not sure*.

1.3 The *to*-infinitive instead of a relative clause

1 Zita wasn't **the first (girl)** to cry.
    (... the first girl who cried)
   I expect **the last (person)** to arrive will be Jo.
    (... the last person who arrives ...)
   We're **the only shop** to offer this service.
    (... the only shop that offers this service)
   Sophie was **the only person/the only one** to say what she thought.
    (... the only person/one who said ...)

2 Who was **the youngest (girl or boy)** to take part in the competition?
    (... the youngest girl or boy who took part ...)

Der *to*-Infinitiv anstelle eines Relativsatzes

Der *to*-Infinitiv kann **anstelle eines Relativsatzes** stehen

1 nach *the first, the last, the next, the only*.

❗ Nach *the only* muss ein Nomen oder *one/ones* stehen.

2 nach einem Superlativ.

Grammar File

1. There were hard **mattresses to sleep** on.
   (... mattresses that we/they could sleep on)
   Philip is **the person to ask** about grammar.
   (... the person who you should ask)
   That's the **place to go** to if you need help.
   (... the place that you must/should go to)
   Look, this is **the way to do** it.
   (... the way that you should do it)

2. There was **no one to help** us.
   (... no one who could help us)
   I'm looking for **someone to share** a flat with.
   (... someone who I can share a flat with)
   Lucy doesn't know **anybody to play** with.
   (... anybody who she can/could play with)
   There's **nowhere to go** in this town.
   (... nowhere that I can go)

▶ Unit 1: P 3–5 (pp. 18–19)

Der *to*-Infinitiv kann **anstelle eines Relativsatzes mit modalem Hilfsverb** stehen

1 nach einem **Nomen** (häufig nach *person, place, way*).

2 nach den Zusammensetzungen mit **some-, any-** und **no-** (*someone, something, somewhere, anybody, no one, nowhere* usw.).

In English: The *to*-infinitive

The *to*-infinitive is used
– after *ask, cause, expect, force, help, tell, want, would like, ...* + object — Dad **would like you to help** him.
– after a question word, instead of a subordinate clause — I don't know **who to ask**.
– after *the first (person), the last (one)*, etc., instead of a relative clause — Sue is always **the first to arrive**.
   Tom was **the oldest to apply**.
– after nouns and *someone, anything, nowhere*, etc., instead of a relative clause — I've got **some letters to write**.
   Is there **anybody to ask**?

Verwende to*-Infinitive, um die folgenden Sätze zu verkürzen.*

1 The first guest **who arrived** at the barbecue was Toby.
2 When I needed help with my new computer, Mel was the only one **who offered**.
3 The person **who you should talk to** about Australia is Jill. Her parents live there.
4 Hurry, please. There are lots of things **that we have to do** today.
5 I need something **that I can wear** at the disco. This top looks good.
6 It's boring on Sundays when there's nobody **that you can hang out with**.

Shall we get help?

No. Dad doesn't want anybody to disturb him when he's working.

*(to) disturb [dɪˈstɜːb] stören

GF 2 The gerund — Das Gerundium

2.1 REVISION The gerund as subject and object

Subject
Riding is fun.
Reiten macht Spaß.

Object
I love riding.
Ich liebe das Reiten. / Ich reite sehr gern.

I like riding my bike. — Ich fahre gern Rad.
Cycling in the rain can be fun too.
Radfahren im Regen kann auch Spaß machen. / Im Regen Rad zu fahren kann auch Spaß machen.

1 Nobody **enjoys** going to the dentist's.
Niemand geht gern zum Zahnarzt.
Imagine living in California!
Stell dir vor, in Kalifornien zu leben!
Tom **suggested** going for an ice cream.
Tom schlug vor, ein Eis essen zu gehen.

2 When it **started** raining / to rain we all went home.
Als es anfing zu regnen, gingen wir alle nach Haus.
Will **loves** doing / to do crazy things.
Will liebt es, verrückte Sachen zu machen.

3 I'll never **forget** talking to Robbie Williams.
Ich werde nie vergessen, wie ich mit Robbie Williams gesprochen habe.
I **forgot** to phone Grandpa. I'm sorry.
Ich habe vergessen, Opa anzurufen. Es tut mir leid.

I **remember** posting the letter last Friday.
Ich erinnere mich daran, letzten Freitag den Brief eingeworfen zu haben.
I must **remember** to post this card tomorrow.
Ich muss daran denken (= ich darf nicht vergessen), morgen diese Karte einzuwerfen.

I've **stopped** talking to Rob. We had a fight.
Ich habe aufgehört, mit Rob zu reden. / Ich rede nicht mehr mit Rob. ...
I **stopped** to talk to Jo. We chatted for a while.
Ich hielt an, um mit Jo zu reden. ...

I can't open the door. — **Try** kicking it.
... Probier mal, dagegen zu treten.
I **tried** to kick the door open and hurt myself.
Ich versuchte/bemühte mich, die Tür aufzutreten ...

▶ Unit 2: P 3, 4 (p. 42)

Das Gerundium als Subjekt und als Objekt

Wenn die -ing-Form eines Verbs die Funktion eines **Nomens** hat, wird sie **Gerundium** (gerund) genannt. Das Gerundium kann **Subjekt** oder **Objekt** eines Satzes sein.

Wie ein Verb kann das Gerundium erweitert werden, z.B. durch ein Objekt (hier: *my bike*) oder eine Orts- oder Zeitangabe (hier: *in the rain*).

! Beachte:

◂ 1 Nach einigen Verben – z.B. **avoid, dislike, enjoy, fancy, finish, imagine, miss, practise, suggest** – muss ein weiteres Verb als Gerundium stehen:
I **enjoy** going ...; He **suggested** going ...
Anders als im Deutschen darf nach diesen Verben **kein Infinitiv** stehen!
Also nicht: I ~~enjoy to go~~ ...; He ~~suggested to go~~ ...

◂ 2 Nach **begin/start, continue, hate, like, love, prefer** kann jedoch – bei gleicher Bedeutung – entweder ein Gerundium oder ein *to*-Infinitiv stehen.

◂ 3 Nach **forget, remember, stop, try** kann entweder ein Gerundium oder ein *to*-Infinitiv stehen, aber mit unterschiedlicher Bedeutung:

– *forget doing* sth.	vergessen, dass/wie man etwas *(in der Vergangenheit)* getan hat
forget to do sth.	vergessen, etwas zu tun
– *remember doing* sth.	sich daran erinnern, dass man etwas *(in der Vergangenheit)* getan hat
remember to do sth.	daran denken, etwas zu tun
– *stop doing* sth.	aufhören, etwas zu tun
stop to do sth.	anhalten, um etwas *(anderes)* zu tun
– *try doing* sth.	etwas (aus)probieren
try to do sth.	versuchen/sich bemühen, etwas zu tun

Grammar File 2

2.2 REVISION The gerund after prepositions — Das Gerundium nach Präpositionen

Boots are made **for walking**. ... zum Wandern
In future, don't use my mobile **without asking**.
... ohne zu fragen
You can save petrol **by driving** more slowly.
... indem man langsamer fährt

Nach einer Präposition *(by, for, of, without, ...)* muss ein Verb als Gerundium stehen.

I'm very **keen on playing** rugby.
Ich spiele leidenschaftlich gern Rugby.

You're just not **used to working** hard.
Du bist es einfach nicht gewohnt, hart zu arbeiten.

Adjektiv/Nomen/Verb + Präposition + Gerundium:

– (to) be	good/bad at interested in keen on sick/tired of used to	doing sth.	Adjektiv + Präposition

Is there any **hope of winning** the final match?
Besteht Hoffnung, das Endspiel zu gewinnen?
What are his **reasons for leaving** school?
Was sind die Gründe dafür, dass er die Schule verlässt?

– the	advantage of chance of hope of reason for	doing sth.	Nomen + Präposition

Sue **is talking about moving** to London.
Sue redet davon, nach London zu ziehen.
I don't **feel like going** out tonight. Do you?
Ich habe keine Lust, heute Abend auszugehen. Und du?

– (to)	dream of feel like talk about think of	doing sth.	Verb + Präposition

▶ Unit 2: P 5 (p. 42)

Additional information

2.3 The gerund with 'its own subject' — Das Gerundium mit „eigenem Subjekt"

1a Ella can't **imagine moving** to Africa.
Ella kann sich nicht vorstellen, nach Afrika zu ziehen.
1b Ella can't **imagine her family moving** to Africa.
Ella kann sich nicht vorstellen, dass ihre Familie nach Afrika zieht.

◀ In Satz **1b** hat das Gerundium ein „eigenes Subjekt": *moving* bezieht sich auf *her family* (und nicht auf *Ella*, das Subjekt des ganzen Satzes).

2a His parents talked **about him going** to Paris.
2b His parents talked **about his going** to Paris.
Seine Eltern redeten davon, dass er nach Paris fährt.

◀ Wenn wie in Satz **2a** das Subjekt des Gerundiums ein Personalpronomen ist, dann steht es in der Objektform: *him* (nicht: *he*). In sehr formellem Englisch wird wie in Satz **2b** oft ein Possessivpronomen bevorzugt: *his going ...*

▶ Unit 2: P 6 (p. 43)

In English: The gerund

1 A **gerund** is an *-ing* form used as a noun.
   It can be the subject or the object of a sentence. — *Singing is fun. I like singing.*
2 After some verbs *(enjoy, imagine, suggest, ...)* we use a gerund, not an infinitive. — *Lucy suggested asking the head teacher.*
3 Verbs which follow a preposition take the form of a gerund. — *Don't cross the road without looking.*
4 Gerunds can have their own subject. — *Is there any chance of Pete/him winning?*

GF 3 Participles   Partizipien

3.1 REVISION Participle forms

Present participle *(-ing)*:
| work | → | **working** | try | → | **trying** |
| dance | → | **dancing** | plan | → | **pla**nn**ing** |

Formen des Partizips

◁ Das **Partizip Präsens** *(present participle)* bildet man durch Anhängen von **-ing** an den Infinitiv. Beachte die Besonderheiten bei der Schreibung.

Past participle, regular verbs *(-ed)*:
| work | → | **worked** | try | → | **tried** |
| dance | → | **danced** | plan | → | **pla**nn**ed** |

◁ Das **Partizip Perfekt** *(past participle)* eines <u>regelmäßigen</u> Verbs wird durch Anhängen von **-ed** an den Infinitiv gebildet. Beachte auch hier die Besonderheiten bei der Schreibung.

Past participle, irregular verbs:
| build | → | **built** | make | → | **made** |
| teach | → | **taught** | write | → | **written** |

<u>Unregelmäßige</u> Verben haben eigene *past participle*-Formen, die man einzeln lernen muss.

▶ *Unregelmäßige Verben (pp. 240–241)*

3.2 REVISION Participle clauses instead of relative clauses

The girl **talking to Leo** is my sister.
    (The girl <u>who is talking</u> to Leo …)
The man **driving the red car** didn't stop.
    (The man <u>who was driving</u> the red car …)

Partizipialsätze anstelle von Relativsätzen

Partizipialsätze können Relativsätze verkürzen und werden daher oft anstelle von Relativsätzen verwendet.

◁ Das **present participle** entspricht einem Relativpronomen + Verb im **Aktiv**:
is talking; was driving.

We often buy strawberries **grown in California**.
    (… strawberries <u>which were grown</u> …)
The girls **chosen for the team** were only 15.
    (The girls <u>who were chosen</u> for the team …)

◁ Das **past participle** entspricht einem Relativpronomen + Verb im **Passiv**:
were grown; were chosen.

▶ *Unit 3: P 1 (p. 59)*

3.3 The present participle after certain verbs

Das Partizip Präsens nach bestimmten Verben

Verb of perception + object + present participle

	Verb	Object	Present participle	
1	I heard	people	shouting.	
2	Rob saw	two men	running	out of the bank.
3	Sue noticed	some men	getting	into a blue car.
4	We watched	the car	driving	down the street.

Mit einem **Verb der Wahrnehmung + Objekt + Partizip Präsens** sagt man, dass man etwas wahrnimmt, das gerade im Verlauf ist.

Verben der Wahrnehmung sind *feel, hear, listen to, notice, see, smell, watch*.

1 Ich hörte Leute schreien.
2 Rob sah zwei Männer aus der Bank laufen.
3 Sue bemerkte, wie/dass einige Männer in ein blaues Auto stiegen.
4 Wir beobachteten, wie das Auto die Straße hinunterfuhr.

Im Deutschen verwendet man einen Infinitiv (1, 2) oder einen Nebensatz mit „wie" oder „dass" (3, 4).

▶ *Unit 3: P 3 (p. 59)*

Grammar File

Wie sagst du das auf Englisch? Verwende present participles.

1 Ich sah, wie ein Junge mit seinem Hund die Straße überquerte. I saw ... with his dog.
2 Ich bemerkte, dass ein blaues Auto um die Ecke fuhr. I noticed ...
3 Plötzlich hörte ich eine Stimme laut rufen. Suddenly I heard ...
4 Dann sah ich den Jungen und den Hund in das Auto einsteigen. Then ...

Additional information

1 Rob **watched the car** <u>stop</u> at the corner.
2 He **saw a man** <u>get out</u>.
3 Rob **heard him** <u>shout</u> something to the others.
4 Then he **watched the car** <u>disappear</u> round the corner.
1 Rob beobachtete, wie das Auto an der Ecke anhielt.
2 Er sah einen Mann aussteigen.
3 Rob hörte, wie er den anderen etwas zurief.
4 Dann beobachtete er, wie/dass das Auto um die Ecke verschwand.

Nach **Verben der Wahrnehmung + Objekt** kann auch ein **Infinitiv** stehen (ohne *to*). Damit drückt man aus, dass das Geschehen **vollständig – von Anfang bis Ende –** wahrgenommen wird. Oft handelt es sich um kurze Handlungen. Vergleiche:
– *I saw a man* **cross** *the street.*
  (Er überquerte die Straße.)
– *I saw a man* **crossing** *the street when a car hit him.*
  (Er war dabei, die Straße zu überqueren, wurde aber angefahren, bevor er die andere Straßenseite erreichte.)

Additional information

We **stood** <u>watching</u> the street artists.
Wir standen da und sahen den Straßenkünstlern zu.

We **sat** <u>chatting</u> in a café.
Wir saßen in einem Café und unterhielten uns.

The dog **came** <u>running</u> towards me.
Der Hund kam auf mich zugerannt.

Das Partizip Präsens kann nach **Verben der Ruhe** *(stand, sit, stay, lie)* und nach **Verben der Bewegung** *(come, go)* stehen.

3.4 Participle clauses instead of adverbial clauses

Partizipialsätze anstelle von adverbialen Nebensätzen

Time

Looking **up,** I saw some small coconuts.
(When I looked up, I saw some small coconuts.)
Als ich aufschaute, sah ich ein paar kleine Kokosnüsse.

Arriving **in Mumbai,** I started to look for a room.
(When I arrived in Mumbai, ...)
Als ich in Mumbai ankam, ...

Asked **to turn down his MP3 player,** the boy started to shout at the bus driver.
(When he was asked to turn down ...)
Als er gebeten wurde, seinen MP3-Spieler leiser zu stellen, ...

Partizipialsätze können **Nebensätze der Zeit** oder **des Grundes** verkürzen.

Solche Partizipialsätze gehen oft dem Hauptsatz voran. Sie sind **typisch für das geschriebene Englisch**.

In gesprochenem Englisch werden meist adverbiale Nebensätze bevorzugt.

▶▶▶

Reason

Feeling tired, I went up to my room.
(Because/Since I felt tired, …)
Weil/Da ich mich müde fühlte, …

Being a doctor, she knew exactly what to do.
Weil/Da sie Ärztin ist, …

Warned by his wife, the man was able to escape.
(Because he was warned by his wife, …)
Von seiner Frau gewarnt, … / Weil er … gewarnt wurde, …

Having + past participle

1 **Having passed** his exams, Mike applied for a job.
(After he had passed his exams, …)
Nachdem Mike seine Prüfungen bestanden hatte, …

2 **Having been** to Italy twice, we decided to go to Spain.
(Because/Since we had been to Italy twice, …)
Da wir schon zweimal in Italien gewesen waren, …

Not having seen the film, I bought the DVD.
(Because/Since I hadn't seen the film, …)
Da ich den Film nicht gesehen hatte, …

▶ Unit 3: P 1, 2 (p. 66); P 5 (p. 67)

Partizipialsätze mit **having** + **Partizip Perfekt** drücken immer **Vorzeitigkeit** aus.

Partizipialsätze mit **having** + **Partizip Perfekt** entsprechen

1 einem adverbialen Nebensatz der **Zeit**, meist mit *after* eingeleitet

2 einem adverbialen Nebensatz des **Grundes**.

Verwende Partizipialsätze anstelle der Nebensätze.

1 **When I arrived at the station**, I bought some sandwiches and a newspaper.
2 **Because he was ill**, Steve couldn't finish his presentation.
3 **When he was asked to stop smoking**, Peter left the room.
4 **As she has spent a lot of time in France**, Sophie can speak French very well.
5 **Since we hadn't been to America**, we booked a holiday in New York.

3.5 Participle clauses giving additional information

I stood in the queue, **waiting** to fill my bucket with water.
Ich stand in der Schlange und wartete darauf, meinen Eimer mit Wasser zu füllen.

Using a knife, he was able to open the door.
Indem er ein Messer benutzte, …

She ran down the stairs, **losing** a shoe.
…, wobei sie einen Schuh verlor.

▶ Unit 3: P 1 (p. 66); P 3, 5 (p. 67)

Partizipialsätze zur Angabe von Zusatzinformationen

Partizipialsätze werden oft verwendet, um Zusatzinformationen zu geben oder die Begleitumstände einer Handlung zu beschreiben. (Meist handelt es sich um zeitgleich oder fast zeitgleich stattfindende Handlungen oder Vorgänge.)

Im Deutschen steht meist ein Hauptsatz mit „und" oder ein Nebensatz mit „indem" oder „wobei".

Grammar File

Verwende einen Partizipialsatz, um die beiden Sätze zu einem Satz zu verbinden. (Manchmal gibt es zwei mögliche Lösungen!)

1. I looked at my watch. I realized that I was late.
2. I hurried down the stairs. I dropped all my books.
3. I hurried into town. I ate a piece of toast on the way.
4. I sat in the classroom alone. I thought all the others were late.
5. I took out my Maths books. Then I remembered it was the English lesson.

3.6 Extra Participle clauses with conjunctions

1a **Reading** a really boring book, I fell asleep.
Als/Weil ich ein wirklich langweiliges Buch las, …
1b **When/While reading** a really boring book, I fell asleep. *or* I fell asleep **when/while reading** a really boring book.

2a I saw a huge black dog **while walking** down the street. (= I was walking down the street)
Ich habe einen riesigen schwarzen Hund gesehen, während ich die Straße hinunterging.
2b I saw a huge black dog **walking** down the street. (= the dog was walking down the street)
Ich habe gesehen, wie ein riesiger schwarzer Hund die Straße hinunterging.
3a **After having** lunch with his girlfriend's parents, Tom fell asleep.
(= first they had lunch, then he fell asleep)
3b **Having** lunch with his girlfriend's parents, Tom fell asleep.
(= he fell asleep while they were having lunch)

4 **Although asked** to stop by the police, the man drove on.
You will have to wait outside **until asked** to enter.
If posted before 12 o'clock, the letter should arrive tomorrow.

▶ *Unit 3: P 4 (p. 67)*

Partizipialsätze mit Konjunktionen

◂ Nicht immer ist eindeutig zu erkennen, ob ein Partizipialsatz einem Nebensatz der Zeit oder einem Nebensatz des Grundes entspricht (Satz **1a**). Erst durch die Konjunktion **when** oder **while** wird deutlich, dass der Satz **zeitlich** zu verstehen ist (**1b**).

◂ Oft gibt es große Bedeutungsunterschiede, je nachdem, ob der Partizipialsatz mit oder ohne Konjunktion verwendet wird – vergleiche **2a** mit **2b** und **3a** mit **3b**.

*She saw an elephant **while** cycling along the road.* | *She saw an elephant cycling along the road.*

◂ Partizipialsätze können auch durch andere Konjunktionen eingeleitet werden, z.B. durch **although, until, if, before** (Sätze **4**).

In English: Participles

Participle clauses can be used
– instead of relative clauses — *The girl **talking to Jack** … / Wine **produced in Australia** …*
– after verbs of perception + object — *I can **see somebody running** down the street.*
 (when the action is not yet completed)
– instead of adverbial clauses of time or reason — ***Travelling** by train, you meet some interesting people.*
 ***Not having** much money, we stayed at a small B&B.*
– to give additional information — *Maggie ran down the road, **singing** her favourite song.*

GF 4 Talking about the future — Über die Zukunft sprechen

The *will*-future

I'll be 15 next October.
It will be cold and windy, and we will get some rain in the afternoon.

I suppose Ella will be late again as usual.
Ich nehme an, Ella kommt wie üblich wieder zu spät.

Just a moment. I'll open the door for you.
Moment. Ich mache Ihnen die Tür auf.
I won't tell anyone what's happened. I promise.
Ich sage niemandem, was passiert ist. …

▶ Unit 4: P 2 (p.83)

Das **Futur mit will** wird verwendet,

◂ um **Vorhersagen** über die Zukunft zu äußern. Oft geht es dabei um Dinge, die man nicht beeinflussen kann, z.B. das Alter oder das Wetter.

◂ um eine **Vermutung** auszudrücken (oft eingeleitet mit *I suppose, I think, I'm sure, I expect, maybe*).

◂ wenn man sich **spontan** – also ohne es im Voraus geplant zu haben – zu etwas **entschließt**. Oft geht es dabei um **Hilfsangebote** oder **Versprechen**.

Hold on, Dad, I'll run and borrow our neighbour's ladder.

The *going to*-future

After school I'm going to study IT – I hope.
Nach der Schule werde ich IT studieren / habe ich vor, IT zu studieren …
My boyfriend says he's going to be an engineer.
Mein Freund sagt, er will Ingenieur werden.

Look at those clouds. There's going to be a storm.
… Es wird ein Gewitter geben.

▶ Unit 4: P 2 (p.83)

Das **Futur mit going to** wird verwendet,

◂ um über **Vorhaben** und **Pläne** für die Zukunft zu sprechen.

◂ um auszudrücken, dass etwas **wahrscheinlich gleich geschehen wird** – es gibt bereits deutliche **Anzeichen** dafür.

The present progressive (future meaning)

We're driving to Scotland next weekend to visit my grandparents.
I'm meeting a friend in town tomorrow at 12.
All my friends are coming to my birthday party on Friday.

▶ Unit 4: P 2 (p.83)

Auch das **present progressive** kann futurische Bedeutung haben. Es wird verwendet, wenn etwas **für die Zukunft fest geplant** oder **fest verabredet** ist (manchmal spricht man vom *diary future*). Durch eine Zeitangabe (*next weekend; tomorrow*) oder aus dem Zusammenhang muss klar sein, dass es um etwas Zukünftiges geht.

Grammar File 4

The simple present (future meaning)

The next train to Bath goes in ten minutes.
Our cookery classes start on 2 September.

▶ Unit 4: P 4 (p. 87)

Auch das **simple present** kann futurische Bedeutung haben. Es wird verwendet, wenn ein **zukünftiges Geschehen** durch einen **Fahrplan**, ein **Programm** oder Ähnliches festgelegt ist (manchmal spricht man vom *timetable future*). Verben wie *arrive, leave, go, open, close, start, stop* werden häufig so verwendet.

The future progressive

This time next week my sister will be flying to Spain – and I'll be doing my Maths exam.
Nächste Woche um diese Zeit wird meine Schwester (gerade) nach Spanien fliegen – und ich werde dabei sein, meine Mathe-Prüfung zu machen.

Das **future progressive** wird verwendet, um über Handlungen und Ereignisse zu sprechen, die **zu einem zukünftigen Zeitpunkt im Gange** sein werden (noch nicht abgeschlossen sein werden).
Typische Zeitangaben sind *a week today* („heute in einer Woche"), *this time next week* oder Ähnliches.

The future perfect

On Friday we will have finished all our exams.
Am Freitag werden wir alle unsere Prüfungen geschafft haben.

And **by the end of next week** we'll have received our results.
Und bis Ende nächster Woche werden wir unsere Ergebnisse erhalten haben.

Das **future perfect** wird verwendet um auszudrücken, dass etwas **zu einem bestimmten Zeitpunkt in der Zukunft geschehen oder getan sein wird**. (Meist wird dieser Zeitpunkt auch genannt – hier: *on Friday; by the end of next week*.)

In English: Talking about the future

will-future:	for predictions or assumptions about the future
	for spontaneous decisions (e.g. offers and promises)
going to-future:	for intentions and plans for the future
	when something will very probably happen (there are already signs of it happening)
Present progressive:	when something is definitely planned or arranged for the future
Simple present:	for future events that are a fixed part of a timetable, programme, schedule, etc.
Future progressive:	when an action or event will be in progress at a point of time in the future
Future perfect:	when an action or event will be complete at a point of time in the future

Vervollständige die Sätze mit der richtigen Zeitform.

1 Our train ... at 10.30 and arrives in Glasgow at 13.35. **(leaves/is going to leave)**
2 I'm sure it ... on time. **(will leave/is leaving)**
3 We ... our cat with the neighbours for two weeks. **(leave/are leaving)**
4 Aidan is good with computers. I suppose he ... IT when he goes to university. **(studies/will study)**
5 Kate wants to travel, so perhaps she ... a year abroad after school. **(will spend/is spending/spends)**
6 Are you free this evening? – No, I ... Bill and Emma. **(meet/am meeting/will meet)**
7 Marie ... 16 next month. **(is/will be)** She ... school and get a job. **(will leave/is going to leave)**

Grammatical terms (Grammatische Fachbegriffe)

English term	German term	Example
active ['æktɪv]	Aktiv	Beckham **scored** the final goal.
activity verb [æk'tɪvəti vɜːb]	Tätigkeitsverb	do, go, make, read, repair
adjective ['ædʒɪktɪv]	Adjektiv	good, red, new, boring
adverb ['ædvɜːb]	Adverb	always, badly, here, really, today
adverb of frequency ['friːkwənsi]	Häufigkeitsadverb	always, often, never
adverb of indefinite time [ɪnˌdefɪnət 'taɪm]	Adverb der unbestimmten Zeit	already, ever, just, never
adverb of manner ['mænə]	Adverb der Art und Weise	badly, happily, quietly, well
adverbial clause [ædˌvɜːbiəl 'klɔːz]	adverbialer Nebensatz	I went to bed **because I was tired**.
article ['ɑːtɪkl]	Artikel	the, a/an
auxiliary [ɔːg'zɪliəri]	Hilfsverb	be, have, do; will, can, must
backshift of tenses ['bækʃɪft]	Verschiebung der Zeitformen (bei der indirekten Rede)	'I'm sorry.' ▶ Sam said he **was** sorry.
command [kə'mɑːnd]	Befehl, Aufforderungssatz	Open your books. Don't talk.
comparison [kəm'pærɪsn]	Steigerung	old – older – oldest
conditional sentence [kənˌdɪʃənl 'sentəns]	Bedingungssatz	I'd call him if I knew his number.
conjunction [kən'dʒʌŋkʃn]	Konjunktion	and, or, but; because, before
contact clause ['kɒntækt klɔːz]	Relativsatz ohne Relativpronomen	She's the girl **I love**.
countable noun ['kaʊntəbl]	zählbares Nomen	girl – girls, pound – pounds
defining relative clause [dɪ'faɪnɪŋ]	bestimmender Relativsatz	There's the girl **who helped me**.
definite article ['defɪnət]	bestimmter Artikel	the
direct speech [ˌdaɪrekt 'spiːtʃ]	direkte Rede, wörtliche Rede	**'I'm sorry.'**
future perfect [ˌfjuːtʃə 'pɜːfɪkt]	vollendete Zukunft, Futur II	On Friday we will have finished our exams.
future progressive [ˌfjuːtʃə prə'gresɪv]	Verlaufsform des *will-future*	A week today I will be lying on the beach.
gerund ['dʒerənd]	Gerundium	I like **dancing**. **Dancing** is fun.
***going to*-future**	Futur mit *going to*	**I'm going to watch** TV tonight.
***if*-clause** ['ɪf klɔːz]	*if*-Satz, Nebensatz mit *if*	**If I see Jack**, I'll tell him.
imperative [ɪm'perətɪv]	Imperativ (Befehlsform)	Open your books. Don't talk.
indirect speech [ˌɪndərekt 'spiːtʃ]	indirekte Rede	Sam said **(that) he was sorry**.
infinitive [ɪn'fɪnətɪv]	Infinitiv (Grundform des Verbs)	(to) open, (to) see, (to) read
irregular verb [ɪˌregjələ 'vɜːb]	unregelmäßiges Verb	(to) go – went – gone
main clause	Hauptsatz	**I like Scruffy** because I like dogs.
modal, modal auxiliary [ˌməʊdl_ɔːg'zɪliəri]	modales Hilfsverb, Modalverb	can, could, may, must
negative statement [ˌnegətɪv 'steɪtmənt]	verneinter Aussagesatz	I don't like bananas.
non-defining relative clause [dɪ'faɪnɪŋ]	nicht bestimmender Relativsatz	Madison, **who lives in Atlanta**, goes to M. L. King High School.
noun [naʊn]	Nomen, Substantiv	Sophie, girl, brother, time
object ['ɒbdʒɪkt]	Objekt	My sister is writing **a letter**.
object form ['ɒbdʒɪkt fɔːm]	Objektform (der Personalpronomen)	me, you, him, her, it, us, them
part of speech [ˌpɑːt_əv 'spiːtʃ]	Wortart	
participle ['pɑːtɪsɪpl]	Partizip	planning, taking; planned, taken
participle clause [ˌpɑːtɪsɪpl 'klɔːz]	Partizipialsatz	I saw a boy **playing in the street**.
passive ['pæsɪv]	Passiv	The goal **was scored** by Beckham.
past participle [ˌpɑːst 'pɑːtɪsɪpl]	Partizip Perfekt	cleaned, planned, gone, taken
past perfect [ˌpɑːst 'pɜːfɪkt]	Plusquamperfekt, Vorvergangenheit	He cried – he **had hurt** his knee.
past perfect progressive [ˌpɑːst ˌpɜːfɪkt prə'gresɪv]	Verlaufsform des *past perfect*	She **had been working** in the garden since 12 o'clock.
past progressive [ˌpɑːst prə'gresɪv]	Verlaufsform der Vergangenheit	At 7.30 I **was having** dinner.
personal passive [ˌpɜːsənl 'pæsɪv]	persönliches Passiv	I was offered a job.

Grammar File

Term	Pronunciation	German	Example
personal pronoun	[ˌpɜːsənl ˈprəʊnaʊn]	Personalpronomen (persönliches Fürwort)	I, you, he, she, it, we, they; me, you, him, her, it, us, them
plural	[ˈplʊərəl]	Plural, Mehrzahl	
positive statement	[ˌpɒzətɪv ˈsteɪtmənt]	bejahter Aussagesatz	I like oranges.
possessive determiner	[pəˌzesɪv dɪˈtɜːmɪnə]	Possessivbegleiter (besitzanzeigender Begleiter)	my, your, his, her, its, our, their
possessive form	[pəˌzesɪv fɔːm]	s-Genitiv	Jo's brother; my sister's room
possessive pronoun	[pəˌzesɪv ˈprəʊnaʊn]	Possessivpronomen	mine, yours, his, hers, ours, theirs
preposition	[ˌprepəˈzɪʃn]	Präposition	after, at, in, next to, under
present participle	[ˌpreznt ˈpɑːtɪsɪpl]	Partizip Präsens	cleaning, planning, going, taking
present perfect	[ˌpreznt ˈpɜːfɪkt]	present perfect	We**'ve made** a cake for you.
present perfect progressive	[ˌpreznt ˌpɜːfɪkt prəˈgresɪv]	Verlaufsform des present perfect	We**'ve been waiting** for an hour.
present progressive	[ˌpreznt prəˈgresɪv]	Verlaufsform der Gegenwart	The Hansons **are having** lunch.
pronoun	[ˈprəʊnaʊn]	Pronomen, Fürwort	
quantifier	[ˈkwɒntɪfaɪə]	Mengenangabe	some, a lot of, many, much
question tag	[ˈkwestʃən tæg]	Frageanhängsel	This place is great, **isn't it?**
question word	[ˈkwestʃən wɜːd]	Fragewort	what?, when?, where?, how?
reflexive pronoun	[rɪˌfleksɪv ˈprəʊnaʊn]	Reflexivpronomen	myself, yourself, themselves
regular verb	[ˌregjələ ˈvɜːb]	regelmäßiges Verb	(to) help – helped – helped
relative clause	[ˌrelətɪv ˈklɔːz]	Relativsatz	There's the girl **who helped me**.
relative pronoun	[ˌrelətɪv ˈprəʊnaʊn]	Relativpronomen	who, that, which, whose
reported speech	[rɪˌpɔːtɪd ˈspiːtʃ]	indirekte Rede	Sam said **(that) he was sorry**.
request	[rɪˈkwest]	Bitte	Can you help me with this?
short answer	[ˌʃɔːt ˈɑːnsə]	Kurzantwort	Yes, I am. / No, I don't.
simple past	[ˌsɪmpl ˈpɑːst]	einfache Form der Vergangenheit	Jo **wrote** two letters yesterday.
simple present	[ˌsɪmpl ˈpreznt]	einfache Form der Gegenwart	I always **go** to school by bike.
singular	[ˈsɪŋgjələ]	Singular, Einzahl	
state verb	[ˈsteɪt vɜːb]	Zustandsverb	be, know, like, own, sound, want
statement	[ˈsteɪtmənt]	Aussagesatz	
subject	[ˈsʌbdʒɪkt]	Subjekt	**My sister** is writing a letter.
subject form	[ˈsʌbdʒɪkt fɔːm]	Subjektform (der Personalpronomen)	I, you, he, she, it, we, they
subordinate clause	[səˌbɔːdɪnət ˈklɔːz]	Nebensatz	I like Scruffy **because I like dogs**.
substitute	[ˈsʌbstɪtjuːt]	Ersatzverb (eines modalen Hilfsverbs)	be able to, be allowed to, have to
tense	[tens]	Zeitform	
uncountable noun	[ʌnˈkaʊntəbl]	nicht zählbares Nomen	bread, milk, money, news, work
verb	[vɜːb]	Verb	hear, open, help, go
verb of perception	[pəˈsepʃn]	Verb der Wahrnehmung	feel, hear, listen to, see, smell
will-future		Futur mit *will*	I think it **will be** cold tonight.
word order	[ˈwɜːd ˌɔːdə]	Wortstellung	
yes/no question		Entscheidungsfrage	Are you 13? Do you like comics?

Lösungen der Grammar-File-Aufgaben

p.155
1. The first guest **to arrive** at the barbecue was Toby.
2. When I needed help with my new computer, Mel was the only one **to offer**.
3. The person **to talk to** about Australia is Jill. Her parents live there.
4. Hurry, please. There are lots of things **to do** today.
5. I need something **to wear** at the disco. This top looks good.
6. It's boring on Sundays when there's nobody **to hang out with**.

p.159
1. I saw a boy crossing the street/the road with his dog.
2. I noticed a blue car driving round the corner.
3. Suddenly I heard a voice shouting loudly.
4. Then I saw the boy and the dog getting in(to) the car.

p.160
1. **Arriving at the station**, I bought some sandwiches and a newspaper.
2. **Being ill**, Steve couldn't finish his presentation.
3. **Asked to stop smoking**, Peter left the room.
4. **Having spent a lot of time in France**, Sophie can speak French very well.
5. **Not having been to America**, we booked a holiday in New York.

p.161
1. **Looking at my watch**, I realized that I was late. / I looked at my watch, **realizing that I was late**.
2. **Hurrying down the stairs**, I dropped all my books. / I hurried down the stairs, **dropping all my books**.
3. I hurried into town, **eating a piece of toast on the way**.
4. **Sitting in the classroom alone**, I thought all the others were late. / I sat in the classroom alone, **thinking all the others were late**.
5. **Taking out my Maths books**, I remembered it was the English lesson.

p.163
1. Our train **leaves** at 10.30 and arrives in Glasgow at 13.35.
2. I'm sure it **will leave** on time.
3. We **are leaving** our cat with the neighbours for two weeks.
4. ... I suppose he **will study** IT when he goes to university.
5. ..., so perhaps she **will spend** a year abroad after school.
6. ... – No, **I'm meeting** Bill and Emma.
7. Marie **will be** 16 next month. She **is going to leave** school and get a job.

Vocabulary

Diese Wörterverzeichnisse findest du in deinem Englischbuch:

- Das **Vocabulary** (S. 167–194) enthält alle neuen Wörter und Wendungen aus Band 5, die du lernen musst. Sie stehen in der Reihenfolge, in der sie in den Units vorkommen.
- Das **Dictionary** (S. 195-236) enthält den Wortschatz der Bände 1 bis 5 in alphabetischer Reihenfolge. Dort kannst du nachschlagen, was ein Wort bedeutet, wie man es ausspricht oder wie es genau geschrieben wird.

So ist das Vocabulary aufgebaut:

- Hier siehst du, wo die Wörter vorkommen.
  p.10 = Seite 10
  p.11/P 3 = Seite 11, Übung 3

- Die Lautschrift zeigt dir, wie ein Wort ausgesprochen und betont wird.

- Eingerückte Wörter lernst du am besten zusammen mit dem vorausgehenden Wort, weil die beiden zusammengehören.

- Die blauen Kästen solltest du dir besonders gut ansehen.

Tipps zum Wörterlernen findest du im Skills File auf Seite 126.

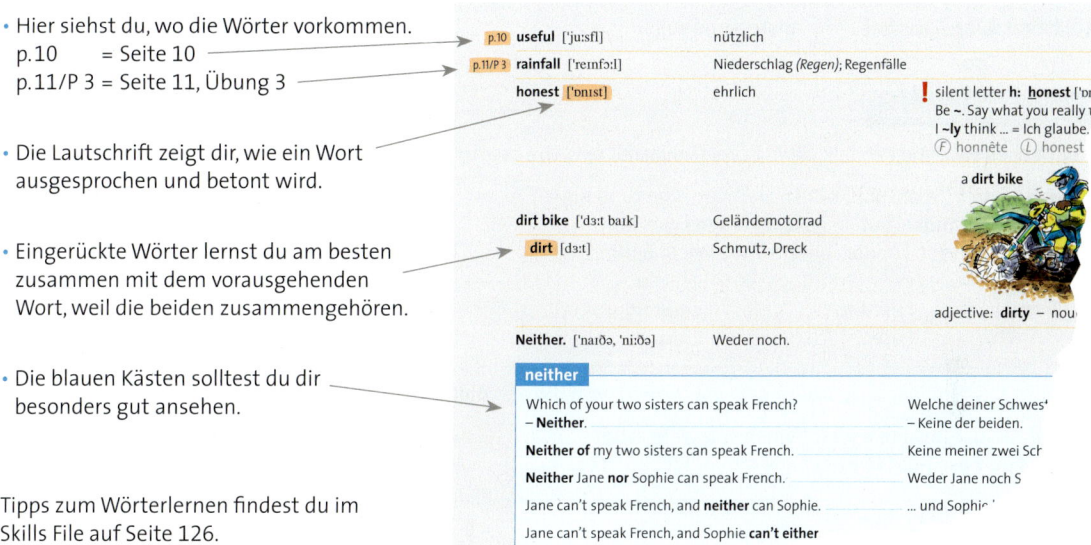

Abkürzungen:

n	= noun	v	= verb	
adj	= adjective	adv	= adverb	
prep	= preposition	conj	= conjunction	
pl	= plural	no pl	= no plural	
p.	= page	pp.	= pages	
sb.	= somebody	sth.	= something	
jn.	= jemanden	jm.	= jemandem	
AE	= American English	infml	= informal	
BE	= British English	fml	= formal	

Symbole:

! Hier stehen Hinweise auf Besonderheiten, bei denen man leicht Fehler machen kann.

◄► ist das „Gegenteil"-Zeichen: **alive** ◄► **dead**
(**alive** ist das Gegenteil von **dead**)

~ Die **Tilde** in den Beispielsätzen steht für das neue Wort.

Ⓕ verwandtes Wort im Französischen
Ⓛ verwandtes Wort im Lateinischen

Unit 1 – Australia

p.6	(to) **subscribe to** sth. [səbˈskraɪb]	etwas abonnieren; etwas abonniert haben	We ~ **to** the *Times*, but my dad sometimes buys another newspaper on the way to work.
	complete [kəmˈpliːt]	komplett, vollständig	My Beatles collection is ~: I have all their CDs!
	(to) **complete** [kəmˈpliːt]	vervollständigen; abschließen, beenden	The gallery was started in 1999 and ~**d** in 2003. I began my education in 1995 and ~**d** it in 2015.
	profile [ˈprəʊfaɪl]	Profil; Beschreibung, Porträt	**!** stress and pronunciation: **profile** [ˈprəʊfaɪl]

Englische Laute → S. 239 · Unregelmäßige Verben → S. 240–241 · Classroom English → S. 242–243

Vocabulary

barbecue [ˈbɑːbɪkjuː]		Grillfest, Grillparty	

(to) **be catching** [ˈkætʃɪŋ]		ansteckend sein	Some diseases **are** ~: they are passed from one person to another.

> **... used to be/do ...**
>
> With **used to ...** you can talk about something that was the case in the past but is not the case today:
>
> I **used to do** a lot of sport, but I haven't got the time now. — Ich habe früher (immer) viel Sport getrieben, ...
> Dad **used to smoke**, but he gave up when I was born. — Dad hat (früher) geraucht, ...
> We **used to live** in London, but now we live in Berlin. — Früher haben wir in London gewohnt, ...
>
> ❗ Pronunciation: I **used to ...**   [juːst tə]
>   I **use ...** („ich benutze")   [juːz]
>
> ❗ Questions and negative statements are formed with **did** and **didn't**:
>
> **Did** you <u>use</u> [juːs] **to cry** a lot when you were little? — Hast du viel geweint, als du klein warst?
> He **didn't** <u>use</u> [juːs] **to be** so rude. What happened? — Er war früher nicht so unhöflich ...

(to) **carry** [ˈkæri]		tragen	❗ • He's **carrying** a suitcase. (Er trägt einen Koffer.) • He's **wearing** jeans and a red shirt. (Er trägt Jeans und ein rotes Hemd.)

instructor [ɪnˈstrʌktə]		Lehrer/in, Ausbilder/in	= a person whose job it is to teach sb. a skill or sport **driving** ~, **flying** ~, **skiing** ~, **swimming** ~ (Fahr-, Flug-, Ski-, Schwimmlehrer/in)
serious [ˈsɪəriəs]		ernst(haft)	She's very funny but always has a ~ face. John has had a ~ accident and is in hospital. Ⓕ sérieux, se Ⓛ serius
seriously [ˈsɪəriəsli]		ernsthaft; *(infml)* sehr	Stop laughing and work ~ now. I love Lucy's jokes: she's a ~ funny girl.
gorgeous [ˈɡɔːdʒəs] *(infml)*		äußerst schön und attraktiv	Her whole face is pretty, and her eyes are ~.
the bush [bʊʃ]		der Busch *(unerschlossenes, „wildes" Land in Australien, Afrika)*	
bush [bʊʃ]		Busch, Strauch	
(to) **freak out** [ˌfriːk ˈaʊt]		ausflippen	
magical [ˈmædʒɪkl]		zauberhaft, wundervoll	Ⓕ magique Ⓛ magicus
No worries! [ˌnəʊ ˈwʌriz] *(bes. australisches Englisch)*		Kein Problem!	Thanks very much for helping me. – **No worries!**

Vocabulary

debate [dɪˈbeɪt]	Debatte	After a long ~, parliament voted for the new law.	*F* le débat
mate [meɪt] *(infml)*	Freund/in, Kumpel	= a good friend	
forever [fərˈevə] *(adv)*	endlos; ewig	That skyscraper is so tall! It seems to go up ~. Will you love me when I'm old? – I'll love you ~!	
mainly [ˈmeɪnli]	vorwiegend, hauptsächlich	The hotel was full of tourists, ~ from Germany.	
dirt road [ˈdɜːt rəʊd]	unbefestigte Straße		
the outback [ˈaʊtbæk]	das Hinterland Australiens		
shock [ʃɒk]	Schock, Schreck	Germany got a ~ when England beat them 5–1.	

PART A   BACKGROUND FILE   Australia

p.8 **flag** [flæɡ]	Fahne, Flagge	The German ~ is black, red and gold.	
shell [ʃel]	Muschel(schale)	shells	
goods *(pl)* [ɡʊdz]	Waren, Güter		
Aborigine [ˌæbəˈrɪdʒəni]	Ureinwohner/in Australiens	noun: **Aborigine** – adjective: **Aboriginal** [ˌæbəˈrɪdʒənl]	
(to) develop (from ... into ...) [dɪˈveləp]	entwickeln; sich entwickeln (aus ... zu ...)	The company ~s and sells software. The village ~ed into a town in only ten years.	
landscape [ˈlændskeɪp]	Landschaft		
(to) create [kriˈeɪt]	(er)schaffen, kreieren		*F* créer *L* creare
figure [ˈfɪɡə]	Zahl, Ziffer	The ~s aren't 100 per cent correct. Please check them again. **!** stress: **figure** [ˈ--]	
despite [dɪˈspaɪt]	trotz	~ the bad news = **although** the news was bad	
convict [ˈkɒnvɪkt]	Sträfling, Strafgefangene(r)	= a prisoner *(nach dem Schuldspruch)*	
former [ˈfɔːmə]	ehemalige(r, s), frühere(r, s)	Australia is a ~ British colony.	
independent [ˌɪndɪˈpendənt]	unabhängig	Australia became ~ from Britain in 1901.	*F* indépendant/e
either ... or ... [ˈaɪðə, ˈiːðə]	entweder ... oder ...		
close [kləʊs]	eng	Australia kept its ~ links to Britain after 1901. We've been ~ friends since kindergarten.	
(to) do business (with) [ˈbɪznəs]	Handel treiben (mit); Geschäfte machen (mit)	Germany **does** a lot of ~ **with** Russia and China. Does your company **do** much ~ **with** Britain?	
business [ˈbɪznəs]	Geschäfte; Unternehmen	Mike started his own ~ when he was 17.	
p.9 **rate** [reɪt]	Rate	If a country's **death** ~ is higher than its **birth** ~, the population usually gets smaller.	
cancer [ˈkænsə]	Krebs *(Krankheit)*	About 25 % of all Germans die from ~.	*F* le cancer *L* cancer
origin [ˈɒrɪdʒɪn]	Herkunft; Ursprung	44 million Americans are **of** German ~. The word 'kangaroo' is **of** Aboriginal ~.	*F* l'origine *(f)* *L* origo *(gen. originis)*

Englische Laute → S. 239 · Unregelmäßige Verben → S. 240–241 · Classroom English → S. 242–243

Vocabulary

fair [feə]	hell *(Haut; Haare)*	
dark [dɑːk]	dunkelhaarig	
equator [ɪˈkweɪtə]	Äquator	
climate [ˈklaɪmət]	Klima	❗ pronunciation: **climate** [ˈklaɪmət] Ⓕ le climat
suntan [ˈsʌntæn]	Sonnenbräune	Despite the dangers to the skin, most people still think they look good with a ~.
ozone hole [ˈəʊzəʊn həʊl]	Ozonloch	
ultraviolet rays *(pl)* [ˌʌltrəˌvaɪələt ˈreɪz]	ultraviolette Strahlen	
earth [ɜːθ]	Erde	❗ on **earth** = auf der Erde Erde = **1.** *(Erdreich)* **soil**; **2.** *(Planet)* **earth**
atmosphere [ˈætməsfɪə]	Atmosphäre; Stimmung	❗ stress: **atmosphere** [ˈ---] The earth's ~ is 78.1% N$_2$ and 20.1% O$_2$. There was an unfriendly ~ in the room.
protective [prəˈtektɪv]	Schutz-, schützend	This work is dangerous, so wear ~ gloves.
sunscreen [ˈsʌnskriːn]	Sonnenschutzmittel	Remember to put on ~ before you go out in the sun.
(to) seek [siːk], **sought**, **sought** [sɔːt] *(fml)*	suchen	Police are still ~ing the convicts who escaped. = (to) **look for**
shade [ʃeɪd]	Schatten	❗ **shade** / **shadow**
unique [juˈniːk]	einzigartig, einmalig	Everybody's eyes are ~: all eyes are different. James has a ~ collection of Frank Zappa CDs. Ⓕ unique Ⓛ unicus
emu [ˈiːmjuː]	Emu	an **emu**
reef [riːf]	Riff	= rocks or a sandbank under the water
naked [ˈneɪkɪd]	nackt	with the **naked** eye = mit dem bloßen Auge ❗ two syllables: **naked** [ˈ--]
species [ˈspiːʃiːz], *pl* **species**	Art *(biologisch)*, Spezies	The grey wolf belongs to the ~ *Canis lupus*.
dolphin [ˈdɒlfɪn]	Delfin	a **whale**
whale [weɪl]	Wal	a **dolphin**

Vocabulary 1

	sadly [ˈsædli]	leider; traurig	**Sadly**, my parents are getting divorced. He shook his head ~ and said no.
	by two degrees/ten per cent	um zwei Grad/zehn Prozent	My pocket money has gone up ~ £1 to £8.
p.10	**statistics** *(pl)* [stəˈtɪstɪks]	Statistik	Government ~ show that the UK's population will be bigger than Germany's by 2050.
	table [ˈteɪbl]	Tabelle	❗ **table** = 1. Tisch; 2. Tabelle
	detailed [ˈdiːteɪld]	ausführlich, detailliert	He drew a very ~ map of the way to his house.
	bar chart [ˈbɑː tʃɑːt]	Balkendiagramm	
	pie chart [ˈpaɪ tʃɑːt]	Tortendiagramm	a **bar chart** a **pie chart**
	(to) **make** sth. **up**	etwas bilden	Immigrants ~ **up** 2.8 % of Saxony's population. This book **is made up of** four units. (= besteht aus)
	percentage [pəˈsentɪdʒ]	Prozentsatz, prozentualer Anteil	What ~ of your pocket money do you spend on sweets? Ⓕ le pourcentage
	(to) **contrast** A **and/with** B [kənˈtrɑːst]	A mit B kontrastieren (= die Unterschiede aufzeigen)	❗ stress: **contr**a**st** *(verb)* [-ˈ-] If you ~ the town **and/with** the country, you'll find lots of differences.
	contrast (to/with sth., **between** two things**)** [ˈkɒntrɑːst]	Gegensatz (zu)	❗ stress: **c**o**ntrast** *(noun)* [ˈ--] **In ~ to** you, I'm not very clever.
	(to) **connect** A **with/to** B [kəˈnekt]	A mit B verbinden	We've ~ed our four computers in a network. = (to) link Ⓛ connectere
	connection [kəˈnekʃn]	Verbindung	Is there a direct ~ from Berlin to New York? = link Ⓛ connexio
	useful [ˈjuːsfl]	nützlich	
	(to) **conclude (**sth. **from** sth.**)** [kənˈkluːd]	(etwas aus etwas) schließen	The meeting ~d with a speech by our boss. **From** his accent, she ~d that he was German. **To ~**, … = Zum Schluss … Ⓕ conclure Ⓛ concludere
	conclusion [kənˈkluːʒn]	Schluss(folgerung)	We can **draw the ~** that … = Wir kommen zu dem Schluss, dass … Ⓕ la conclusion Ⓛ conclusio
p.11/P 3	**rainfall** [ˈreɪnfɔːl]	Niederschlag *(Regen)*; Regenfälle	

PART B Two Australian teenagers

p.12	**nowhere** [ˈnəʊweə]	nirgendwo(hin)	It's the only hotel. There's ~ else to stay. Jeannie lives miles away from the nearest town in **the middle of ~**. *(etwa: … am Ende der Welt)*
	honest [ˈɒnɪst]	ehrlich	❗ silent letter **h: h**onest [ˈɒnɪst] Be ~. Say what you really think. I **~ly** think … = Ich glaube, ehrlich gesagt, dass … Ⓕ honnête Ⓛ honestus

Englische Laute → S. 239 · Unregelmäßige Verben → S. 240–241 · Classroom English → S. 242–243

Vocabulary

	racing ['reɪsɪŋ]	Rennsport	car/motor/Formula 1/boat/motorbike ~ **!** If the word stands alone, it means **horse racing**.
	(to) race (sb./sth.) [reɪs]	(mit jm./etwas) um die Wette laufen/schwimmen/fahren/…	Let's ~ to that tree to see who's fastest.
	race [reɪs]	Rennen, (Wett-)Lauf	= a competition to see who is fastest
	dirt bike ['dɜːt baɪk]	Geländemotorrad	a **dirt bike**
	dirt [dɜːt]	Schmutz, Dreck	adjective: **dirty** – noun: **dirt**
	(to) attach (to) [əˈtætʃ]	anhängen, anheften (an) *(an Brief, Mail)*	You can ~ the photos and mail them to me. I'm ~ing some photos of Ashley's party. Ⓕ attacher (à)
p.14/P 1	(to) react (to/against sth.) [riˈækt]	reagieren (auf etwas)	noun: **reaction** – verb: (to) **react**
	(to) be on *(in the cinema, theatre, etc.)* [ɒn]	laufen *(im Kino, Theater usw.)*	What's ~ at the cinema this week?
p.15/P 2	wetsuit ['wetsuːt]	Nassanzug *(Tauch- oder Surfanzug)*	
	private ['praɪvət]	privat	**!** stress and pronunciation: **pr**i**vate** ['praɪvət] **private** ◄► **public**
p.15/P 3	tricky ['trɪki]	verzwickt, heikel	a **tricky** situation/problem/question
p.15/P 4	jealous (of) ['dʒeləs]	neidisch (auf); eifersüchtig (auf)	You get so much pocket money! I'm really ~. Sarah is really ~ **of** her baby brother. She thinks her parents love him more. Ⓕ jaloux, se

PART C   The Aboriginal people of Australia

p.16	(to) exist [ɪgˈzɪst]	existieren	Some people believe that life ~s on Mars. Ⓕ exister
	lizard ['lɪzəd]	Eidechse	a **lizard**
	track [træk]	Spur, Fährte; Pfad, Weg	The police followed the convict's ~ in the snow. I went along a ~ through the fields (= **path**).
	(to) make love	miteinander schlafen, sich lieben	(to) **make love** = (to) **have sex**
	(to) sink [sɪŋk], sank [sæŋk], sunk [sʌŋk]	sinken	The ship **is sinking**.
	cave [keɪv]	Höhle	Ⓕ la caverne Ⓛ cavus
	culture ['kʌltʃə]	Kultur	
	(to) respect sb./sth. (for sth.) [rɪˈspekt]	jn./etwas (wegen einer Sache) achten, respektieren	You are always honest, and I ~ you **for** that. Ⓕ respecter
	respect (for) [rɪˈspekt]	Achtung, Respekt (vor)	**With** ~ (= *Bei allem Respekt*), you're wrong.

Tipps zum Wörterlernen → S.126 · Alphabetisches Wörterverzeichnis → S.195–236 · Personen-, Orts- und Ländernamen → S.237–239

Vocabulary 1

p.17	**generation** [ˌdʒenəˈreɪʃn]	Generation	❗ stress: gener**a**tion [ˌ--'--]	Ⓕ la génération
	racist [ˈreɪsɪst]	rassistisch; Rassist/in		Ⓕ raciste; le/la raciste
	race [reɪs]	Rasse		Ⓕ la race
	ideal [aɪˈdiːəl]	Ideal, Idealvorstellung	❗ stress and pronunciation: id**ea**l [aɪˈdiːəl]	Ⓕ l'idéal (m)
	orphan [ˈɔːfən]	Waise, Waisenkind	= a child without living parents	Ⓕ l'orphelin,e Ⓛ orbus, orba
	(to) **run** sth. [rʌn], **ran** [ræn], **run**	etwas leiten (Hotel, Firma usw.)	My aunt ~s an old people's home (= Altenheim).	
	nun [nʌn]	Nonne		
	monk [mʌŋk]	Mönch		
	(to) **trick** sb. **into** doing sth. [trɪk]	jn. mit einer List / einem Trick dazu bringen, etwas zu tun	The thief ~ed the girl **into** opening the door.	
	(to) **trick** sb.	jn. austricksen, reinlegen	I saw he had ~ed me and I felt embarrassed.	
	truck [trʌk]	Lastwagen, LKW	a **truck**	
	mattress [ˈmætrəs]	Matratze	❗ stress: m**a**ttress ['--]	
	blanket [ˈblæŋkɪt]	Decke (zum Zudecken)		
	(to) **apologize (to** sb. **for** sth.) [əˈpɒlədʒaɪz]	sich (bei jm. für etwas) entschuldigen	= (to) say sorry He ~d for not writing sooner.	
	rabbit-proof [ˈræbɪt pruːf]	kaninchen-sicher, kaninchen-fest	Words with **-proof**: a **weatherproof/windproof/rainproof** jacket; a **waterproof** watch; a **fireproof** door; a **childproof** bottle	

PART D In the outback

p.20	**lonely** [ˈləʊnli]	einsam		
	heat [hiːt]	Hitze	adjective: **hot** – noun: **heat**	
	(to) **break down** [ˌbreɪk ˈdaʊn]	eine Panne haben; zusammenbrechen	We were late because our car **broke** ~. When she saw the accident, she **broke** ~ and cried.	
	(to) **crash (into** sth.**)** [kræʃ]	gegen etwas fahren/laufen; abstürzen	The car ~ed **into** a wall. The plane ~ed **into** a hill and 50 people died. My computer ~ed and I lost lots of work.	
p.21	**fly** [flaɪ]	Fliege	a **fly**	

Vocabulary

	(to) **fall asleep** [əˈsliːp]	einschlafen	The lesson was so boring that I almost **fell ~**.
	frightening [ˈfraɪtnɪŋ]	schrecklich, erschreckend	His face was so **~** that I went white with fear. The rate of skin cancer in Australia is **~**.
	(to) **frighten** [ˈfraɪtn]	verängstigen, erschrecken	Don't look at me like that: it **~s** me. I was **~ed** by a noise in the middle of the night.
	tin [tɪn]	Dose	You **eat** food that was in a **tin**: tuna, meat, vegetables, soup, beans, etc.
	can [kæn]	Dose	You **drink** drinks that were in a **can**.
	(to) **kneel (down)** [niːl], **knelt, knelt** [nelt]	sich hinknien	She went into the church, **knelt ~** and prayed.
	beside [bɪˈsaɪd]	neben	There's a shop **~** our house, on the right. = next to
p.22	**poison** [ˈpɔɪzn]	Gift	a **poisonous** snake Ⓕ le poison
	poisonous [ˈpɔɪzənəs]	giftig	Be careful! That snake could be **~**. If you eat **~** plants, you might die.
	salt [sɔːlt]	Salz	Too much **~** on your food is unhealthy.
	pepper [ˈpepə]	Pfeffer	Not enough **~** on your food is boring.
p.23	**nearby** [ˌnɪəˈbaɪ]	(adj) nahegelegen; (adv) in der Nähe	If you visit Berlin, you should also go to the **~** city of Potsdam. Our house is in a good location: there are parks, a school and lots of shops **~**. ❗ (not: in the near)
	apart from [əˈpɑːt]	außer	Everybody had finished **~ from** me: I was last. = except
	strength [streŋθ]	Kraft, Stärke	adjective: **strong** – noun: **strength**
	conscious (of sth.**)** [ˈkɒnʃəs]	(sich einer Sache) bewusst; bei Bewusstsein	We are **~ of** the problem and will solve it soon. Help, Jo's fallen from a tree. – Is he **~**? ❗ **conscious ◄► unconscious** (= bewusstlos) Ⓛ conscius
p.24	**literature** [ˈlɪtrətʃə]	Literatur	❗ stress: **li**terature [ˈ---]
	plot [plɒt]	Handlung	= the story in a play, book, film, etc.
	flashback [ˈflæʃbæk]	Rückblende	Many events in this film are not in order, but **~s**.
p.25	**setting** [ˈsetɪŋ]	Schauplatz	The **~** of the play is 11th-century Scotland.
	(to) **be set in** [set]	spielen in	*Marienhof* **is ~ in** Cologne but filmed in Munich.

Tipps zum Wörterlernen → S.126 · Alphabetisches Wörterverzeichnis → S.195–236 · Personen-, Orts- und Ländernamen → S.237–239

imagery [ˈɪmɪdʒəri]		Metaphorik	= language that creates pictures in your head and helps you to imagine things
image [ˈɪmɪdʒ]		Bild, Vorstellung	Whenever I hear a bell, I have an ~ of food in my head. Ⓕ l'image (f) Ⓛ imago
author [ˈɔːθə]		Autor/in	The narrator of *A prayer for Blue Delaney* is called Colm, but the ~ is Kirsty Murray.
metaphor [ˈmetəfə, ˈmetəfɔː]		Metapher	❗ stress: m**e**taphor [ˈ---]
easy-going [ˌiːzi ˈɡəʊɪŋ]		gelassen, unbeschwert	She never gets angry but is always very ~-~.
stupid [ˈstjuːpɪd]		blöd, dämlich	**stupid** ◄► **clever** Ⓕ stupide Ⓛ stupidus

Unit 2 – The road ahead

p.32	**ahead (of** sb./sth.**)** [əˈhed]	(jm./etwas) voraus	Darwin's ideas were ~ **of** his time.
	the road ahead	die Straße vor uns	
	A-level exams, A-levels *(pl)* [ˈeɪ ˌlevl]	*die höchsten Abschlussprüfungen des Schulsystems in England, Wales und Nordirland*	After he had passed his **A-levels** (*oder* **A-level exams**), he worked abroad for a year, then went to university. **A** = **advanced** [ədˈvɑːnst] (fortgeschritten)
	level [ˈlevl]	(Lern-)Stand, Niveau	What ~ is this course? – It's for beginners. The crime ~ in this city is very high.
	exam [ɪɡˈzæm]	Prüfung	She got good results in her ~s.
	qualification [ˌkwɒlɪfɪˈkeɪʃn]	Abschluss, Qualifikation	❗ stress: qualific**a**tion [ˌ---ˈ--] mostly plural: What ~s do you need for this job? Ⓕ la qualification
	university [ˌjuːnɪˈvɜːsəti]	Universität, Hochschule	The oldest **universities** in the UK are Oxford (1167) and Cambridge (1209).
	(to) inherit sth. **(from** sb.**)** [ɪnˈherɪt]	etwas (von jm.) erben	When his grandmother died, Peter ~ed £2,000,000 and a large house **from** her.
	fortune [ˈfɔːtʃuːn]	Vermögen; Glück	He made his ~ in the cotton industry. The king sent the prince away to seek his ~.
	(to) pass [pɑːs]	bestehen *(Test, Prüfung usw.)*	Did you ~ the test? – Yes, I got a B.
	scientist [ˈsaɪəntɪst]	Naturwissenschaftler/in	= someone who studies or has studied science

a **scientist**

Ⓕ le/la scientifique Ⓛ sciens

PART A Personality quiz: Where are you heading?

p.34	personality [ˌpɜːsəˈnæləti]	Persönlichkeit	Ⓕ la personnalité
	(to) head for/to/towards sth. [hed]	auf etwas zugehen, -fahren, -steuern	I was ~ing towards the bus when I realized I had forgotten my homework. Be careful with that old car: you're ~ing for an accident!
	stranger [ˈstreɪndʒə]	Unbekannte(r), Fremde(r)	Young children shouldn't speak to ~s. Ⓕ l'étranger, -ère
	strange [streɪndʒ]	fremd	It's easy to get lost in a ~ city. ❗ strange = 1. seltsam; 2. fremd
	Neither. [ˈnaɪðə, ˈniːðə]	Weder noch.	

neither – neither ... nor – not either

Which of your two sisters can speak French? – **Neither**.	Welche deiner Schwestern kann Französisch? – Keine der beiden.
Neither of my two sisters can speak French.	Keine meiner zwei Schwestern kann Französisch.
Neither Jane **nor** Sophie can speak French.	Weder Jane noch Sophie ...
Jane can't speak French, and **neither** can Sophie.	... und Sophie auch nicht.
Jane can't speak French, and Sophie **can't either**.	... und Sophie auch nicht.

	(to) be in charge of sth./sb. [tʃɑːdʒ]	für etwas/jn. verantwortlich sein; etwas leiten	When Mum's away, I'm in ~ of my little sisters. Who is in ~ of this project?
	Christmas [ˈkrɪsməs]	Weihnachten	We always stay at home at ~. = an/zu Weihnachten What presents did you get for ~? = zu Weihnachten

a **Christmas** tree

	(to) get sidetracked [ˈsaɪdtrækt]	abgelenkt werden	Our teacher stopped talking because he got ~ for a moment by a bird at the window.
	landline [ˈlændlaɪn]	Festnetzleitung	**landline** phone ◄► **mobile** phone
	(to) cancel sth. (BE: -ll-) [ˈkænsəl]	etwas absagen	The concert was ~led because of the rain. ❗ jm. absagen = (to) tell sb. you can't come
	civilization [ˌsɪvəlaɪˈzeɪʃn]	Zivilisation	❗ stress: **civilization** [ˌ---ˈ--]
p.35	confident [ˈkɒnfɪdənt]	selbstbewusst, (selbst)sicher	I felt ~ before the test because I'd revised well. My dad isn't ~ when he drives in strange cities. Ⓕ confident,e Ⓛ confidens
	energetic [ˌenəˈdʒetɪk]	dynamisch, tatkräftig, energisch	He's an active and ~ person who loves sport. Ⓕ énergique
	flexible [ˈfleksəbl]	flexibel, anpassungsfähig	I'll come whenever you want: I'm very ~.
	annoying [əˈnɔɪɪŋ]	ärgerlich, lästig	I find people who know everything very ~.
	(to) annoy [əˈnɔɪ]	ärgern, verärgern	It ~s me when people don't say hello.
	(to) be/get annoyed (with sb., about sth.)	sich ärgern (über jn./etwas)	I was ~ with my friend because he was so late. My dad often gets ~ about the government.

Vocabulary

at once [ət 'wʌns]	gleichzeitig, zugleich, auf einmal	Some women say men can't do two things **at ~**.
(to) give (sth.) **up** [ˌgɪv ˈʌp]	(etwas) aufgeben	Don't **~ up** yet, try again!
freedom ['friːdəm]	Freiheit	= liberty ❗ *If we talk about a specific case, we usually use the word* **freedom** *and not* **liberty**: freedom of speech, ~ of thought, ~ of expression, ~ of religion, ~ of information.
calm [kɑːm]	ruhig, still	Don't panic in an emergency: just **keep ~**. Ⓕ calme
anyone ['eniwʌn]	jede(r) (beliebige)	

any, anyone, etc.

The words **any**, **anyone**, etc. are

in questions:	Do you know **anybody** here? Would you like **anything** else to eat?	
in negative statements:	We're **not** going **anywhere** this summer: we're staying at home.	
They can also be used in positive statements:	You're wrong. **Anybody** can see that. I've finished my work. Now I can do **anything** I want. If I had enough money, I could go **anywhere**.	*Jeder Beliebige alles, egal was überall hin*
They are often used in *if*-clauses:	If I could choose **any** job, I'd be a fireman.	*irgendeinen*

(to) be keen to do sth., **on doing** sth. [kiːn]	wild darauf sein, etwas zu tun	I'm not very **~ on going / ~ to go** to the concert because there's a party on at the weekend.
punctual ['pʌŋktʃuəl]	pünktlich	You're late again. You must try to be more **~**.
logical ['lɒdʒɪkl]	logisch	a **~** person *(ein logisch denkender Mensch)* Ⓕ logique
technology [tekˈnɒlədʒi]	Technologie	❗ stress: **technology** [-'---]
practical ['præktɪkl]	praktisch	
(to) settle down [ˌsetl ˈdaʊn]	zur Ruhe kommen, sesshaft werden	OK, everybody, be quiet now and **~ down**! After a wild youth, he is **settling ~** now.
particular [pəˈtɪkjələ]	bestimmte(r, s), spezielle(r, s)	= specific Is there a **~** style of music you like? Ⓕ particulier, -ière
(to) mind sth. [maɪnd]	etwas dagegen haben	

(to) mind

You **won't mind** if they disagree.	Es wird dir nichts ausmachen, ...
I **don't mind helping** in our shop, but I hate having to get up so early.	Es macht mir nichts aus, ...
I'd like to ask you a few questions, **if you don't mind**.	..., wenn Sie nichts dagegen haben.
Do you mind if I open the window?	Stört es dich, ...
Would you mind waiting outside, please?	Würden Sie bitte draußen warten?

	necessary ['nesəsri]	notwendig, nötig	Water is ~ for life. You can phone me on my mobile if ~. ⓕ nécessaire ⓛ necessarius
	goal [gəʊl]	Ziel	= aim ❗ **goal** = 1. Tor *(im Sport)*; 2. Ziel
p.36/P 2	**interview** ['ɪntəvjuː]	Vorstellungsgespräch	❗ **interview** = 1. Interview *(TV, Zeitung usw.)* 2. Vorstellungsgespräch
	(to) **chew** [tʃuː]	kauen	After going to the dentist's I couldn't ~ for a day.
	(**chewing**) **gum** ['tʃuːɪŋ gʌm]	Kaugummi	I'm not eating, I'm just chewing ~. (= ... ich kaue Kaugummi.)
p.37/P 3	(to) **confirm** [kən'fɜːm]	bestätigen	Please ~ that you have received this e-mail. ⓕ confirmer ⓛ confirmare
	impolite [ˌɪmpə'laɪt]	unhöflich	= rude ⓕ impoli,e

Negative prefixes

A negative prefix in front of an adjective or participle changes the meaning to 'not ~' or 'the opposite of ~'. Most adjectives (mostly of German or French origin) use the prefix 'un-':

un- **unable, unafraid, unavailable, uncomfortable, unequal, unfair, unfriendly, unhappy, unimportant, unlucky, unpopular, unreal, unrealistic, unreliable, unsafe**
and adjectives formed from participles, e.g. **unintere**s**ting** or **unans**w**ered**.

Others (mostly of Latin origin) use 'in-': **inaccurate, incorrect, indirect, inexact, inexpensive**

❗ 'in-' changes to:

il- in front of the letter **l**: **illegal**
im- in front of the letter **p**: **impossible, imperfect, impersonal, impolite**
ir- in front of the letter **r**: **irregular**

❗ The stress is never on the prefix but stays on the same syllable as in the original adjective:
s**a**fe, uns**a**fe; **a**ble, un**a**ble; p**o**ssible, imp**o**ssible. This is different from German.

PART B A year abroad

p.38	**CV** [ˌsiː 'viː] (**curriculum vitae** [kəˌrɪkjələm 'viːtaɪ]) *(BE)*	Lebenslauf	= the history of your life that you send when you apply for a job
	résumé ['rezəmeɪ] *(AE)*	Lebenslauf	
	application [ˌæplɪ'keɪʃn]	Bewerbung	**letter of** ~ = Bewerbungsschreiben
	applicant ['æplɪkənt]	Bewerber/in	
	as [æz]	weil, da	= because
	valuable ['væljuəbl]	wertvoll; nützlich	This book only cost £1 but is far more ~ to me. Thank you, that was very ~ help.
	to date	bis heute	We need ten people to help with the party, but ~ ~ only six have volunteered.
	secondary school ['sekəndri]	weiterführende Schule	ⓕ l'école *(f)* secondaire
	primary school ['praɪməri] *(BE)*	Grundschule *in GB, von 4 oder 5 bis 11 Jahren*	= **elementary school** *(AE)* ⓕ l'école *(f)* primaire

Vocabulary

badge [bædʒ]	Abzeichen, Button	**badges**	
		a **button** (Knopf)	
basic ['beɪsɪk]	Grund-, grundlegend; einfach, elementar	the **Basic Law** of Germany = das Grundgesetz Sorry, my French is very ~: what does *ami* mean?	
written ['rɪtn]	schriftliche(r, s)	We're doing a three-hour ~ test in Maths tomorrow.	
spoken ['spəʊkn]	mündliche(r, s)	**Spoken** language is often more informal than written language.	
placement ['pleɪsmənt]	Praktikum	Students often do a ~ to get work experience.	
reference ['refrəns]	Referenz, Empfehlung	**!** stress: **reference** ['--] I got a ~ when my placement finished.	
request [rɪ'kwest]	Bitte, Wunsch	**on request** = auf Anfrage	
p.39 **candidate** ['kændɪdət]	Kandidat/in; Bewerber/in	**!** stress: **candidate** ['---] (F) le/la candidat,e (L) candidatus	
effective [ɪ'fektɪv]	effektiv, wirksam, wirkungsvoll	**!** stress: **effective** [-'--] noun: **effect** – adjective: **effective**	
employer [ɪm'plɔɪə]	Arbeitgeber/in	(F) l'employeur, -euse	
employee [ɪm'plɔɪiː]	Arbeitnehmer/in	(F) l'employé,e	
nationality [ˌnæʃə'næləti]	Staatsangehörigkeit, Nationalität	**!** stress: **nationality** [ˌ--'---] My parents **are** different **nationalities**. Dad's French and Mum's Canadian.	
suitable ['suːtəbl]	geeignet, passend	Jeans aren't ~ clothes for a job interview. Dress **suitably** when you go for a job interview.	
(to) deserve [dɪ'zɜːv]	verdienen *(zu Recht bekommen)*	**!** pronunciation: (to) **deserve** [dɪ'zɜːv]	
successful [sək'sesfəl]	erfolgreich		
achievement [ə'tʃiːvmənt]	Leistung, Errungenschaft	verb: (to) **achieve** – noun: **achievement**	
recent ['riːsnt]	jüngst, aktuell	Their most ~ CD was released last month. This news is very ~: the event happened a minute ago. (F) récent,e (L) recens	
recently ['riːsntli]	vor kurzem, kürzlich, neulich; in letzter Zeit	I met my old English teacher in London ~. I haven't done much sport ~. (F) récemment	
certificate [sə'tɪfɪkət]	Urkunde, Zeugnis, Bescheinigung	Do you get a ~ at the end of the course?	
award [ə'wɔːd]	Auszeichnung, Preis		
brief [briːf]	kurz (gefasst), knapp, von kurzer Dauer	Please be **brief**. = Fasse dich bitte kurz. He died after a ~ illness at the age of 23. (F) bref, brève (L) brevis	
membership (of sth.**)** ['membəʃɪp]	Mitgliedschaft (in etwas)	What does ~ **of** the golf club cost?	

responsibility (for) [rɪˌspɒnsəˈbɪləti]	Verantwortung (für)	The car driver **took ~ for** the accident. *(übernahm die Verantwortung)* (F) la responsabilité
responsible (for) [rɪˈspɒnsəbl]	verantwortlich (für)	(F) responsable
driving licence [ˈdraɪvɪŋ ˌlaɪsəns]	Führerschein, Fahrerlaubnis	In the UK you can have a **driving ~** for a car at the age of 17.
foreign [ˈfɒrɪn]	ausländisch	a **~ language** = eine Fremdsprache
foreigner [ˈfɒrɪnə]	Ausländer/in	
intermediate [ˌɪntəˈmiːdiət]	Mittel-; für fortgeschrittene Anfänger/innen	My mum did a Polish course for beginners last year, and this year she'll do the **~** course.
positive [ˈpɒzətɪv]	positiv	Jenny is always happy and has a very **~** attitude. ❗ stress: **p**o**sitive** [ˈ---]
negative [ˈnegətɪv]	negativ	❗ stress: **n**e**gative** [ˈ---] **negative** ◀▶ **positive**
(to) avoid [əˈvɔɪd]	vermeiden	This area is dangerous and should be **~ed**.
spelling [ˈspelɪŋ]	Rechtschreibung	Some peeple make lots of misstakes with there spelling.
format [ˈfɔːmæt]	Format	❗ stress: **format** [ˈ--]
font [fɒnt]	Schrift(art)	Times, *Shelley Script* and **STENCIL** are all **~s**.
bold (type) [ˌbəʊld ˈtaɪp]	Fettdruck	To show a word is important, print it in **~**.
p.40 **formal** [ˈfɔːml]	formell, förmlich	❗ stress: **formal** [ˈ--]
informal [ɪnˈfɔːml]	informell; umgangssprachlich	**formal** ◀▶ **informal**
typical (of) [ˈtɪpɪkl]	typisch (für)	❗ That's **typical of** you = Das ist typisch **für** dich.
opportunity [ˌɒpəˈtjuːnəti]	Gelegenheit, Chance, Möglichkeit	(F) l'opportunité (f) (L) opportunitas

German „Möglichkeit"

There are several ways to translate the word „Möglichkeit".

The word **possibility** is used when „Möglichkeit" means „nicht sicher, unwahrscheinlich".

There is a	**possibility**	of snow in May, but it's very unlikely.
Is there a	**possibility**	of seeing the Queen when we go to London?
Have you thought about the	**possibility**	that I might be right?

German learners often use **possibility** too much. If „Möglichkeit" means „Gelegenheit, Zeit", we can use **chance** or **opportunity** (**opportunity** is a little more formal).

Did you find the	**chance/opportunity**	of finishing / to finish	your book?
My dad says he has a better	**chance/opportunity**	of getting / to get	a job if he moves abroad.
I have been given the	**chance/opportunity**	of going / to go	to Australia for a year.

If „Möglichkeit" means „Art und Weise", we can also use **way**.

There are several	**ways**	of translating / to translate	„Möglichkeit".
There's no other	**way**	of solving / to solve	this problem.

electrical engineer [ɪˌlektrɪkəl ˌendʒɪˈnɪə]	Elektrotechniker/in
(to) remember doing sth. [rɪˈmembə]	sich daran erinnern, etwas getan zu haben

Vocabulary

Same verb, different meaning

Some verbs can be used with the gerund *and* the infinitive, but the meaning is different:

Please **remember to buy** water tomorrow.	Denk daran, morgen Wasser zu kaufen.
I **remember buying** it, but I left it in the shop.	Ich erinnere mich daran, dass ich es gekauft habe, ...
Don't **forget to visit** John tomorrow.	Vergiss nicht, morgen John zu besuchen.
I'll never **forget visiting** John for the first time.	Ich werde nie vergessen, wie ich John zum ersten Mal besucht habe.
I think you should **stop buying** so many CDs.	Ich denke, du solltest aufhören, so viele CDs zu kaufen.
Look, a petrol station: let's **stop to buy** some drinks.	Guck, eine Tankstelle: halten wir an, um Getränke zu kaufen.
The phone rang but Pete **went on reading.**	Das Telefon klingelte, aber Pete las weiter.
After finishing the *Harry Potter* series, Pete **went on to read** a book by Philip Pullman.	... las er dann (als Nächstes) ein Buch von Philip Pullman.
If you can't play an instrument, **try singing**.	..., probiere es mal mit Singen.
I **tried to sing** the song but had forgotten the words.	Ich versuchte, das Lied zu singen ...

grateful ['greɪtfl]		dankbar	Thank you: I'm very ~ to you all for your help.
interest ['ɪntrəst]		Interesse	verb: (to) **interest** – noun: **interest**
community [kə'mjuːnəti]		Gemeinde, Gemeinschaft	The Asian ~ makes up 4% of the UK population. MySpace and Facebook are online **communities**. Ⓕ la communauté Ⓛ communitas
by asking		indem du fragst	I got his number **by looking** on the internet. *(indem ich gesucht habe; durch Suchen)* **learning by doing** = Lernen durch Handeln/Tun
p.41/P 1	**orchestra** ['ɔːkɪstrə]	Orchester	❗ stress: <u>orchestra</u> ['---]

	advertisement [əd'vɜːtɪsmənt, AE: ˌædvə'taɪzmənt] *(infml:* **ad** [æd]*, BE auch:* **advert** ['ædvɜːt]*)*	Anzeige, Inserat; *(im Fernsehen)* Werbespot	You find job ~s in newspapers or on the internet. Lots of people change channels during the ~**s**.
	(to) **advertise** ['ædvətaɪz]	Werbung machen (für); inserieren	❗ English: (to) **advertise** clothes/cars/furniture German: **für** Kleidung/Autos/Möbel **werben**
	advertising ['ædvətaɪzɪŋ] *(no pl)*	Werbung	The company spends millions on ~ so that people will buy their products.
	advertiser ['ædvətaɪzə]	Inserent/in; Werbekunde/-kundin	
	(to) **enclose** [ɪn'kləʊz]	etwas *(einem Brief)* beilegen	I **enclose** my CV. *or* My CV **is enclosed**.
p.42/P 3	**mind** [maɪnd]	Verstand, Kopf	Grandpa is very old but his ~ is still very active.
p.42/P 4	**likes and dislikes** *(pl)* ['dɪslaɪks]	Vorlieben und Abneigungen	Finding out about a person's ~ **and** ~ is a good way to get to know them.

Englische Laute → S. 239 · Unregelmäßige Verben → S. 240–241 · Classroom English → S. 242–243

	(to) **fancy** sth. ['fænsi] (infml)	Lust auf/zu etwas haben	Do you ~ going to a gig tonight?
p.42/P 5	**committee** [kə'mɪti]	Ausschuss, Komitee	! spelling: co**mm**i**tt**ee

Collective nouns („Sammelnamen")

Collective nouns like *band*, *class* and *family* describe a *group of people*.

After a **collective noun** in the *singular*, the **verb** can be in the *singular* or the *plural* without much difference in meaning.

The orchestra **is** very good.
The orchestra **are** very good.

Examples:

band	My favourite band **is/are** Coldplay. *also:* Coldplay **is/are** my favourite band.	**family**	My family **doesn't/don't** live in London any more.
class	9 GE **is/are** probably the best class in the school.	**government**	The government **looks/look** after the population very well.
club	The drama club **is/are** looking for actors. *also:* Spurs **is/are** the best club in England.	**group**	A group of teenagers **was/were** standing in front of the building.
committee	What **has/have** the committee decided to do?	**staff**	The staff **doesn't/don't** earn much.
		team	The team **hopes/hope** to win.

We use a singular verb if we mean the group as a *whole group*:

The orchestra **has played** five times in four days and **is flying** home tomorrow.

We use a plural verb if we mean the *members of the group*:

The orchestra **have picked up** their instruments and **are leaving** the theatre.

p.43/P 6	**table of contents** ['kɒntents]	Inhaltsverzeichnis	The **table of ~** is usually at the front of a book ...
	index ['ɪndeks]	Index, Register	... and the ~ is usually at the back.

PART C   The business: A reality TV show

p.44	(to) **impress** [ɪm'pres]	beeindrucken	Ⓕ impressionner Ⓛ imprimere
	weakness ['wi:knəs]	Schwäche, Schwachpunkt	A typical interview question is 'What are your strengths and **~es**?'
	assessment [ə'sesmənt]	Einschätzung, Beurteilung	Here is my ~ of the situation: ...
	(to) **assess** [ə'ses]	einschätzen, beurteilen	Interviewers try to ~ a candidate's qualities.
	sheet [ʃi:t]	Blatt, Bogen (Papier)	**sheets** of paper
p.45/P 1	**visual aids** (pl) [ˌvɪʒuəl_'eɪdz]	Anschauungsmaterialien	a **video projector** a **slide**
	transparency [træns'pærənsi]	Folie	
	overhead projector, OHP [ˌəʊvəhed prə'dʒektə, ˌəʊ_ˌeɪtʃ 'pi:]	Tageslichtprojektor, Polylux	
	video projector ['vɪdiəʊ prə'dʒektə]	Videoprojektor, Beamer	! 'beamer' does not exist in English
	slide [slaɪd]	Folie (bei Präsentationsprogrammen)	a **transparency** an **OHP**

Vocabulary

(to) **focus (on)** ['fəʊkəs]	sich konzentrieren (auf)	You're getting sidetracked again. Try to ~!	
focus ['fəʊkəs]	Schwer-, Mittel-, Hauptpunkt	The ~ of tomorrow's lesson will be grammar.	
audience ['ɔːdɪəns]	Zuschauer/innen, Zuhörer/innen, Publikum	At the end of the concert, the ~ stood up and clapped for five minutes. (F) l'audience (f) (L) audiens	
one by one	eins nach dem anderen	I explained my reasons slowly and ~ by ~.	

PART D How to be a teenage millionaire

p.46	(to) **earn (money)** [ɜːn]	(Geld) verdienen	! verdienen = 1. (to) **deserve** (what you should get) 2. (to) **earn** (what you actually get)
	(to) **vote** [vəʊt]	zur Wahl gehen, wählen	Only 23 % of the population ~d in the elections. (F) voter
			! (to) **vote for** sb. = für jn. stimmen
	design [dɪˈzaɪn]	Muster, Entwurf; Design, Gestaltung	This website has free ~s for dresses and skirts. After school he wants to study ~ at art college.
	within [wɪˈðɪn]	innerhalb (von)	We were asked to finish our project ~ four weeks, but I had already done it after one day.
p.47	(to) **trust** [trʌst]	trauen, vertrauen	He isn't honest, you know. You can't ~ him at all.
	adviser [ədˈvaɪzə]	Berater/in	The president has many ~s to help him.
	(to) **advise** sb. [ədˈvaɪz]	jn. beraten	! (to) **advise** sb. **to do** sth. = jm. raten, etwas zu tun
	advice (no pl) [ədˈvaɪs]	Rat, Ratschlag, Ratschläge	Take my ~: go and see a doctor. (Hör auf meinen Rat: …) ! She gave me **some** / <u>lots of</u> / <u>a piece of</u> advice. Never: She gave me ~~an advice~~ / lots of ~~advices~~.
	set [set]	Reihe, Set, Satz	
	minimum [ˈmɪnɪməm]	Minimum	Will says he needs **a ~ of** (= at least) £100 pocket money a month to survive.
	maximum [ˈmæksɪməm]	Maximum	Will's parents say their ~ is £40.
	ambition [æmˈbɪʃn]	Ehrgeiz	My ~ is to be a famous author. (F) l'ambition (f) (L) ambitio
	ambitious [æmˈbɪʃəs]	ehrgeizig	Her dad is very ~ for her and helps her a lot. (F) ambitieux, -euse (L) ambitiosus
	determination [dɪˌtɜːmɪˈneɪʃn]	Entschlossenheit	We admired his ~ to beat his illness. (F) la détermination
	determined [dɪˈtɜːmɪnd]	(fest) entschlossen	Nothing will stop me: I am ~ to win.
	faith (in sth./sb.**)** [feɪθ]	Vertrauen (in jn./etwas); Glaube	I have no ~ in you: I don't trust you at all. Do you have a ~? – Yes, I'm Jewish.
	stressful [ˈstresfl]	anstrengend, stressig	Having a bath is nice at the end of a ~ day.
	definite [ˈdefɪnət]	fest, bestimmt; endgültig, eindeutig	Have you got any ~ plans for the future? I need a ~ answer by tomorrow. (L) definitus
p.48	**artistic** [ɑːˈtɪstɪk]	künstlerisch	! He's **artistic**. (Er ist künstlerisch begabt.) nouns: **art** (Kunst), **artist** (Künstler/in) – adjective: **artistic** (F) artistique

Englische Laute → S.239 · Unregelmäßige Verben → S.240–241 · Classroom English → S.242–243

greedy ['gri:di]	gierig; habgierig	A ~ person wants more food or money than they really need.	
formula ['fɔ:mjələ]	Formel	The ~ to work out the area of a circle is πr^2.	
role model ['rəʊl ˌmɒdl]	Vorbild	Doctors who smoke are bad ~ **models**.	

Unit 3 – Life in the big city

p.50	**ancient** ['eɪnʃənt]	antik; alt	the ~ world, ~ cities, in ~ Rome, ~ history
	modern ['mɒdn]	modern	❗ stress: m**o**dern ['--]
	waste [weɪst]	Abfall	❗ waste = 1. Verschwendung; 2. Abfall
	epidemic [ˌepə'demɪk]	Epidemie	Over 50 million people all over the world died in the flu ~ of 1918–1919.
	(to) attract [ə'trækt]	anziehen, anlocken	I was first ~**ed** to her by her smile. London ~**s** millions of tourists every year. Ⓛ attrahere
	attractive [ə'træktɪv]	attraktiv, verlockend	She looks nice and has a very ~ personality too.
	progress *(no pl)* ['prəʊgres]	Fortschritt(e)	My teacher says I have made good ~ since I started learning the piano.
	urban ['ɜ:bən]	städtisch, Stadt-	**Urban** planners think about the future of towns and cities. Ⓕ urbain,e Ⓛ urbanus
	rural ['rʊərəl]	ländlich, Land-	**rural** ◄► **urban** Ⓕ rural,e
	growth [grəʊθ]	Wachstum, Zunahme	We need to plan the ~ of big cities. The ~ of air transport is a big environmental problem.
	inhabitant [ɪn'hæbɪtənt]	Einwohner/in, Bewohner/in	Bristol is a city of over 400,000 ~**s**. The most famous ~ of Berlin Zoo is called Knut. Ⓕ l'habitant,e Ⓛ inhabitantes *(pl)*
	(to) inhabit [ɪn'hæbɪt]	bewohnen, leben in	Before the arrival of the English colonists, Massachusetts was ~**ed** by the Wampanoag.
	developing country [dɪ'veləpɪŋ]	Entwicklungsland	

PART A   Hong Kong: Full speed ahead

p.52	**global** ['gləʊbl]	weltweit, Welt-	One of the biggest environmental problems is ~ **warming** *(Erwärmung der Erdatmosphäre)*. Ⓕ global,e
	life expectancy ['laɪf_ɪkˌspektənsi]	Lebenserwartung	The ~ ~ of women is usually higher than men's.
	drug [drʌg]	Droge; Medikament	He doesn't smoke, drink alcohol or take ~**s**. Scientists have found a new ~ for AIDS.
	in the **mid**-1800s [mɪd]	Mitte des 19. Jahrhunderts	He's in his ~-forties = Er ist Mitte vierzig. in the ~-1970s = Mitte der 70er Jahre ~-June = Mitte Juni

Vocabulary

Religions

Religion	Person	Adjective	Building
Buddhism [ˈbʊdɪzm]	**Buddhist** [ˈbʊdɪst]	Buddhist	temple [ˈtempl]
Christianity [ˌkrɪstiˈænəti]	**Christian** [ˈkrɪstʃən]	Christian	church, chapel [ˈtʃæpl]
Hinduism [ˈhɪndu:ɪzm]	**Hindu** [ˈhɪndu:]	Hindu	temple
Islam [ˈɪzlɑ:m]	**Muslim** [ˈmʊzlɪm]	Muslim	mosque
Judaism [ˈdʒu:deɪɪzm]	**Jew** [dʒu:]	Jewish	synagogue
Taoism [ˈtaʊɪzm]	**Taoist** [ˈtaʊɪst]	Taoist	temple
atheism [ˈeɪθi:ɪzəm]	**atheist** [ˈeɪθi:ɪst]	**atheistic** [ˌeɪθiˈɪstɪk]	

possession [pəˈzeʃən] — Besitz; Eigentum — France used to have many ~s in northern Africa. The family lost all their ~s in the fire. Ⓕ la possession Ⓛ possessio

powerful [ˈpaʊəfl] — mächtig, einflussreich; stark, kräftig — Bill Gates is a rich and ~ man. Pavarotti had a beautiful and ~ voice.

  power [ˈpaʊə] — Macht; Stärke — A new government came to ~ after the election. Electric cars don't have the ~ to drive very fast.

agreement [əˈgri:mənt] — Abkommen, Vertrag — The two sides worked out an ~ to end the war.

(to) govern [ˈgʌvən] — regieren — After the war, Germany was at first ~ed by Britain, the USA, France and Russia. Ⓕ gouverner Ⓛ gubernare

(to) trade (in sth.**)** [treɪd] — Handel (mit etwas) treiben — He became rich by ~ing in slaves.

(to) support [səˈpɔ:t] — unterstützen, befürworten

official [əˈfɪʃl] — amtlich, Amts- — Canada's ~ languages are English and French. ❗ stress: off**i**cial [-ˈ--] Ⓕ officiel, le Ⓛ officialis

dialect [ˈdaɪəlekt] — Dialekt, Mundart — = a form of a language where words, grammar and pronunciation can be different ❗ stress: **di**alect [ˈ---] Ⓕ le dialecte

port [pɔ:t] — (Handels-)Hafen, Hafen(stadt) — Rotterdam is one of the biggest ~s in Europe. Ⓕ le port Ⓛ portus

finance (no pl) [ˈfaɪnæns] — Geld; Finanzwesen — We need to get some ~ for our new project. Wall Street is the centre of global ~.

  financial [faɪˈnænʃl] — finanziell, Finanz- — ❗ stress: fin**a**ncial [-ˈ--] Ⓕ financier, -ère

magnet [ˈmægnət] — Magnet — ❗ stress: **ma**gnet [ˈ--]

p.53 **energy** [ˈenədʒi] — Energie, Kraft — Wind ~ is very good for the environment. Ⓕ l'énergie (f)

p.54 **tuition** [tjuˈɪʃn] — (Nachhilfe-)Unterricht — My Latin marks were so bad that I need extra ~.

p.55/P 1 **polluted** [pəˈlu:tɪd] — verseucht, verunreinigt

a **polluted** river
Ⓕ pollué, e
Ⓛ pollutus

suburb [ˈsʌbɜ:b] — Vorort — It's so noisy in the town centre that my parents have decided to move to a ~. Ⓛ suburbium

poverty [ˈpɒvəti] — Armut — poverty ◄► wealth Ⓕ la pauvreté Ⓛ paupertas

Englische Laute → S.239 · Unregelmäßige Verben → S.240–241 · Classroom English → S.242–243

PART B Johannesburg: city of contrasts

p.56	(to) **unite (with** sb./sth.**)** [juːˈnaɪt]	sich (mit jm./etwas) vereinigen, vereinen	The thirteen colonies ~d to form the USA. *F* unir
	economic [ˌiːkəˈnɒmɪk]	wirtschaftliche(r, s); Wirtschafts-	Can the government solve our ~ problems? *F* économique
	economy [ɪˈkɒnəmi]	(Volks-)Wirtschaft, Ökonomie	*F* l'économie *(f)*
	(to) **result in** sth. [rɪˈzʌlt]	zu etwas führen, etwas zur Folge haben	The war ~ed in millions of deaths.
	oppressive [əˈpresɪv]	repressiv, unterdrückerisch	We can't support ~ governments. *F* oppressif, ve
	(to) **separate** [ˈsepəreɪt]	trennen	! adjective: **separate** [ˈseprət] [´--] – verb: (to) **separate** [ˈsepəreɪt] [´---] *F* séparer *L* separare
	uprising [ˈʌpraɪzɪŋ]	Aufstand	A small ~ can result in a revolution.
	(to) **educate** [ˈedʒukeɪt]	unterrichten, erziehen; aufklären	She was ~d at the University of Oxford. The aim of the flyer is to ~ the public about the dangers of AIDS. *F* éduquer *L* educare
	rapid [ˈræpɪd]	rapide, schnell	

English 'so' = German „auch"

John **is** very clever.	So **is** Peter.	
He**'s got** a lovely flat.	So **has** Peter.	
He **can** speak lots of languages.	So **can** Peter.	
He **earns** quite a lot of money.	So **does** Peter.	Peter auch.
He **has been** to the USA.	So **has** Peter.	
He **went** to New York.	So **did** Peter.	
He **would like** to visit Cuba.	So **would** Peter.	

| | **security** [sɪˈkjʊərəti] | Sicherheit(svorkehrungen) | *L* securitas |

„Sicherheit"

They'll be safe if they stay in the car.   A **security** check at the airport

safety = Sicherheit *(das Sichersein vor Gefahr)*   **security** = Sicherheit, Sicherheitsvorkehrungen

| | **overseas** [ˌəʊvəˈsiːz] | ausländisch; im Ausland | Lots of ~ visitors are expected at the Olympics. I don't know where he lives: somewhere ~. ! *The adj* **overseas** *sounds nicer than* **foreign**. |

Tipps zum Wörterlernen → S.126 · Alphabetisches Wörterverzeichnis → S.195–236 · Personen-, Orts- und Ländernamen → S.237–239

Vocabulary

p.57	**imaginable** [ɪˈmædʒɪnəbl]	vorstellbar	I looked in every ~ place but couldn't find it. ❗ the best song **imaginable** = das beste Lied, das man sich vorstellen kann: *When used with a superlative,* **imaginable** *comes* **after** *the noun.*
	welcoming [ˈwelkəmɪŋ]	(gast)freundlich	My host family was very ~ when I arrived.
	(to) treat [triːt]	behandeln	Minority cultures should be ~ed with respect. Ⓕ traiter Ⓛ tractare
	thunderstorm [ˈθʌndəstɔːm]	Gewitter	There are lots of ~s here in the summer.
	the fearless [ˈfɪələs]	die Furchtlosen	
	prostitute [ˈprɒstɪtjuːt]	Prostituierte(r)	
	(to) mug (-gg-) [mʌg]	überfallen	He was ~ged on his way home from the cinema.
	(to) party *(infml)* [ˈpɑːti]	feiern	Jan's birthday was so cool: we **partied** all night.
p.58	**disposable** [dɪˈspəʊzəbl]	Einweg-, Wegwerf-	You have to keep a pair of ~ gloves in your car.
p.59 /P 1	**law** *(no pl)* [lɔː]	Jura, Rechtswissenschaften	She wants to study ~ in Paris. ❗ **law** = 1. Gesetz; 2. Jura
	campaign [kæmˈpeɪn]	Kampagne	
	(to) free [friː]	freilassen	He was ~d from prison after ten years.
	democracy [dɪˈmɒkrəsi]	Demokratie	❗ stress: **dem**o**cr**acy [-ˈ---] Ⓕ la démocratie
	democrat [ˈdeməkræt]	Demokrat/in	❗ stress: **dem**ocrat [ˈ---] Ⓕ le/la démocrate
	democratic [ˌdeməˈkrætɪk]	demokratisch	Ⓕ démocratique

Different forms of government

Name:		The power is with:
absolute monarchy [ˈmɒnəki]		a **monarch** [ˈmɒnək], who has absolute power
anarchy [ˈænəki]		no one
constitutional monarchy [ˌkɒnstɪˈtjuːʃənl]		a monarch (but with little power)
democracy		the citizens
dictatorship [dɪkˈteɪtəʃɪp]		a single person, a **dictator** [dɪkˈteɪtə]
junta [ˈdʒʌntə, ˈhʊntə]		the army
oligarchy [ˈɒlɪgɑːki]		a small number of people
plutocracy [pluːˈtɒkrəsi]		the rich people
theocracy [θiˈɒkrəsi]		religious leaders

	(to) retire [rɪˈtaɪə]	sich zurückziehen; in den Ruhestand gehen	At the age of 32, he ~d from the national team. Most people ~ when they are about 65.
p.59 /P 2	**professor** [prəˈfesə]	Professor/in	❗ 'Professor' stands alone as a title: Herr Professor Schwarz = ~~Mr~~ **Professor** Schwarz
p.59 /P 3	**memorial (to** sb./sth.**)** [məˈmɔːriəl]	Denkmal (für jn./etwas)	Nelson's Column in London is a ~ to Admiral Horatio Nelson, 1758–1805.
	tap [tæp]	Wasserhahn	a **tap**
	dusty [ˈdʌsti]	staubig	noun: **dust** – adjective: **dusty**
p.60 /P 4	**hunger** [ˈhʌŋgə]	Hunger	adjective: **hungry** – noun: **hunger**

Englische Laute → S. 239 · Unregelmäßige Verben → S. 240–241 · Classroom English → S. 242–243

Vocabulary

	nature ['neɪtʃə]	Natur	❗ stress: **na**ture ['--] (F) la nature Er ist gerne in der Natur. = He likes to be outside. *Not*: He likes to be ~~in the nature~~.
	trend [trend]	Mode, Trend	It costs a lot of money to follow the latest **~s**.
p. 60/P 5	**witness (to** sth.**)** ['wɪtnəs]	Zeuge, Zeugin (für/von etwas)	The police are looking for **~s to** the accident.
	at once [ət 'wʌns]	sofort	= immediately ❗ **at once** = 1. gleichzeitig; 2. sofort
	control [kən'trəʊl]	Kontrolle	under **~**, out of **~**, (to) lose **~** (F) le contrôle
p. 61/P 6	**(to) summarize** ['sʌməraɪz]	zusammenfassen	Can you **~** the main points of the book?
	(to) get sth. **across (to** sb.**)** [ə'krɒs]	(jm.) etwas rüberbringen/klarmachen	I tried hard to **get** it **~ to** her that she was wrong, but she refused to understand.
	tone of voice [təʊn]	Ton(fall)	He said 'OK', but from his **~ of ~** he meant 'No'.
	(to) stress [stres]	betonen	❗ noun: **stress** – verb: (to) **stress**
	posh [pɒʃ]	vornehm, edel *(etwas abwertend)*	Your mum has a Rolls-Royce? Very **~**!
	lady ['leɪdi]	Dame	
	gentleman ['dʒentlmən], *pl* **-men** ['dʒentlmən]	Herr	**Ladies** and **gentlemen** = Meine Damen und Herren
	childhood ['tʃaɪldhʊd]	Kindheit	We've known each other since our **~**.

PART C   Mumbai: people of the city

p. 62	**steady** ['stedi]	stetig	The police are making slow but **~** progress and are hoping to find the criminal soon.
	(to) experience [ɪk'spɪəriəns]	erfahren, erleben	Have you ever **~d** bullying at school?
	common ['kɒmən]	weit verbreitet, häufig	The most **~** name for baby boys in the UK today is Jack. (L) communis
	office ['ɒfɪs]	Büro	
	office worker ['ɒfɪs ˌwɜːkə]	Büroangestellte(r)	
	billion ['bɪliən]	Milliarde (1 000 000 000)	❗ stress: **bi**llion ['--] a **billion** people = one thousand million people
	trillion ['trɪliən]	Billion (1 000 000 000 000)	a **trillion** dollars = one million million dollars
	a sixth [sɪksθ]	ein Sechstel	❗ *Fast alle Bruchteile sind von der Schreibweise mit den Ordinalzahlen identisch, z. B.:* **third**: dritte(r, s) – a **third**: ein Drittel **fifth**: fünfte(r, s) – a **fifth**: ein Fünftel *Die Ausnahmen:* **second**: zweite(r, s) – a **half**: eine Hälfte **fourth**: vierte(r, s) – a **quarter**: ein Viertel
p. 63	**squatter** ['skwɒtə]	Haus-, Landbesetzer/in	Empty houses in cities are attractive to **~s**.
	(to) occupy ['ɒkjupaɪ]	besetzen	The seat was **occupied** by the biggest man I had ever seen. (F) occuper (L) occupare
	ceiling ['siːlɪŋ]	(Zimmer-)Decke	The **~** in this room is 3.5 metres high. (L) caelum
	landlord ['lændlɔːd], **landlady** ['lændleɪdi]	Vermieter/in	Mum's phoning the **~** because there's no hot water in our flat.

Tipps zum Wörterlernen → S. 126 · Alphabetisches Wörterverzeichnis → S. 195–236 · Personen-, Orts- und Ländernamen → S. 237–239

Vocabulary

concrete [ˈkɒŋkriːt]	Beton, Beton-	! stress: **c**oncrete [ˈ--]
cell [sel]	Zelle	a prison ~, a monk's ~, a nun's ~
perhaps [pəˈhæps]	vielleicht	= maybe
kind [kaɪnd]	freundlich	It was **kind** of you to offer to help, thanks.
fan [fæn]	Ventilator	! **fan** = 1. Anhänger/in; 2. Ventilator
mosquito [mɒsˈkiːtəʊ]	Stechmücke, Moskito	a **mosquito**
upper-class [ˌʌpəˈklɑːs]	der Oberschicht zugehörig, vornehm, edel	
neighbourhood *(BE)*, **neighborhood** *(AE)* [ˈneɪbəhʊd]	Gegend, Stadtbereich, Nachbarschaft	We live in the same ~, but we've never spoken.
bucket [ˈbʌkɪt]	Eimer	a **bucket**
rush [rʌʃ]	Ansturm	As soon as the doors opened, there was a ~ for the places nearest the stage.
(to) bathe [beɪð] *(bes. AE)*	baden *(sich waschen)*	= BE (to) have a bath
underwear *(no pl)* [ˈʌndəweə]	Unterwäsche	= clothes you <u>wear</u> <u>under</u> your other clothes
(to) manage a problem [ˈmænɪdʒ]	mit einem Problem umgehen, ein Problem lösen	The government needs to decide how to ~ the economic crisis.
p.64 **besides** [bɪˈsaɪdz]	außer	**Besides** the clothes I'm wearing, I own nothing. ! **besides** = 1. außerdem; 2. außer
balcony [ˈbælkəni]	Balkon	! stress: **b**alcony [ˈ---]
sheet [ʃiːt]	Laken	! **sheet** = 1. Blatt (Papier); 2. Laken
single bed [ˌsɪŋglˈbed]	Einzelbett	sheet — single bed — double bed — **duvet** [ˈduːveɪ] or **quilt** [kwɪlt]
palm tree [pɑːm]	Palme	! silent letter **l**: pa**l**m [pɑːm]
coconut [ˈkəʊkənʌt]	Kokosnuss	
(to) matter [ˈmætə]	wichtig sein	Money **matters** to me. = It's important to me. It doesn't **matter** any more. = Es ist jetzt egal.
scent [sent]	Duft	! silent letter **c**: **s**cent [sent] = an attractive smell
p.65 **air conditioning** *(no pl)* [ˈeə kənˌdɪʃnɪŋ]	Klimatisierung, Klimaanlage	Does your car have **air conditioning**? *(not: ... ~~a~~ air conditioning)*

Englische Laute → S.239 · Unregelmäßige Verben → S.240–241 · Classroom English → S.242–243

3–4 Vocabulary

	horizon [həˈraɪzn]	Horizont	**!** stress: ho**ri**zon [-ˈ--]
	muddy [ˈmʌdi]	schlammig, matschig	
	mud [mʌd]	Schlamm, Matsch	mud
	pond [pɒnd]	Teich	Our neighbour has built a little ~ for his fish. She works across the ~ now, in New York.
	judge [dʒʌdʒ]	Richter/in	Ⓕ le/la juge Ⓛ iudex a **judge**
	fancy [ˈfænsi]	schick, ausgefallen *(etwas abwertend)*	
	(to) **stare (at** sb./sth.**)** [steə]	(jn./etwas an)starren	You mustn't ~ at people. It's rude.
p.66/P 2	**commuter** [kəˈmjuːtə]	Pendler/in	Many ~s live in the suburbs and travel to work in the city centre.
	destination [ˌdestɪˈneɪʃn]	(Reise-)Ziel	At the border, we were asked what our final ~ was. Ⓕ la déstination
p.67/P 3	**beggar** [ˈbegə]	Bettler/in	**!** spelling: begg**a**r
	(to) **beg** [beg]	betteln	
p.67/P 5	**travel guide** [ˈtrævl gaɪd]	Reiseführer *(Buch)*	I could lend you a ~ **guide** for your trip to Paris.
	(to) **fascinate** [ˈfæsəneɪt]	faszinieren	Work fascinates me. I can sit and look at it for hours.
p.69/P 8	**column** [ˈkɒləm]	Spalte	**!** column = 1. Säule; 2. Spalte Ⓕ la colonne Ⓛ columna

Unit 4 – Teen world

PART A   Mobile life and love

p.80	**behaviour** [bɪˈheɪvjə]	Verhalten, Benehmen	He used to make trouble in class but his ~ is improving now.
	(to) **behave** [bɪˈheɪv]	sich verhalten, sich benehmen	He ~d as if he hadn't seen me. **Behave** yourself, or you can go to your room.
	questionnaire (on sth.**)** [ˌkwestʃəˈneə]	Fragebogen (zu etwas)	Our teacher asked us to complete a ~ **on** fashion. Ⓕ le questionnaire

Tipps zum Wörterlernen → S.126 · Alphabetisches Wörterverzeichnis → S.195–236 · Personen-, Orts- und Ländernamen → S.237–239

Vocabulary

secretly ['siːkrətli]	heimlich, insgeheim	! *(adv)* She **secretly** put some poison into his tea. *(adj)* We had a **secret** meeting. *(geheim)* *(n)* I can't tell you. It's a **secret**. *(Geheimnis)* Ⓕ en secret	
(to) **ask** sb. **out (on a date)**	sich mit jm. verabreden; jn. einladen, mit einem auszugehen	If you really like him, why don't you ~ him **out**?	
date [deɪt]	Verabredung, Date	(to) **go on a ~** with sb. *(mit jm. ausgehen)*	
(to) **end** sth. [end]	etwas beenden	! (to) **end** = 1. zu Ende gehen; 2. beenden	
relationship [rɪˈleɪʃnʃɪp]	Verhältnis, Beziehung	(to) **end a ~** *(= Schluss machen)*	
unwanted [ˌʌnˈwɒntɪd]	unerwünscht, ungewollt	If you don't ask him to join you, he'll feel ~. an **unwanted** baby *(ein ungewolltes Baby)*	
(to) **go by**	vergehen, vorübergehen *(Zeit)*	She said she'd be back in a minute, but a whole hour went ~ before she came.	
(to) **chuck** *(infml, bes. BE)* [tʃʌk]	werfen, schmeißen	= (to) throw	
(to) **chuck** sb. *(infml, bes. BE)*	mit jm. Schluss machen	Jack and Olivia aren't together any more. – Who ~**ed** who?	
(to) **ruin** [ˈruːɪn]	verderben; ruinieren	Too much rain can ~ camping trips. He was ~**ed** in the economic crisis. Ⓕ ruiner	
(to) **cheat** sb. [tʃiːt]	jn. betrügen	A thief ~**ed** me and stole all my money.	
(to) **cheat on** sb. *(infml)*	jn. betrügen, jm. untreu sein	He ~**ed on** his wife twice before she left him.	
p.82/P 1 **argumentative writing** *(no pl)* [ˌɑːgjuˈmentətɪv]	Erörterung		
opposite [ˈɒpəzɪt]	entgegengesetzt; gegenüberliegende(r, s)	You're going the wrong way. You have to go in the ~ direction. She lives on the ~ side of the street.	
(to) **sum** (sth.) **up** (-mm-) [ˌsʌmˈʌp]	(etwas) zusammenfassen	**To sum up**, this is what we have learned: … *(Resümee: …/ Zusammenfassend: …)*	
(to) **rate** [reɪt]	bewerten, einschätzen	How do you ~ your spoken English?	
p.83/P 2 (to) **persuade** [pəˈsweɪd]	überreden	I didn't want to go at first, but Paul ~**d** me that it would be fun. Ⓕ persuader Ⓛ persuadere	
p.83/P 3 **handsome** [ˈhænsəm]	attraktiv, gut aussehend		

German „schön" usw.

attractive	used to describe a place or a person (the way they look *and* their personality)
beautiful	used to describe a place, a woman or a girl (but not usually a man)
good-looking	used to describe a person (the way they look but *not* their personality)
gorgeous	used informally to describe a very attractive person
handsome	usually only used to describe a man
lovely	used to describe a place, situation or a person; if you are describing a person, it often shows you like or love them
pretty	used to describe a place and a baby or a girl – or a woman who looks like a girl

(to) **be/feel flattered** [ˈflætəd]	sich geschmeichelt fühlen	When I said he was handsome, he was both ~ and embarrassed.	

PART B   Teens in trouble

p.84	troublemaker ['trʌbl‚meɪkə]	Unruhestifter/in	
	social ['səʊʃl]	sozial, Sozial-, gesellschaftlich	! stress: **s**ocial ['--] (F) social,e
	order ['ɔːdə]	Befehl, Anweisung, Anordnung	(F) un ordre
	(to) order ['ɔːdə]	befehlen	The soldier ~ed me to get out of the car. (L) ordinare
	(to) ban (-nn-) [bæn]	verbieten; sperren; ein (Aufenthalts-)Verbot erteilen	The British parliament ~ned slavery in 1807. He was ~ned from racing as he had taken drugs. The song has been ~ned because of its lyrics.
	(to) train as … [treɪn]	eine Ausbildung machen zu …	She has ~ed as a hairdresser and is looking for a job now.
	builder ['bɪldə]	Bauarbeiter/in	
	(to) straighten sth. up [‚streɪtn_'ʌp]	etwas aufräumen, etwas in Ordnung bringen	We'll have to ~ up the flat before the guests arrive. Give up smoking and drinking and try to ~ up your life.
	(to) punish ['pʌnɪʃ]	bestrafen	When you did something wrong as a child, how were you ~ed? (F) punir (L) punire
	punishment ['pʌnɪʃmənt]	Bestrafung, Strafe	Feeling sick was a kind of ~ for eating too much. (F) la punition (L) punitio
	under age [‚ʌndər_'eɪdʒ]	minderjährig	
	vandalism ['vændəlɪzəm]	Vandalismus, Zerstörungswut	! stress: **v**andalism ['----] (F) le vandalisme
	(to) vandalize ['vændəlaɪz]	mutwillig beschädigen, mutwillig zerstören	Cars and shop windows in the city centre have been ~d again.
p.85	boot camp ['buːt kæmp]	Erziehungslager (für junge Straftäter/innen)	
	eagle ['iːgl]	Adler	
	military ['mɪlətri]	militärisch, Militär-	**military-style** fashion (Mode im Militärstil) (F) militaire (L) militaris
	(to) make sb. do sth.	jn. zwingen, etwas zu tun; jn. dazu bringen, etwas zu tun	I didn't want to go to Grandma's party, but my dad **made** me **go**.

Tipps zum Wörterlernen → S.126 · Alphabetisches Wörterverzeichnis → S.195–236 · Personen-, Orts- und Ländernamen → S.237–239

Vocabulary

	discipline ['dɪsəplɪn]	Disziplin	! stress: d**i**scipline ['---] (F) la discipline (L) disciplina
p.86/P 1	(to) **express** [ɪk'spres]	äußern, zum Ausdruck bringen, ausdrücken	John always ~es his opinion in a very direct way. I ~ed sadness at the news of his wife's death. He's not good at English so he can't ~ himself well. (F) exprimer (L) exprimere
	clarification [ˌklærəfɪ'keɪʃn]	Klarstellung, Klärung	
	unless [ən'les]	es sei denn, außer (wenn)	You'll get into trouble with your parents ~ you work harder. (= ... if you don't work harder)
p.87/P 2	(to) **harass** ['hærəs, hə'ræs]	belästigen	He got an ASBO for ~ing his neighbours.
p.87/P 3	(to) **pass a law** [pɑːs]	ein Gesetz verabschieden	
	force [fɔːs]	Gewalt	(F) la force

PART C   Get involved

p.88	**along with** sb./sth. [ə'lɒŋ]	neben jm./etwas, (zusammen) mit jm./etwas	We walked onto the ferry ~ **with** hundreds of other travellers.
	diver ['daɪvə]	Taucher/in	The body was found in a canal by ~s.
	trash (AE) [træʃ]	Abfall, Müll	= BE rubbish
	(bottle) cap [kæp]	(Flaschen-)Deckel	! **cap** = 1. Mütze, Kappe; 2. Deckel
	turtle ['tɜːtl]	Wasserschildkröte	a **turtle**
	by far [baɪ 'fɑː]	bei weitem; mit Abstand	Of the whole class, he got **by** ~ the best marks.
	(to) **donate** [dəʊ'neɪt]	spenden, schenken	My dad ~s blood every six months. Our neighbours have ~d their old clothes to Oxfam. (F) donner (L) donare
	coin [kɔɪn]	Münze	
	bill (AE) [bɪl], **note** (BE) [nəʊt]	(Geld-)Schein, Banknote	some **coins** and **bills** (AE) **/ notes** (BE)
	altogether [ˌɔːltə'geðə]	insgesamt	£3.75 for the postcards and £5.50 for the stamps. That's £9.25 ~.
	store (AE) [stɔː]	Laden	= BE shop
	beef [biːf]	Rindfleisch	(F) le boeuf a **cow** **beef**
	(to) **have** sth. **done**	etwas machen lassen	You hair looks nice. Did you ~ it **cut** or did you cut it yourself?

Englische Laute → S.239 · Unregelmäßige Verben → S.240–241 · Classroom English → S.242–243

p.89	**community service** [kəˈmjuːnəti ˌsɜːvɪs]	gemeinnützige Arbeit	Naomi wasn't sent to prison. Instead, her punishment was to do 200 hours' **~ service**.
	(to) require sb. **to do** sth. [rɪˈkwaɪə]	von jm. verlangen, etwas zu tun	STUDENTS ARE REQUIRED TO TURN OFF THEIR MOBILES DURING LESSONS. Ⓛ requirere
	(to) encourage [ɪnˈkʌrɪdʒ]	*(jn.)* ermutigen, ermuntern; *(etwas)* fördern	My parents **~d** me to apply for the job. We'd like to **~** interest in local history.
p.90/P1	**privilege** [ˈprɪvəlɪdʒ]	Privileg	❗ stress: **pri**vilege ['---] Ⓕ le privilège
	(to) do a paper round [ˈpeɪpə raʊnd]	Zeitungen austragen	He **does a paper ~** every morning before school to earn a bit of money.
	(to) walk the dog [wɔːk]	den Hund ausführen	Dogs should be **~ed** three times a day.

PART D   The caller

p.92	**ugly** [ˈʌgli]	hässlich	**ugly** ◄► **beautiful**
	(to) bump into sb./sth. [bʌmp]	sich an etwas stoßen; gegen jn. stoßen	It was dark and I **~ed into** my desk. A man **~ed into** me in the street and I fell down.
	impatient [ɪmˈpeɪʃnt]	ungeduldig	I get **~** when I have to wait for a long time. Ⓕ impatient, e Ⓛ impatiens
	patient [ˈpeɪʃnt]	geduldig	Be **~**, I'm doing it as fast as I can. Ⓛ patiens
	(to) lie (to sb.**)** [laɪ]	(jn. an)lügen	❗ (to) **lie, lay, lain** = liegen (to) **lie, lied, lied** = lügen
	diamond [ˈdaɪəmənd]	Diamant	❗ stress: **di**amond ['---]
	darling [ˈdɑːlɪŋ]	Liebling, Schatz	= dear, love, sweetheart
	(to) search sth./sb. **(for** sth./sb.**)** [sɜːtʃ]	etwas/jn. (nach etwas/jm.) durchsuchen	The police **~ed** the flat **for** the dealers and their drugs.
	mood [muːd]	Laune, Stimmung	The **~** of the meeting got angry after a while.
	(to) be in a good/bad **mood** [muːd]	gute/schlechte Laune haben	Natalie **is in a** terrible **~** every Monday morning.
p.93	**(to) pretend** [prɪˈtend]	so tun, als ob	He **~ed** to be ill so that he could miss school. Ⓕ prétendre Ⓛ praetendere
	ghost [gəʊst]	Gespenst, Geist	You look scared, as if you've just seen a **~**.
	Anyway, ... [ˈeniweɪ]	Aber egal, ... / Wie dem auch sei, ...	Sorry, I still don't agree. **Anyway**, let's talk about something else.
p.95	**suspense** [səˈspens]	Spannung	Ⓕ le suspense
	repetition [ˌrepəˈtɪʃn]	Wiederholung	verb: (to) **repeat** – noun: **repetition** Ⓕ la répétition Ⓛ repetitio
	climax [ˈklaɪmæks]	Höhepunkt	❗ Höhepunkt = **1. highlight** *(schönster Teil von etwas)* **2. climax** *(spannendster Moment in einem Roman, Film usw.)*
	quotation [kwəʊˈteɪʃn]	Zitat	My favourite **~** is by George Bernard Shaw: 'Youth is a wonderful thing. What a crime to waste it on children.'

Dictionary (English – German)

Das **Dictionary** (S. 195–236) enthält den Wortschatz der Bände 1 bis 5 von *English G 21*.
Wenn du wissen möchtest, was ein Wort bedeutet, wie man es ausspricht oder wie es genau geschrieben wird, kannst du hier nachschlagen.

Im **Dictionary** werden folgende **Abkürzungen und Symbole** verwendet:

jm. = jemandem	sb. = somebody	pl = plural	AE = American English
jn. = jemanden	sth. = something	no pl = no plural	infml = informal

° Mit diesem Kringel sind Wörter markiert, die nicht zum Lernwortschatz gehören.
▶ Der Pfeil verweist auf Kästchen im **Vocabulary** (S. 167–194), in denen du weitere Informationen zu diesem Wort findest.

Die **Fundstellenangaben** zeigen, wo ein Wort zum ersten Mal vorkommt.
Die Ziffern in Klammern bezeichnen Seitenzahlen:

I = Band A1 • II = Band A2 • III = Band A3 • IV = Band A4 • V = Band A5
V 1 (15) = Band 5, Unit 1, Seite 15
V 1 (29/200) = Band 5, Unit 1, Seite 200 (im Vocabulary, zu Seite 29)

Tipps zur Arbeit mit einem Wörterbuch findest du im Skills File auf Seite 124.

> **Tipp**
> Auf der **Audio-CD im Workbook** findest du sowohl dieses englisch-deutsche Wörterverzeichnis als auch ein deutsch-englisches Wörterverzeichnis mit dem Lernwortschatz der Bände 1–5.

1

1800s [ˌeɪtiːn ˈhʌndrədz]: **in the mid-1800s** Mitte des 19. Jahrhunderts V 3 (52)
1950s [ˌnaɪntiːnˈfɪftiz] die Fünfzigerjahre (des 20. Jahrhunderts) III
9/11 [ˌnaɪn ˈɪˈlevn] Nine Eleven *(der Terroranschlag am 11. September 2001)* IV

A

a [ə]
1. ein, eine I
2. **once/twice a week** einmal/zweimal pro Woche III • **a bit** ein bisschen, etwas II • **a few** ein paar, einige II • **a lot (of)** eine Menge, viel, viele II • **He likes her a lot.** Er mag sie sehr. I
abbey [ˈæbi] Abtei II
abbreviation [əˌbriːviˈeɪʃn] Abkürzung IV
able [ˈeɪbl]: **be able to do sth.** etwas tun können; fähig sein/in der Lage sein, etwas zu tun II
Aboriginal [ˌæbəˈrɪdʒənəl] Aborigine- *(die Ureinwohner/innen Australiens betreffend)* V 1 (8/169) • **the Aboriginal people** die Ureinwohner/innen Australiens V 1 (8/169)
Aborigine [ˌæbəˈrɪdʒəni] Ureinwohner/in Australiens V 1 (8)
about [əˈbaʊt]
1. über I
2. ungefähr II
ask about sth. nach etwas fragen I • **know about sth.** von etwas wissen; über etwas Bescheid wissen II • **learn about sth.** etwas über etwas erfahren, etwas über etwas herausfinden II • **This is about Mr Green.** Es geht um Mr Green. I • **What about ...? 1.** Was ist mit ...? / Und ...? I; **2.** Wie wär's mit ...? I • **What are you talking about?** Wovon redest du? I **What was the best thing about ...?** Was war das Beste an ...? II
above [əˈbʌv] über, oberhalb (von) III
°**abridge** [əˈbrɪdʒ] kürzen
abroad [əˈbrɔːd] im Ausland II
go abroad ins Ausland gehen/fahren II
absolute [ˈæbsəluːt] absolut V 3 (59/187)
absolutely [ˌæbsəˈluːtli] absolut, völlig IV
AC [ˌeɪˈsiː] siehe **air conditioning**
°**academy** [əˈkædəmi] Akademie
accent [ˈæksənt] Akzent II
accident [ˈæksɪdənt] Unfall II
accommodation [əˌkɒməˈdeɪʃn] Unterkunft IV
accurate [ˈækjərət] genau, akkurat
°**ac/dc** [ˌeɪ siː ˈdiː siː] *(infml)* Strom
achieve [əˈtʃiːv] erreichen, erzielen, zustande bringen IV • **achieve an end** ein Ziel erreichen IV
achievement [əˈtʃiːvmənt] Leistung, Errungenschaft V 2 (39)
acid [ˈæsɪd] Säure IV
acrobat [ˈækrəbæt] Akrobat/in III
across [əˈkrɒs]
1. (quer) über II
2. hinüber, herüber III
°**acrostic** [əˈkrɒstɪk] Akrostichon
act [ækt] aufführen, spielen I
°**acting** [ˈæktɪŋ] Schauspielerei
action [ˈækʃn] Action; Handlung, Tat III
active [ˈæktɪv] aktiv III
activist [ˈæktəvɪst] Aktivist/in IV
activity [ækˈtɪvəti] Aktivität, Tätigkeit I
actor [ˈæktə] Schauspieler/in II
actually [ˈæktʃuəli] eigentlich, tatsächlich, übrigens, zwar IV
ad [æd] Anzeige, Inserat; *(im Fernsehen)* Werbespot IV
AD [ˌeɪ ˈdiː] *(from Latin: Anno Domini)* nach Christus III
°**adapt** [əˈdæpt] adaptieren
add (to) [æd] hinzufügen, ergänzen, addieren (zu) I • °**Added to that ...** Hinzu kommt, dass ...
address [əˈdres] Anschrift, Adresse II
adjust (to sth.) [əˈdʒʌst] sich (an etwas) gewöhnen, sich (auf etwas) einstellen IV
admire [ədˈmaɪə] bewundern IV
adult [ˈædʌlt] Erwachsene(r) III
adult life das Leben als Erwachsene(r) III
advanced [ədˈvɑːnst] fortgeschritten; für Fortgeschrittene V 2 (32/175)
advantage (over sb./sth.) [ədˈvɑːntɪdʒ] Vorteil (gegenüber jm./etwas) IV
adventure [ədˈventʃə] Abenteuer II
advert [ˈædvɜːt] Anzeige, Inserat; *(im Fernsehen)* Werbespot II
advertise [ˈædvətaɪz] Werbung machen (für); inserieren V 2 (41)

advertisement [əd'vɜːtɪsmənt] Anzeige; Inserat; *(im Fernsehen)* Werbespot V 2 (41)
advertiser ['ædvətaɪzə] Inserent/in; Werbekunde/-kundin V 2 (46)
advertising ['ædvətaɪzɪŋ] Werbung V 2 (41) • °**advertising company** Werbefirma
advice *(no pl)* [əd'vaɪs] Rat, Ratschlag, Ratschläge V 2 (47) • **Take my advice.** Hör auf meinen Rat. V 2 (47/183)
advise sb. [əd'vaɪz] jn. beraten V 2 (47)
adviser [əd'vaɪzə] Berater/in V 2 (47)
afraid [ə'freɪd]
1. **be afraid (of)** Angst haben (vor) I
2. **I'm afraid** leider III
°**Afrikaans** [ˌæfrɪ'kɑːnz] Afrikaans *(eine der elf Amtssprachen Südafrikas, aus dem Niederländischen entstanden)*
after ['ɑːftə] nach *(zeitlich)* I **after that** danach I • **after-school** nach dem Unterricht stattfindende(r, s) V 2 (38)
after ['ɑːftə] nachdem II
°**aftercare** ['ɑːftəkeə] Resozialisierungshilfe *(bsp. nach einem Gefängnisaufenthalt)*
afternoon [ˌɑːftə'nuːn] Nachmittag I • **in the afternoon** nachmittags, am Nachmittag I • **on Friday afternoon** freitagnachmittags, am Freitagnachmittag I
again [ə'gen] wieder; noch einmal I **now and again** ab und zu, von Zeit zu Zeit III
against [ə'genst] gegen I
age [eɪdʒ] Alter III • **at (the age of) 16** mit 16; im Alter von 16 III **she's my age** sie ist in meinem Alter V 2 (47) • **under age** minderjährig V 4 (84)
agency ['eɪdʒənsi]: **news agency** Nachrichtenagentur IV
ago [ə'gəʊ]: **a minute ago** vor einer Minute I
agree [ə'griː]: **agree (on)** sich einigen (auf) I • **agree (to sth.)** sich (zu etwas) bereit erklären V 3 (52) **agree (with sb.)** (jm.) zustimmen I
agreement [ə'griːmənt] Abkommen, Vertrag V 3 (52)
agriculture ['ægrɪkʌltʃə] Landwirtschaft IV
ahead (of sb./sth.) [ə'hed] (jm./ etwas) voraus V 2 (32) • **the road ahead** die Straße vor uns V 2 (32)
AIDS [eɪdz] AIDS V 3 (56)

aim [eɪm] Ziel III
air [eə] Luft II
°**air-conditioner** ['eəkənˌdɪʃənə] Klimagerät
air conditioning *(no pl)* ['eə kənˌdɪʃənɪŋ] Klimatisierung, Klimaanlage V 3 (65)
airport ['eəpɔːt] Flughafen III
alarm clock [ə'lɑːm klɒk] Wecker I
album ['ælbəm] Album II
alcohol ['ælkəhɒl] Alkohol III
A-level exams, A-levels *(pl)* ['eɪ ˌlevl] die höchsten Abschlussprüfungen des Schulsystems in England, Wales und Nordirland V 2 (32)
alive [ə'laɪv]: **be alive** leben, am Leben sein IV • °**come alive** lebendig werden • **keep sth. alive** etwas am Leben halten IV
all [ɔːl] alle; alles I • **2 all** 2 beide (2:2 unentschieden) III • **all day** den ganzen Tag (lang) I • **all over the world** auf der ganzen Welt III
all right [ɔːl 'raɪt] gut, in Ordnung II • **All the best** Viele Grüße IV
all the time die ganze Zeit I • **all we have to do now ...** alles, was wir jetzt (noch) tun müssen, ... II **from all over the world** aus der ganzen Welt II • **This is all wrong.** Das ist ganz falsch. I • **all year round** das ganze Jahr hindurch IV
allergic (to sth.) [ə'lɜːdʒɪk] allergisch (gegen etwas) III
allow [ə'laʊ] erlauben, zulassen II **be allowed to do sth.** [ə'laʊd] etwas tun dürfen II
almost ['ɔːlməʊst] fast, beinahe II
alone [ə'ləʊn] allein I
along [ə'lɒŋ]: **along the road** entlang der Straße / die Straße entlang II • **get along** zurechtkommen IV
along with sb./sth. [ə'lɒŋ] neben jm./etwas, (zusammen) mit jm./ etwas V 4 (88)
alphabet ['ælfəbet] Alphabet I
already [ɔːl'redi] schon, bereits II
also ['ɔːlsəʊ] auch IV • **not only ... but also ...** nicht nur ... sondern auch ... IV
although [ɔːl'ðəʊ] obwohl III
altogether [ˌɔːltə'geðə] insgesamt V 4 (88)
always ['ɔːlweɪz] immer I
am [eɪ 'em]: **7 am** 7 Uhr morgens/ vormittags I
amazing [ə'meɪzɪŋ] erstaunlich, unglaublich II
ambition ['æmbɪʃn] Ehrgeiz V 2 (47)
ambitious [æm'bɪʃəs] ehrgeizig V 2 (47)

ambulance ['æmbjələns] Krankenwagen III
American football [əˌmerɪkən 'fʊtbɔːl] Football I
among [ə'mʌŋ] unter, zwischen *(mehreren Personen oder Dingen)* IV
an [ən] ein, eine I
anarchy ['ænəki] Anarchie V 3 (59/187)
▶ S.187 Different forms of government
ancestor ['ænsestə] Vorfahr/in IV
ancient ['eɪnʃənt] antik; alt V 3 (50) **ancient cities** antike Städte V 3 (50/184) • **in ancient Rome** im antiken/alten Rom V 3 (50/184) **the ancient world** die Antike V 3 (50/184)
and [ənd, ænd] und I • **and now for** und jetzt ... *(kündigt ein neues Thema an)* III • **nice and cool/ clean/...** schön kühl/sauber/... I
angel ['eɪndʒl] Engel II
angry (about sth./with sb.) ['æŋgri] wütend, böse (über etwas/auf jn.) II
animal ['ænɪml] Tier I
°**annex** ['æneks] Nebengebäude
anniversary [ˌænɪ'vɜːsəri] Jahrestag IV • **anniversary of sb.'s death** Todestag IV
announce [ə'naʊns] bekanntgeben III
announcement [ə'naʊnsmənt] Bekanntgabe, Ankündigung; Durchsage; Ansage III
annoy [ə'nɔɪ] ärgern, verärgern V 2 (35) • **be/get annoyed (with sb., about sth.)** sich (über jn./ etwas) ärgern V 2 (35)
annoying [ə'nɔɪɪŋ] ärgerlich, lästig V 2 (35)
anorak ['ænəræk] Anorak, Windjacke III
another [ə'nʌðə] ein(e) andere(r, s); noch ein(e) I • **another 70 metres** weitere 70 Meter, noch 70 Meter II
answer ['ɑːnsə] (be)antworten I **answer (the phone)** rangehen *(ans Telefon)* II
answer (to) ['ɑːnsə] Antwort (auf) I
anti- ['ænti] anti-, gegen- V 3 (56) **anti-social** asozial, antisozial V 4 (84)
antonym ['æntənɪm] Antonym IV
any ['eni]: **any ...?** (irgend)welche ...? I • **not (...) any** kein(e) I **not (...) any more** nicht mehr II **any** irgendeine(r) V 2 (35/177)
anybody ['enibɒdi]: **anybody?** (irgend)jemand? II • **not (...) anybody** niemand II • **anybody** jede(r) (beliebige) V 2 (35)

Dictionary

anyone ['enıwʌn]: **anyone?** (irgend) jemand? III • **not (...) anyone** niemand III • **anyone** jede(r) (beliebige) V 2 (35)
anything ['enıθıŋ]: **anything?** (irgend)etwas? II • **Did you do anything special?** Habt ihr irgendetwas Besonderes gemacht? I • **not (...) anything** nichts II • **anything** alles, egal was V 2 (35/177)
▶ S.177 any, anyone, etc.
anyway ['enıweı]
1. sowieso I
2. trotzdem II
Anyway, ... ['enıweı] Aber egal, ... / Wie dem auch sei, ... V 4 (93)
anywhere ['enıweə]: **anywhere?** irgendwo(hin)? II • **not (...) anywhere** nirgendwo(hin) II • **anywhere** überall hin V 2 (35/177)
▶ S.177 any, anyone, etc.
apart [ə'pɑːt] voneinander getrennt, auseinander IV
apart from [ə'pɑːt] außer V 1 (23)
°**apartheid** [ə'pɑːthaıt] Apartheid *(Rassentrennung in Südafrika, bis 1994)*
apartment [ə'pɑːtmənt] Wohnung IV • °**one-bedroom apartment** Wohnung mit einem Schlafzimmer
apologize (to sb. for sth.) [ə'pɒlədʒaız] sich (bei jm. für etwas) entschuldigen V 2 (17)
appear [ə'pıə] erscheinen, auftauchen II
appetite ['æpıtaıt] Appetit III
apple ['æpl] Apfel I
applicant ['æplıkənt] Bewerber/in V 2 (39)
application [ˌæplı'keıʃn] Bewerbung V 2 (38) • **letter of application** Bewerbungsschreiben V 2 (38/178)
apply for [ə'plaı] sich bewerben (um/für etwas); etwas beantragen IV
appointment [ə'pɔıntmənt] Termin, Verabredung I
April ['eıprəl] April I
architect ['ɑːkıtekt] Architekt/in III
°**architecture** ['ɑːkıtektʃə] Architektur
archive ['ɑːkaıv] Archiv IV
are [ɑː] bist; sind; seid I • **How are you?** Wie geht es dir/Ihnen/euch? II • **The pencils are 35 p.** Die Bleistifte kosten 35 Pence. I
area ['eərıə] Gebiet, Gegend; Bereich III
argue ['ɑːgjuː] sich streiten, sich zanken I

argument ['ɑːgjumənt]
1. Streit, Auseinandersetzung II • **have an argument** eine Auseinandersetzung haben, sich streiten II
°**2.** Argument
argumentative writing [ˌɑːgju'mentətıv] Erörterung V 4 (82)
arm [ɑːm] Arm I
armchair ['ɑːmtʃeə] Sessel I
army ['ɑːmi] Armee, Heer IV
around [ə'raʊnd] in ... umher, durch, um ... (herum) III • **around six** um sechs Uhr herum, gegen sechs III **around the lake** um den See (herum) III • **around the town** in der Stadt umher, durch die Stadt III • **look around** sich umsehen III **turn around** sich umdrehen IV **walk/run/jump around** herumgehen/-rennen/-springen, umhergehen/-rennen/-springen III
°**arrange a date** [ə'reındʒ] eine Verabredung planen
arrival [ə'raıvl] Ankunft III
arrive [ə'raıv] ankommen, eintreffen II
arrow ['ærəʊ] Pfeil IV • **bow and arrow** Pfeil und Bogen IV
art [ɑːt] Kunst I • **rock art** *(no pl)* Felsmalerei(en) V 1 (8)
article ['ɑːtıkl] (Zeitungs-)Artikel I
artificial [ˌɑːtı'fıʃl] künstlich, Kunst- III
artistic [ɑː'tıstık] künstlerisch; künstlerisch begabt V 2 (48)
as [əz, æz]
1. als, während II
2. wie II • **as you know** wie du weißt II
3. **as nice/big/exciting as** so schön/groß/aufregend wie II **just as ... as** ebenso ... wie IV **as soon as** sobald, sowie II
4. weil V 2 (38)
°**ASBO** ['æzbəʊ] einstweilige Verfügung wegen asozialen Verhaltens
as if [əz_'ıf] als ob IV
ask [ɑːsk] fragen I • **ask about sth.** nach etwas fragen I • **ask questions** Fragen stellen I • **ask sb. for sth.** jn. um etwas bitten II • **ask someone out (on a date)** sich mit jm. verabreden; jn. einladen, mit einem auszugehen V 4 (80) **ask sb. the way** jn. nach dem Weg fragen II
asleep [ə'sliːp]: **be asleep** schlafen II • **fall asleep** einschlafen V 1 (21)
°**aspect** ['æspekt] Aspekt
assess [ə'ses] einschätzen, beurteilen V 2 (44)

assessment [ə'sesmənt] Einschätzung, Beurteilung V 2 (44)
assignment [ə'saınmənt] *(AE)* Hausaufgabe IV
assistant [ə'sıstənt] Verkäufer/in I
at [ət, æt]: **at 7 Hamilton Street** in der Hamiltonstraße 7 I • **at 8.45** um 8.45 I • **at (the age of) 16** mit 16; im Alter von 16 III • **at break** in der Pause *(zwischen Schulstunden)* II • **at home** zu Hause, daheim I • **at last** endlich, schließlich I • **at least** zumindest, wenigstens I • **at night** nachts, in der Nacht I • **at school** in der Schule I • **at sea** auf See II • **at that table** an dem Tisch (dort) / an den Tisch (dort) I • **at the back (of the room)** hinten, im hinteren Teil (des Zimmers) II • **at the bottom (of)** unten, am unteren Ende (von) II • **at the chemist's/doctor's/hairdresser's** beim Apotheker/Arzt/Friseur III • **at the end (of)** am Ende (von) I • **at the moment** im Moment, gerade, zurzeit I • **at the Shaws' house** im Haus der Shaws, bei den Shaws zu Hause I • **at the station** am Bahnhof I • **at the top (of)** oben, am oberen Ende, an der Spitze (von) I • **at the weekend** am Wochenende I • **at work** bei der Arbeit / am Arbeitsplatz I
ate [et, eıt] *siehe* eat
atheism ['eıθıızəm] Atheismus V 3 (52/185)
atheist ['eıθııst] Atheist(in) V 3 (52/185)
atheistic [ˌeıθi'ıstık] atheistisch V 3 (52/185)
▶ S.185 Religions
athletics [æθ'letıks] Leichtathletik III
atmosphere ['ætməsfıə] Atmosphäre; Stimmung V 1 (9)
°**atom** ['ætəm] Atom
attach to [ə'tætʃ] anhängen, anheften (an) *(an Brief, Mail)* V 1 (12)
attack [ə'tæk] Angriff III • **heart attack** Herzinfarkt IV
attack [ə'tæk] angreifen III
°**attention** [ə'tenʃn]: **attract sb.'s attention** jm. ins Auge fallen
attitude to/towards ['ætıtjuːd] Haltung gegenüber, Einstellung zu IV
attract [ə'trækt] anziehen, anlocken V 3 (50) • °**attract sb.'s attention** jm. ins Auge fallen
attractive [ə'træktıv] attraktiv, verlockend V 3 (50)
▶ S.191 German „schön" usw.

audience ['ɔːdɪəns] Zuschauer/innen, Zuhörer/innen, Publikum V 2 (45)
August ['ɔːɡəst] August I
aunt [ɑːnt] Tante I • **auntie** ['ɑːnti] Tante II
°**Aussie** ['ɒzi] (infml) Australier/in; australisch
°**Aussie rules football** Australian Football
author ['ɔːθə] Autor/in V 1 (25)
auto ['ɔːtəʊ] (AE) Auto, PKW IV
autobiography [ˌɔːtəʊbaɪ'ɒɡrəfi] Autobiografie IV
autumn ['ɔːtəm] Herbst I
available [ə'veɪləbl] erhältlich; vorrätig IV
avenue ['ævənjuː] Allee, Boulevard IV
average ['ævərɪdʒ] Durchschnitt; durchschnittlich IV
avoid [ə'vɔɪd] vermeiden V 2 (39)
award [ə'wɔːd] Auszeichnung, Preis V 2 (39)
away [ə'weɪ] weg, fort I • **get away from sth./sb.** von etwas/jm. weggehen, sich entfernen III • **put sth. away** wegräumen IV
awesome ['ɔːsəm] (AE, infml) klasse, großartig IV
awful ['ɔːfl] furchtbar, schrecklich II

B

baby ['beɪbi] Baby I • **have a baby** ein Baby/Kind bekommen II
back [bæk]: **at the back (of the room)** hinten, im hinteren Teil (des Zimmers) II • **back home** zurück zu Hause IV
back door [ˌbæk 'dɔː] Hintertür II
background ['bækɡraʊnd] Hintergrund II • **background file** etwa: Hintergrundinformation II
bacon ['beɪkən] Schinkenspeck II
bacteria (pl) [bæk'tɪəriə] Bakterien IV
bad [bæd] schlecht, schlimm I • **bad timing** schlechtes Timing, schlechte Wahl des Zeitpunkts IV
badge [bædʒ] Abzeichen, Button V 2 (38)
badminton ['bædmɪntən] Badminton, Federball I • **badminton racket** Federballschläger III
bag [bæɡ] Tasche, Beutel, Tüte I; Handtasche III
bagel ['beɪɡl] Bagel (ringförmiges Brötchen) IV

balcony ['bælkəni] Balkon V 3 (64)
ball [bɔːl]
1. Ball (zum Sport) I
2. Ball (Tanz) II
balloon [bə'luːn] Heißluftballon; Luftballon II
ban (-nn) [bæn] sperren; ein (Aufenthalts-)Verbot erteilen V 4 (84)
banana [bə'nɑːnə] Banane I
band [bænd] Band, (Musik-)Gruppe I
▶ S.182 Collective nouns
banjo ['bændʒəʊ] Banjo III
bank [bæŋk] Bank, Sparkasse I
bank robber ['bæŋk ˌrɒbə] Bankräuber/in I
bar [bɑː] Bar II
bar chart ['bɑː tʃɑːt] Balkendiagramm V 1 (10)
barbecue ['bɑːbɪkjuː] Grillfest, Grillparty V 1 (6)
°**barbie** ['bɑːbi] (infml) Grillfest, Grillparty
°**bare** [beə] kahl
bark [bɑːk] bellen II
baseball ['beɪsbɔːl] Baseball I
baseball cap Baseballmütze I
basic ['beɪsɪk] grundlegend, Grund-; einfach, elementar V 2 (38)
Basic Law Grundgesetz (der Bundesrepublik) V 2 (38/179)
basket ['bɑːskɪt] Korb I • **a basket of apples** ein Korb Äpfel I
basketball ['bɑːskɪtbɔːl] Basketball I
bass [beɪs] Kontrabass; Bassgitarre III • **bass guitar** Bassgitarre III • **double bass** Kontrabass III
bat [bæt]: **table tennis bat** Tischtennisschläger III
bath [bɑːθ] Bad, Badewanne II • **have a bath** baden, ein Bad nehmen II
bathe [beɪð] (AE) baden (sich waschen) V 3 (63)
bathroom ['bɑːθruːm; 'bɑːθrʊm] Badezimmer I
bay [beɪ] Bucht III
BC [ˌbiː 'siː] v. Chr. IV
be [biː], **was/were, been** sein I • **be into sth.** (infml) etwas mögen III • **be a farmer, a teacher, …** Bauer/Bäuerin, Lehrer/in, … werden IV
beach [biːtʃ] Strand II • **on the beach** [biːtʃ] am Strand II
°**beacon** ['biːkən] Leuchtfeuer
bean [biːn] Bohne IV
bear [beə] Bär II • **teddy bear** Teddybär III
beat [biːt], **beat, beaten** schlagen; besiegen III

beaten ['biːtn] siehe beat
beautiful ['bjuːtɪfl] schön I
▶ S.191 German „schön" usw.
beauty ['bjuːti] Schönheit III
became [bɪ'keɪm] siehe become
because [bɪ'kɒz] weil I
because of [bɪ'kɒz_əv] wegen IV
become [bɪ'kʌm], **became, become** werden II • °**become law** Rechtskraft erlangen
bed [bed] Bett I • **Bed and Breakfast (B&B)** [ˌbed_ən 'brekfəst] Frühstückspension I • **double bed** Doppelbett V 3 (64/189) • **go to bed** ins Bett gehen I • **put sb. to bed** jn. ins Bett bringen III • **single bed** Einzelbett V 3 (64)
bedroom ['bedruːm; 'bedrʊm] Schlafzimmer I • °**one-bedroom apartment** Wohnung mit einem Schlafzimmer
beef [biːf] Rindfleisch V 4 (88)
been [biːn] siehe be
before [bɪ'fɔː] vor (zeitlich) I • **the day before yesterday** vorgestern II
before [bɪ'fɔː] bevor II
before [bɪ'fɔː] (vorher) schon mal II
beg [beɡ] betteln V 3 (67)
began [bɪ'ɡæn] siehe begin
beggar ['beɡə] Bettler/in V 3 (67)
begin (-nn-) [bɪ'ɡɪn], **began, begun** beginnen, anfangen (mit) I
beginner [bɪ'ɡɪnə] Anfänger/in V 1 (15)
beginning [bɪ'ɡɪnɪŋ] Anfang, Beginn II
begun [bɪ'ɡʌn] siehe begin
behave [bɪ'heɪv] sich verhalten, sich benehmen V 4 (80)
behaviour [bɪ'heɪvjə] Verhalten, Benehmen V 4 (80)
behind [bɪ'haɪnd] hinter I • **leave behind** zurücklassen IV
believe [bɪ'liːv] glauben III • **believe in sth.** an etwas glauben IV • **She couldn't believe her eyes.** Sie traute ihren Augen kaum. III
bell [bel] Klingel, Glocke I
belong (to) [bɪ'lɒŋ] gehören (zu) II
below [bɪ'ləʊ] unter, unterhalb (von) III
beside [bɪ'saɪd] neben V 1 (21)
besides [bɪ'saɪdz] außerdem IV
besides [bɪ'saɪdz] außer V 3 (64)
best [best] am besten II • **All the best** Viele Grüße IV • **Best wishes** Viele Grüße IV • **the best** … der/die/das beste …; die besten … I
What was the best thing about …? Was war das Beste an …? II

Dictionary

bet (-tt-) [bet]**, bet, bet** wetten III • **You bet!** *(infml)* Aber klar! / Und ob! IV
better [ˈbetə] besser I • **like sth. better** etwas lieber mögen II
between [bɪˈtwiːn] zwischen II • °**(in) between** dazwischen IV
°**beyond** [bɪˈjɒnd] jenseits (von), über ... hinaus
°**bhelpuri** [belˈpʊəri] *indisches Gericht mit Puffreis*
Bible [ˈbaɪbl] Bibel IV
big [bɪɡ] groß I • **big wheel** Riesenrad III
bike [baɪk] Fahrrad I • **bike tour** Radtour II • **ride a bike** Rad fahren I
bilingual [ˌbaɪˈlɪŋɡwəl] zweisprachig IV
bill [bɪl] *(AE)* (Geld-)Schein, Banknote V 4 (88)
billion [ˈbɪliən] Milliarde V 3 (62)
bin [bɪn] Mülltonne II
binoculars *(pl)* [bɪˈnɒkjʊləz] Fernglas IV
biography [baɪˈɒɡrəfi] Biografie III
biological [ˌbaɪəˈlɒdʒɪkl] biologisch IV
biology [baɪˈɒlədʒi] Biologie I
bird [bɜːd] Vogel I
birth [bɜːθ] Geburt IV • **birth rate** Geburtsrate V 1 (9/169) • **date of birth** Geburtsdatum IV • °**give birth to sb.** jn. gebären
birthday [ˈbɜːθdeɪ] Geburtstag I • **Happy birthday.** Herzlichen Glückwunsch zum Geburtstag. I • **My birthday is in May.** Ich habe im Mai Geburtstag. I • **My birthday is on 13th June.** Ich habe am 13. Juni Geburtstag. I • **When's your birthday?** Wann hast du Geburtstag? I • **for his birthday** zu seinem Geburtstag III
biscuit [ˈbɪskɪt] Keks, Plätzchen I
bit [bɪt]: **a bit** ein bisschen, etwas II
black [blæk] schwarz I
blame sb. (for) [bleɪm] jm. die Schuld geben (an); jm. Vorwürfe machen (wegen) III
blanket [ˈblæŋkɪt] Decke *(zum Zudecken)* V 1 (17)
bled [bled] *siehe* **bleed**
bleed [bliːd]**, bled, bled** bluten IV
bleep [bliːp] piepsen II
bleep [bliːp] Piepton II
blessing [ˈblesɪŋ] Segen IV
blew [bluː] *siehe* **blow**
blind [blaɪnd] blind III
block [blɒk] blockieren, (ver)sperren IV

block [blɒk] (Häuser-, Wohn-)Block IV
blog [blɒɡ] Blog *(Weblog, digitales Tagebuch)* IV
blond *(bei Frauen oft:* **blonde***)* [blɒnd] blond IV
blood [blʌd] Blut III
°**bloom** [bluːm]: **in bloom** blühend
blouse [blaʊz] Bluse II
blow [bləʊ]**, blew, blown** pusten, blasen; wehen III
blown [bləʊn] *siehe* **blow**
blue [bluː] blau I
blues [bluːz] Blues III
board [bɔːd] (Wand-)Tafel I • **on the board** an der/die Tafel I
boat [bəʊt] Boot, Schiff I
body [ˈbɒdi] Körper I
bodyguard [ˈbɒdiɡɑːd] Bodyguard, Leibwächter/in, Leibwache IV
°**Boer** [bɔː] Bure/Burin *(Südafrikaner/in niederländischer Herkunft)*
boil [bɔɪl] kochen *(Flüssigkeit, Speise)* IV
°**bold** [bəʊld] kräftig, auffallend
bold (type) [ˌbəʊld ˈtaɪp] Fettdruck V 2 (39)
bone [bəʊn] Knochen IV
bomb [bɒm] Bombe IV
book [bʊk] Buch I
booklet [ˈbʊklət] Broschüre II
°**boom** [buːm] Boom, Aufschwung
boot [buːt] Stiefel II
boot camp [ˈbuːt kæmp] Erziehungslager *(für junge Straftäter/innen)* V 4 (85)
border [ˈbɔːdə] Grenze IV
bored [bɔːd]: **get bored** sich langweilen; gelangweilt sein IV
boring [ˈbɔːrɪŋ] langweilig I
born [bɔːn]: **be born** geboren sein/werden II
borough [ˈbʌrə, *AE:* ˈbɜːrəʊ] (Stadt-)Bezirk III
borrow sth. [ˈbɒrəʊ] sich etwas (aus)leihen, etwas entleihen II
boss [bɒs] Boss, Chef/in I
both [bəʊθ] beide I
bottle [ˈbɒtl] Flasche I • **a bottle of milk** eine Flasche Milch I
bottle cap (Flaschen-)Deckel V 4 (88)
bottom [ˈbɒtəm] unteres Ende II • **at the bottom (of)** unten, am unteren Ende (von) II
bought [bɔːt] *siehe* **buy**
bow [bəʊ] Bogen *(Waffe und zum Musizieren)* IV • **bow and arrow** Pfeil und Bogen IV
bowl [bəʊl] Schüssel I • **a bowl of cornflakes** eine Schale Cornflakes I

box [bɒks] Kasten, Kästchen, Kiste I
box office [ˈbɒks ˌɒfɪs] (Theater-, Kino-)Kasse III
boy [bɔɪ] Junge I • **boy!** *(AE, infml)* Mann! Mensch! III
boycott [ˈbɔɪkɒt] Boykott IV
bracket [ˈbrækɪt] Klammer *(in Texten)* IV • **round brackets** runde Klammern IV • **square brackets** eckige Klammern IV
brainstorm [ˈbreɪnstɔːm] brainstormen *(so viele Ideen wie möglich sammeln)* III
brave [breɪv] tapfer, mutig IV
bread *(no pl)* [bred] Brot I
break [breɪk]**, broke, broken** (zer)brechen; kaputt machen; kaputt gehen II • **break a rule/order** gegen eine Regel/Anordnung verstoßen IV • **break sth. open** etwas aufbrechen IV
break [breɪk] Pause I • **at break** in der Pause *(zwischen Schulstunden)* II • **take a break** eine Pause machen IV
break down [ˌbreɪk ˈdaʊn]
1. eine Panne haben V 1 (20)
2. zusammenbrechen V 1 (20)
breakfast [ˈbrekfəst] Frühstück I • **have breakfast** frühstücken I
breathe [briːð] atmen IV
bridge [brɪdʒ] Brücke I
bridle path [ˈbraɪdl ˌpɑːθ] Reitweg III
bright [braɪt] hell, leuchtend II
brief [briːf] kurz (gefasst), knapp, von kurzer Dauer V 2 (39) • **be brief** sich kurz fassen V 2 (39/179)
°**brilliant** [ˈbrɪliənt] glänzend; strahlend
bring [brɪŋ]**, brought, brought** (mit-, her)bringen I • °**bring in** einbringen
British [ˈbrɪtɪʃ] britisch II
broadcast [ˈbrɔːdkɑːst]**, broadcast, broadcast** senden; *(eine Sendung)* ausstrahlen IV
broke [brəʊk] *siehe* **break**
broken [ˈbrəʊkən] *siehe* **break**
broken [ˈbrəʊkən] gebrochen; zerbrochen, kaputt II
brother [ˈbrʌðə] Bruder I
brought [brɔːt] *siehe* **bring**
brown [braʊn] braun I
bucket [ˈbʌkɪt] Eimer V 3 (63)
Buddhism [ˈbʊdɪzm] Buddhismus V 3 (52/185)
Buddhist [ˈbʊdɪst] Buddhist/in, buddhistisch V 3 (52/185)
▶ S.185 Religions
budgie [ˈbʌdʒi] Wellensittich I

build [bɪld], **built, built** bauen II **the ship was built in Bristol** das Schiff wurde in Bristol gebaut II
builder [ˈbɪldə] Bauarbeiter/in V 4 (84)
building [ˈbɪldɪŋ] Gebäude II
built [bɪlt] siehe **build**
bulletin board [ˈbʊlətɪn bɔːd] schwarzes Brett, Anschlagtafel IV
bully [ˈbʊli] einschüchtern, tyrannisieren II
bully [ˈbʊli] (Schul-)Tyrann III
bummer [ˈbʌmə]: **What a bummer!** (infml) So ein Mist! Wie schade! III
bump into sb./sth. [bʌmp] sich an etwas stoßen; gegen jn. stoßen V 4 (92)
bunk (bed) [bʌŋk] Etagenbett, Koje II
°**bunsen burner** [ˌbʌnsn ˈbɜːnə] Bunsenbrenner
burn [bɜːn] brennen; verbrennen IV
bury [ˈberi] begraben, vergraben; beerdigen IV
bus [bʌs] Bus I
bush [bʊʃ] Busch, Strauch V 1 (6)
bus pass [ˈbʌs pɑːs] Bus-Monatskarte III
bus stop [ˈbʌs stɒp] Bushaltestelle III
bush [bʊʃ]: **the bush** der Busch (unkultiviertes, „wildes" Land in Australien, Afrika) V 1 (6)
business [ˈbɪznəs] Unternehmen; Geschäfte V 1 (8) • **business people** (pl) Geschäftsleute V 3 (55) • **do business (with)** Geschäfte machen (mit); Handel treiben (mit) V 1 (8) • °**get down to business** an die Arbeit gehen • **Mind your own business.** Das geht dich nichts an! / Kümmere dich um deine eigenen Angelegenheiten! II • **start a business** ein Unternehmen gründen V 2 (46)
°**businesswoman** [ˈbɪznəswʊmən], pl **businesswomen** Geschäftsfrau
busy [ˈbɪzi]
1. beschäftigt I
2. belebt, verkehrsreich; hektisch III
but [bət, bʌt]
1. aber I
2. sondern IV • **not only ... but also ...** nicht nur ... sondern auch ... IV
butter [ˈbʌtə] Butter IV
button [ˈbʌtn] Knopf III
buy [baɪ], **bought, bought** kaufen I
by [baɪ]
1. von I
2. an; (nahe) bei II

3. **by two degrees/ten per cent** um zwei Grad/zehn Prozent V 1 (9)
°4. neben
by asking indem du fragst V 2 (40)
by car/bike/... mit dem Auto/Rad/... II • **by day and by night** bei Tag und bei Nacht V 3 (67)
by far bei weitem; mit Abstand V 4 (88) • **by the end of the song** (spätestens) bis zum Ende des Lieds III • **by the way** übrigens; nebenbei (bemerkt) III
Bye. [baɪ] Tschüs! I

C

cabin [ˈkæbɪn] Hütte III
café [ˈkæfeɪ] (kleines) Restaurant, Imbissstube, Café I
cafeteria [ˌkæfəˈtɪəriə] Cafeteria, Selbstbedienungsrestaurant II
cage [keɪdʒ] Käfig I
cake [keɪk] Kuchen, Torte I
calendar [ˈkælɪndə] Kalender I
call [kɔːl] rufen; anrufen; nennen I **be called** heißen, genannt werden II • **call for help** um Hilfe rufen V 4 (94) • **call sb. names** jn. mit Schimpfwörtern hänseln, jm. Schimpfwörter nachrufen III
call [kɔːl] Ruf, Schrei; Anruf II **give sb. a call** jn. anrufen V 4 (83) • **make a call** ein Telefongespräch führen, telefonieren V 4
calm [kɑːm] ruhig, still V 2 (35) **keep calm** ruhig/still bleiben; Ruhe bewahren V 2 (35/177)
calm down [ˌkɑːm ˈdaʊn] sich beruhigen II • **calm sb. down** jn. beruhigen II
came [keɪm] siehe **come**
camel [ˈkæml] Kamel II
camera [ˈkæmərə] Kamera, Fotoapparat I
camp [kæmp] zelten III
camp [kæmp] Camp, Lager IV
campaign [kæmˈpeɪn] Kampagne V 3 (59)
campground [ˈkæmpˌɡraʊnd] (AE) Zeltplatz III
camping gear [ˈkæmpɪŋ ˌɡɪə] Campingausrüstung IV
campsite [ˈkæmpsaɪt] Zeltplatz III
can [kæn] Dose V 1 (21)
can [kən, kæn]
1. können I
2. dürfen I
Can I help you? Kann ich Ihnen helfen? / Was kann ich für Sie tun? (im Geschäft) I
canal [kəˈnæl] Kanal III

cancel [ˈkænsəl] absagen V 2 (34)
cancer [ˈkænsə] Krebs (Krankheit) V 1 (9)
candidate [ˈkændɪdət] Kandidat/in; Bewerber/in V 2 (39)
candle [ˈkændl] Kerze IV
cannot [ˈkænɒt] kann nicht IV
canoe [kəˈnuː] Kanu III
canoe [kəˈnuː] paddeln, Kanu fahren III
canyon [ˈkænjən] Cañon IV
cap [kæp] Mütze, Kappe II
capital [ˈkæpɪtl] Hauptstadt III
capital letter [ˌkæpɪtl ˈletə] Großbuchstabe II
captain [ˈkæptɪn] Kapitän/in III
caption [ˈkæpʃn] Bildunterschrift IV
car [kɑː] Auto I
caravan [ˈkærəvæn] Wohnwagen II
card [kɑːd] (Spiel-, Post-)Karte I
care (about) [keə] sich interessieren (für); sich kümmern (um); wichtig nehmen III • **I care about the environment.** Die Umwelt liegt mir am Herzen. III • **I don't care about money.** Geld ist mir egal. III • **Who cares?** Ist doch egal! / Na und? III
care [keə]: **take care of sth.** sich um etwas kümmern III
career [kəˈrɪə] Karriere III
careful [ˈkeəfl] vorsichtig I
caretaker [ˈkeəteɪkə] Hausmeister/in II
°**carjack** [ˈkɑːdʒæk] unter Androhung von Gewalt ein Auto stehlen
°**carjacker** [ˈkɑːdʒækə] Autodieb/in
car park [ˈkɑː pɑːk] Parkplatz III
carrot [ˈkærət] Möhre, Karotte I
carry [ˈkæri] tragen V 1 (6)
cart [kɑːt] Wagen, Karren IV
cartoon [kɑːˈtuːn] Cartoon (Zeichentrickfilm; Bilderwitz) II
case [keɪs] Fall II • °**just in case** falls; für den Fall, dass
casino [kəˈsiːnəʊ] (Spiel)kasino IV
castle [ˈkɑːsl] Burg, Schloss II
cat [kæt] Katze I
catch [kætʃ], **caught, caught** fangen; erwischen II • **be catching** ansteckend sein V 1 (6)
cathedral [kəˈθiːdrəl] Kathedrale, Dom II
cattle (pl) [ˈkætl] Vieh, Rinder IV
caught [kɔːt] siehe **catch**
cause [kɔːz] verursachen IV
cause [kɔːz] Ursache IV
cave [keɪv] Höhle V 1 (16)
CD [ˌsiːˈdiː] CD I • **CD player** CD-Spieler I

ceilidh ['keɪlɪ] Musik- und Tanzveranstaltung, vor allem in Schottland und Irland III
ceiling ['siːlɪŋ] (Zimmer-) Decke V 3 (63)
celebrate ['selɪbreɪt] feiern IV
celebration [ˌseləˈbreɪʃn] Feier IV
celebrity [səˈlebrəti] berühmte Persönlichkeit, Prominente(r) III
cell [sel] Zelle V 3 (63)
cello ['tʃeləʊ] Cello III
cellphone ['selfəʊn] (AE) Mobiltelefon, Handy III
cent (c) [sent] Cent I
cent: per cent [pəˈsent] Prozent III
centimetre (cm) ['sentɪmiːtə] Zentimeter III
central ['sentrəl] Zentral-, Mittel- III
centre ['sentə] Zentrum, Mitte I
century ['sentʃəri] Jahrhundert II
certificate [səˈtɪfɪkət] Urkunde, Zeugnis, Bescheinigung V 2 (39)
chair [tʃeə] Stuhl I
champion ['tʃæmpiən] Meister/in, Champion I
championship ['tʃæmpiənʃɪp] Meisterschaft III
chance [tʃɑːns] Chance II
change [tʃeɪndʒ]
  1. Wechselgeld I
  2. (Ver-)Änderung, Wechsel IV
change [tʃeɪndʒ]
  1. umsteigen III
  2. (sich) (ver-)ändern IV
  3. wechseln IV
  4. umtauschen IV
  5. umwandeln IV
  6. **change stations** (Radio) umschalten IV
  7. sich umziehen IV
chapel ['tʃæpl] Kapelle, Kirche (für manche protestantische Gemeinden) V 3 (52/185)
  ▶ S.185 Religions
character ['kærəktə] Charakter, Persönlichkeit IV
characteristic [ˌkærəktəˈrɪstɪk] (charakteristisches) Merkmal IV
charge (at sb.) [tʃɑːdʒ] stürmen; (jn.) angreifen IV
charge [tʃɑːdʒ]: **be in charge of sth./sb.** für etwas/jn. verantwortlich sein; etwas leiten V 2 (34)
charity ['tʃærəti] Wohlfahrtsorganisation II
chart [tʃɑːt] Diagramm I
chase sb. [tʃeɪs] jn. jagen; jm. hinterherjagen IV
chat (-tt-) [tʃæt] chatten, plaudern II
chat [tʃæt] Chat, Unterhaltung II
chat room ['tʃæt ruːm] Chatroom III
chat show Talkshow II

cheap [tʃiːp] billig, preiswert II
cheat [tʃiːt]: **cheat sb.** jn. betrügen V 4 (80) • **cheat on sb.** jn. betrügen, jm. untreu sein V 4 (80)
check [tʃek] (über)prüfen, kontrollieren I • °**check up on sb.** jn. kontrollieren
checklist ['tʃeklɪst] Checkliste III
check out (of a hotel) [ˌtʃek ˈaʊt] (aus einem Hotel) auschecken, abreisen V 1 (18)
checkpoint ['tʃekpɔɪnt] Kontrollpunkt (zur Selbstüberprüfung) I
°**cheeky** ['tʃiːki] (BE, infml) frech
cheer [tʃɪə] jubeln II
cheerleader ['tʃɪəliːdə] Cheerleader (Stimmungsanheizer/in bei Sportereignissen) IV
cheese [tʃiːz] Käse I
chemist ['kemɪst] Drogerie, Apotheke II • **at the chemist's** beim Apotheker III
°**cheque (for)** [tʃek] Scheck (über)
chew [tʃuː] kauen V 2 (36) • **chew gum** Kaugummi kauen V 2 (36/178)
chewing gum [ˈɡʌm] Kaugummi V 2 (36)
chicken ['tʃɪkɪn] Huhn; (Brat-)Hähnchen I
chief [tʃiːf] Häuptling IV
child [tʃaɪld], pl **children** ['tʃɪldrən] Kind I • **children's home** Kinderheim V 1 (19)
childhood ['tʃaɪldhʊd] Kindheit V 3 (61)
childproof ['tʃaɪldpruːf] kindersicher V 1 (17/173)
chill out [ˌtʃɪl ˈaʊt] (infml) sich entspannen, relaxen III
Chinese [tʃaɪˈniːz] chinesisch IV
chips (pl) [tʃɪps]
  1. (BE) Pommes frites I
  2. (AE) Chips IV
chocolate ['tʃɒklət] Schokolade I
°**choice** [tʃɔɪs] (Aus-)Wahl
choir [ˈkwaɪə] Chor I
choose [tʃuːz], **chose, chosen** (sich) aussuchen, (aus)wählen I
chose [tʃəʊz] siehe **choose**
chosen ['tʃəʊzn] siehe **choose**
Christ [kraɪst] Christus IV
Christian ['krɪstʃən] Christ/in, christlich V 3 (52/185)
Christianity [ˌkrɪstiˈænəti] Christentum V 3 (52/185)
  ▶ S.185 Religions
Christmas ['krɪsməs] Weihnachten V 2 (34) • **at Christmas** an/zu Weihnachten V 2 (34/176) • **Christmas tree** Christ-, Weihnachtsbaum V 2 (34/176) • **for Christmas** zu Weihnachten V 2 (34/176)

chuck sb. [tʃʌk] (infml) mit jm. Schluss machen V 4 (80)
church [tʃɜːtʃ] Kirche I • **go to church** in die Kirche gehen III
  ▶ S.185 Religions
cinema ['sɪnəmə] Kino II • **go to the cinema** ins Kino gehen II
circle ['sɜːkl] Kreis III • °**double circle** Doppelkreis
circus ['sɜːkəs] (runder) Platz III
city ['sɪti] Stadt, Großstadt I
  city centre [ˌsɪti ˈsentə] Stadtzentrum, Innenstadt I
civilization [ˌsɪvəlaɪˈzeɪʃn] Zivilisation V 2 (34)
civil rights (pl) [ˌsɪvl ˈraɪts] Bürgerrechte IV
civil war [ˌsɪvl ˈwɔː] Bürgerkrieg IV
°**claim sth. (for sb.)** [kleɪm] etwas in Besitz nehmen (für jn.)
clap (-pp-) [klæp] (Beifall) klatschen IV
clarification [ˌklærɪfɪˈkeɪʃn] Klarstellung, Klärung V 4 (86)
clarinet [ˌklærɪˈnet] Klarinette III
class [klɑːs]
  1. (Schul-)Klasse I • **class teacher** Klassenlehrer/in I
  ▶ S.182 Collective nouns
  2. Unterricht; Kurs IV
classic ['klæsɪk] klassisch III
classical ['klæsɪkl] klassisch III
classmate ['klɑːsmeɪt] Klassenkamerad/in, Mitschüler/in I
classroom ['klɑːsruːm; 'klɑːsrʊm] Klassenzimmer I
clause [klɔːz] (Teil-, Glied-)Satz III
clean [kliːn] sauber I
clean [kliːn] sauber machen, putzen I • **clean one's teeth** sich die Zähne putzen III
cleaner ['kliːnə] Putzfrau, -mann II
°**clean-up** ['kliːnʌp] Säuberung
clear [klɪə] klar, deutlich I
clever ['klevə] klug, schlau I
cleverness ['klevənəs] Klugheit, Schlauheit IV
click on sth. [klɪk] etwas anklicken II
cliff [klɪf] Klippe III
climate ['klaɪmət] Klima V 1 (9)
climax ['klaɪmæks] Höhepunkt V 4 (95)
climb [klaɪm] klettern; hinaufklettern (auf) I • **Climb a tree.** Klettere an einen Baum. I
clinic ['klɪnɪk] Klinik II
clock [klɒk] (Wand-, Stand-, Turm-) Uhr I
°**clockwise** ['klɒkwaɪz] im Uhrzeigersinn

close (to) [kləʊs]
 1. nahe (bei, an) III
 2. eng V 1(8)
 That was close. Das war knapp. II
close [kləʊz] schließen, zumachen I
closed [kləʊzd] geschlossen II
closely [ˈkləʊsli]: **look closely at sth.** etw. genau anschauen III
clothes (pl) [kləʊðz, kləʊz] Kleider, Kleidungsstücke I
clothing [ˈkləʊðɪŋ] Kleidung IV
 piece of clothing Kleidungsstück IV
cloud [klaʊd] Wolke II • °**with one's head in the clouds** mit seinen Gedanken ganz woanders
cloudy [ˈklaʊdi] bewölkt II
clown [klaʊn] Clown/in I
club [klʌb] Klub; Verein I
 ▶ S.182 Collective nouns
coach [kəʊtʃ] Trainer/in III • **life coach** Lebensberater/in V 2 (44)
coast [kəʊst] Küste II
coconut [ˈkəʊkənʌt] Kokosnuss V 3 (64)
coffee [ˈkɒfi] Kaffee IV • **coffee to go** Kaffee zum Mitnehmen IV
coin [kɔɪn] Münze V 4 (88)
cola [ˈkəʊlə] Cola I
cold [kəʊld] kalt I • **be cold** frieren I
cold [kəʊld] Erkältung II • **have a cold** erkältet sein, eine Erkältung haben II
collapse [kəˈlæps] zusammenbrechen; einstürzen IV
collect [kəˈlekt] sammeln I
collection [kəˈlekʃn] Sammlung IV
collector [kəˈlektə] Sammler/in II
college [ˈkɒlɪdʒ] Hochschule, Fachschule III
collocation [ˌkɒləˈkeɪʃn] Kollokation (Wörter, die oft zusammen vorkommen) IV
°**colonial building** [kəˈləʊniəl] Gebäude aus der britischen Kolonialzeit
colonist [ˈkɒlənɪst] Kolonist/in; Siedler/in IV
colony [ˈkɒləni] Kolonie IV
colour [ˈkʌlə] Farbe I • **What colour is …?** Welche Farbe hat …? I
°**Coloured** [ˈkʌləd] in Südafrika: gemischtrassig
colourful [ˈkʌləfl] bunt IV
column [ˈkɒləm]
 1. Säule III
 2. Spalte V 3 (69)
come [kʌm], **came, come** kommen I • °**come across sth.** etwas finden IV
°**come alive** lebendig werden

come from stammen von/aus IV
come home nach Hause kommen I • **come in** hereinkommen I
°**come on** angehen • **Come on. 1.** Na los, komm. II; **2.** Ach komm! / Na hör mal! II • **come together** zusammenkommen IV • **come true** wahr werden II • °**come up** erscheinen • **come up with sth.** sich etwas ausdenken, sich etwas einfallen lassen IV
comedy [ˈkɒmədi] Comedyshow, Komödie II
comfort [ˈkʌmfət] trösten IV
comfortable [ˈkʌmftəbl] bequem I
comic [ˈkɒmɪk] Comic-Heft I
comment [ˈkɒment] Kommentar IV
commit (-tt-) [kəˈmɪt]: **commit a crime** ein Verbrechen begehen IV
committee [kəˈmɪti] Ausschuss, Komitee V 2 (42) • °**Head of the Committee** Ausschussvorsitzende(r)
 ▶ S.182 Collective nouns
common [ˈkɒmən] weit verbreitet, häufig V 3 (62)
Commonwealth [ˈkɒmənwelθ]: **the Commonwealth** Gemeinschaft der Länder des ehemaligen Britischen Weltreichs III
°**communications** [kəˌmjuːnɪˈkeɪʃnz] Kommunikationsnetz, Kommunikationswissenschaft
community [kəˈmjuːnəti] Gemeinschaft, Gemeinde V 2 (40) • **community hall** Gemeinschaftshalle, -saal / Gemeindehalle, -saal III
community service gemeinnützige Arbeit V 4 (89)
commuter [kəˈmjuːtə] Pendler/in V 3 (66)
company [ˈkʌmpəni] Firma, Gesellschaft III
compare [kəmˈpeə] vergleichen II
comparison [kəmˈpærɪsn] Steigerung; Vergleich II
competition [ˌkɒmpəˈtɪʃn] Wettbewerb III
complete [kəmˈpliːt] komplett, vollständig V 1(6)
complete [kəmˈpliːt] vervollständigen; abschließen, beenden V 1(6)
°**complex** [ˈkɒmpleks] Anlage
computer [kəmˈpjuːtə] Computer I
°**computer geek** [giːk] (bes. AE, infml) Computerfreak • **computer science** Computerwissenschaft, Informatik III
°**con** [kɒn]: **pros and cons** (pl) Vor- und Nachteile
°**concentrate on sth.** [ˈkɒnsntreɪt] sich auf etwas konzentrieren

concern [kənˈsɜːn]: **To whom it may concern** (bes. AE) Sehr geehrte Damen und Herren IV
concert [ˈkɒnsət] Konzert II
conclude (sth. from sth.) [kənˈkluːd] (etwas aus etwas) schließen V 1(10)
conclusion [kənˈkluːʒn] Schluss(folgerung) V 1(10) • **draw a conclusion** einen Schluss ziehen V 1 (10/171)
concrete [ˈkɒŋkriːt] Beton, Beton- V 3 (63)
confident [ˈkɒnfɪdənt] selbstbewusst, (selbst)sicher V 2 (35)
confirm [kənˈfɜːm] bestätigen V 2 (37)
confuse [kənˈfjuːz] verwirren IV
confusion [kənˈfjuːʒn] Verwirrung IV
Congratulations! [kənˌɡrætʃuˈleɪʃnz] Herzlichen Glückwunsch! III
connect A with/to B [kəˈnekt] A mit B verbinden V 1(10)
connection [kəˈnekʃn] Verbindung V 1(10)
conscious [ˈkɒnʃəs] bei Bewusstsein V 1 (23) • **conscious of sth.** sich einer Sache bewusst V 1 (23)
consequence [ˈkɒnsɪkwəns] Folge, Konsequenz IV
°**consider** [kənˈsɪdə] nachdenken über, berücksichtigen, in Betracht ziehen
console [ˈkɒnsəʊl]: **game console** Spielkonsole V 2 (34)
constitutional monarchy [ˌkɒnstɪˈtjuːʃənl] konstitutionelle Monarchie V 3 (59/187)
 ▶ S.187 Different forms of government
°**construction industry** [kənˈstrʌkʃn] Baugewerbe
contact sb. [ˈkɒntækt] sich mit jm. in Verbindung setzen; mit jm. Kontakt aufnehmen III
contact [ˈkɒntækt] Kontakt IV
 contact details Kontaktdaten V 2 (39)
context [ˈkɒntekst] Zusammenhang, Kontext IV
continent [ˈkɒntɪnənt] Kontinent IV
continue [kənˈtɪnjuː] weitermachen (mit); weiterreden; weitergehen II
contrast (to/with sth., between two things) [ˈkɒntrɑːst] Gegensatz (zu) V 1 (10)
contrast sth. and/with sth. [kənˈtrɑːst] A mit B kontrastieren (die Unterschiede aufzeigen) V 1 (10)
control (over) [kənˈtrəʊl] Kontrolle (über) V 3 (60) • **under control** unter Kontrolle IV • °**take control** die Kontrolle übernehmen

conversation [ˌkɒnvəˈseɪʃn] Gespräch, Unterhaltung II
convict [ˈkɒnvɪkt] Sträfling, Strafgefangene(r) V 1 (8)
cook [kʊk] kochen, zubereiten II
cook [kʊk] Koch, Köchin II
cooker [ˈkʊkə] Herd I
cookie [ˈkʊki] (AE) Keks IV
cool [kuːl]
1. kühl I
2. cool II
°**cool** [kuːl] (ab)kühlen
copy [ˈkɒpi] kopieren II
copy [ˈkɒpi] Kopie, Abschrift IV
°**coral** [ˈkɒrəl] Koralle
corner [ˈkɔːnə] Ecke I • **on the corner of Sand Street and London Road** Sand Street, Ecke London Road II
corn [kɔːn] (AE, no pl) Mais IV
cornflakes [ˈkɔːnfleɪks] Cornflakes I
correct [kəˈrekt] korrigieren, verbessern II
correct [kəˈrekt] richtig, korrekt II
correction [kəˈrekʃn] Korrektur, Berichtigung IV
°**correspond with sth.** [ˌkɒrəˈspɒnd] mit etwas übereinstimmen
cost [kɒst], cost, cost kosten III
cost [kɒst] Preis, Kosten IV
costume [ˈkɒstjuːm] Kostüm, Verkleidung I
cotton [ˈkɒtn] Baumwolle IV
°**couch potato** [ˈkaʊtʃ pəˌteɪtəʊ] Dauerglotzer/in
could [kəd, kʊd]: **he could ...** er konnte ... II
could [kəd, kʊd]: **we could ...** wir könnten ... II
°**could** [kəd, kʊd]: °**it could have cut ...** es hätte ... schneiden können
count [kaʊnt] zählen II
countdown [ˈkaʊntdaʊn] Countdown III
counter [ˈkaʊntə]
1. Spielstein II
2. Theke, Ladentisch IV
country [ˈkʌntri] Land (auch als Gegensatz zur Stadt) II • **in the country** auf dem Land II
couple [ˈkʌpl]: **a couple of** ein paar/Paar II
course [kɔːs] Kurs, Lehrgang III
course: of course [əv ˈkɔːs] natürlich, selbstverständlich I
court [kɔːt]
1. Platz, Court III
2. Gericht(shof) IV
cousin [ˈkʌzn] Cousin, Cousine I

cover [ˈkʌvə]
1. zudecken, bedecken IV
°2. sich erstrecken über
cover [ˈkʌvə] (CD-)Hülle I
°**covering letter** [ˈkʌvərɪŋ] Begleitbrief
cow [kaʊ] Kuh II
°**coz** [kəz] = **because**
°**crack** [kræk] Spalt, Schlitz
°**crafts** (pl) [krɑːfts] Kunsthandwerk
crash [kræʃ] abstürzen III • **crash in(to) sth.** gegen etwas fahren/laufen V 1 (20)
crazy [ˈkreɪzi] verrückt III
cream [kriːm] Sahne; Creme IV
cream cheese [ˌkriːm ˈtʃiːz] Frischkäse IV
create [kriˈeɪt] (er)schaffen, kreieren V 1 (8)
creative [kriˈeɪtɪv] kreativ, einfallsreich IV
crew [kruː] Crew, (Schiffs-)Mannschaft III
cricket [ˈkrɪkɪt] Kricket III
crime [kraɪm] Verbrechen; Kriminalität IV • **commit a crime** ein Verbrechen begehen IV • **crime film** Krimi IV • **crime rate** Kriminalität(srate) V 3 (56) • **crime story** Krimi IV
crisis [ˈkraɪsɪs] Krise IV
crisps (pl) [krɪsps] Kartoffelchips I
critic [ˈkrɪtɪk] Kritiker/in IV
crocodile [ˈkrɒkədaɪl] Krokodil II
cross [krɒs] überqueren; (sich) kreuzen II
crosswalk [ˈkrɒswɔːk] (AE) Fußgängerüberweg II
crowd [kraʊd] (Menschen-)Menge III
crowded [ˈkraʊdɪd] voller Menschen, überfüllt III
°**crown-of-thorns starfish** [kraʊn ˌɒv ˌtɔːnz ˈstɑːfɪʃ] Dornenkronenseestern
cruel [ˈkruːəl] grausam IV
cry [kraɪ]
1. schreien I • **cry in pain** vor Schmerzen schreien I
2. weinen III
°**crystal-clear** [ˌkrɪstəl ˈklɪə] kristallklar
culture [ˈkʌltʃə] Kultur V 1 (16)
cup [kʌp]
1. Tasse II • **a cup of tea** eine Tasse Tee II
2. Pokal III
cupboard [ˈkʌbəd] Schrank I
curriculum vitae [kəˌrɪkjələm ˈviːtaɪ] (BE) Lebenslauf V 2 (38)
cut (-tt-) [kʌt], cut, cut schneiden II • **cut sth. off** etwas abschneiden, abtrennen III • **cut sth. out** ausschneiden III • **cut the grass** Rasen mähen IV
cut [kʌt] Schnitt IV
CV [ˌsiː ˈviː] (BE) Lebenslauf V 2 (38)
cycle [ˈsaɪkl] (mit dem) Rad fahren II
cycle path [ˈsaɪkl pɑːθ] Radweg II

D

dad [dæd] Papa, Vati; Vater I
daily [ˈdeɪli] täglich IV
damn [dæm] verdammt IV
dance [dɑːns] tanzen I
dance [dɑːns] Tanz I • **dance floor** Tanzfläche III
dancer [ˈdɑːnsə] Tänzer/in II
dancing [ˈdɑːnsɪŋ] Tanzen I
dancing lessons Tanzstunden, Tanzunterricht I
danger (to) [ˈdeɪndʒə] Gefahr (für) I °**stop a danger** einer Gefahr Einhalt gebieten
dangerous [ˈdeɪndʒərəs] gefährlich II
dark [dɑːk]
1. dunkel I
2. dunkelhaarig V 1 (9)
dark [dɑːk]: **after dark** nach Einbruch der Dunkelheit IV
darling [ˈdɑːlɪŋ] Liebling, Schatz V 4 (92)
date [deɪt]
1. Datum I • **date of birth** Geburtsdatum IV • **to date** bis heute, bis dato V 2 (38)
2. Verabredung, Date V 4 (80) • **go on a date with sb.** mit jm. ausgehen V 4 (80/191)
date [deɪt] (bes. AE) mit jm. (aus)gehen; sich (regelmäßig) mit jm. treffen III
daughter [ˈdɔːtə] Tochter I
day [deɪ] Tag I • **by day and by night** bei Tag und bei Nacht V 3 (67) **one day** eines Tages I • **days of the week** Wochentage I • **the day before yesterday** vorgestern II • **that day** an jenem Tag III
dead [ded] tot I
deaf [def] taub, gehörlos III
deal with sb./sth. [diːl], dealt, dealt sich mit jm./etwas beschäftigen; handeln von etwas IV • °**deal drugs** mit Drogen handeln
deal [diːl] Angebot IV • **make a deal** ein Abkommen/eine Abmachung treffen III • **It's a deal!** Abgemacht! III
dealt [delt] siehe **deal**

dear [dɪə] Schatz, Liebling I • **Oh dear!** Oje! II
dear [dɪə]: **Dear Jay …** Lieber Jay, … I **Dear Sir or Madam …** Sehr geehrte Damen und Herren IV
death [deθ] Tod IV • **death rate** Sterberate V 1 (9/169) • **death sentence** Todesstrafe IV • **fall to one's death** zu Tode stürzen IV
debate [dɪˈbeɪt] Debatte V 1 (6)
debts (pl) [dets] Schulden IV
December [dɪˈsembə] Dezember I
decide (on sth.) [dɪˈsaɪd] sich entscheiden (für etwas), (etwas) beschließen II
°**decision** [dɪˈsɪʒn] Entscheidung II
°**declaration** [ˌdekləˈreɪʃn] Erklärung II
deep [diːp] tief IV
deer, pl **deer** [dɪə] Reh, Hirsch II
defence [dɪˈfens] Verteidigung III
definite [ˈdefɪnət] fest, bestimmt; endgültig, eindeutig V 2 (47)
degree [dɪˈɡriː] Grad II
delay [dɪˈleɪ] aufhalten IV
delay [dɪˈleɪ] Verspätung IV
deli [ˈdeli] Deli (Lebensmittelgeschäft mit Fastfoodrestaurant) IV
delicious [dɪˈlɪʃəs] köstlich, lecker II
deliver [dɪˈlɪvə] (aus)liefern, austragen IV
democracy [dɪˈmɒkrəsi] Demokratie; demokratischer Staat V 3 (59)
▶ S.187 Different forms of government
democrat [ˈdeməkræt] Demokrat/in V 3 (59)
democratic [ˌdeməˈkrætɪk] demokratisch V 3 (59)
dentist [ˈdentɪst] Zahnarzt, -ärztin IV
°**department** [dɪˈpɑːtmənt] Abteilung
department store [dɪˈpɑːtmənt stɔː] Kaufhaus II
departure [dɪˈpɑːtʃə] Abfahrt; Abflug IV
depend on sth./sb. [dɪˈpend] sich auf etwas/jn verlassen IV
dependable [dɪˈpendəbl] zuverlässig IV
describe sth. (to sb.) [dɪˈskraɪb] (jm.) etwas beschreiben II
description [dɪˈskrɪpʃn] Beschreibung II
desert [ˈdezət] Wüste IV
deserve [dɪˈzɜːv] verdienen (zu Recht bekommen) V 2 (39)
design [dɪˈzaɪn] Muster, Entwurf; Design, Gestaltung V 2 (46)
design school Kunsthochschule V 2 (47)
design [dɪˈzaɪn] entwickeln, entwerfen I

°**desire** [dɪˈzaɪə] Wunsch, Verlangen
desk [desk] Schreibtisch I
despite [dɪˈspaɪt] trotz V 1 (8)
destination [ˌdestɪˈneɪʃn] (Reise-)Ziel V 3 (66)
destroy [dɪˈstrɔɪ] zerstören III
detail [ˈdiːteɪl] Detail, Einzelheit III • **contact details** Kontaktdaten V 2 (39)
detailed [ˈdiːteɪld] ausführlich, detailliert V 1 (10)
detective [dɪˈtektɪv] Detektiv/in I
determination [dɪˌtɜːmɪˈneɪʃn] Entschlossenheit V 2 (47)
determined [dɪˈtɜːmɪnd] (fest) entschlossen V 2 (47)
develop (from … into …) [dɪˈveləp] entwickeln; sich (aus … zu …) entwickeln V 1 (8)
developing country [dɪˈveləpɪŋ] Entwicklungsland V 3 (50)
diagonal [daɪˈæɡənəl] diagonal, schräg IV
dial (-ll-) [ˈdaɪəl] wählen (Telefonnummer) II
dialect [ˈdaɪəlekt] Dialekt, Mundart V 3 (52)
diamond [ˈdaɪəmənd] Diamant V 4 (92)
diary [ˈdaɪəri] Tagebuch; Terminkalender I
dice, pl **dice** [daɪs] Würfel II • **throw the dice** würfeln II
°**dictate** [dɪkˈteɪt] diktieren
dictator [dɪkˈteɪtə] Diktator/in V 3 (59/187)
dictatorship [ˌdɪkˈteɪtəʃɪp] Diktatur V 3 (59/187)
▶ S.187 Different forms of government
dictionary [ˈdɪkʃənri] Wörterbuch, (alphabetisches) Wörterverzeichnis I
did [dɪd] siehe **do** • **Did you go?** Bist du gegangen? / Gingst du? I **we didn't go** [ˈdɪdnt] wir sind nicht gegangen/wir gingen nicht I
die (of) (-ing form: **dying**) [daɪ] sterben (an) II
difference [ˈdɪfrəns] Unterschied III
different (from) [ˈdɪfrənt] verschieden, unterschiedlich; anders (als) I
difficult [ˈdɪfɪkəlt] schwierig, schwer I
°**diner** [ˈdaɪnə] Restaurantgast
dining room [ˈdaɪnɪŋ ruːm, ˈdaɪnɪŋ rʊm] Esszimmer I
dinner [ˈdɪnə] Abendessen, Abendbrot I • **have dinner** Abendbrot essen I
dinosaur [ˈdaɪnəsɔː] Dinosaurier III
direct [dəˈrekt] direkt V 2 (37)
direct [dəˈrekt] Regie führen III

direct speech [dəˈrekt] direkte Rede III
directions (pl) [dəˈrekʃnz] Wegbeschreibung(en) II
director [dəˈrektə] Regisseur/in III
dirt [dɜːt] Schmutz, Dreck V 1 (12)
dirt bike [ˈdɜːt baɪk] Geländemotorrad V 1 (12)
dirt road [ˈdɜːt rəʊd] unbefestigte Straße V 1 (6)
dirty [ˈdɜːti] schmutzig II • °**get one's hands dirty** sich die Hände schmutzig machen
disabled [dɪsˈeɪbld] (körper)behindert III
disadvantage [ˌdɪsədˈvɑːntɪdʒ] Nachteil IV
disagree (with) [ˌdɪsəˈɡriː] anderer Meinung sein (als), nicht übereinstimmen (mit) II
disappear [ˌdɪsəˈpɪə] verschwinden II
disappoint sb. [ˌdɪsəˈpɔɪnt] jn. enttäuschen IV
disappointed (with/in sb., with/about sth.) [ˌdɪsəˈpɔɪntɪd] enttäuscht (von jm./etwas) IV
discipline [ˈdɪsəplɪn] Disziplin V 4 (85)
disc jockey [ˈdɪsk dʒɒki] Diskjockey III
disco [ˈdɪskəʊ] Disko I
discover [dɪˈskʌvə] entdecken; herausfinden II
discriminate against sb. [dɪˈskrɪmɪneɪt] jn. diskriminieren, jn. benachteiligen IV
discrimination (against) [dɪˌskrɪmɪˈneɪʃn] Diskriminierung (von), Benachteiligung (von) IV
°**race discrimination** Diskriminierung aufgrund der Rasse, der ethnischen Gruppe
discussion [dɪˈskʌʃn] Diskussion II
disease [dɪˈziːz] (ansteckende) Krankheit IV
dish [dɪʃ] Gericht (Speise) III
dishes (pl) [ˈdɪʃɪz] Geschirr I • **do the dishes** das Geschirr abwaschen I
dishwasher [ˈdɪʃwɒʃə] Geschirrspülmaschine I
dislikes (pl) [ˈdɪslaɪks]: **likes and dislikes** (pl) Vorlieben und Abneigungen V 2 (42)
display [dɪˈspleɪ] Display IV • **be on display** ausgestellt sein IV
°**display** [dɪˈspleɪ] zeigen, ausstellen
°**disposable** [dɪˈspəʊzəbl] Einweg-, Wegwerf-
°**disposal** [dɪˈspəʊzl] Beseitigung, Entsorgung

distance [ˈdɪstəns] Entfernung IV
diver [ˈdaɪvə] Taucher/in V 4 (88)
divide (into) [dɪˈvaɪd] (sich) teilen (in), (sich) aufteilen (in) II
divorced [dɪˈvɔːst] geschieden I
DJ [ˈdiːdʒeɪ] Diskjockey III
DJ [ˈdiːdʒeɪ] (Musik/CDs/Platten) auflegen *(in der Disko)* III
do [duː], **did, done** tun, machen I • **do a gig** einen Auftritt haben, ein Konzert geben III • **do a good job** gute Arbeit leisten II • **do an exercise** eine Übung machen II • **do a project** ein Projekt machen, durchführen II • **do sb. a favour** jm. einen Gefallen tun IV • **do sport** Sport treiben I • °**do sth. wrong** etwas Verbotenes tun • **do the dishes** das Geschirr abwaschen I • **How am I doing?** Wie komme ich voran? (Wie sind meine Fortschritte?) III • **learning by doing** Lernen durch Handeln/Tun V 2 (40/181)
doctor [ˈdɒktə] Arzt/Ärztin, Doktor I • **at/to the doctor's** beim/zum Arzt III
°**document** [ˈdɒkjuːmənt] dokumentieren
documentary [ˌdɒkjuˈmentri] Dokumentarfilm II
°**doer** [ˈduːə] Macher/in
dog [dɒɡ] Hund I • **walk the dog** den Hund ausführen V 4 (90)
doll [dɒl] Puppe IV
dollar ($) [ˈdɒlə] Dollar IV
dolphin [ˈdɒlfɪn] Delfin V 1 (9)
°**domain** [dəˈmeɪn] Domain, Domäne
donate [dəʊˈneɪt] spenden, schenken V 4 (88)
done [dʌn] *siehe* **do**
don't [dəʊnt]: **Don't listen to Dan.** Hör/Hört nicht auf Dan. I • **I don't like ...** Ich mag ... nicht. / Ich mag kein(e) ... I
door [dɔː] Tür I
doorbell [ˈdɔːbel] Türklingel I
°**doorway** [ˈdɔːweɪ] Eingang
dossier [ˈdɒsieɪ] Mappe, Dossier *(des Sprachenportfolios)* I
double [ˈdʌbl] zweimal, doppelt, Doppel- I • **double bed** Doppelbett V 3 (64/189) • °**double circle** Doppelkreis
double bass [ˌdʌbl ˈbeɪs] Kontrabass III
°**double-decker** [ˌdʌblˈdekə] Doppeldecker
dough [dəʊ] Teig IV
down [daʊn] hinunter, herunter, nach unten I • **down there** (nach) dort unten II

download [ˌdaʊnˈləʊd] runterladen, downloaden II
downstairs [ˌdaʊnˈsteəz] unten; nach unten I
downtown [ˌdaʊnˈtaʊn] Stadtzentrum IV • **downtown bus** *(AE)* Bus in Richtung Stadtzentrum IV
°**Down Under** [ˌdaʊnˈʌndə] umgangssprachliche Bezeichnung für Australien
Dr., Dr [ˈdɒktə] Dr. IV
draft [drɑːft] Entwurf IV
dragon [ˈdræɡən] Drache III
drama [ˈdrɑːmə]
1. Schauspiel, darstellende Kunst I
2. Fernsehspiel; Drama IV
drank [dræŋk] *siehe* **drink**
draw [drɔː], **drew, drawn** zeichnen III
draw a conclusion [drɔː] einen Schluss ziehen V 1 (10/171)
draw [drɔː] Unentschieden III
drawing [ˈdrɔːɪŋ] Zeichnung III
drawn [drɔːn] *siehe* **draw**
dream [driːm] Traum I • **dream house** Traumhaus I
dream (of, about) [driːm] träumen (von) III • **dream on** weiterträumen III • °**the Dreaming** die Traumzeit
dress [dres] sich kleiden, sich anziehen IV
dress [dres] Kleid I
dressed [drest]: **get dressed** sich anziehen I
drew [druː] *siehe* **draw**
°**drill** [drɪl] Waffendrill
drink [drɪŋk] Getränk I
drink [drɪŋk], **drank, drunk** trinken I
°**drinking water** [ˈdrɪŋkɪŋ wɔːtə] Trinkwasser
drive [draɪv], **drove, driven** (ein Auto / mit dem Auto) fahren II
°**drive off** davonfahren • **driving instructor** Fahrlehrer/in V 1 (6/168)
drive [draɪv] (Auto)fahrt IV
driven [ˈdrɪvn] *siehe* **drive**
driver [ˈdraɪvə] Fahrer/in II
driving licence [ˈdraɪvɪŋ ˌlaɪsəns] Führerschein, Fahrerlaubnis V 2 (39)
drop (-pp-) [drɒp]
1. fallen lassen I
2. fallen I
drop sb. off jn. absetzen (aussteigen lassen) IV
drove [drəʊv] *siehe* **drive**
drown [draʊn] ertrinken IV
drug [drʌɡ] Droge; Medikament V 3 (52) • **drug dealer** Dealer/in V 3 (57)
drum [drʌm] Trommel; Schlagzeug III • **drumstick** Trommelstock III

play the drums Schlagzeug spielen III
drunk [drʌŋk]
1. *siehe* **drink**
2. betrunken IV • **get drunk** sich betrinken V 4 (87)
dry [draɪ] trocken III
°**dryer** [ˈdraɪə] Trockner
°**Dunno.** [dəˈnəʊ] *(infml)* = **I don't know.**
during *(prep)* [ˈdjʊərɪŋ] während III
dust [dʌst] Staub IV
dustbin [ˈdʌstbɪn] Mülltonne II
dusty [ˈdʌsti] staubig V 3 (59)
duvet [ˈduːveɪ] Bettdecke, Federbett V 3 (64/189)
DVD [ˌdiː viː ˈdiː] DVD I

E

each [iːtʃ] jeder, jede, jedes (einzelne) I • **each other** einander, sich (gegenseitig) III
eagle [ˈiːɡl] Adler V 4 (85)
ear [ɪə] Ohr I
earache [ˈɪəreɪk] Ohrenschmerzen II
early [ˈɜːli] früh I
earn money [ɜːn] Geld verdienen V 2 (46)
earring [ˈɪərɪŋ] Ohrring I
earth [ɜːθ] Erde V 1 (9)
earthquake [ˈɜːθkweɪk] Erdbeben IV
earthworm [ˈɜːθwɜːm] Regenwurm IV
east [iːst] Osten; nach Osten; östlich II • **eastbound** [ˈiːstbaʊnd] Richtung Osten III • **eastern** [ˈiːstən] östlich, Ost- III
easy [ˈiːzi] leicht, einfach I • **easy-to-read** leicht zu lesende(r, s) V 2 (39)
easy-going [ˌiːzi ˈɡəʊɪŋ] gelassen, unbeschwert V 1 (25)
eat [iːt], **ate, eaten** essen I
eaten [ˈiːtn] *siehe* **eat**
°**ebony** [ˈebəni] Ebenholz
economic [ˌiːkəˈnɒmɪk] wirtschaftliche(r, s); Wirtschafts- V 3 (56)
economy [ɪˈkɒnəmi] (Volks-)Wirtschaft V 3 (56)
edit [ˈedɪt] redigieren III
editor [ˈedɪtə] Redakteur/in III
educate [ˈedʒukeɪt] unterrichten; erziehen; aufklären V 3 (56)
education [ˌedʒuˈkeɪʃn] (Schul-, Aus-)Bildung; Erziehung IV
effect (on) [ɪˈfekt] Wirkung, Auswirkung (auf) IV

effective [ɪˈfektɪv] effektiv, wirksam, wirkungsvoll V 2 (39)
e-friend [ˈiːfrend] Brieffreund/in *(im Internet)* I
egg [eg] Ei I
eightish [ˈeɪtɪʃ] ungefähr acht (Jahre/Uhr) IV
either [ˈaɪðə, ˈiːðə]: **either … or …** entweder … oder … V 1 (8) • **not (…) either** auch nicht II
▶ S.176 neither
elect sb. sth. [ɪˈlekt] jn. zu etwas wählen IV
election [ɪˈlekʃn] Wahl *(von Kandidaten bei einer Abstimmung)* IV
electric [ɪˈlektrɪk] elektrisch, Elektro- III
electrical engineer [ɪˌlektrɪkəl ˌendʒɪˈnɪə] Elektrotechniker/in V 2 (40)
electricity [ɪˌlekˈtrɪsəti] Strom, Elektrizität III • **static electricity** elektrische Auflaudung IV
electronic [ɪˌlekˈtrɒnɪk] elektronisch III
elementary school [ˌelɪˈmentri skuːl] *(USA)* Grundschule *(für 6- bis 11-Jährige)* IV
elephant [ˈelɪfənt] Elefant I
elevator [ˈelɪveɪtə] *(AE)* Fahrstuhl, Aufzug II
else [els]: **anybody/anything else** sonst (noch) jemand/etwas • **anywhere else** sonst (noch) irgendwo(hin) • **somebody else** jemand anders • **something else** etwas anderes • **somewhere else** woanders(hin) • **who/what/where/why/… else?** wer/was/wo/warum/… (sonst) noch? III
e-mail [ˈiːmeɪl] E-Mail I
embarrassed [ɪmˈbærəst] verlegen IV
embarrassing [ɪmˈbærəsɪŋ] peinlich IV
emergency [ɪˈmɜːdʒənsi] Notfall, Not- IV
employer [ɪmˈplɔɪə] Arbeitgeber/in V 2 (39)
empty [ˈempti] leer I
emu [ˈiːmjuː] Emu V 1 (9)
enclose [ɪnˈkləʊz] etwas *(einem Brief)* beilegen V 2 (41)
encourage [ɪnˈkʌrɪdʒ] (jn.) ermutigen, ermuntern; (etwas) fördern V 4 (89)
encyclopedia [ɪnˌsaɪkləˈpiːdiə] Enzyklopädie, Lexikon II
end [end] Ende; Schluss I • **at the end (of)** am Ende (von) I • **achieve an end** ein Ziel erreichen IV

end [end]
1. zu Ende gehen IV
2. (etwas) beenden V 4 (80) • **end a relationship** mit jm. Schluss machen V 4 (80/191)
ending [ˈendɪŋ] Ende, (Ab-)Schluss *(einer Geschichte, eines Films usw.)* III • **happy ending** Happyend II
endless [ˈendləs] endlos V 1 (6)
enemy [ˈenəmi] Feind/in II
energetic [ˌenəˈdʒetɪk] dynamisch, tatkräftig, energisch V 2 (35)
energy [ˈenədʒi] Energie, Kraft V 3 (53)
engineer [ˌendʒɪˈnɪə] Ingenieur/in II
English [ˈɪŋglɪʃ] Englisch; englisch I
enjoy [ɪnˈdʒɔɪ] genießen I
enough [ɪˈnʌf] genug I
enroll for/in/on sth. [ɪnˈrəʊl] sich (für etwas) anmelden IV
enter [ˈentə]
1. betreten IV • **enter a country** in ein Land einreisen IV
2. eingeben, eintragen II
entertain sb. [ˌentəˈteɪn] jn. unterhalten IV
entertainment [ˌentəˈteɪnmənt] Unterhaltung (Vergnügen) IV
entry [ˈentri]
1. Eintrag, Eintragung *(im Wörterbuch/Tagebuch)* III
2. Einsendung, Beitrag *(zu einem Wettbewerb)* III
environment [ɪnˈvaɪrənmənt] Umwelt IV
environmental [ɪnˌvaɪrənˈmentl] Umwelt- IV
epidemic [ˌepəˈdemɪk] Epidemie V 3 (50)
equal [ˈiːkwəl] gleich IV
equalize [ˈiːkwəlaɪz] ausgleichen; das Ausgleichstor erzielen III
equator [ɪˈkweɪtə] Äquator V 1 (9)
equipment [ɪˈkwɪpmənt] Ausrüstung III
eraser [ɪˈreɪzə(r), ɪˈreɪsə(r)] *(AE)* Radiergummi IV
°**escalator** [ˈeskəleɪtə] Rolltreppe
escape from sb./sth. [ɪˈskeɪp] vor jm./aus etwas fliehen; entkommen IV
°**especially** [ɪˈspeʃli] besonders
essay (about, on) [ˈeseɪ] Aufsatz (über) I
etc. (et cetera) [etˈsetərə] usw. (und so weiter) IV
ethnic [ˈeθnɪk] ethnisch, Volks- IV
euro (€) [ˈjʊərəʊ] Euro I
even [ˈiːvn]
1. sogar II
2. (sogar) schon III

evening [ˈiːvnɪŋ] Abend I • **in the evening** abends, am Abend I • **on Friday evening** freitagabends, am Freitagabend I
event [ɪˈvent] Ereignis II
ever [ˈevə] je, jemals III • **ever?** je? / jemals? / schon mal? II • **more than ever** mehr als je (zuvor), mehr denn je V 3 (50)
every [ˈevri] jeder, jede, jedes I
everybody [ˈevrɪbɒdi] jeder, alle II
everyday *(adj)* [ˈevrɪdeɪ] Alltags-; alltäglich IV
everyone [ˈevrɪwʌn] jeder; alle III
everything [ˈevrɪθɪŋ] alles I
everywhere [ˈevrɪweə] überall I
exact [ɪɡˈzækt] genau III
exam [ɪɡˈzæm] Prüfung V 2 (32)
example (of) [ɪɡˈzɑːmpl] Beispiel (für) I • **for example** zum Beispiel I
excellent [ˈeksələnt] ausgezeichnet, hervorragend IV
except [ɪkˈsept] außer, bis auf IV
exchange [ɪksˈtʃeɪndʒ] (Schüler-)Austausch III
exchange [ɪksˈtʃeɪndʒ] aus-, umtauschen III; *(Geld)* wechseln III
excited [ɪkˈsaɪtɪd] *(positiv)* aufgeregt, begeistert II
exciting [ɪkˈsaɪtɪŋ] aufregend, spannend II
Excuse me, … [ɪkˈskjuːz miː] Entschuldigung, … / Entschuldigen Sie, … I
execution [ˌeksɪˈkjuːʃn] Hinrichtung IV
exercise [ˈeksəsaɪz] Übung, Aufgabe I • **do an exercise** eine Übung machen II • **exercise book** Schulheft, Übungsheft I • **pre-writing exercise** Übung vor dem Schreiben III
exhibition (on) [ˌeksɪˈbɪʃn] Ausstellung (über) IV
exist [ɪɡˈzɪst] existieren V 1 (16)
expect [ɪkˈspekt] erwarten, annehmen, vermuten IV
expectancy [ɪkˈspektənsi]: **life expectancy** Lebenserwartung V 3 (52)
expensive [ɪkˈspensɪv] teuer I
experience [ɪkˈspɪəriəns] Erfahrung; Erlebnis IV • **work experience** *(no pl)* Arbeits-, Praxiserfahrung(en) V 2 (38)
experience [ɪkˈspɪəriəns] erfahren, erleben V 3 (62)
experienced [ɪkˈspɪəriənst] erfahren IV
explain sth. to sb. [ɪkˈspleɪn] jm. etwas erklären, erläutern II

explanation [ˌeksplə'neɪʃn] Erklärung II
explore [ɪk'splɔː] erkunden, erforschen I
explorer [ɪk'splɔːrə] Entdecker/in, Forscher/in II
explosion [ɪk'spləʊʒn] Explosion IV
express [ɪk'spres] äußern, zum Ausdruck bringen, ausdrücken V 4 (86)
expression [ɪk'spreʃn] Ausdruck III
extra ['ekstrə] zusätzlich I
°**extract** ['ekstrækt] Auszug *(aus einem Buch, Text, Film usw.)*
extracurricular activities *(kurz:* **extracurriculars)** [ˌekstrəkə'rɪkjələz] schulische Angebote außerhalb des regulären Unterrichts, oft als Arbeitsgemeinschaften IV
extraordinary [ɪk'strɔːdnri] außergewöhnlich IV
°**extreme** [ɪk'striːm] extrem
eye [aɪ] Auge I • **keep an eye on sth./sb.** nach jm./etwas Ausschau halten IV • **She couldn't believe her eyes.** Sie traute ihren Augen kaum. III

F

face [feɪs] Gesicht I
°**face** [feɪs]
  1. **face sth.** *(Zimmer)* zu etwas liegen
  2. **face a problem** mit einem Problem konfrontiert sein
fact [fækt] Tatsache, Fakt III
factory ['fæktri] Fabrik II
factual text ['fæktʃuːl] Sachtext IV
failure ['feɪljə] ungenügend IV
fair [feə]
  1. fair, gerecht II
  2. hell *(Haut; Haare)* V 1 (9)
°**fair dinkum** [ˌfeə 'dɪŋkəm] *(Australisches E)* echt, wahr(haftig)
faith (in sb./sth.) [feɪθ] Vertrauen (in jn./etwas); Glaube V 2 (47)
faithfully ['feɪθfəli]: **Yours faithfully** *(BE)* mit freundlichen Grüßen IV
fall [fɔːl], **fell, fallen** fallen, stürzen; hinfallen II • **fall asleep** einschlafen V 1 (21) • **fall down** runterfallen; hinfallen II • **fall in love (with sb.)** sich verlieben (in jn.) IV • **fall off** herunterfallen (von) II • **fall to one's death** zu Tode stürzen IV
fallen ['fɔːlən] *siehe* **fall**
family ['fæməli] Familie I • **family man** Familienmensch IV • **family tree** (Familien-)Stammbaum I
  ▶ S.182 Collective nouns

famous (for) ['feɪməs] berühmt (für, wegen) II
fan [fæn] Fan, Anhänger/in III
fan [fæn] Ventilator V 3 (63)
fancy sth. ['fænsi] *(infml)* Lust auf/zu etwas haben V 2 (42)
fancy ['fænsi] schick, ausgefallen *(etwas abwertend)* V 3 (65)
fantastic [fæn'tæstɪk] fantastisch, toll I
fantasy ['fæntəsi] Fantasy *(Genre)* V 2 (34)
far [fɑː] weit (entfernt) I • **by far** bei weitem; mit Abstand V 4 (88) • **far and wide** weit und breit IV • **so far** bis jetzt, bis hierher III
faraway ['fɑːrəweɪ] abgelegen III
farm [fɑːm] Bauernhof, Farm II
farmer ['fɑːmə] Bauer/Bäuerin, Landwirt/in; (Fisch-)Züchter/in III
farmhouse ['fɑːmhaʊs] Bauernhaus III
fascinate ['fæsəneɪt] faszinieren V 3 (67)
fashion ['fæʃn] Mode II • **military-style fashion** Mode im Militärstil V 4 (85/192)
fast [fɑːst] schnell II
°**fast and furious** ['fjʊəriəs] rasant, intensiv
fat [fæt] dick IV
father ['fɑːðə] Vater I
fault [fɔːlt] Schuld, Fehler IV • **it's your fault** du hast Schuld IV
favour ['feɪvə] : **do sb. a favour** jm. einen Gefallen tun IV
favourite ['feɪvrɪt] Lieblings- I • **my favourite colour** meine Lieblingsfarbe I
favourite ['feɪvrɪt] Favorit/in; Liebling III
fear (of) [fɪə] Furcht, Angst (vor) III
fearless ['fɪələs] furchtlos V 3 (57) • **the fearless** die Furchtlosen V 3 (57)
°**feature** ['fiːtʃə] Merkmal
February ['februəri] Februar I
fed [fed] *siehe* **feed**
feed [fiːd], **fed, fed** füttern I
feel [fiːl], **felt, felt** fühlen; sich fühlen II; sich anfühlen II • **I feel sick.** Mir ist schlecht. II
feeling ['fiːlɪŋ] Gefühl III
feet [fiːt] *Plural von „foot"* I
fell [fel] *siehe* **fall**
felt [felt] *siehe* **feel**
felt tip ['felt tɪp] Filzstift I
female ['fiːmeɪl] Weibchen II
fence [fens] Zaun IV
ferry ['feri] Fähre III
festival ['festɪvl] Fest, Festival II
fetch [fetʃ] holen, abholen IV

few [fjuː] wenige IV • **a few** ein paar, einige II
fewer ['fjuːə] weniger IV
fiction ['fɪkʃn] Belletristik; Prosaliteratur IV
fiddle ['fɪdl] *(infml)* Fiedel, Geige III • **play the fiddle** Geige spielen III
field [fiːld] Feld, Acker, Weide II • **in the field** auf dem Feld II
fight (for) [faɪt], **fought, fought** kämpfen (für, um) III • °**fight a war** einen Krieg führen
fight [faɪt] Kampf IV
figure ['fɪgə] Zahl, Ziffer, Betrag V 1 (8)
file [faɪl]: **background file** etwa: Hintergrundinformation II • **grammar file** Grammatikanhang I • **skills file** Anhang mit Lern- und Arbeitstechniken I
fill sth. (with sth.) [fɪl] etwas (mit etwas) (aus)füllen IV
filling ['fɪlɪŋ] (Brot-)Belag IV
film [fɪlm] Film I • **crime film** Krimi IV • **film star** Filmstar I
film [fɪlm] filmen III
final ['faɪnl] Finale, Endspiel III
final ['faɪnl] letzte(r, s); End- III
finally ['faɪnəli] endlich, schließlich IV
finance ['faɪnæns] Finanzwesen V 3 (52)
financial [faɪ'nænʃl] finanziell, Finanz- V 3 (52)
find [faɪnd], **found, found** finden I • **find out (about)** herausfinden (über) I
°**finding** ['faɪndɪŋ] Ergebnis
fine [faɪn]
  1. gut, ausgezeichnet; in Ordnung II
  2. *(gesundheitlich)* gut II **I'm/He's fine.** Es geht mir/ihm gut. II
fine [faɪn] Geldstrafe IV
finger ['fɪŋgə] Finger I
finish ['fɪnɪʃ] beenden, zu Ende machen; enden I
fire ['faɪə] Feuer, Brand II • **There's no smoke without fire.** Wo Rauch ist, ist auch Feuer. IV
°**fire** ['faɪə]: **fire a gun** mit einer Schusswaffe schießen
firefighter ['faɪəfaɪtə] Feuerwehrmann, -frau IV
°**firefighting** ['faɪəˌfaɪtɪŋ] Brandbekämpfung
fireman ['faɪəmən] Feuerwehrmann II
fireproof ['faɪəpruːf] feuerbeständig, -fest V 1 (17/173)

fire station [ˈfaɪə ˌsteɪʃn] Feuerwache IV
firewoman [ˈfaɪəˌwʊmən], *pl* **firewomen** Feuerwehrfrau II
first [fɜːst]
1. erste(r, s) I
2. zuerst, als Erstes I
be first der/die Erste sein I
°**come first** den Vorrang haben
for the first time zum ersten Mal II • **First Nations** die Ersten Nationen *(indianische Ureinwohner/innen Kanadas)* III
first floor [ˌfɜːst ˈflɔː] erster Stock *(BE)* / Erdgeschoss *(AE)* IV
fish, *pl* **fish/fishes** [fɪʃ] Fisch I
fish [fɪʃ] fischen, angeln III
fisherman [ˈfɪʃəmən], *pl* **fishermen** [ˈfɪʃəmən] Angler, Fischer III
fist [fɪst] Faust IV
fit (-tt-) [fɪt] passen I
flag [flæɡ] Fahne, Flagge V 1 (8)
flash [flæʃ] aufblitzen; leuchten IV
flash [flæʃ] Lichtblitz III
flashback [ˈflæʃbæk] Rückblende V 1 (24)
flat [flæt] Wohnung I
flat [flæt] flach, eben II
flattered [ˈflætəd]: **be/feel flattered** sich geschmeichelt fühlen V 4 (83)
flavour [ˈfleɪvə] Geschmack, Geschmacksrichtung II
flea market [ˈfliː ˌmɑːkɪt] Flohmarkt III
flew [fluː] *siehe* **fly**
flexible [ˈfleksəbl] flexibel, anpassungsfähig V 2 (35)
flight [flaɪt] Flug II
floor [flɔː]
1. Fußboden I • **dance floor** Tanzfläche III
2. Stock(werk) IV • **first floor** erster Stock *(BE)* / Erdgeschoss *(AE)* IV
ground floor *(BE)* Erdgeschoss IV
on the second floor im zweiten Stock *(BE)* / im ersten Stock *(AE)* IV
flow [fləʊ] fließen IV
flow chart [ˈfləʊ tʃɑːt] Flussdiagramm I
flower [ˈflaʊə] Blume; Blüte II
flown [fləʊn] *siehe* **fly**
flu [fluː] Grippe II
flute [fluːt] Querflöte III
fly [flaɪ], **flew, flown** fliegen II
flying instructor Fluglehrer/in V 1 (6/168)
fly [flaɪ] Fliege V 1 (21)
flyer [ˈflaɪə] Flugblatt, Flyer IV
focus [ˈfəʊkəs] Schwerpunkt, Mittelpunkt, Hauptpunkt V 2 (45)
focus (on) [ˈfəʊkəs] sich konzentrieren (auf) V 2 (45)

fog [fɒɡ] Nebel II
foggy [ˈfɒɡi] neblig II
folk (music) [ˈfəʊk ˌmjuːzɪk] Folk *(meist englischsprachige, volkstümliche Musik mit Elementen der Rockmusik)* III
folks [fəʊks] *(infml, bes. AE)* Leute III • °**old folks' home** *(infml)* Altenheim, Seniorenresidenz
follow [ˈfɒləʊ] folgen; verfolgen I
°**follow rules** [ˈfɒləʊ] sich an die Regeln halten • **the following ...** die folgenden ... III
font [fɒnt] Schrift(art) V 2 (39)
food [fuːd] Essen; Lebensmittel; Futter I
foot [fʊt], *pl* **feet** [fiːt]
1. Fuß I • **on foot** zu Fuß III
2. Fuß *(Längenmaß; ca. 30 cm)* IV
football [ˈfʊtbɔːl] Fußball I
football boots Fußballschuhe, -stiefel I • **football pitch** Fußballplatz, -feld II
footballer [ˈfʊtbɔːlə] Fußballspieler/in III
footnote [ˈfʊtnəʊt] Fußnote, Anmerkung IV
for [fə, fɔː] für I • **for a moment** einen Moment lang II • **for a while** eine Weile, einige Zeit IV • **for breakfast/lunch/dinner** zum Frühstück/Mittagessen/Abendbrot III • **for example** zum Beispiel I • **for his birthday** zu seinem Geburtstag III • **for lots of reasons** aus vielen Gründen I • **for miles** meilenweit II • **(in prison) for murder** (im Gefängnis) wegen Mordes IV • **for sale** *(auf Schild)* zu verkaufen IV **for the first time** zum ersten Mal II • **for three days** drei Tage (lang) I • **for years** seit Jahren III • **just for fun** nur zum Spaß I • **What for?** [ˌwɒt ˈfɔː] Wofür? II • **What's for homework?** Was haben wir als Hausaufgabe auf? I
force [fɔːs] Gewalt V 4 (87) • **use force** Gewalt anwenden V 4 (87)
force sb. to do sth. [fɔːs] jn. dazu bringen/jn. zwingen, etwas zu tun IV
foreground [ˈfɔːɡraʊnd] Vordergrund II
forehead [ˈfɔːhed, ˈfɒrɪd] Stirn IV
foreign [ˈfɒrɪn] ausländisch V 2 (39)
foreign language Fremdsprache V 2 (39)
foreigner [ˈfɒrɪnə] Ausländer/in V 2 (39)
forest [ˈfɒrɪst] Wald II
°**forestry** [ˈfɒrɪstri] Forstwirtschaft
forever [fərˈevə] endlos; ewig V 1 (6)

forgave [fəˈɡeɪv] *siehe* **forgive**
forget (-tt-) [fəˈɡet], **forgot, forgotten** vergessen III
▶ S. 181 Same verb, different meaning
forgive sb. for sth. [fəˈɡɪv], **forgave, forgiven** jm. etwas vergeben, verzeihen IV
forgiven [fəˈɡɪvn] *siehe* **forgive**
forgot [fəˈɡɒt] *siehe* **forget**
forgotten [fəˈɡɒtn] *siehe* **forget**
fork [fɔːk] Gabel III
form [fɔːm] bilden IV
form [fɔːm] (Schul-)Klasse I • **form teacher** Klassenlehrer/in I
formal [ˈfɔːml] formell, förmlich V 2 (40)
format [ˈfɔːmæt] Format V 2 (39)
former [ˈfɔːmə] ehemalige(r, s), frühere(r, s) V 1 (8)
formula [ˈfɔːmjələ] Formel V 2 (48)
fort [fɔːt] Fort III
fortune [ˈfɔːtʃuːn] Vermögen; Glück V 2 (32)
forum [ˈfɔːrəm] Forum IV
forward [ˈfɔːwəd]: **look forward to sb./sth.** sich auf jn./etwas freuen IV
fought [fɔːt] *siehe* **fight**
foul [faʊl] foulen III
found [faʊnd] *siehe* **find**
found [faʊnd] gründen IV
fox [fɒks] Fuchs II
freak out [ˌfriːk ˈaʊt] ausflippen V 1 (6)
free [friː]
1. frei I • **free time** Freizeit, freie Zeit I • **free-time activities** Freizeitaktivitäten II
2. kostenlos I
free [friː] freilassen V 3 (59)
freedom [ˈfriːdəm] Freiheit V 2 (35)
freeway [ˈfriːweɪ] *(USA, Australien)* Autobahn IV
French [frentʃ] Französisch I
French fries [ˌfrentʃ ˈfraɪz] *(bes. AE)* Pommes frites IV
°**freshwater** [ˈfreʃwɔːtə] Süßwasser-
Friday [ˈfraɪdeɪ, ˈfraɪdi] Freitag I
fridge [frɪdʒ] Kühlschrank I
friend [frend] Freund/in I • **make friends (with)** Freunde finden; sich anfreunden (mit) II
friendliness [ˈfrendlinəs] Freundlichkeit IV
friendly [ˈfrendli] freundlich II
°**friendship** [ˈfrendʃɪp] Freundschaft
fries [fraɪz]: **(French) fries** *(bes. AE)* Pommes frites IV
frighten [ˈfraɪtn] verängstigen, erschrecken V 1 (21)
frightening [ˈfraɪtnɪŋ] schrecklich, erschreckend V 1 (21)

frisbee ['frɪzbi] Frisbee IV
frog [frɒg] Frosch II
from [frəm, frɒm]
1. aus I
2. von I
dresses from the 60s Kleider aus den 60ern / aus den 60er Jahren II
from all over the UK / England aus dem gesamten Vereinigten Königreich / aus ganz England II
from all over the world aus der ganzen Welt II • **from Monday to Friday** von Montag bis Freitag III • **from my point of view** aus meiner Sicht; von meinem Standpunkt aus gesehen II • **I'm from ...** Ich komme/bin aus ... I • **Where are you from?** Wo kommst du her? I
front [frʌnt]: **at the front** vorne, im vorderen Teil III • **in front of** vor (räumlich) I • **to the front** nach vorn I • **front door** [ˌfrʌnt 'dɔː] Wohnungstür, Haustür I • **front page** Titelseite III
fruit [fruːt] Obst, Früchte; Frucht I
fruit salad Obstsalat I • **pick fruit** Obst pflücken IV
fry [fraɪ] braten III
full [fʊl] voll I
°**full speed ahead** volle Kraft voraus
fun [fʌn]
1. Spaß I • **have fun** Spaß haben, sich amüsieren I • **Have fun!** Viel Spaß! I • **just for fun** nur zum Spaß I • **Riding is fun.** Reiten macht Spaß. I
2. lustige(r, s) V 4 (83)
funeral ['fjuːnərəl] Trauerfeier IV
funny ['fʌni] witzig, komisch I
furniture (no pl) ['fɜːnɪtʃə] Möbel III
future ['fjuːtʃə] Zukunft I

G

gallery ['gæləri] Galerie III
game [geɪm] Spiel I • **a game of football** ein Fußballspiel II
game console Spielkonsole V 2 (34)
gang [gæŋ] Bande, Gang V 4 (87)
garage ['gærɑːʒ] Garage II
garbage ['gɑːbɪdʒ] (AE) Müll, Abfall IV
garden ['gɑːdn] Garten I
gas [gæs]
1. Gas IV
2. (AE) Benzin IV • **gas station** (AE) Tankstelle IV
gate [geɪt] Flugsteig III
gave [geɪv] siehe **give**

gear (no pl) [gɪə] Ausrüstung IV
camping gear Campingausrüstung IV • **sports gear** Sportausrüstung, Sportsachen II
°**geek** [giːk]: **computer geek** (bes. AE, infml) Computerfreak
general ['dʒenrəli] allgemeine(r, s) III
generally ['dʒenrəli] im Allgemeinen III
generation [ˌdʒenə'reɪʃn] Generation V 1 (17)
gentleman ['dʒentlmən], pl **gentlemen** ['dʒentlmən] Herr V 4 (61) • **Ladies and gentlemen** Meine Damen und Herren V 3 (61/188)
geography [dʒi'ɒgrəfi] Geografie, Erdkunde I
German ['dʒɜːmən] Deutsch; deutsch; Deutsche(r) I
Germany ['dʒɜːməni] Deutschland I
get (-tt-) [get], **got, got**
1. bekommen, kriegen II
2. holen, besorgen II
3. gelangen, (hin)kommen I
4. get angry/hot/... wütend/ heiß/... werden II
5. get off (the train/bus) (aus dem Zug/Bus) aussteigen I • **get on (the train/bus)** (in den Zug/Bus) einsteigen I
6. get up aufstehen I
I don't get it. Das versteh ich nicht. / Das kapier ich nicht. II
get sth. across (to sb.) (jm.) etwas klarmachen/rüberbringen V 3 (61)
get along zurechtkommen IV
get away from sth./sb. von etwas/ jm. weggehen, sich entfernen III
get bored sich langweilen, gelangweilt sein IV • °**get down to business** an die Arbeit gehen
get dressed sich anziehen I • **get drunk** sich betrinken V 4 (87) • **get involved (in)** sich engagieren (für, bei); sich beteiligen (an) IV • **get lost** sich verlaufen III • **get married** heiraten V 3 (64) • °**get one's hands dirty** sich die Hände schmutzig machen • **get out (of a car)** (aus einem Auto) aussteigen V 3 (60) • **Get out of my sight.** Geh mir aus den Augen. IV • **get ready (for)** sich fertig machen (für), sich vorbereiten (auf) I • °**get someone married** jn. verheiraten • **get sth. right** etwas richtig machen III • **get sth. wrong** etwas falsch machen III • **get things ready** Dinge fertig machen, vorbereiten I • **get used to sth./sb.** sich gewöhnen an jn./etwas IV • **What**

can I get you? Was kann/darf ich euch/Ihnen bringen? II
getting by in English [ˌgetɪŋ 'baɪ] etwa: auf Englisch zurechtkommen I
ghost [gəʊst] Gespenst, Geist V 4 (93)
giant ['dʒaɪənt] riesige(r, s), Riesen- IV
gig [gɪg] (infml) Gig, Auftritt III
do a gig einen Auftritt haben, ein Konzert geben III
giraffe [dʒɪ'rɑːf] Giraffe II
girl [gɜːl] Mädchen I
girlfriend ['gɜːlfrend] Freundin III
gist [dʒɪst] das Wesentliche III
give [gɪv], **gave, given** geben I
give sth. back etwas zurückgeben I • **give sb. a call** jn. anrufen V 4 (83) • **give sb. a hug** jn. umarmen IV • **give information** Information(en) angeben V 2 (39)
give a smile lächeln IV • **give sb. a smile** jn. anlächeln IV • **give a source** eine Quelle angeben IV
give a speech eine Rede halten IV
give (sth./sb.) up (etwas/jn.) aufgeben V 2 (35)
given ['gɪvn] siehe **give**
glad [glæd] froh, dankbar IV
°**glamour** ['glæmə] Glanz, Glamour
glass [glɑːs] Glas I • **a glass of water** ein Glas Wasser I
glasses (pl) ['glɑːsɪz] (eine) Brille I
global ['gləʊbl] weltweit, Welt- V 3 (52) • **global warming** Erwärmung der Erdatmosphäre V 3 (52/184)
gloves (pl) [glʌvz] Handschuhe II
glue [gluː] (auf-, ein)kleben II
glue [gluː] Klebstoff I • **glue stick** ['gluː stɪk] Klebestift I
go [gəʊ], **went, gone**
1. gehen I; fahren II
2. go hard/bad/deaf/blind/crazy/... hart/schlecht/taub/blind/verrückt/... werden III • **go red in the face** rot werden V 4 (92)
go abroad ins Ausland gehen/ fahren II • **go ahead** in Führung gehen III • **go by** vergehen, vorübergehen (Zeit) V 4 (80) • **go by car/bike/...** mit dem Auto/Rad/... fahren IV • **go for a run** laufen gehen IV • **go for a walk** spazieren gehen, einen Spaziergang machen II • **go home** nach Hause gehen I • **go off 1.** losfahren, -gehen IV; **2.** (Waffe) losgehen; (Bombe) explodieren IV • **go on 1.** weitergehen; weiterreden III; **2.** angehen (Licht) III; °**3.** sich erstrecken • **go**

on a date with sb. mit jm. ausgehen V 4 (80/191) • **go on a hike** eine Wanderung machen IV • **go on a trip** einen Ausflug machen II • **go on a walk** eine Wanderung / einen Spaziergang machen IV • **go on doing sth.** etwas weiter tun IV 2 (40/181) • **go on holiday** in Urlaub fahren II • **go on to do sth.** dann etwas tun IV 2 (40/181)
▶ S.181 Same verb, different meaning
go out weg-, raus-, ausgehen I • **go out with sb.** mit jm. (aus)gehen V 4 (83) • **go riding/shopping/swimming** reiten/einkaufen/schwimmen gehen I • **go skiing** Ski laufen/fahren III • **go surfing** wellenreiten gehen, surfen gehen II • **go to** führen nach *(Straße, Weg)* II • **go to bed** ins Bett gehen I • **go to mass** die Messe besuchen IV • **go to the cinema** ins Kino gehen II • **go to university** mit dem Studium anfangen V 2 (43) **go well** gut (ver)laufen, gutgehen II • **go with** gehören zu, passen zu III • **Let's go.** Auf geht's! *(wörtlich: Lass uns gehen.)* I • **coffee to go** Kaffee zum Mitnehmen IV **What are you going to do?** Was wirst du tun? / Was hast du vor zu tun? I
goal [gəʊl]
1. Tor *(im Sport)* III • **score a goal** ein Tor schießen, einen Treffer erzielen III
2. Ziel V 2 (35)
goalkeeper ['gəʊlkiːpə] Torwart, Torfrau III
goat [gəʊt] Ziege IV
God [gɒd] Gott IV
gold [gəʊld] Gold III • °**gold rush** Goldrausch
gone [gɒn]
1. *siehe* **go**
2. **be gone** weg sein, nicht da sein II
°**gonna** ['gʌnə] *(infml)* = **going to**
good [gʊd]
1. gut I • **Good afternoon.** Guten Tag. *(nachmittags)* I • **Good luck (with …)!** Viel Glück (bei/mit …)! I **Good morning.** Guten Morgen. I
2. brav I
Goodbye. [ˌgʊd'baɪ] Auf Wiedersehen. I • **say goodbye** sich verabschieden I
good-looking [ˌgʊd'lʊkɪŋ] gut aussehend V 3 (83/191)
▶ S.191 German „schön" usw.
goods *(pl)* [gʊdz] Waren, Güter V 1 (8)

goose bumps *(pl)* ['guːs ˌbʌmps] Gänsehaut *(AE)* IV
goose pimples *(pl)* ['guːs 'pɪmpəlz] *(BE)* Gänsehaut IV
gorge [gɔːdʒ] Schlucht IV
gorgeous ['gɔːdʒəs] *(infml)* äußerst schön und attraktiv V 1 (6)
▶ S.191 German „schön" usw.
gorilla [gə'rɪlə] Gorilla IV
gossip ['gɒsɪp] schwatzen, klatschen, tratschen II
°**gossip** ['gɒsɪp] Klatsch (und Tratsch)
got [gɒt] *siehe* **get**
got [gɒt]: **I've got …** Ich habe … I **I haven't got a chair.** Ich habe keinen Stuhl. I
govern ['gʌvən] regieren V 3 (52)
government ['gʌvənmənt] Regierung *(als Schulfach etwa:* Staatskunde*)* IV
▶ S.182 Collective nouns
governor ['gʌvənə] Gouverneur/in IV
grab (-bb-) [græb] schnappen, packen III
grade [greɪd]
1. *(AE)* Jahrgangsstufe, Klasse IV
2. (Schul-)Note, Zensur IV
graduate ['grædʒueɪt] *(AE)* den Schulabschluss machen IV *(BE)* den Hochschulabschluss machen I
graffiti [grə'fiːti] Graffiti V 4 (84)
grammar ['græmə] Grammatik I **grammar file** Grammatikanhang I **grammar school** Gymnasium III
grand [grænd] eindrucksvoll, beeindruckend IV
grandchild ['græntʃaɪld], *pl* **grandchildren** ['-tʃɪldrən] Enkel/in I
granddaughter ['grændɔːtə] Enkelin II
grandfather ['grænfɑːðə] Großvater I
grandma ['grænmɑː] Oma I
grandmother ['grænmʌðə] Großmutter I
grandpa ['grænpɑː] Opa I
grandparents ['grænpeərənts] Großeltern I
grandson ['grænsʌn] Enkel II
granny ['græni] Oma II
grape [greɪp] Weintraube IV
grass [grɑːs] Gras, Rasen IV • **cut the grass** Rasen mähen IV
grateful ['greɪtfl] dankbar V 2 (40)
great [greɪt] großartig, toll I
great-grandmother/-father [ˌgreɪt 'grænmʌðə], [ˌgreɪt 'grænfɑːðə] Urgroßmutter/-vater III
greedy ['griːdi] gierig; habgierig V 2 (48)

green [griːn] grün I
greet [griːt] begrüßen IV
grew [gruː] *siehe* **grow**
grey [greɪ] grau II
grid [grɪd] Gitter; Rechteckschema IV
ground [graʊnd] (Erd-)Boden III
ground floor [ˌgraʊnd 'flɔː] *(BE)* Erdgeschoss IV
Ground Zero [ˌgraʊnd 'zɪərəʊ] Bodennullpunkt *(Bezeichnung für das zerstörte World Trade Center in New York)* IV
group [gruːp] Gruppe I • **group word** Oberbegriff II
▶ S.182 Collective nouns
grow [grəʊ], **grew, grown**
1. wachsen II • **grow up** erwachsen werden; aufwachsen III °**grow rich** reich werden
2. *(Getreide usw.)* anbauen, anpflanzen IV
grown [grəʊn] *siehe* **grow**
growth [grəʊθ] Wachstum, Zunahme V 3 (50)
grumble ['grʌmbl] murren, nörgeln II
guard [gɑːd] Wachposten IV
guess [ges] raten, erraten, schätzen II • **Guess what!** [ˌges 'wɒt] Stell dir vor! / Stellt euch vor! II
guest [gest] Gast II
guide [gaɪd] Fremdenführer/in, Reiseleiter/in IV • **(travel) guide** Reiseführer *(Buch)* V 3 (67)
guided tour [ˌgaɪdɪd 'tʊə] Führung IV
guinea pig ['gɪni pɪg] Meerschweinchen I
guitar [gɪ'tɑː] Gitarre I • **play the guitar** Gitarre spielen I
°**Gujarati** [ˌgʊdʒə'rɑːti] Gujarati *(Sprache oder Bewohner/in des indischen Bundesstaats Gujarat)*
gum [gʌm]: **chewing gum** Kaugummi V 2 (36) • **chew gum** Kaugummi kauen V 2 (36/178)
gun [gʌn] Schusswaffe IV • °**fire a gun** [faɪə] mit einer Schusswaffe schießen
guy [gaɪ] Typ, Kerl II • **guys** *(pl)* Leute II
gym [dʒɪm] Sporthalle, Turnhalle; Fitnessstudio IV

H

had [hæd] *siehe* **have**
hair *(no pl)* [heə] Haar, Haare I
hairdresser ['heədresə] Friseur/in III **at the hairdresser's** beim Friseur III

half [hɑːf], *pl* **halves** [hɑːvz]
1. Hälfte III
2. Halbzeit III

half [hɑːf] halbe(r, s) II • **half an hour** eine halbe Stunde II • **half past 11** halb zwölf (11.30 / 23.30) I

half-time Halbzeit(pause) III

three and a half days/weeks dreieinhalb Tage/Wochen IV

half-pipe [ˈhɑːfpaɪp] Halfpipe *(halbierte Röhre für Inlineskater)* III

hall [hɔːl]
1. Flur, Diele I
2. Halle, Saal III • **community hall** Gemeinschaftshalle, -saal III
sports hall Sporthalle III

hallway [ˈhɔːlweɪ] *(AE)* Korridor, Gang IV

hamburger [ˈhæmbɜːɡə] Hamburger I

hamster [ˈhæmstə] Hamster I

hand sb. sth. [hænd] jm. etwas reichen IV

hand [hænd] Hand I • °**get one's hands dirty** sich die Hände schmutzig machen • °**put one's hand up, raise one's hand** sich melden • **second-hand** gebraucht; aus zweiter Hand III

handkerchief [ˈhæŋkətʃɪf] Taschentuch IV

handout [ˈhændaʊt] Arbeitsblatt, Informationsblatt, Handout IV

handsome [ˈhænsəm] attraktiv, gut aussehend V 4 (83)
▶ S.191 German „schön" usw.

hang sb. [hæŋ] jn. hängen IV

hang sth. (up) [hæŋ], **hung, hung** etwas aufhängen IV

hang out [ˌhæŋˈaʊt], **hung, hung** *(infml)* hängen, rumhängen, abhängen III

happen (to) [ˈhæpən] geschehen, passieren (mit) I

happiness [ˈhæpɪnəs] Glück III

happy [ˈhæpi] glücklich, froh I
Happy birthday. Herzlichen Glückwunsch zum Geburtstag. I
happy ending Happyend II

harass [ˈhærəs, həˈræs] belästigen V 4 (87)

harbour [ˈhɑːbə] Hafen III

hard [hɑːd] hart; schwer, schwierig II • **work hard** hart arbeiten II

hard-working [ˌhɑːdˈwɜːkɪŋ] fleißig V 2 (48)

harvest [ˈhɑːvɪst] Ernte IV

hat [hæt] Hut I

hate [heɪt] hassen, gar nicht mögen I

have [həv, hæv], **had, had** haben, besitzen II • **have an argument** eine Auseinandersetzung haben, sich streiten II • **have a baby** ein Baby/Kind bekommen II • **have a bath** baden, ein Bad nehmen II • **have a cold** erkältet sein, eine Erkältung haben II • **have a massage** sich massieren lassen II • **have a sauna** in die Sauna gehen II • **have a shower** (sich) duschen I • **have a sore throat** Halsschmerzen haben II • **have a temperature** Fieber haben II • **have breakfast** frühstücken I • **have dinner** Abendbrot essen I • **have ... for breakfast** ... zum Frühstück essen/trinken I • **have fun** Spaß haben, sich amüsieren I • **Have fun!** Viel Spaß! I • **have a good/great time** sich gut amüsieren III • **have sex** miteinander schlafen, sich lieben V 1 (16/172) • **have sth. done** etwas machen lassen V 4 (88) • **have to do** tun müssen I

have got: I've got ... [aɪvˈɡɒt] Ich habe ... I • **I haven't got a chair.** Ich habe keinen Stuhl. I

he [hiː] er I

head [hed] Kopf I • **nod (one's head)** (mit dem Kopf) nicken III **shake one's head** den Kopf schütteln III • °**with one's head in the clouds** mit seinen Gedanken ganz woanders • °**Head of the Committee** Ausschussvorsitzende(r)

head for/to/towards sth. [hed] auf etwas zugehen, -fahren, -steuern V 2 (34)

headache [ˈhedeɪk] Kopfschmerzen II

heading [ˈhedɪŋ] Überschrift IV

headline [ˈhedlaɪn] Schlagzeile III

headphones *(pl)* [ˈhedfəʊnz] Kopfhörer III

head teacher [ˌhedˈtiːtʃə] Schulleiter/in III

health [helθ] Gesundheit; Gesundheitslehre IV

healthy [ˈhelθi] gesund II

hear [hɪə], **heard, heard** hören I

heard [hɜːd] *siehe* **hear**

heart [hɑːt] Herz I • **heart attack** Herzinfarkt IV • °**learn sth. by heart** etwas auswendig lernen

heat [hiːt] Hitze V 1 (21)

heaven [ˈhevn] Himmel *(im religiösen Sinn)* IV

heavy metal [ˌheviˈmetl] Heavymetal III

hedgehog [ˈhedʒhɒɡ] Igel II

held [held] *siehe* **hold**

helicopter [ˈhelɪkɒptə] Hubschrauber, Helikopter II

°**hell** [hel]: **like hell** wie verrückt **make sb.'s life hell** jm. das Leben zur Hölle machen

Hello. [həˈləʊ] Hallo. / Guten Tag. I

helmet [ˈhelmɪt] Helm III

help [help] helfen I • **Can I help you?** Kann ich Ihnen helfen? / Was kann ich für Sie tun? *(im Geschäft)* I • **help (sb.) out** (jm.) aushelfen V 4 (79)

help [help] Hilfe I

helpful [ˈhelpfl] hilfreich, nützlich IV

helpless [ˈhelpləs] hilflos IV

her [hə, hɜː]
1. ihr, ihre I
2. sie; ihr I

herb [hɜːb] (Gewürz-)Kraut III

here [hɪə]
1. hier I • **round here** hier (in der Gegend) IV
2. hierher I
Here you are. Bitte sehr. / Hier bitte. I

heritage [ˈherɪtɪdʒ] Erbe IV

hero [ˈhɪərəʊ], *pl* **heroes** [ˈhɪərəʊz] Held/in IV

hers [hɜːz] ihrer, ihre, ihrs II

herself [hɜːˈself]
1. sich III
2. selbst IV

Hey! [heɪ] Hallo! III

Hi! [haɪ] Hallo! I • **Say hi to your parents for me.** Grüß deine Eltern von mir. I

hid [hɪd] *siehe* **hide**

hidden [ˈhɪdn] *siehe* **hide**

hide [haɪd], **hid, hidden** sich verstecken; (etwas) verstecken I

high [haɪ] hoch III

highlight [ˈhaɪlaɪt] Höhepunkt III

°**high-rise** [ˈhaɪraɪz] Hochhaus-

high school [ˈhaɪ skuːl] *(USA)* Schule für 14- bis 18-Jährige IV

highway [ˈhaɪweɪ] *(USA)* Fernstraße *(oft mit vier oder mehr Spuren)* IV

hijacker [ˈhaɪdʒækə] (Flugzeug-)-Entführer/in IV

hike [haɪk] wandern IV

hike [haɪk] Wanderung, Marsch IV

hill [hɪl] Hügel II

hilly [ˈhɪli] hügelig III

him [hɪm] ihn; ihm I

himself [hɪmˈself]
1. sich III
2. selbst IV

°**Hindi** [ˈhɪndi] Hindi

Hindu [ˈhɪnduː] Hindu V 3 (52/185)

Hinduism [ˈhɪnduːɪzm] Hinduismus V 3 (52/185)
▶ S.185 Religions

hip hop [ˈhɪp ˌhɒp] Hiphop IV

hippo [ˈhɪpəʊ] Flusspferd II

his [hɪz]
1. sein, seine I
2. seiner, seine, seins II

history ['hɪstri] Geschichte I • °**make history of one's own** selbst Geschichte machen

hit (-tt-) [hɪt], **hit, hit**
1. schlagen III
2. treffen IV
°3. **hit sb.** jn. angreifen

°**HIV** [ˌeɪtʃˌaɪ 'viː] HIV, Menschliches Immunschwäche-Virus

hobby ['hɒbi] Hobby I

hockey ['hɒki] Hockey I • **hockey pitch** Hockeyplatz, -feld II • **hockey shoes** Hockeyschuhe I

hold [həʊld], **held, held** halten II • **hold a competition** einen Wettbewerb veranstalten III • °**hold sth. in store** etwas bereithalten • °**hold sth. out** etwas hinhalten

hole [həʊl] Loch I

holiday(s) ['hɒlədeɪ] Ferien I • **be on holiday** in Urlaub sein II • **go on holiday** in Urlaub fahren II • **holiday home** Ferienhaus, -wohnung III

home [həʊm] Heim, Zuhause I • **at home** daheim, zu Hause I • **children's home** Kinderheim V 1 (19) • **come home** nach Hause kommen II • **get home** nach Hause kommen II • **go home** nach Hause gehen I • °**old folks' home** (infml) Altenheim, Seniorenresidenz • **old people's home** Altenheim, Seniorenresidenz V 1 (17/173)

homeland ['həʊmlænd] Heimat(land) IV

homeless ['həʊmləs] obdachlos IV

homeowner ['həʊmˌəʊnə] Eigenheimbesitzer/in IV

°**homestead** ['həʊmsted] Anwesen, Gehöft

hometown ['həʊmˌtaʊn] Heimat(stadt) IV

homework (no pl) ['həʊmwɜːk] Hausaufgabe(n) I • **do homework** die Hausaufgabe(n) machen I • **What's for homework?** Was haben wir als Hausaufgabe auf? I

honest ['ɒnɪst] ehrlich V 1 (12)

Hooray! [huˈreɪ] Hurra! II

hope [həʊp] hoffen I • **I hope so.** Ich hoffe es. II

hope (of) [həʊp] Hoffnung (auf) III

hopeful ['həʊpfʊl] hoffnungsvoll IV

hopeless ['həʊpləs] hoffnungslos IV • **You're hopeless.** Dir ist nicht zu helfen. IV

horizon [həˈraɪzn] Horizont V 3 (65)

horrible ['hɒrəbl] scheußlich, grauenhaft II

horror ['hɒrə] Entsetzen, Grauen, Horror III

horse [hɔːs] Pferd I • **(horse) racing** Pferderennsport V 1 (12/172)

hose [həʊz] Schlauch IV

hospital ['hɒspɪtl] Krankenhaus II • **He's gone to hospital.** Er ist ins Krankenhaus gegangen. III • **He's in hospital.** Er ist im Krankenhaus. III

host [həʊst] Gastgeber IV

hostess ['həʊstes] Gastgeberin (in USA auch: Frau, die in einem Restaurant die Gäste in Empfang nimmt) IV

hostel ['hɒstl] Herberge, Wohnheim III • **youth hostel** Jugendherberge III

hot [hɒt] heiß I • **hot chocolate** heiße Schokolade I • **hot-water bottle** Wärmflasche II

hotel [həʊˈtel] Hotel II

hotline ['hɒtlaɪn] Hotline II

hour ['aʊə] Stunde I • **half an hour** eine halbe Stunde II • **a 24-hour supermarket** ein Supermarkt, der 24 Stunden geöffnet ist III • **a two-hour operation** eine zweistündige Operation III

house [haʊs] Haus I • **at the Shaws' house** im Haus der Shaws / bei den Shaws zu Hause I

°**housing department** ['haʊzɪŋ] Wohnungsamt

how [haʊ] wie I • **How about you grabbing that table?** Wie wär's, wenn ihr den Tisch dort schnappt? IV • **How are you?** Wie geht es dir/Ihnen/euch? II • **How do you know …?** Woher weißt/kennst du …? I • **how many?** wie viele? I • **how much?** wie viel? I • **How much is/are …?** Was kostet/kosten …? / Wie viel kostet/kosten …? I • **How old are you?** Wie alt bist du? I • **How was …?** Wie war …? I • **How shall I put it?** Wie soll ich es formulieren/ausdrücken? IV • **how to do sth.** wie man etwas tut / tun kann / tun soll IV

however [haʊˈevə] trotzdem IV

°**HTML** Hypertext-Auszeichnungssprache (Formatierungssprache zur Erstellung von Hypertextseiten im WWW)

hug (-gg-) [hʌg] umarmen IV

hug [hʌg] Umarmung IV • **give sb. a hug** jn. umarmen IV

huge [hjuːdʒ] riesig, sehr groß III

human ['hjuːmən] Mensch, menschliches Wesen IV

hundred ['hʌndrəd] hundert, Hundert I

hung [hʌŋ] siehe **hang**

hunger ['hʌŋɡə] Hunger V 3 (60)

hungry ['hʌŋɡri] hungrig I • **be hungry** Hunger haben, hungrig sein I

hunt [hʌnt] Jagd III

hunt [hʌnt] jagen III

hurry ['hʌri] eilen; sich beeilen II • **hurry up** sich beeilen I

hurry ['hʌri]: **be in a hurry** in Eile sein, es eilig haben I

hurt [hɜːt], **hurt, hurt** wehtun; verletzen I

hurt [hɜːt] verletzt II

husband ['hʌzbənd] Ehemann II

hut [hʌt] Hütte IV

hutch [hʌtʃ] (Kaninchen-)Stall I

I

I [aɪ] ich I • **I'm** [aɪm] ich bin I • **I'm from …** Ich komme aus … / Ich bin aus … I • **I'm … years old.** Ich bin … Jahre alt. I • **I'm sorry.** Entschuldigung. / Tut mir leid. I

ice [aɪs] Eis II

ice cream [ˌaɪs ˈkriːm] (Speise-)Eis I

ice hockey ['aɪs hɒki] Eishockey III

ice rink ['aɪs rɪŋk] Schlittschuhbahn II

ID [ˌaɪ ˈdiː] Ausweis IV

idea [aɪˈdɪə] Idee, Einfall I

ideal [aɪˈdiːəl] Ideal, Idealvorstellung V 1 (17)

identification [aɪˌdentɪfɪˈkeɪʃn] Ausweis IV

°**identify with** [aɪˈdentɪfaɪ] (sich) identifizieren (mit)

identity [aɪˈdentɪti] Identität IV

if [ɪf]
1. wenn, falls II
2. ob II

ill [ɪl] krank II

illegal [ɪˈliːɡl] illegal, ungesetzlich IV

illness ['ɪlnəs] Krankheit IV

illustrate ['ɪləstreɪt] veranschaulichen, illustrieren IV

image ['ɪmɪdʒ] Bild V 1 (25)

imagery ['ɪmɪdʒəri] Metaphorik V 1 (25)

imaginable [ɪˈmædʒɪnəbl] vorstellbar, erdenklich V 3 (57)

imagination [ɪˌmædʒɪˈneɪʃn] Fantasie, Vorstellung(skraft) IV

imagine sth. [ɪˈmædʒɪn] sich etwas vorstellen III • **imagine doing sth.**

sich vorstellen, etwas zu tun V 3 (65)
imitate ['ɪmɪteɪt] nachmachen III
immediately [ɪ'miːdɪətli] sofort IV
immigrant ['ɪmɪɡrənt] Einwanderer/Einwanderin IV
immigrate ['ɪmɪɡreɪt] einwandern IV
immigration [ˌɪmɪ'ɡreɪʃn] Einwanderung IV • °**immigration station** Einwanderungsstelle
impatient [ɪm'peɪʃnt] ungeduldig V 4 (92)
imperfect [ɪm'pɜːfɪkt] unvollkommen, mangelhaft V 2 (37/178)
impersonal [ɪm'pɜːsənl] unpersönlich V 2 (37/178)
impolite [ˌɪmpə'laɪt] unhöflich V 2 (37)
▶ S.178 Negative prefixes
important [ɪm'pɔːtnt] wichtig II
impossible [ɪm'pɒsəbl] unmöglich II
▶ S.178 Negative prefixes
impress [ɪm'pres] beeindrucken V 2 (44)
°**impression** [ɪm'preʃn] Eindruck
impressive [ɪm'presɪv] beeindruckend, eindrucksvoll III
improve [ɪm'pruːv] (sich) verbessern III
in [ɪn] in I • **the best view in the world** die beste Aussicht der Welt IV • **in 2050** im Jahr 2050 II • **in ... Street** in der ...straße I • **in English** auf Englisch I • **in front of** vor (räumlich) I • **in here** hier drinnen I • **in next to no time** im Nu III • **in other places** an anderen Orten, anderswo III • **in school** (AE) in der Schule IV • **in the afternoon** nachmittags, am Nachmittag I • **in the country** auf dem Land II • **in the evening** abends, am Abend I • **in the field** auf dem Feld II • **in the morning** am Morgen, morgens I • **in the photo/picture** auf dem Foto/Bild I • **in there** dort drinnen I • **in the sky** am Himmel II • **in the world** auf der Welt II • **in the yard** auf dem Hof II • **in time** [ɪn 'taɪm] rechtzeitig II
inaccurate [ɪn'ækjərət] ungenau V 2 (37/178)
inactive [ɪn'æktɪv] inaktiv, untätig V 2 (37/178)
▶ S.178 Negative prefixes
include [ɪn'kluːd] einschließen IV
incorrect [ˌɪnkə'rekt] inkorrekt, falsch V 2 (37/178)
▶ S.178 Negative prefixes

incredible [ɪn'kredɪbl] unglaublich IV
independent [ˌɪndɪ'pendənt] unabhängig V 1 (8)
index ['ɪndeks] Index, Register V 2 (43)
Indian ['ɪndiən]
1. Inder/in I
2. Indianer/in IV
indirect [ˌɪndə'rekt] indirekt V 2 (37/178) • **indirect speech** indirekte Rede III
▶ S.178 Negative prefixes
industrial [ɪn'dʌstriəl] industriell III
industry ['ɪndəstri] Industrie III
inexact [ˌɪnɪɡ'zækt] ungenau V 2 (37/178)
inexpensive [ˌɪnɪk'spensɪv] preiswert V 2 (37/178)
▶ S.178 Negative prefixes
infinitive [ɪn'fɪnətɪv] Infinitiv (Grundform des Verbs) I
inform sb. (about/of sth.) [ɪn'fɔːm] jn. (über etwas) informieren IV
informal [ɪn'fɔːml] informell; umgangssprachlich V 2 (40)
information (about/on) (no pl) [ˌɪnfə'meɪʃn] Information(en) (über) I • **give information** Information(en) angeben V 2 (39)
inhabit [ɪn'hæbɪt] bewohnen, leben in V 3 (50)
inhabitant [ɪn'hæbɪtənt] Einwohner/in, Bewohner/in V 3 (50)
inherit sth. (from sb.) [ɪn'herɪt] etwas (von jm.) erben V 2 (32)
injury ['ɪndʒəri] Verletzung II
innovation [ˌɪnə'veɪʃn] Innovation, Neuerung IV
insect ['ɪnsekt] Insekt IV
inside [ˌɪn'saɪd]
1. innen (drin), drinnen I; Innen- IV
2. nach drinnen II
3. **inside the car** ins Auto (hinein), ins Innere des Autos II
install [ɪn'stɔːl] installieren, einrichten II
installation [ˌɪnstə'leɪʃn] Installation, Einrichtung II
instant message [ˌɪnstənt 'mesɪdʒ] Nachricht, die man im Internet austauscht (in Echtzeit) III
instead of [ɪn'sted ˌəv] anstelle von, statt IV
instructions (pl) [ɪn'strʌkʃnz] (Gebrauchs-)Anweisung(en), Anleitung(en) II
instructor [ɪn'strʌktə] Lehrer/in, Ausbilder/in V 1 (6)
instrument ['ɪnstrəmənt] Instrument III
interest ['ɪntrəst] Interesse V 2 (40)

interest sb. ['ɪntrəst] jn. interessieren IV
interested [ɪntrəstɪd]: **be interested (in)** interessiert sein (an), sich interessieren (für) III
interesting ['ɪntrəstɪŋ] interessant I
intermediate [ˌɪntə'miːdɪət] Mittel-, für fortgeschrittene Anfänger/innen V 2 (39)
international [ˌɪntə'næʃnəl] international II
internet ['ɪntənet] Internet I • **surf the internet** im Internet surfen II
interrupt [ˌɪntə'rʌpt] unterbrechen IV
interview ['ɪntəvjuː] befragen, interviewen IV
interview ['ɪntəvjuː]
1. Interview (Zeitung, TV, usw.) V 2 (36/178)
2. Vorstellungsgespräch V 2 (36)
into ['ɪntə, 'ɪntʊ]
1. in ... (hinein) I
2. **be into sth.** (infml) etwas mögen III
introduce sb. (to sb.) [ˌɪntrə'djuːs] jn. (jm.) vorstellen IV
introduce sb. to sth. [ˌɪntrə'djuːs] jn. in etwas einführen IV
introduction (to) [ˌɪntrə'dʌkʃn] Einführung (in) III
invent [ɪn'vent] erfinden III
inventor [ɪn'ventə] Erfinder/in III
invitation (to) [ˌɪnvɪ'teɪʃn] Einladung (zu) I
invite (to) [ɪn'vaɪt] einladen (zu) I
involved [ɪn'vɒlvd]: **get involved (in)** sich engagieren (für, bei); sich beteiligen (an) IV
°**iron filings** (pl) [ˌaɪən 'faɪlɪŋz] Eisenspäne
irregular [ɪ'reɡjələ] unregelmäßig III
is [ɪz] ist I
Islam ['ɪzlɑːm] Islam V 3 (52/185)
▶ S.185 Religions
island ['aɪlənd] Insel II
it [ɪt] er/sie/es I • **It's £1.** Er/Sie/Es kostet 1 Pfund. I
IT [ˌaɪ 'tiː], **information technology** IT (Informationstechnologie) II
its [ɪts] sein/seine; ihr/ihre I
itself [ɪt'self]
1. sich III
2. selbst IV

J

°**jacaranda** [ˌdʒækə'rændə] Jacaranda, Palisanderholzbaum
jacket ['dʒækɪt] Jacke, Jackett II

January [ˈdʒænjuəri] Januar I
jazz [dʒæz] Jazz III
jealous (of) [ˈdʒeləs] neidisch (auf); eifersüchtig (auf) V 1 (15)
jeans *(pl)* [dʒiːnz] Jeans I
jet lag [ˈdʒet ˌlæg] Jetlag IV
Jew [dʒuː] Jude/Jüdin V 3 (52/185)
Jewish [ˈdʒuːɪʃ] jüdisch IV
▶ S.185 Religions
job [dʒɒb] Aufgabe, Job I • **do a good job** gute Arbeit leisten II
join sb./sth. [dʒɔɪn] sich jm. anschließen; bei jm./etwas mitmachen II
join in [ˌdʒɔɪn ˈɪn] mitmachen III
joke [dʒəʊk] Witz I
joke [dʒəʊk] scherzen, Witze machen II
journalist [ˈdʒɜːnəlɪst] Journalist/in IV
journey [ˈdʒɜːni] Reise, Fahrt III
Judaism [ˈdʒuːdeɪɪzm] Judaismus V 3 (52/185)
▶ S.185 Religions
judge [dʒʌdʒ] Richter/in V 3 (65)
judge sb. (by) [dʒʌdʒ] jn. beurteilen, einschätzen (nach) IV
judo [ˈdʒuːdəʊ] Judo I • **do judo** Judo machen I
jug [dʒʌg] Krug I • **a jug of milk** ein Krug Milch I
juice [dʒuːs] Saft I
July [dʒuˈlaɪ] Juli I
jumble sale [ˈdʒʌmbl seɪl] Wohltätigkeitsbasar I
jump [dʒʌmp] springen II
June [dʒuːn] Juni I
jungle [ˈdʒʌŋgl] Dschungel IV
junior [ˈdʒuːniə]
1. Junioren-, Jugend- I
2. **junior (to sb.)** jm. untergeordnet IV
junta [ˈdʒʌntə, ˈhʊntə] Junta V 3 (59/187)
▶ S.187 Different forms of government
just [dʒʌst]
1. (einfach) nur, bloß I
2. gerade (eben), soeben II
just then genau in dem Moment; gerade dann II
3. **just like you** genau wie du II
just as … as ebenso … wie IV
4. einfach III

K

kangaroo [ˌkæŋgəˈruː] Känguru II
keen to do sth. / on doing sth. [kiːn] wild darauf sein, etwas zu tun V 2 (35)

keep [kiːp], **kept, kept** (be)halten; aufbewahren III • **keep an eye on sth./sb.** nach jm./etwas Ausschau halten IV • **keep calm** ruhig/still bleiben; Ruhe bewahren V 2 (35/177)
keep (on) doing sth. etwas weiter tun; etwas ständig tun IV • **keep in touch** in Verbindung bleiben, Kontakt halten III • **keep quiet** still sein, leise sein IV • **keep sth. alive** etwas am Leben halten IV • **keep sb./sth. out of sth.** jn./etwas (aus etwas) heraushalten V 4 (84) • **keep sth. warm/cool/open/…** etwas warm/kühl/offen/… halten II
keeper [ˈkiːpə] Torwart, Torfrau III
kept [kept] *siehe* **keep**
ketchup [ˈketʃəp] Ketchup IV
key [kiː] Schlüssel I • **key word** Stichwort, Schlüsselwort I • **key ring** Schlüsselring IV
key [kiː] Haupt-, entscheidende(r, s) V 2 (39)
keyboard [ˈkiːbɔːd] Keyboard *(elektronisches Tasteninstrument)* III
kick [kɪk] *(mit dem Fuß)* treten *(gegen)* IV
kid [kɪd] Kind, Jugendliche(r) I
kill [kɪl] töten I
kilogram (kg) [ˈkɪləgræm], **kilo** [ˈkiːləʊ] Kilogramm, Kilo IV • **a kilogram of oranges** ein Kilogramm Orangen III • **a 150-kilogram bear** ein 150 Kilogramm schwerer Bär III
kilometre (km) [ˈkɪləmiːtə] Kilometer III • **a ten-kilometre walk** eine Zehn-Kilometer-Wanderung III • **square kilometre** Quadratkilometer III
kind (of) [kaɪnd] Art (von) III
kind of scary *(infml)* irgendwie unheimlich III
kind [kaɪnd] freundlich V 3 (63)
kindergarten [ˈkɪndəgɑːtn] Kindergarten; *(USA)* Vorschule *(für 5- bis 6-Jährige)* IV
°**kinetic** [kɪˈnetɪk] kinetisch
king [kɪŋ] König I
kiss [kɪs] (sich) küssen IV
kiss [kɪs] Kuss IV
kitchen [ˈkɪtʃɪn] Küche I
kite [kaɪt] Drachen I
knee [niː] Knie I
kneel (down) [niːl], **knelt, knelt** sich hinknien V 1 (21)
knelt [nelt] *siehe* **kneel**
knew [njuː] *siehe* **know**
knife [naɪf], *pl* **knives** [naɪvz] Messer III
knock (on) [nɒk] (an)klopfen (an) I

know [nəʊ], **knew, known**
1. wissen I
2. kennen I
How do you know …? Woher weißt du …?/Woher kennst du …? I • **know about sth.** von etwas wissen; über etwas Bescheid wissen II • **…, you know.** …, wissen Sie. / …, weißt du. I • **You know what, Sophie?** Weißt du was, Sophie? I
known [nəʊn]
1. *siehe* **know**
2. bekannt IV
koala [kəʊˈɑːlə] Koala V 1 (9)
°**kookaburra** [ˈkʊkəbʌrə] Jägerliest, Lachender Hans *(australische Vogelart)*
°**koyal** [kɔɪəl] Koel *(Vogelart)*

L

ladder [ˈlædə] *(die)* Leiter IV
lady [ˈleɪdi] Dame V 3 (61) • **Ladies and gentlemen** Meine Damen und Herren V 3 (61/188)
laid [leɪd] *siehe* **lay**
lain [leɪn] *siehe* **lie**
lake [leɪk] (Binnen-)See II
lamp [læmp] Lampe I
land [lænd] landen II
land [lænd] Land III • **on land** auf dem Land III
landlady [ˈlændleɪdi] Vermieterin V 3 (63)
landline [ˈlændlaɪn] Festnetzleitung V 2 (34)
landlord [ˈlændlɔːd] Vermieter V 3 (63)
landscape [ˈlændskeɪp] Landschaft V 1 (8)
lane [leɪn] Gasse, Weg III
language [ˈlæŋgwɪdʒ] Sprache I • **foreign language** Fremdsprache V 2 (39)
laptop [ˈlæptɒp] Laptop V 1 (12)
large [lɑːdʒ] groß III
lasagne [ləˈzænjə] Lasagne I
last [lɑːst] letzte(r, s) I • **the last day** der letzte Tag I • **at last** endlich, schließlich I
last-minute [ˌlɑːst ˈmɪnɪt]: **a last-minute shot** ein Schuss in der letzten Minute III
late [leɪt] spät; zu spät I • **be late** zu spät sein/kommen I • **late at night** spät abends V 4 (84) • **Sorry, I'm late.** Entschuldigung, dass ich zu spät bin/komme. I
later [ˈleɪtə] später I
latest [ˈleɪtɪst] neueste(r, s) III

laugh [lɑːf] lachen I • **laugh at sb.** jn. anlachen V 4 (83) • **laugh out loud** laut lachen II
laughter [ˈlɑːftə] Gelächter II
°**lavatory** [ˈlævətri] Toilette
law [lɔː]
1. Gesetz IV • **Basic Law** Grundgesetz (der Bundesrepublik) V 2 (38/179) • °**become law** Rechtskraft erlangen • **pass a law** ein Gesetz verabschieden V 4 (87)
2. Jura V 3 (59) • °**law firm** Anwaltskanzlei
lay [leɪ] siehe **lie**
lay the table [leɪ], **laid, laid** den Tisch decken I
layer [ˈleɪə] Schicht IV
°**layout** [ˈleɪaʊt] Anordnung, Layout V
lead (to sth.) [liːd], **led, led** (zu etwas) führen IV
leader [ˈliːdə] (An-)Führer/in, Leiter/in IV
learn [lɜːn] lernen I • **learn about sth.** etwas über etwas erfahren, etwas über etwas herausfinden II • °**learn sth. by heart** etwas auswendig lernen • **learning by doing** Lernen durch Handeln/Tun V 2 (40/181)
least [liːst] am wenigsten IV • **at least** zumindest, wenigstens I
leather [ˈleðə] Leder III
leave [liːv], **left, left**
1. (weg)gehen; abfahren II
2. verlassen II
3. **leave (behind)** zurücklassen IV
4. **leave sth. out** etwas auslassen V 3 (63)
led [led] siehe **lead**
left [left] siehe **leave** • **be left** übrig sein II
left [left] linke(r, s) I • **look left** nach links schauen I • **on the left** links, auf der linken Seite I • **take a left** (AE) nach links/rechts abbiegen IV • **to the left** nach links III • **turn left** (nach) links abbiegen II
leg [leg] Bein I
legal [ˈliːgl] legal IV
leisure centre [ˈleʒə sentə] Freizeitzentrum, -park II
lemonade [ˌleməˈneɪd] Limonade I
lend sb. sth. [lend], **lent, lent** jm. etwas leihen II
lent [lent] siehe **lend**
lentil [ˈlentəl] Linse (Hülsenfrucht) III
leotard [ˈliːətɑːd] Gymnastikanzug; Turnanzug III
less [les] weniger IV • **more or less** mehr oder weniger IV

lesson [ˈlesn] (Unterrichts-)Stunde I • **lessons** (pl) Unterricht I
let [let], **let, let** lassen II • **Let's ...** Lass uns ... / Lasst uns ... • **Let's go.** Auf geht's! (wörtlich: Lass uns gehen.) I • **Let's look at the list.** Sehen wir uns die Liste an. / Lasst uns die Liste ansehen. I • **let sb. do sth.** jm. erlauben, etwas zu tun; zulassen, dass jd. etwas tut III
letter [ˈletə]
1. Buchstabe I • **capital letter** Großbuchstabe III • **small letter** Kleinbuchstabe III
2. **letter (to)** [ˈletə] Brief (an) II • °**covering letter** Begleitbrief **letter of application** Bewerbungsschreiben V 2 (38/178)
lettuce [ˈletɪs] (Kopf-)Salat II
level [ˈlevl] (Lern-)Stand, Niveau, Grad V 2 (32)
liberty [ˈlɪbəti] Freiheit IV
library [ˈlaɪbrəri] Bibliothek, Bücherei I
license plate [ˈlaɪsns pleɪt] (AE) Nummernschild IV
lie (-ing form: **lying**) [laɪ], **lay, lain** liegen IV
lie (to sb.) (-ing form: **lying**) [laɪ] jn. (an)lügen V 4 (92)
life [laɪf], pl **lives** [laɪvz] Leben I **life coach** Lebensberater/in V 2 (44) **life expectancy** Lebenserwartung V 3 (52) • **life sentence** lebenslängliche Haftstrafe IV • **way of life** Lebensart III
lift [lɪft] (an-, hoch)heben IV
lift [lɪft] Fahrstuhl, Aufzug II
light [laɪt] Licht III
°**light** [laɪt]: **light blue** hellblau
°**light** [laɪt], **lit, lit** [lɪt] beleuchten, anzünden
like [laɪk]
1. wie I • **just like you** genau wie du II • **language like that** solche Sprache IV • **like what?** wie zum Beispiel? IV • **What was the weather like?** Wie war das Wetter? II
2. (infml) als ob III
like [laɪk] mögen, gernhaben I **like sth. better** etwas lieber mögen II • **like sth. very much** etwas sehr mögen II • **I like dancing/swimming…** Ich tanze/schwimme… gern. I • **I'd like …** (= **I would like …**) Ich hätte gern … / Ich möchte gern … I • **I'd like to go** (= **I would like to go**) Ich würde gern gehen / Ich möchte gehen I **I wouldn't like to go** Ich würde nicht gern gehen / Ich möchte

nicht gehen I • **Would you like …?** Möchtest du …? / Möchten Sie …? I
likes and dislikes (pl) [laɪks, ˈdɪslaɪks] Vorlieben und Abneigungen V 2 (42)
limit [ˈlɪmɪt] Begrenzung, Beschränkung III • **speed limit** Geschwindigkeitsbegrenzung, -beschränkung III
line [laɪn]
1. Zeile II
2. (U-Bahn-)Linie III
3. Schlange, Reihe (wartender Menschen) IV • **Line starts here.** Hier anstellen. IV • °**wait in line (for sth.)** sich (nach etwas) anstellen IV **line of work** Beruf, berufliche Richtung IV • **be in a line of work** einen Beruf ausüben IV
link [lɪŋk] verbinden, verknüpfen I
link [lɪŋk] Verbindung III
linking word [ˈlɪŋkɪŋ wɜːd] Bindewort II
lion [ˈlaɪən] Löwe II
lip [lɪp] Lippe IV
list [lɪst] auflisten, aufzählen II
list [lɪst] Liste I • **put one's name on a list** sich eintragen IV
listen (to) [ˈlɪsn] zuhören; sich etwas anhören I • **listen for sth.** auf etwas horchen, achten III
listener [ˈlɪsnə] Zuhörer/in II
°**lit** [lɪt] siehe **light**
literature [ˈlɪtrətʃə] Literatur V 1 (24)
litter [ˈlɪtə] Abfälle zurücklassen IV
litter [ˈlɪtə] Abfall IV
little [ˈlɪtl]
1. klein I
2. wenig IV • **a little** ein bisschen, ein wenig IV
live [lɪv] leben, wohnen I **standard of living** Lebensstandard V 3 (56)
live [laɪv]: **live concert** Livekonzert III • **live music** Livemusik II
lives [laɪvz] Plural von „life" I
living-history museum Freilichtmuseum IV
living room [ˈlɪvɪŋ ruːm; rʊm] Wohnzimmer I
lizard [ˈlɪzəd] Eidechse V 1 (16)
load [ləʊd] beladen III
lobby [ˈlɒbi] Eingangshalle IV
local [ˈləʊkl] örtlich, Lokal-; am/vom Ort III
location [ləʊˈkeɪʃn] (Einsatz-)Ort, Platz III
loch [lɒx] (Binnen-)See in Schottland III
lock [lɒk] Schleuse III
lock [lɒk] abschließen, zuschließen I • **lock up** abschließen II

logical ['lɒdʒɪkl] logisch (denkend) V 2 (35)
logo ['ləʊgəʊ] Logo, Markenzeichen III
lonely ['ləʊnli] einsam V 1 (20)
long [lɒŋ] lang I • **a long way (from)** weit entfernt (von) I • **a long time** lange III
look [lʊk]
1. schauen, gucken I
2. **look different/great/old** anders/toll/alt aussehen I • **look after sth./sb.** sich um etwas/jn. kümmern; auf etwas/jn. aufpassen II • **look at** ansehen, anschauen I **look at sth. closely** etwas genau anschauen III • **look for** suchen II • **look forward to sb./sth.** sich auf jn./etwas freuen IV • **look left and right** nach links und rechts schauen I • **look around/round** sich umsehen I • **look up (from)** hochsehen, aufschauen (von) II **look up to sb.** zu jm. aufsehen IV **look up words** Wörter nachschlagen III
Lord [lɔːd] Herr(gott) IV
lose [luːz], **lost, lost** verlieren II
lost [lɒst]
1. siehe **lose**
2. **get lost** sich verlaufen III
lot [lɒt]: **a lot (of), lots of** eine Menge, viel, viele I / II • **He likes her a lot.** Er mag sie sehr. I • **lots more** viel mehr I • **Thanks a lot!** Vielen Dank! I
°**lottery** ['lɒtəri] Lotterie
loud [laʊd] laut I
love [lʌv] lieben, sehr mögen I **love sth. very much** etwas sehr lieben II
love [lʌv]
1. Liebe II
2. „Liebes", „Liebling" III
fall in love (with sb.) sich verlieben (in jn.) IV • **be in love** verliebt sein V 4 (79)
Love ... Liebe Grüße, ... (Grußformel am Ende eines Briefes) I • **make love** miteinander schlafen, sich lieben V 1 (16)
lovely ['lʌvli] schön, hübsch, wunderbar I
▶ S.191 German „schön" usw.
luck [lʌk]: **Good luck (with ...)!** Viel Glück (bei/mit ...)! I
luckily ['lʌkɪli] zum Glück, glücklicherweise II
lucky ['lʌki]: **be lucky** Glück haben III
lunch [lʌntʃ] Mittagessen I • **for lunch** zum Mittagessen III

lunch break Mittagspause I
lunchtime ['lʌntʃtaɪm] Mittagszeit III
lyrics (pl) ['lɪrɪks] Liedtext(e) III

M

machine [məˈʃiːn] Maschine, Gerät II
mad [mæd] verrückt I • **mad about** verrückt nach III
madam ['mædəm]: **Dear Sir or Madam ...** Sehr geehrte Damen und Herren IV
made [meɪd]
1. siehe **make**
2. **be made of sth.** aus etwas (gemacht) sein III • **be made up of sth.** aus etwas bestehen V 1 (10/171)
magazine [ˌmæɡəˈziːn] Zeitschrift, Magazin I
magical ['mædʒɪkl] zauberhaft, wundervoll V 1 (6)
magnet ['mæɡnət] Magnet V 3 (52)
°**Maharashtrian** [ˌmɑːhəˈræʃtrɪən] Bewohner/in des indischen Bundesstaats Maharashtra
mail sb. [meɪl] jn. anmailen II **mail sb. sth.** jm. etwas schicken, senden (vor allem per E-Mail) III
main [meɪn] Haupt- III
mainly ['meɪnli] hauptsächlich, vorwiegend V 1 (6)
maize (no pl) [meɪz] (BE) Mais IV
majority [məˈdʒɒrəti] Mehrheit IV
make [meɪk], **made, made** machen; bauen I • **make a call** ein Telefongespräch führen, telefonieren II **make a deal** ein Abkommen/eine Abmachung treffen III • **make a mess** alles durcheinanderbringen, alles in Unordnung bringen I **make a speech** eine Rede halten IV • **make friends (with)** Freunde finden; sich anfreunden (mit) II °**make it** es schaffen • °**make it out of sth.** etwas überleben **make love** miteinander schlafen, sich lieben V 1 (16) • °**make one's way** sich begeben • **make sb. do sth.** jn. zwingen, etwas zu tun; jn. dazu bringen, etwas zu tun V 4 (85) • °**make sb.'s life hell** jm. das Leben zur Hölle machen • **make sth. up** etwas bilden V 1 (10)
make sure sich vergewissern IV
make-up ['meɪkʌp] Make-up II
make-up artist Maskenbildner/in
male [meɪl] Männchen II

mall [mɔːl, BE auch mæl] (großes) Einkaufszentrum III
man [mæn], pl **men** [men] Mann I
manage a problem ['mænɪdʒ] mit einem Problem umgehen, ein Problem lösen V 3 (63)
manager ['mænədʒə] Manager/in III
°**manatee** [ˌmænəˈtiː] Seekuh
°**mango** ['mæŋɡəʊ] Mango
many ['meni] viele I • **how many?** wie viele? I
map [mæp] Landkarte, Stadtplan II
°**Marathi** [məˈrɑːti] Marathi (Sprache des indischen Bundesstaats Maharashtra)
March [mɑːtʃ] März I
march [mɑːtʃ] Marsch, Demonstration IV
mark [mɑːk] (Schul-)Note, Zensur IV
mark [mɑːk]: **quotation marks** Anführungszeichen, -striche III
mark sth. (up) [ˌmɑːk ˈʌp] etwas markieren, kennzeichnen II
market ['mɑːkɪt] Markt II
marmalade ['mɑːməleɪd] Orangenmarmelade I
married (to) ['mærɪd] verheiratet (mit) I • **get married** heiraten V 3 (64) • °**get someone married** jn. verheiraten
marry ['mæri] heiraten III
mass [mæs] Messe (Gottesdienst) IV
massage ['mæsɑːʒ] Massage II **have a massage** sich massieren lassen II
match [mætʃ] Spiel, Wettkampf I
°**match sth. (to sth.)** [mætʃ] etwas (zu etwas) zuordnen
mate [meɪt] (infml) Freund/in, Kumpel V 1 (6)
material [məˈtɪəriəl] Material, Stoff II • °**raw material** Rohstoff
maths [mæθs] Mathematik I
matter ['mætə]: **What's the matter?** Was ist los? / Was ist denn? II
matter ['mætə] wichtig sein V 3 (64)
mattress ['mætrəs] Matratze V 1 (17)
may [meɪ] dürfen I
May [meɪ] Mai I
maybe ['meɪbi] vielleicht I
mayor [meə] Bürgermeister/in IV
maximum ['mæksɪməm] Maximum V 2 (47)
me [miː] mir; mich I • **Me too.** Ich auch. I • **more than me** mehr als ich II • **That's me.** Das bin ich. I **Why me?** Warum ich? I
meal [miːl] Mahlzeit, Essen III **set meal** Menü III

mean [miːn], **meant, meant**
 1. bedeuten II
 2. meinen, sagen wollen I
mean [miːn] gemein IV
meaning [ˈmiːnɪŋ] Bedeutung I
°**meaningful** [ˈmiːnɪŋfʊl] aussagekräftig
meant [ment] siehe **mean**
meat [miːt] Fleisch I
medal [ˈmedl] Medaille III
media (pl) [ˈmiːdiə] Medien III
mediate [ˈmiːdieɪt] vermitteln IV
mediation [ˌmiːdiˈeɪʃn] Vermittlung, Sprachmittlung, Mediation II
medium [ˈmiːdiəm] mittel-, mittlere(r, s); mittelgroß III
meet [miːt], **met, met**
 1. treffen; kennenlernen I
 2. sich treffen I
meeting [ˈmiːtɪŋ] Versammlung, Besprechung IV
member [ˈmembə]: **member of staff** (BE), **staff member** (AE) Mitarbeiter/in IV
membership (of sth.) [ˈmembəʃɪp] Mitgliedschaft (in etwas) V 2 (39)
memorial (to sb./sth.) [məˈmɔːriəl] Denkmal (für jn./etwas) V 3 (59)
men [men] Plural von „man" I
menu [ˈmenjuː] Speisekarte; Menü (Computer) III
°**mention** [ˈmenʃn] erwähnen
°**merchant** [ˈmɜːtʃənt] Kaufmann
merry-go-round [ˈmerɪɡəʊˌraʊnd] Karussel IV
mess [mes]: **make a mess** alles durcheinanderbringen, alles in Unordnung bringen I
message [ˈmesɪdʒ]
 1. **instant message** Nachricht, die man im Internet austauscht (in Echtzeit) III
 °**2.** Botschaft, Aussage
met [met] siehe **meet**
metaphor [ˈmetəfə, ˈmetəfɔː] Metapher V 1 (25)
method [ˈmeθəd] Methode IV
metre [ˈmiːtə] Meter II
mice [maɪs] Plural von „mouse" I
microphone [ˈmaɪkrəfəʊn] Mikrofon III
mid [mɪd]: **in the mid-1800s** Mitte des 19. Jahrhunderts V 3 (52)
middle (of) [ˈmɪdl] Mitte; Mittelteil I • **the middle of nowhere** (infml) etwa: das Ende der Welt V 1 (12/171)
middle school [ˈmɪdl ˌskuːl] (USA) Schule für 11- bis 14-Jährige IV
might [maɪt]: **you might need help** du könntest (vielleicht) Hilfe brauchen III

migrant worker [ˌmaɪɡrənt ˈwɜːkə] Wanderarbeiter/in IV
mild [maɪld] mild III
mile [maɪl] Meile (= ca. 1,6 km) II • **for miles** meilenweit II
military [ˈmɪlətri] militärisch, Militär- V 4 (85) • **military-style fashion** Mode im Militärstil V 4 (85/192)
milk [mɪlk] melken IV
milk [mɪlk] Milch I
milkshake [ˈmɪlkʃeɪk] Milchshake I
°**milky** [ˈmɪlki] milchig
million [ˈmɪljən] Million III
millionaire [ˌmɪljəˈneə] Millionär/in IV
mime [maɪm] vorspielen, pantomimisch darstellen II
mind (doing) sth. [maɪnd]
 1. etwas dagegen haben (etwas zu tun) V 2 (35) • **Do you mind?** Stört es dich/Sie? V 2 (35/177) • **I don't mind** Es macht mir nichts aus V 2 (35/177) • **if you don't mind** wenn Sie nichts dagegen haben V 2 (35/177) • **Would you mind ...?** Würden Sie bitte ...? V 2 (35/177)
 ▶ S.177 (to) mind
 2. (sich kümmern) **Mind your own business.** Das geht dich nichts an! / Kümmere dich um deine eigenen Angelegenheiten! II **Never mind.** Kümmere dich nicht drum. / Macht nichts. II
mind [maɪnd] Verstand, Kopf V 2 (42)
mind map [ˈmaɪnd mæp] Mindmap („Gedankenkarte", „Wissensnetz") I
mine [maɪn] meiner, meine, meins II
minimum [ˈmɪnɪməm] Minimum V 2 (47)
minister [ˈmɪnɪstə]
 1. Minister/in IV • **prime minister** Premierminister/in IV
 2. Pfarrer/in, Pastor/in IV
minority [maɪˈnɒrəti] Minderheit IV
mints (pl) [mɪnts] Pfefferminzbonbons I
minute [ˈmɪnɪt] Minute I • **Wait a minute.** Warte mal! / Moment mal! II • **a 30-minute ride** eine 30-minütige Fahrt III
Minuteman [ˈmɪnɪtˌmæn] Angehöriger der amerikanischen Miliz V
mirror [ˈmɪrə] Spiegel II
Miss White [mɪs] Frau White (unverheiratet) I
miss [mɪs]
 1. vermissen II
 2. verpassen II
Miss a turn. Einmal aussetzen. II
missing [ˈmɪsɪŋ]: **be missing** fehlen II

mistake [mɪˈsteɪk] Fehler I • **by mistake** aus Versehen IV
mix [mɪks] mischen, mixen III
mixed-race [ˌmɪkst ˈreɪs] gemischtrassig V 1 (17)
mixture [ˈmɪkstʃə] Mischung III
mobile (phone) [ˈməʊbaɪl] Mobiltelefon, Handy I
model [ˈmɒdl] Modell(-flugzeug, -schiff usw.) I; (Foto-)Modell II
modern [ˈmɒdən] modern V 3 (50)
mole [məʊl] Maulwurf II
mom [mɑːm] (AE) Mutti, Mama; Mutter III
moment [ˈməʊmənt] Augenblick, Moment I • **at the moment** im Moment, gerade, zurzeit I • **for a moment** einen Moment lang II
monarch [ˈmɒnək] Monarch/in V 3 (59/187)
monarchy [ˈmɒnəki] Monarchie V 3 (59/187)
▶ S.187 Different forms of government
Monday [ˈmʌndeɪ, ˈmʌndi] Montag I • **Monday morning** Montagmorgen I
money [ˈmʌni] Geld I • **Money doesn't grow on trees.** Redensart: Geld wächst nicht auf Bäumen; Geld liegt nicht auf der Straße. III • **raise money (for)** Geld sammeln (für) IV
monitor [ˈmɒnɪtə] Bildschirm, Monitor III
monk [mʌŋk] Mönch V 1 (17)
monkey [ˈmʌŋki] Affe II
°**monsoon** [ˌmɒnˈsuːn] Regenzeit
monster [ˈmɒnstə] Monster, Ungeheuer III
month [mʌnθ] Monat I
mood [muːd] Laune V 4 (92) • **be in a good/bad mood** gute/schlechte Laune haben V 4 (92)
moon [muːn] Mond II
moped [ˈməʊped] Moped V 3 (67)
°**moral** [ˈmɒrəl] Lehre, Moral
more [mɔː] mehr I • **lots more** viel mehr I • **more boring (than)** langweiliger (als) II • **more or less** mehr oder weniger IV • **more quickly (than)** schneller (als) II • **more than ever** mehr als je (zuvor), mehr denn je V 3 (50) • **more than me** mehr als ich II • **no more music** keine Musik mehr I • **not (...) any more** nicht mehr II • **one more** noch ein(e), ein(e) weitere(r, s) I
morning [ˈmɔːnɪŋ] Morgen, Vormittag I • **in the morning** morgens, am Morgen I • **Monday morning** Montagmorgen I • **on**

Friday morning freitagmorgens, am Freitagmorgen I
°**mortuary science** ['mɔːtʃərɪ, AE mɔːtʃʊəri] Bestattungswissenschaft
mosque [mɒsk] Moschee III
▶ S.185 Religions
mosquito [mɒs'kiːtəʊ] Stechmücke, Moskito V 3 (63)
most [məʊst] (der/die/das) meiste ...; am meisten II • **most people** die meisten Leute I • **(the) most boring ...** der/die/das langweiligste ...; am langweiligsten II
motel [məʊ'tel] Motel III
mother ['mʌðə] Mutter I
motorway ['məʊtəweɪ] (BE) Autobahn IV
mountain ['maʊntən] Berg II
mouse [maʊs], pl **mice** [maɪs] Maus I
mouth [maʊθ] Mund I
move [muːv]
1. bewegen; sich bewegen II **Move back one space.** Geh ein Feld zurück. II • **Move on one space.** Geh ein Feld vor. II • °**be on the move** in Bewegung sein
2. **move (to)** umziehen (nach, in) II • **move in** einziehen II • **move out** ausziehen II
move [muːv] Umzug IV
movement ['muːvmənt] Bewegung II
movie ['muːvi] Film IV
MP3 player [ˌempiːˈθriː ˌpleɪə] MP3-Spieler I
Mr, Mr. ... ['mɪstə] Herr ... I
Mrs, Mrs. ... ['mɪsɪz] Frau ... I
Ms, Ms. ... [mɪz, məz] Frau ... II
much [mʌtʃ] viel I • **how much?** wie viel? I • **How much is/are ...?** Was kostet/kosten ...? / Wie viel kostet/kosten ...? I • **like/love sth. very much** etwas sehr mögen / sehr lieben II • **Thanks very much!** Danke sehr! / Vielen Dank! II
mud [mʌd] Schlamm, Matsch V 3 (65/190)
muddy ['mʌdi] schlammig, matschig V 3 (65)
muesli ['mjuːzli] Müsli I
mug (-gg-) [mʌg] überfallen V 3 (57)
mule [mjuːl] Maultier IV • **mule train** Maultierkarawane IV
°**mulga-tree** ['mʌlgə] Mulgabaum
multi- ['mʌltɪ] viel-, mehr-; multi-, Multi- IV • **multi-coloured** mehrfarbig IV • **multi-millionaire** Multimillionär(in) IV

mum [mʌm], **mummy** ['mʌmi], Mama, Mutti; Mutter I
murderer ['mɜːdərə] Mörder/in III
murder ['mɜːdə] (er)morden III
murder ['mɜːdə] Mord III
museum [mjuːˈziːəm] Museum I
music ['mjuːzɪk]
1. Musik I • **Music is for dancing.** etwa: Musik ist zum Tanzen da. III
2. Noten III • **I can read music.** Ich kann Noten lesen. III
musical ['mjuːzɪkl] Musical I
musician [mjuːˈzɪʃn] Musiker/in III
Muslim ['mʊzlɪm] Muslim/Muslima, Muslimin; muslimisch V 3 (52/185)
▶ S.185 Religions
must [mʌst] müssen I
mustard ['mʌstəd] Senf IV
mustn't do ['mʌsnt] nicht tun dürfen II
my [maɪ] mein/e I • **My name is ...** Ich heiße ... / Mein Name ist ... I
It's my turn. Ich bin dran / an der Reihe. I
myself [maɪˈself]
1. mir/mich III
2. selbst IV
mystery ['mɪstri] Rätsel, Geheimnis II

N

naked ['neɪkɪd] nackt V 1 (9) • **with the naked eye** mit dem bloßen Auge V 1 (9/170)
name [neɪm] Name I • **My name is ...** Ich heiße ... / Mein Name ist ... I • **What's your name?** Wie heißt du? I • **call sb. names** jn. mit Schimpfwörtern hänseln, jm. Schimpfwörter nachrufen III
put one's name on a list sich eintragen IV
name [neɪm] nennen; benennen II
narrator [nəˈreɪtə] Erzähler/in IV
nation ['neɪʃn] Nation, Volk III
the First Nations die Ersten Nationen (indianische Ureinwohner/innen Kanadas) III
national ['næʃnəl] national III
national park Nationalpark IV
nationality [ˌnæʃəˈnæləti] Staatsangehörigkeit, Nationalität V 2 (39)
Native American [ˌneɪtɪv əˈmerɪkən] amerikanische(r) Ureinwohner/in, Indianer/in IV
natural ['nætʃrəl] natürlich, Natur- II
nature ['neɪtʃə] Natur V 3 (60)

near [nɪə] in der Nähe von, nahe (bei) I
nearby [ˌnɪəˈbaɪ] (adj) nahegelegen; (adv) in der Nähe V 1 (23)
nearly ['nɪəli] fast, beinahe IV
neat [niːt]
1. gepflegt II • **neat and tidy** schön ordentlich II
2. (AE, infml) großartig, toll, klasse III
necessary ['nesəsri] notwendig, nötig V 2 (35)
neck [nek] Hals IV
need [niːd] brauchen, benötigen I
needn't do ['niːdnt] nicht tun müssen, nicht zu tun brauchen II
°**need** [niːd]: **people in need** Notleidende
negative ['negətɪv] negativ V 2 (39)
neighbour ['neɪbə] Nachbar/in I
neighbourhood ['neɪbəhʊd] Gegend, Stadtbereich; Nachbarschaft V 3 (63)
Neither. ['naɪðə, 'niːðə] Weder noch.; Keiner der beiden. V 2 (34)
▶ S.176 neither
nervous ['nɜːvəs] nervös, aufgeregt I
network ['netwɜːk] (Fernseh-/ Radio-) Sendernetz IV
never ['nevə] nie, niemals I
Never mind. Kümmere dich nicht drum. / Macht nichts. II
new [njuː] neu I • °**the New World** die Neue Welt (Amerika)
news (no pl) [njuːz] Nachrichten I
news agency ['njuːz ˌeɪdʒənsi] Nachrichtenagentur IV
newspaper ['njuːspeɪpə] Zeitung I
do a (news)paper round Zeitungen austragen V 4 (90)
next [nekst]: **be next** der/die Nächste sein I • °**the boy next door** der Junge von nebenan
the next day am nächsten Tag I • **the next photo** das nächste Foto I • **What have we got next?** Was haben wir als Nächstes? I
next to [nekst] neben I
nice [naɪs] schön, nett I • **nice and cool/clean/...** schön kühl/sauber/... I • **Nice to meet you.** Nett, dich/ euch/Sie kennenzulernen. III
night [naɪt] Nacht, später Abend I
at night nachts, in der Nacht I
by day and by night bei Tag und bei Nacht V 3 (67) • **late at night** spät abends V 4 (84) • **on Friday night** freitagnachts, Freitagnacht I
nightclub ['naɪtklʌb] Nachtklub III
nil [nɪl] null III

no [nəʊ] nein I
no [nəʊ] kein, keine I • **no more music** keine Musik mehr I • **no people at all** überhaupt keine Menschen IV • **No way!** [ˌnəʊ 'weɪ] Auf keinen Fall! / Kommt nicht in Frage! II; Was du nicht sagst! / Das kann nicht dein Ernst sein! III
no., *pl* **nos.** ['nʌmbə] Nr. III
noble ['nəʊbl] ehrenhaft; adlig IV
nobody ['nəʊbədi] niemand II
nod (-dd-) [nɒd] nicken (mit) II
nod (one's head) (mit dem Kopf) nicken III
noise [nɔɪz] Geräusch; Lärm I
noisy ['nɔɪzi] laut, lärmend II
no one ['nəʊ wʌn] niemand III
°**not listening to no one** *(infml)* = not listening to anyone
non-fiction ['nɒnˌfɪkʃn] Sachliteratur IV
non-violent [ˌnɒn 'vaɪələnt] gewaltlos, gewaltfrei IV
north [nɔːθ] Norden; nach Norden; nördlich II • **northbound** ['nɔːθbaʊnd] Richtung Norden III • **north-east** [ˌnɔːθ'iːst] Nordosten; nach Nordosten; nordöstlich II • **northern** ['nɔːðən] nördlich, Nord- III • **north-west** [ˌnɔːθ'west] Nordwesten; nach Nordwesten; nordwestlich II
nose [nəʊz] Nase I
not [nɒt] nicht I • **not (…) any** kein, keine I • **not (…) any more** nicht mehr II • **not (…) anybody** niemand II • **not (…) anything** nichts II • **not (…) anywhere** nirgendwo(hin) II • **not at all** gar nicht, überhaupt nicht, überhaupt kein(e) IV • **not (…) either** auch nicht II • **not only … but also …** nicht nur … sondern auch … IV
not (…) yet noch nicht II
▶ S.176 neither
note [nəʊt]
1. Mitteilung, Notiz I • **take notes (on)** sich Notizen machen (über, zu) I
2. Ton III
3. *(BE)* (Geld-)Schein, Banknote V 4 (88)
°**note sth. down** [ˌnəʊt 'daʊn] (sich) etwas notieren
nothing ['nʌθɪŋ] nichts III
nothing at all gar nichts, überhaupt nichts IV
notice ['nəʊtɪs] (be)merken III
notice board ['nəʊtɪs bɔːd] schwarzes Brett, Anschlagtafel III
novel ['nɒvl] Roman IV

November [nəʊ'vembə] November I
now [naʊ] nun, jetzt I • **(and) now for …** und jetzt … *(kündigt ein neues Thema an)* III • **now and again** ab und zu, von Zeit zu Zeit III
nowadays ['naʊədeɪz] heutzutage IV
nowhere ['nəʊweə] nirgendwo(hin) V 1 (12) • **the middle of nowhere** *(infml) etwa:* das Ende der Welt V 1 (12/171)
number ['nʌmbə] Zahl, Ziffer, Nummer I
number plate ['nʌmbə ˌpleɪt] Nummernschild IV
nun [nʌn] Nonne V 1 (17)
°**nurse** [nɜːs] Krankenschwester, Krankenpfleger/in
nut [nʌt] Nuss III

O

o [əʊ] null I
°**obelisk** ['ɒbəlɪsk] Obelisk
obey [ə'beɪ] gehorchen; sich halten an IV
objective [əb'dʒektɪv] objektiv V 3 (60)
observatory [əb'zɜːvətri] Aussichtsplattform IV
occupy ['ɒkjuːpaɪ] besetzen V 3 (63)
ocean ['əʊʃn] Ozean IV
o'clock [ə'klɒk]: **eleven o'clock** elf Uhr I
October [ɒk'təʊbə] Oktober I
of [əv, ɒv] von I • **of the summer holidays** der Sommerferien I • **a kilogram of oranges** ein Kilogramm Orangen III
of course [əv 'kɔːs] natürlich, selbstverständlich I
off [ɒf]: **take 10 c off** 10 Cent abziehen I
offer ['ɒfə] (an)bieten IV
office ['ɒfɪs] Büro V 3 (62)
office worker ['ɒfɪs ˌwɜːkə] Büroangestellte(r) V 3 (62)
official [ə'fɪʃl] amtlich, Amts- V 3 (52)
often ['ɒfn] oft, häufig I
Oh dear! Oje! II
OHP [ˌəʊ ˌeɪtʃ 'piː] Tageslichtprojektor, Polylux V 2 (45)
Oh well … [əʊ 'wel] Na ja … / Na gut … I
OK [ˌəʊ'keɪ] okay, gut, in Ordnung I
old [əʊld] alt I • **How old are you?** Wie alt bist du? I • **I'm … years old.** Ich bin … Jahre alt. I • °**old folks' home** *(infml)* Altenheim,

Seniorenresidenz • **old people's home** Altenheim, Seniorenresidenz V 1 (17/173)
old-fashioned [ˌəʊld'fæʃnd] altmodisch IV
oldie ['əʊldi] *(infml)* Oldie III
oligarchy ['ɒlɪɡɑːki] Oligarchie V 3 (59/187)
▶ S.187 Different forms of government
Olympic Games [əˌlɪmpɪk 'ɡeɪmz] Olympische Spiele IV
on [ɒn]
1. auf I
2. weiter III
3. *(Radio, Licht usw.)* an, eingeschaltet II
be on *(in the cinema, theatre, etc.)* laufen *(im Kino, Theater, usw.)* V 1 (14) • **go on** angehen III • **on a/my shift** in einer/meiner Schicht IV • **on 13th June** am 13. Juni I • **on foot** zu Fuß III • **on Friday** am Freitag I • **on Friday afternoon** freitagnachmittags, am Freitagnachmittag I • **on Friday evening** freitagabends, am Freitagabend I • **on Friday morning** freitagmorgens, am Freitagmorgen I • **on Friday night** freitagnachts, Freitagnacht I • **on his street** in seiner Straße III • **on the beach** am Strand II • **on the board** an die Tafel I • **on the left** links, auf der linken Seite I • **on the Missouri River** am Missourifluss IV • **on the phone** am Telefon I • **on the plane** im Flugzeug II • **on the radio** im Radio I • **on the right** rechts, auf der rechten Seite I • **on the scene** vor Ort, zur Stelle IV • **on the second floor** im zweiten Stock *(BE)* / im ersten Stock *(AE)* IV • **on the train** im Zug I • **on their/your/the way (to)** unterwegs (nach) IV • **on the weekend** *(AE)* am Wochenende IV • **on top of** oben auf IV • **on TV** im Fernsehen I • **What page are we on?** Auf welcher Seite sind wir? I • **be on holiday** in Urlaub sein II • **go on holiday** in Urlaub fahren II
straight on geradeaus weiter II
once [wʌns] einmal III • **once/twice a week** (einmal/zweimal) pro Woche III • **at once 1.** gleichzeitig, zugleich, auf einmal V 2 (35)
2. sofort V 3 (60)
one [wʌn] eins, ein, eine I • **one day** eines Tages I • **one more** noch ein/e, ein/e weitere(r, s) I • **a new one** ein neuer / eine neue / ein neues II • **my old ones** meine

alten II • **one by one** eins nach dem anderen V 2 (45) • **one tough girl** *(AE, infml) etwa:* ein wirklich toughes Mädchen III
onion [ˈʌnjən] Zwiebel III
online [ˌɒnˈlaɪn] online, Online- III
only [ˈəʊnli]
1. nur, bloß I • **not only ... but also ...** nicht nur ... sondern auch ... IV
2. erst II
3. **the only guest** der einzige Gast I
onto [ˈɒntə, ˈɒntʊ] auf (... hinauf) III
open [ˈəʊpən]
1. öffnen, aufmachen I
2. sich öffnen I
open [ˈəʊpən] geöffnet, offen I
open-air concert [ˌəʊpənˈeə ˌkɒnsət] Open-Air-Konzert, Konzert im Freien II • **opening times** Öffnungszeiten IV
°**opening** [ˈəʊpənɪŋ] Öffnung
opera [ˈɒprə] Oper III
opera house [ˈɒprə haʊs] Oper, Opernhaus III
operation (on) [ˌɒpəˈreɪʃn] Operation (an) III
opinion (on/of) [əˈpɪnjən] Meinung (zu/von) IV • **in my opinion** meiner Meinung nach IV
°**opium** [ˈəʊpiəm] Opium
opponent [əˈpəʊnənt] Gegner/in IV
opportunity [ˌɒpəˈtjuːnəti] Gelegenheit, Chance, Möglichkeit V 2 (40)
▶ S.180 German „Möglichkeit"
opposite [ˈɒpəzɪt] gegenüber (von) II
opposite [ˈɒpəzɪt] entgegengesetzt; gegenüberliegende(r, s) V 4 (82)
opposite [ˈɒpəzɪt] Gegenteil IV
°**oppression** [əˈpreʃn] Unterdrückung
oppressive [əˈpresɪv] repressiv, unterdrückerisch V 3 (56)
or [ɔː] oder I
orange [ˈɒrɪndʒ] orange(farben) I
orange [ˈɒrɪndʒ] Orange, Apfelsine I • **orange juice** [ˈɒrɪndʒ dʒuːs] Orangensaft I
orchestra [ˈɔːkɪstrə] Orchester V 2 (41)
▶ S.182 Collective nouns
order [ˈɔːdə]
1. Befehl, Anweisung, Anordnung V 4 (84) • **break an order** gegen eine Anordnung verstoßen V 4 (84)
°2. Reihenfolge
order [ˈɔːdə]
1. bestellen II
2. befehlen V 4 (84)

organization [ˌɔːɡənaɪˈzeɪʃn] Organisation IV
organize [ˈɔːɡənaɪz] organisieren, veranstalten III
organized [ˈɔːɡənaɪzd] (gut) organisiert V 2 (35)
origin [ˈɒrɪdʒɪn] Herkunft, Abstammung V 1 (9)
original *(n; adj)* [əˈrɪdʒənl] Original; Original-, ursprünglich IV
original version Originalfassung IV
orphan [ˈɔːfən] Waise, Waisenkind V 1 (17)
°**Oscar** [ˈɒskə]: **an Oscar-winning film** ein mit einem Oscar ausgezeichneter Film
other [ˈʌðə] andere(r, s) I • **the others** die anderen I • **the other way round** anders herum II
otherwise [ˈʌðəwaɪz] sonst IV
Ouch! [aʊtʃ] Autsch! I
our [ˈaʊə] unser, unsere I
ours [ˈaʊəz] unsere(r, s) II
ourselves [aʊəˈselvz]
1. uns III
2. selbst IV
out [aʊt] heraus, hinaus; draußen II
be out weg sein, nicht da sein I
out of ... aus ... (heraus/hinaus) I
outback [ˈaʊtbæk]: **the outback** *(Australien)* das Hinterland V 1 (6)
outfit [ˈaʊtfɪt] Outfit *(Kleidung; Ausrüstung)* II
outdoor [ˈaʊtdɔː] im Freien, Außen- III
outline [ˈaʊtlaɪn] Gliederung IV
outside [ˌaʊtˈsaɪd]
1. draußen I; Außen- IV; in der Natur V 3 (60/188)
2. nach draußen II
3. **outside the room** vor dem Zimmer; außerhalb des Zimmers I
oven [ˈʌvn] Ofen, Backofen III
over [ˈəʊvə]
1. über, oberhalb von I • **all over the world** auf der ganzen Welt III **from all over the world** aus der ganzen Welt II • **over here** herüber V 4 (83) • **over there** da drüben I • **over to ...** hinüber zu/nach ... II • **over time** [ˌəʊvə ˈtaɪm] im Laufe der Zeit IV
2. **be over** vorbei sein, zu Ende sein I
°**overfishing** [ˌəʊvəˈfɪʃɪŋ] Überfischung
overhead projector [ˌəʊvəhed prəˈdʒektə] Tageslichtprojektor, Polylux V 2 (45)
overseas [ˌəʊvəˈsiːz] ausländisch; im Ausland V 3 (56)

own [əʊn] besitzen IV
own [əʊn]: **our own pool** unser eigenes Schwimmbecken II • **on our/my/... own** allein, selbstständig *(ohne Hilfe)* IV
owner [ˈəʊnə] Besitzer/in, Eigentümer/in IV
ozone hole [ˈəʊzəʊn həʊl] Ozonloch V 1 (9)

P

pack [pæk] packen, einpacken II
packet [ˈpækɪt] Päckchen, Packung, Schachtel I • **a packet of mints** ein Päckchen/eine Packung Pfefferminzbonbons I
paddle [ˈpædl] paddeln III
paddle [ˈpædl] Paddel III
pads [pædz] Knieschützer; Schulterpolster III
page [peɪdʒ] (Buch-, Heft-)Seite I **What page are we on?** Auf welcher Seite sind wir? I
paid [peɪd] *siehe* pay
pain [peɪn] Schmerz(en) I • **cry in pain** vor Schmerzen schreien I
paint [peɪnt] (an)malen I; anstreichen II
paint [peɪnt] Farbe, Lack IV
painter [ˈpeɪntə] Maler/in II
painting [ˈpeɪntɪŋ] Gemälde, Bild; Malerei II
pair [peə]: **a pair (of)** ein Paar II
palace [ˈpæləs] Palast, Schloss III
palm tree [pɑːm] Palme V 3 (64)
panic *(-ing form:* **panicking***)* [ˈpænɪk] in Panik geraten III
pants *(pl)* [pænts] *(AE)* Hose IV
paper [ˈpeɪpə]
1. Papier I
2. Zeitung V 4 (90)
do a paper round Zeitungen austragen V 4 (90)
°**Pappa** [ˈpæpə] Vati
parade [pəˈreɪd] Parade, Umzug IV
paradise [ˈpærədaɪs] Paradies III
paragraph [ˈpærəɡrɑːf] Absatz *(in einem Text)* II
Paralympics [ˌpærəˈlɪmpɪks] Paralympische Spiele *(Olympische Spiele für Sportler/innen mit körperlicher Behinderung)* III
paramedic [ˌpærəˈmedɪk] Sanitäter/in II
paraphrase [ˈpærəfreɪz] umschreiben, anders ausdrücken III
parcel [ˈpɑːsl] Paket I
pardon [ˈpɑːdn] begnadigen IV
parent [ˈpeərənt]: **a single parent** ein(e) Alleinerziehende(r) II

Dictionary

parents ['peərənts] Eltern I
park [pɑːk] Park I • **car park** Parkplatz III • **national park** Nationalpark IV
park [pɑːk] parken V 3 (60)
parking lot ['pɑːkɪŋ lɒt] (AE) Parkplatz IV
parliament ['pɑːləmənt] Parlament III
parrot ['pærət] Papagei I
part [pɑːt] Teil I • **take part in sth.** teilnehmen an etwas III
participate (in) [pɑːˈtɪsɪpeɪt] teilnehmen (an) IV
particular [pəˈtɪkjələ] bestimmte(r, s), spezielle(r, s) V 2 (35)
partner ['pɑːtnə] Partner/in I
party ['pɑːti] Party I
party ['pɑːti] (infml) feiern V 3 (57)
pass [pɑːs]
1. (herüber)reichen, weitergeben I **pass sth. on** etwas weiterleiten, -geben IV • **pass round** herumgeben I
2. bestehen (Test, Prüfung usw.) V 2 (32)
3. genehmigen, verabschieden (Gesetz usw.) V 4 (87)
passenger ['pæsɪndʒə] Passagier/in, Fahrgast III
passive ['pæsɪv] Passiv III
past [pɑːst] Vergangenheit II
past [pɑːst] vorbei (an), vorüber (an) II • **half past 11** halb zwölf (11.30 / 23.30) I • **quarter past 11** Viertel nach 11 (11.15 / 23.15) I
path [pɑːθ] Pfad, Weg II • **bridle path** ['braɪdl ˌpɑːθ] Reitweg III
patient ['peɪʃnt] geduldig V 4 (92)
patrol [pəˈtrəʊl] Streife, Patrouille IV
pavement ['peɪvmənt] Gehweg, Bürgersteig IV
pay (for) [peɪ], **paid, paid** bezahlen II
PE [ˌpiːˈiː], **Physical Education** [ˌfɪzɪkəl_edʒuˈkeɪʃn] Sportunterricht, Turnen I
pedestrian [pəˈdestrɪən] Fußgänger/in IV
pedestrian crossing [pəˌdestrɪən ˈkrɒsɪŋ] Fußgängerüberweg IV
pen [pen] Kugelschreiber, Füller I
penalty ['penlti] Strafstoß; Elfmeter (Fußball) III
pence (p) (pl) [pens] Pence (Plural von „penny") I
pencil ['pensl] Bleistift I • **pencil case** ['pensl keɪs] Federmäppchen I • **pencil sharpener** ['pensl ˌʃɑːpnə] Bleistiftanspitzer I

penny ['peni] kleinste britische Münze I
people ['piːpl] Menschen, Leute I °**people in need** Notleidende **old people's home** Altenheim, Seniorenresidenz V 1 (17/173)
pepper ['pepə] Pfeffer V 1 (22)
per [pɜː, pə] pro III
per cent (%) [pəˈsent] Prozent III
percentage [pəˈsentɪdʒ] Prozentsatz, prozentualer Anteil V 1 (10)
perfect ['pɜːfɪkt] perfekt; ideal; vollkommen I
performer: **(street) performer** [pəˈfɔːmə] Straßenkünstler/in III
perhaps [pəˈhæps] vielleicht V 3 (63)
period ['pɪəriəd] (Unterrichts-/ Schul-)Stunde IV
person ['pɜːsn] Person I
personal ['pɜːsənl] persönlich III
personality [ˌpɜːsəˈnæləti] Persönlichkeit V 2 (34)
persuade [pəˈsweɪd] überreden V 4 (83)
pet [pet] Haustier I • **pet shop** Tierhandlung I
°**petrochemicals** (pl) [ˌpetrəʊˈkemɪkəlz] die petrochemische Industrie
petrol ['petrəl] Benzin IV
petrol station ['petrəl ˌsteɪʃn] Tankstelle IV
phone [fəʊn] anrufen I
phone [fəʊn] Telefon I • **on the phone** am Telefon I • **phone number** Telefonnummer I • **pick up the phone** den Hörer abnehmen II
photo ['fəʊtəʊ] Foto I • **in the photo** auf dem Foto I • **take photos** Fotos machen, fotografieren I
photographer [fəˈtɒgrəfə] Fotograf/in II
phrase [freɪz] Ausdruck, (Rede-)Wendung II
piano [piˈænəʊ] Klavier, Piano I **play the piano** Klavier spielen I
pick [pɪk]: **pick fruit/flowers** Obst/ Blumen pflücken IV • **pick sb. up** jn. abholen III • **pick sth. up** etwas hochheben, aufheben III • **pick up the phone** den Hörer abnehmen II
picnic ['pɪknɪk] Picknick II
picture ['pɪktʃə] Bild I • **in the picture** auf dem Bild I
pie [paɪ] Obstkuchen; Pastete II
pie chart ['paɪ tʃɑːt] Tortendiagramm V 1 (10)
piece [piːs]: **a piece of** ein Stück I **a piece of paper** ein Stück Papier I

a piece of clothing Kleidungsstück IV
pilgrim ['pɪlgrɪm] Pilger/in IV
pilot ['paɪlət] Pilot/in IV
°**pinboard** ['pɪnbɔːd] Pinnwand
pink [pɪŋk] pink(farben), rosa I
pipe [paɪp] Pfeife III
pirate ['paɪrət] Pirat, Piratin I
pitch [pɪtʃ]: **football/hockey pitch** Fußball-/Hockeyplatz, -feld II
pity ['pɪti] **It's a pity (that ...)** Es ist schade, dass ... II
pizza ['piːtsə] Pizza I
place [pleɪs] Ort, Platz I • **place of birth** Geburtsort IV • **take place** stattfinden II • **in other places** an anderen Orten, anderswo III
placement ['pleɪsmənt] Praktikum V 2 (38)
plain [pleɪn] einfach, schlicht IV
plan [plæn] Plan I
plan (-nn-) [plæn] planen II
plane [pleɪn] Flugzeug II • **on the plane** im Flugzeug II
planet ['plænɪt] Planet II
plant [plɑːnt] (ein-, aus-, be-)pflanzen IV
plant [plɑːnt] Pflanze IV
plastic ['plæstɪk] Plastik, Kunststoff IV
plate [pleɪt] Teller I • **a plate of chips** ein Teller Pommes frites I **license plate** (AE) Nummernschild IV • **number plate** Nummernschild IV
platform ['plætfɔːm] Bahnsteig, Gleis III
play [pleɪ] spielen I • **play a trick on sb.** jm. einen Streich spielen II **play football** Fußball spielen I **play the drums** Schlagzeug spielen III • **play the fiddle** Geige spielen III • **play the guitar** Gitarre spielen I • **play the piano** Klavier spielen I • **play the violin** Geige spielen III
play [pleɪ] Theaterstück I
°**play area** ['pleɪ ˌeərɪə] Spielplatz
player ['pleɪə] Spieler/in I
please [pliːz] bitte (in Fragen und Aufforderungen) I
pleased [pliːzd]: **be pleased** sich freuen IV
plenty of ['plenti_əv] reichlich, viel(e) II
plot [plɒt] Handlung V 1 (24)
plug [plʌg] Stecker III
plutocracy [pluːˈtɒkrəsi] Plutokratie V 3 (59/187)
▶ S.187 Different forms of government
pm [ˌpiːˈem]: **7 pm** 7 Uhr abends/ 19 Uhr I

pocket ['pɒkɪt] Tasche *(an Kleidungsstück)* II • **pocket money** ['pɒkɪt mʌni] Taschengeld II
poem ['pəʊɪm] Gedicht I
point [pɔɪnt] Punkt II • **11.4 (eleven point four)** 11,4 (elf Komma vier) II • **point of view** Standpunkt II • **from my point of view** aus meiner Sicht; von meinem Standpunkt aus gesehen II • **That's a good point.** Das ist ein gutes Argument. V 4 (86) • **There was no point.** Es hatte keinen Sinn. III **What's the point?** Was soll das? III
point (at/to sth.) [pɔɪnt] zeigen, deuten (auf etwas) II
poison ['pɔɪzn] Gift V 1 (22)
poisonous ['pɔɪzənəs] giftig V 1 (22)
police *(pl)* [pə'liːs] Polizei I • **police station** Polizeiwache, Polizeirevier II
polite [pə'laɪt] höflich IV
politician [ˌpɒlə'tɪʃn] Politiker/in IV
politics ['pɒlətɪks] (die) Politik IV
polluted [pə'luːtɪd] verseucht, verunreinigt V 3 (55)
pollution [pə'luːʃn] Verschmutzung IV
poltergeist ['pəʊltəgaɪst] Poltergeist I
pond [pɒnd] Teich V 3 (65)
ponytail ['pəʊniteɪl] Pferdeschwanz *(Frisur)* III
pool [puːl] Schwimmbad, Schwimmbecken II
poor [pɔː, pʊə] arm I • **poor Sophie** (die) arme Sophie I
pop siehe **population**
pop (music) [pɒp] Pop(musik) III
popcorn ['pɒpkɔːn] Popcorn II
popular ['pɒpjələ] populär, beliebt III
population [ˌpɒpju'leɪʃn] Bevölkerung, Einwohner(zahl) III
port [pɔːt] Hafen(stadt) V 3 (52)
posh [pɒʃ] vornehm, edel *(etwas abwertend)* V 3 (61)
positive ['pɒzətɪv] positiv V 2 (39)
possession [pə'zeʃn] Besitz, Besitzung; Eigentum V 3 (52)
possibility [ˌpɒsə'bɪlɪti] Möglichkeit IV
▶ S.180 German „Möglichkeit"
possible ['pɒsəbl] möglich II
post [pəʊst] Post *(Briefe, Päckchen, ...)* III
post office ['pəʊst ˌɒfɪs] Postamt II
postcard ['pəʊstkɑːd] Postkarte II
poster ['pəʊstə] Poster I
postscript ['pəʊstskrɪpt] Postskript III

potato [pə'teɪtəʊ], *pl* **potatoes** Kartoffel I • °**couch potato** [kaʊtʃ] Dauerglotzer/in • **potato chips** *(AE)* Kartoffelchips IV
pound (£) [paʊnd] Pfund *(britische Währung)* I
pound [paʊnd] Pfund *(Gewichtseinheit)*: **a three-pound ball** ein drei Pfund schwerer Ball III
poverty ['pɒvəti] Armut V 3 (55)
power ['paʊə] Macht; Stärke V 3 (52)
powerful ['paʊəfl] mächtig, einflussreich V 3 (52)
°**powerhouse** ['paʊəˌhaʊs]: **economic powerhouse** wirtschaftliche Macht
practical ['præktɪkl] praktisch; praxisnah, praxisbezogen V 2 (35)
practice ['præktɪs] *im Lehrwerk:* Übungsteil I
practice ['præktɪs] *(AE)* üben; trainieren IV
practise ['præktɪs] üben; trainieren I
pray [preɪ] beten IV
prayer [preə] Gebet IV
precinct ['priːsɪŋkt]: **shopping precinct** Einkaufsviertel, Einkaufsstraße III
prefer sth. (to sth.) (-rr-) [prɪ'fɜː] etwas (einer anderen Sache) vorziehen; etwas lieber tun (als etwas) IV
prefix ['priːfɪks] Präfix III
prejudice (against) ['predʒʊdɪs] Voreingenommenheit (gegen), Vorurteil (gegenüber) IV
prejudiced: ['predʒʊdɪst]: **be prejudiced (against)** voreingenommen sein (gegen), Vorurteile haben (gegenüber) IV
prepare [prɪ'peə] vorbereiten; sich vorbereiten II • **prepare for** sich vorbereiten auf II
present ['preznt]
1. Gegenwart I
2. Geschenk I
present sth. (to sb.) [prɪ'zent] (jm.) etwas präsentieren, vorstellen I; überreichen III
presentation [ˌprezn'teɪʃn] Präsentation, Vorstellung I
present-day [ˌpreznt 'deɪ] heutige(r, s) IV
presenter [prɪ'zentə] Moderator/in II
president ['prezɪdənt] Präsident/in IV
pretend [prɪ'tend] so tun, als ob V 4 (93)
pretty ['prɪti]
1. hübsch I

▶ S.191 German „schön" usw.
2. **pretty cool/good/...** ziemlich cool/gut/... II
prevent sth. [prɪ'vent] etwas verhindern IV • **prevent sb./sth. from doing sth.** jn./etwas daran hindern, etwas zu tun IV
prewriting exercise [ˌpriː'raɪtɪŋ] Übung vor dem Schreiben III
price [praɪs] (Kauf-)Preis I
primary school ['praɪməri] Grundschule in GB, von 4–5 bis 11 Jahren V 2 (38)
prime minister [ˌpraɪm 'mɪnɪstə] Premierminister/in IV
principal ['prɪnsəpl] *(bes. AE)* Schulleiter/in IV
print sth. out [ˌprɪnt 'aʊt] etwas ausdrucken II
prison ['prɪzn] Gefängnis IV • **in prison for murder** im Gefängnis wegen Mordes IV
prisoner ['prɪznə] Gefangene(r) IV
private ['praɪvət] privat V 1 (15)
privilege ['prɪvəlɪdʒ] Privileg V 4 (90)
prize [praɪz] Preis, Gewinn I
°**pro** [prəʊ]: **pros and cons** *(pl)* Vor- und Nachteile
probably ['prɒbəbli] wahrscheinlich II
problem ['prɒbləm] Problem II °**face a problem** mit einem Problem konfrontiert sein • **manage a problem** mit einem Problem umgehen, ein Problem lösen V 3 (63)
produce [prə'djuːs] produzieren, erzeugen, herstellen II
°**producer** [prə'djuːsə] Produzent/in
professional [prə'feʃnl] professionell IV
professor [prə'fesə] Professor/in V 3 (59)
profile ['prəʊfaɪl] Profil; Beschreibung, Porträt V 1 (6)
program ['prəʊɡræm] *(AE)* Programm IV
programme ['prəʊɡræm] programmieren; planen IV
programme ['prəʊɡræm]
1. Programm I
2. (Fernseh-/Radio-)Sendung IV
progress ['prəʊɡres] Fortschritt V 3 (50)
project (about, on) ['prɒdʒekt] Projekt (über, zu) I • **do a project** ein Projekt machen, durchführen II
projector [prə'dʒektə]: **video projector** Videoprojektor, Beamer V 2 (45)
promise ['prɒmɪs] versprechen II
pronunciation [prəˌnʌnsi'eɪʃn] Aussprache I

proof *(no pl)* [pruːf] Beweis(e) II
prostitute [ˈprɒstɪtjuːt] Prostituierte(r) V 3 (57)
protect sb./sth. (from sb./sth.) [prəˈtekt] jn./etwas (be)schützen (vor jm./etwas) IV
protective [prəˈtektɪv] Schutz-, schützend V 1 (9)
protest (against/about) [prəˈtest] protestieren (gegen) IV
protest [ˈprəʊtest] Protest IV
proud (of sb./sth.) [praʊd] stolz (auf jn./etwas) II
PS [ˌpiːˈes] **(postscript** [ˈpəʊstskrɪpt]) PS, Postskript *(Nachschrift unter Briefen)* III
pub [pʌb] Kneipe, Lokal II
public [ˈpʌblɪk] öffentlich IV
public transport öffentlicher Verkehr IV
public [ˈpʌblɪk]: **the public** die Öffentlichkeit IV
publish [ˈpʌblɪʃ] veröffentlichen III
pull [pʊl] ziehen I
pullover [ˈpʊləʊvə] Pullover II
punctual [ˈpʌŋktʃuəl] pünktlich V 2 (35)
punish [ˈpʌnɪʃ] bestrafen V 4 (84)
punishment [ˈpʌnɪʃmənt] Bestrafung, Strafe V 4 (84)
punk [pʌŋk] Punker/in II
purple [ˈpɜːpl] violett; lila I
purse [pɜːs] Geldbörse I
push [pʊʃ] drücken, schieben, stoßen I
put (-tt-) [pʊt]**, put, put** legen, stellen, (etwas wohin) tun I • **put sth. away** wegräumen IV • **put sth. in order** etwas in Ordnung bringen IV • **put sb. to bed** jn. ins Bett bringen III • **put sth. on** etwas anziehen *(Kleidung)*; etwas aufsetzen *(Hut, Helm)* II • **put out a fire** ein Feuer löschen IV • °**put one's hand up** sich melden • **put one's name on a list** sich eintragen IV **You know how to put it.** Sie wissen, wie man es formuliert/ausdrückt. IV
puzzled [ˈpʌzld] verwirrt II
pyjamas *(pl)* [pəˈdʒɑːməz] Schlafanzug II

Q

qualification [ˌkwɒlɪfɪˈkeɪʃn] Abschluss, Qualifikation V 2 (32)
quality [ˈkwɒləti] Eigenschaft; Qualität IV
quarter [ˈkwɔːtə]: **quarter past 11** Viertel nach 11 (11.15 / 23.15) I

quarter to 12 Viertel vor 12 (11.45 / 23.45) I
quay [kiː] Kai III
queen [kwiːn] Königin III
question [ˈkwestʃn] Frage I • **ask questions** Fragen stellen I
questionnaire (on sth.) [ˌkwestʃəˈneə] Fragebogen (zu etwas) V 4 (80)
queue [kjuː] Schlange, Reihe *(wartender Menschen)* IV
quick [kwɪk] schnell I
quiet [ˈkwaɪət] leise, still, ruhig I **keep quiet** still sein, leise sein IV
quilt [kwɪlt] Bettdecke, Federbett V 3 (64/189)
°**quit (-tt-)** [kwɪt]**, quit, quit** verlassen
quite [kwaɪt] ziemlich; ganz III
quiz [kwɪz]**,** *pl* **quizzes** [ˈkwɪzɪz] Quiz, Ratespiel I
quotation [kwəʊˈteɪʃn] Zitat V 4 (95)
quotation marks [kwəʊˈteɪʃn ˌmɑːks] Anführungszeichen, -striche III

R

rabbit [ˈræbɪt] Kaninchen I
°**rabbit hole** Eingang zum Kaninchenbau
rabbitproof [ˈræbɪtpruːf] kaninchensicher, kaninchen-fest V 1 (17)
race (sb./sth.) [reɪs] (mit jm./etwas) um die Wette laufen/schwimmen/fahren/... V 1 (12)
race [reɪs] Rennen, (Wett-)Lauf V 1 (12)
race [reɪs] Rasse V 1 (17) • **mixed-race** gemischtrassig V 1 (17) • °**race discrimination** Diskriminierung aufgrund der Rasse • °**race relations** *(pl)* Beziehungen zwischen den Rassen
racing [ˈreɪsɪŋ] (Pferde-)Rennsport V 1 (12)
racist [ˈreɪsɪst] Rassist/in; rassistisch V 1 (17)
racket [ˈrækɪt] Schläger *(Badminton, Tennis, Squash)* III
radio [ˈreɪdiəʊ] Radio I • **on the radio** im Radio I
raft [rɑːft] Schlauchboot, Floß IV
raft [rɑːft] mit einem Schlauchboot/Floß fahren IV
°**railroad** [ˈreɪlrəʊd] *(AE)* Eisenbahn
railway [ˈreɪlweɪ] Eisenbahn II
rain [reɪn] Regen II
rain [reɪn] regnen II
rainfall [ˈreɪnfɔːl] Niederschlag *(Regen)*; Regenfälle V 1 (11)

rainproof [ˈreɪnpruːf] regendicht V 1 (17/173)
rainy [ˈreɪni] regnerisch II • **rainy season** Regenzeit II
raise [reɪz]: **raise money (for)** Geld sammeln (für) IV • °**raise one's hand** sich melden
ran [ræn] *siehe* **run**
rang [ræŋ] *siehe* **ring**
ranger [ˈreɪndʒə] Ranger/in, Aufseher/in III
rap [ræp] Rap(musik) *(rhythmischer Sprechgesang)* I
rapid [ˈræpɪd] rapide, schnell V 3 (56)
rapids *(pl)* [ˈræpɪdz] Stromschnellen III
rapper [ˈræpə] Rapper/in IV
rat [ræt] Ratte III
rate [reɪt] Rate V 1 (9) • **birth rate** Geburtsrate V 1 (9/169) • **death rate** Sterberate V 1 (9/169)
rate [reɪt] bewerten, einschätzen V 4 (82)
°**rating** [ˈreɪtɪŋ] Einschätzung
ray [reɪ] (Licht-)Strahl V 1 (9) **ultraviolet rays** *(pl)* ultraviolette Strahlen V 1 (9)
RE [ˌɑːrˈiː]**, Religious Education** [rɪˌlɪdʒəs ˌedʒuˈkeɪʃn] Religion, Religionsunterricht I
reach [riːtʃ] erreichen III
react (to sth.) [riˈækt] reagieren (auf/gegen etwas) V 1 (14)
reaction (to) [riˈækʃn] Reaktion (auf) IV
read [riːd]**, read, read** lesen I
°**read aloud** [əˈlaʊd] vorlesen **easy-to-read** leicht zu lesende(r, s) V 2 (39)
reader [ˈriːdə] Leser/in II
ready [ˈredi] bereit, fertig I • **get ready (for)** sich fertig machen (für), sich vorbereiten (auf) I • **get things ready** Dinge fertig machen, vorbereiten I
real [rɪəl] echt, wirklich I • **real late** *(AE, infml)* wirklich spät, echt spät III
realistic [ˌriːəˈlɪstɪk] realistisch, wirklichkeitsnah III
reality [riˈæləti] Wirklichkeit, Realität IV • **reality show** Reality-Show IV
realize [ˈrɪəlaɪz] erkennen, merken I
really [ˈrɪəli] wirklich I
reason [ˈriːzn] Grund, Begründung I • **the reason why** der Grund, warum IV • **for lots of reasons** aus vielen Gründen I
receive [rɪˈsiːv] erhalten III
recent [ˈriːsnt] jüngst, aktuell V 2 (39)

recently [ˈriːsntli] vor kurzem, kürzlich, neulich; in letzter Zeit V 2 (39)
recess [ˈriːses] *(AE)* Pause *(zwischen Schulstunden)* IV • **during recess** in der Pause IV
recognize [ˈrekəgnaɪz] erkennen IV
record [rɪˈkɔːd] aufnehmen, aufzeichnen III
recorder [rɪˈkɔːdə] Blockflöte III
recording [rɪˈkɔːdɪŋ] Aufnahme, Aufzeichnung III
recover (from) [rɪˈkʌvə] sich erholen (von) II
recycled [ˌriːˈsaɪkld] wiederverwertet, wiederverwendet, recycelt II
recycling [ˌriːˈsaɪklɪŋ] Wiederverwertung, Recycling II
red [red] rot I
reddish [ˈredɪʃ] rötlich IV
reduce sth. (by) [rɪˈdʒuːs] etwas reduzieren (um) IV
reef [riːf] Riff V 1 (9)
referee [ˌrefəˈriː] Schiedsrichter/in III
reference [ˈrefrəns] Referenz, Empfehlung V 2 (38)
reflex [ˈriːfleks] Reflex IV
regular [ˈregjələ] regelmäßig III
rehearsal [rɪˈhɜːsl] Probe *(am Theater)* I
rehearse [rɪˈhɜːs] proben *(am Theater)* I
relations *(pl)* [rɪˈleɪʃnz] Beziehungen IV • °**race relations** *(pl)* Beziehungen zwischen den Rassen, den ethnischen Gruppen
relationship [rɪˈleɪʃnʃɪp] Verhältnis, Beziehung V 4 (80) • **end a relationship** mit jm. Schluss machen V 4 (80/191)
relative [ˈrelətɪv] Verwandte(r) II
relax [rɪˈlæks] (sich) entspannen, sich ausruhen II
relaxed [rɪˈlækst] entspannt V 2 (44)
release [rɪˈliːs] *(CD, Film usw.)* herausbringen, auf den Markt bringen III
reliable [rɪˈlaɪəbl] zuverlässig IV
religion [rɪˈlɪdʒən] Religion IV
religious [rɪˈlɪdʒəs] gläubig, religiös IV
remember sth. [rɪˈmembə]
1. sich an etwas erinnern I
2. sich etwas merken I
▸ S.181 Same verb, different meaning
repair [rɪˈpeə] reparieren, ausbessern III
repeat [rɪˈpiːt] wiederholen II
repetition [ˌrepəˈtɪʃn] Wiederholung V 4 (95)
replace sth. (with) [rɪˈpleɪs] etwas ersetzen (durch) III

reply (to) [rɪˈplaɪ] antworten (auf), beantworten; erwidern III
report (on) [rɪˈpɔːt] Bericht, Reportage (über) I
report (to sb.) [rɪˈpɔːt] jm. berichten, sich bei jm. melden II
reporter [rɪˈpɔːtə] Reporter/in II
represent [ˌreprɪˈzent] repräsentieren, vertreten III
request [rɪˈkwest] Bitte, Wunsch V 2 (38) • **on request** auf Wunsch V 2 (38/179)
require sb. to do sth [rɪˈkwaɪə] von jm. verlangen, etwas zu tun V 4 (89)
rescue [ˈreskjuː] Rettung, Rettungsdienst IV
research *(no pl)* [rɪˈsɜːtʃ, ˈriːsɜːtʃ] Recherche, Forschung(en) III
researcher [rɪˈsɜːtʃə, ˈriːsɜːtʃə] Rechercheur/in III
reservation [ˌrezəˈveɪʃn] Reservat IV
resources *(pl)* [rɪˈzɔːsɪs, rɪˈsɔːsɪz] Mittel, Ressourcen IV
respect (for) [rɪˈspekt] Achtung, Respekt (vor) V 1 (16) • **With respect, ...** Bei allem Respekt, ... V 1 (16/172)
respect sb./sth. (for sth.) [rɪˈspekt] jn./etwas (wegen einer Sache) achten, respektieren V 1 (16)
responsibility (for) [rɪˌspɒnsəˈbɪləti] Verantwortung (für) V 2 (39) • **take responsibility (for)** Verantwortung (für) übernehmen V 2 (39)
responsible (for) [rɪˈspɒnsəbl] verantwortlich (für) V 2 (39)
rest [rest] Rest II
restart [ˌriːˈstɑːt] neu starten *(Computer)* II
restaurant [ˈrestrɒnt] Restaurant II
restroom [ˈrest.ruːm] *(AE)* (öffentliche) Toilette IV
result [rɪˈzʌlt] Ergebnis, Resultat I
result in sth. [rɪˈzʌlt] zu etwas führen V 3 (56)
résumé [ˈrezəmeɪ] *(AE)* Lebenslauf V 2 (38)
retire [rɪˈtaɪə] in den Ruhestand gehen; sich zurückziehen V 3 (59)
°**return** [rɪˈtɜːn] zurückkehren
°**return** [rɪˈtɜːn] Rückkehr
°**reverse** [rɪˈvɜːs] umgekehrte(r, s) **in reverse** umgekehrt
revise [rɪˈvaɪz] überarbeiten IV
revision [rɪˈvɪʒn] Wiederholung (des Lernstoffs) I
revolution [ˌrevəˈluːʃn] Revolution IV
°**rewrite** [ˌriːˈraɪt] neu schreiben, umschreiben
rhino [ˈraɪnəʊ] Nashorn II

rhythm [ˈrɪðəm] Rhythmus III
rich [rɪtʃ] reich II
ridden [ˈrɪdn] *siehe* ride
riddle [ˈrɪdl] Rätsel, Scherzfrage III
ride [raɪd], **rode, ridden** reiten I
ride a (motor)bike (Motor-)Rad fahren I
ride [raɪd]: **(bike) ride** (Rad-)Fahrt, (Rad-)Tour II • **(bus) ride** (Bus-)Fahrt II • **take a ride** eine Spritztour/Fahrt machen II
riding [ˈraɪdɪŋ] Reiten, Reitsport I
go riding [ˈraɪdɪŋ] reiten gehen I
riding boots *(pl)* Reitstiefel III • **riding hat** Reitkappe, Reiterhelm III
right [raɪt] richtig I • **all right** [ɔːl ˈraɪt] gut, in Ordnung II • **be right** Recht haben I • **get sth. right** etwas richtig machen III • **That's right.** Das ist richtig. / Das stimmt. I • **You need a school bag, right?** Du brauchst eine Schultasche, stimmt's? / nicht wahr? I
right [raɪt] Recht IV • **civil rights** *(pl)* Bürgerrechte IV • °**Bill of Rights** Zusatzartikel 1–10 zu den Grundrechten der USA
right [raɪt] rechte(r, s) I • **look right** nach rechts schauen I • **on the right** rechts, auf der rechten Seite I • **to the right** nach rechts III • **turn right** (nach) rechts abbiegen II • **take a right** *(AE)* nach links/rechts abbiegen IV
right [raɪt]: **right behind you** direkt/genau hinter dir II • **right now** jetzt sofort; jetzt gerade I
rim [rɪm] Rand, Kante IV
ring [rɪŋ] Ring II
ring [rɪŋ], **rang, rung** klingeln, läuten II
ringtone [ˈrɪŋtəʊn] Klingelton III
riot [ˈraɪət] Aufruhr, Krawall IV
ripe [raɪp] reif IV
rise [raɪz], **rose, risen**
1. (auf)steigen IV
°2. *(Baum)* sich erheben
risen [ˈrɪzn] *siehe* rise
river [ˈrɪvə] Fluss II
road [rəʊd] Straße I • **Park Road** [ˌpɑːk ˈrəʊd] Parkstraße I
rock [rɒk] Fels, Felsen II • **rock art** *(no pl)* Felsmalerei(en) V 1 (8)
rock (music) [rɒk] Rock(musik) III
rode [rəʊd] *siehe* ride
role [rəʊl] Rolle III
role model [ˈrəʊl ˌmɒdl] Vorbild V 2 (48)
roll [rəʊl] Brötchen II
Roman [ˈrəʊmən] römisch; Römer, Römerin II
roof [ruːf] Dach II

Dictionary

room [ruːm, rʊm] Raum, Zimmer I
rope [rəʊp] Seil IV
rose [rəʊz] siehe **rise**
round [raʊnd] rund II • **round brackets** runde Klammern IV
round [raʊnd] um ... (herum); in ... umher II • **round here** hier (in der Gegend) IV • **the other way round** anders herum II
round [raʊnd] • **do a paper round** Zeitungen austragen V 4 (90)
route [ruːt] Strecke, Route IV
routine [ruːˈtiːn] Routine IV
row [rəʊ] Reihe IV
royal [ˈrɔɪəl] königlich, Königs II
rubber [ˈrʌbə] Radiergummi I
rubbish [ˈrʌbɪʃ] (Haus-)Müll, Abfall II • **rubbish collection** Müllabfuhr II
rucksack [ˈrʌksæk] Rucksack III
rude [ruːd] unhöflich, unverschämt II
rugby [ˈrʌgbi] Rugby III
ruin [ˈruːɪn] Ruine IV
ruin [ˈruːɪn] verderben; ruinieren V 4 (80)
rule [ruːl] Regel, Vorschrift III **break a rule** gegen eine Regel verstoßen IV • °**follow rules** sich an die Regeln halten • **set of rules** Regelwerk V 2 (47)
ruler [ˈruːlə] Lineal I
run [rʌn] (Wett-)Lauf • **go for a run** laufen gehen IV • °**on the run** (infml) auf Trab
run (-nn-) [rʌn], **ran, run**
1. laufen, rennen I • **run away** weglaufen V 3 (67)
2. verlaufen (Straße; Grenze) IV
3. etwas leiten (Hotel, Firma usw.) V 1 (17) • °**run one's own affairs** sich selbst verwalten
rung [rʌŋ] siehe **ring**
runner [ˈrʌnə] Läufer/in III
running shoes [ˈrʌnɪŋ ʃuːz] Laufschuhe III
running track [ˈrʌnɪŋ træk] Laufbahn (Sport) III
°**rupee** [ruːˈpiː] Rupie I
rural [ˈrʊərəl] ländlich, Land- V 3 (50)
rush [rʌʃ] Ansturm V 3 (63) • °**gold rush** Goldrausch

S

sad [sæd] traurig II
saddle [ˈsædl] Sattel III
sadly [ˈsædli] leider; traurig V 3 (9)
sadness [ˈsædnəs] Traurigkeit IV
safe [seɪf] Tresor, Safe IV

safe (from) [seɪf] sicher, in Sicherheit (vor) II
safety [ˈseɪfti] Sicherheit IV
▶ S. 186 „Sicherheit"
said [sed] siehe **say**
sail [seɪl] (mit dem Schiff) fahren; segeln IV
saint [seɪnt] Heilige(r) IV
salad [ˈsæləd] Salat (als Gericht oder Beilage) I
sale [seɪl] (Aus-, Schluss-)Verkauf IV
salmon [ˈsæmən], pl **salmon** Lachs III
salt [sɔːlt] Salz V 1 (22)
°**saltwater** [ˈsɔːltwɔːtə] Salzwasser-, Meereswasser- • **saltwater crocodile** Leisten- oder Salzwasserkrokodil
same [seɪm] • **the same ...** der-/die-/dasselbe ...; dieselben ... I • **be/look the same** gleich sein/aussehen I
°**sandbank** [ˈsændˌbæŋk] Sandbank
sandwich [ˈsænwɪtʃ, ˈsænwɪdʒ] Sandwich, (zusammengeklapptes) belegtes Brot I
sandy [ˈsændi] sandig IV
sang [sæŋ] siehe **sing**
sank [sæŋk] siehe **sink**
°**sari** [ˈsɑːri] Sari
sat [sæt] siehe **sit**
Saturday [ˈsætədeɪ, ˈsætədi] Samstag, Sonnabend I
sauce [sɔːs] Soße III
sauna [ˈsɔːnə] Sauna II • **have a sauna** in die Sauna gehen II
sausage [ˈsɒsɪdʒ] (Brat-, Bock-)Würstchen, Wurst I
save [seɪv]
1. retten II
2. sparen II
saw [sɔː] siehe **see**
saxophone [ˈsæksəfəʊn] Saxophon III
say [seɪ], **said, said** sagen I • **It says here: ...** Hier steht: ... / Es heißt hier: ... II • **say goodbye** sich verabschieden I • **Say hi to your parents for me.** Grüß deine Eltern von mir. I • **say sorry** sich entschuldigen II • **They say ...** Man sagt, ... II
scan (-nn-) [skæn]: **scan a text** einen Text schnell nach bestimmten Wörtern/Informationen absuchen II
°**scar** [skɑː] Narbe
scared [skeəd] verängstigt I • **be scared (of)** Angst haben (vor) I
scary [ˈskeəri] unheimlich; gruselig I • **kind of scary** (infml) irgendwie unheimlich III

scene [siːn] Szene I • **on the scene** vor Ort, zur Stelle IV
scenery [ˈsiːnəri] Landschaft III
scent [sent] Duft V 3 (64)
schedule [AE: ˈskedʒuːl, BE: ˈʃedjuːl] (bes. AE) Stundenplan IV
school [skuːl] Schule I • **at school** in der Schule I • **from school** aus der Schule III • **in school** (AE) in der Schule IV • **school bag** Schultasche I • **school office** Sekretariat IV • **school subject** Schulfach I
science [ˈsaɪəns] Naturwissenschaft I
science fiction [ˌsaɪəns ˈfɪkʃn] Sciencefiction V 2 (34)
scientist [ˈsaɪəntɪst] Naturwissenschaftler/in V 2 (32)
score [skɔː] Spielstand; Punktestand III • **final score** Endstand (beim Sport) III • **What's the score?** Wie steht es? (beim Sport) III
score (a goal) [skɔː], [gəʊl] ein Tor schießen, einen Treffer erzielen III
Scottish [ˈskɒtɪʃ] schottisch III
scrapbook [ˈskræpbʊk] Sammelalbum IV
scream [skriːm] schreien IV
scream [skriːm] Schrei IV
°**screenplay** [ˈskriːnpleɪ] Drehbuch
°**screw up** [ˌskruː ˈʌp] (infml) Mist bauen; alles vermasseln
°**scrub** [skrʌb] Gebüsch, Gestrüpp
sea [siː] Meer, (die) See I • **at sea** auf See II
search sth./sb. (for sth./sb.) [sɜːtʃ] etwas/jn. (nach etwas/jm.) durchsuchen V 4 (92)
°**sea snake** [ˈsiː ˌsneɪk] Seeschlange
season [ˈsiːzn] Jahreszeit II • **rainy season** Regenzeit II
seat [siːt] Sitz, Platz IV
second [ˈsekənd] Sekunde I
°**second hand** [ˈsekənd hænd] Sekundenzeiger
second [ˈsekənd] zweite(r, s) I
second-hand [ˌsekənd ˈhænd] gebraucht; aus zweiter Hand III
a second-half goal ein Tor in der zweiten Hälfte/Halbzeit III
secondary school [ˈsekəndri] weiterführende Schule V 2 (38)
secret (n) [ˈsiːkrət] Geheimnis IV
secret (adj) [ˈsiːkrət] geheim IV
secretly [ˈsiːkrətli] heimlich, insgeheim V 4 (80)
section [ˈsekʃn] Abschnitt, Teil II; (Themen-)Bereich III

security [sɪˈkjʊərəti] Sicherheit(svorkehrungen) V 3 (56)
▶ S.186 „Sicherheit"
see [siː], **saw, seen**
1. sehen I
2. see sb. jn. besuchen, jn. aufsuchen II
See? Siehst du? I • **See you.** Bis bald. / Tschüs. I
seek [siːk], **sought, sought,** suchen V 1 (9)
seem (to be / to do) [siːm] (zu sein/tun) scheinen III
seen [siːn] siehe **see**
see-through [ˈsiːθruː] durchsichtig IV
segregate [ˈsegrɪgeɪt] trennen (nach Rasse, Religion, Geschlecht) IV
segregation [ˌsegrɪˈgeɪʃn] Trennung (nach Rasse, Religion, Geschlecht) IV
selection (of) [sɪˈlekʃn] Auswahl (an) II
sell [sel], **sold, sold** verkaufen I
semester [sɪˈmestə] Semester (Schulhalbjahr in den USA) IV
semi-final [ˌsemiˈfaɪnl] Halbfinale III
send [send], **sent, sent** senden, schicken II • °**send sb. flying** jn. zu Boden schicken
senior [ˈsiːniə]
1. senior (to sb.) (rang)höher (als jd.) IV
2. leitende(r, s) IV
senior [ˈsiːniə] Rentner/in, Senior/in IV
sent [sent] siehe **send**
sentence sb. (to sth.) [ˈsentəns] jn. verurteilen (zu etwas) IV
sentence [ˈsentəns]
1. Satz I • **sentence for sentence** Satz um Satz III
2. Urteil, Strafe IV • **death sentence** Todesstrafe IV • **life sentence** lebenslängliche Haftstrafe IV
separate [ˈseprət] getrennt, separat, extra IV
separate [ˈsepəreɪt] trennen V 3 (56)
September [sepˈtembə] September I
series, pl **series** [ˈsɪəriːz] (Sende-)Reihe, Serie II
serious [ˈsɪəriəs] ernst(haft) V 1 (6)
seriously [ˈsɪəriəs] ernsthaft; (infml) sehr V 1 (6)
service [ˈsɜːvɪs]
1. Dienst (am Kunden), Service II • **social services** Sozialeinrichtungen V 4 (89)
2. Gottesdienst IV

session [ˈseʃn]: **training session** Trainingsstunde, -einheit III
set (-tt-) [set], **set, set**
1. set a trap (for sb.) (jm.) eine Falle stellen II • **set sth. up** etwas aufstellen, aufbauen III • °**set a trend** einen Trend bestimmen/auslösen
2. be set in spielen in V 1 (25)
set [set] Reihe, Set, Satz V 2 (47)
set of rules Regelwerk V 2 (47)
set meal [ˌset ˈmiːl] Menü II
setting [ˈsetɪŋ] Schauplatz V 1 (25)
settle down [ˌsetl ˈdaʊn] zur Ruhe kommen, sesshaft werden V 2 (35)
settler [ˈsetlə] Siedler/in IV
several [ˈsevrəl] mehrere, verschiedene IV
sew (on) [səʊ], **sewed, sewn** (an)nähen IV
sewn [səʊn] siehe **sew**
sex [seks]: **have sex** miteinander schlafen, sich lieben V 1 (16/172)
shade [ʃeɪd] Schatten (von der Sonne geschützt) V 1 (9)
shadow [ˈʃædəʊ] Schatten (Umriss) III
shake [ʃeɪk], **shook, shaken** zittern; schütteln IV • **shake one's head** den Kopf schütteln III
Shall we ...? [ʃæl] Wollen wir ...? / Sollen wir ...? III
shape [ʃeɪp] Form, Gestalt II
share sth. (with sb.) [ʃeə]
1. sich etwas teilen (mit jm.) I; etwas gemeinsam (mit jm.) haben/nutzen IV
2. jm. etwas mitteilen IV
she [ʃiː] sie I
sheep, pl **sheep** [ʃiːp] Schaf II
°**sheep station** Schaffarm (in Australien)
sheet [ʃiːt]
1. Blatt, Bogen (Papier) V 2 (44)
2. Laken V 3 (64)
shelf [ʃelf], pl **shelves** [ʃelvz] Regal(brett) I
shell [ʃel] Muschel(schale) V 1 (8)
shift [ʃɪft] Schicht (bei der Arbeit) IV
shine [ʃaɪn], **shone, shone**
1. scheinen (Sonne) II
2. glänzen IV
ship [ʃɪp] Schiff I
shirt [ʃɜːt] Hemd I • **football shirt** (Fußball-)Trikot III
shiver [ˈʃɪvə] zittern II
shock [ʃɒk] Schock, Schreck V 1 (6)
shocked [ʃɒkt] schockiert III
shocking [ˈʃɒkɪŋ] schockierend V 4 (85)
shoe [ʃuː] Schuh I

shone [ʃɒn, AE ʃəʊn] siehe **shine**
shoot [ʃuːt] **shot, shot**
1. (er)schießen IV • **shoot at sth./sb.** auf jn./etwas schießen V 3 (61)
2. (Film) drehen; fotografieren IV
shop [ʃɒp] Laden, Geschäft I
shop assistant [ˈʃɒp əˌsɪstənt] Verkäufer/in I
shop (-pp-) [ʃɒp] einkaufen (gehen) I
shopping [ˈʃɒpɪŋ] (das) Einkaufen I
go shopping einkaufen gehen I
shopping list Einkaufsliste I
shopping mall (großes) Einkaufszentrum III • **shopping precinct** Einkaufsviertel, -straße (autofrei) III
short [ʃɔːt] kurz I • **a short time** kurz IV
°**shorten** [ˈʃɔːtən] kürzen
shorts (pl) [ʃɔːts] Shorts, kurze Hose I
shot [ʃɒt] siehe **shoot**
shot [ʃɒt] Schuss III
should [ʃəd, ʃʊd]: **you should ...** du solltest ... / ihr solltet ... I • **you should have asked** du hättest fragen sollen IV
shoulder [ˈʃəʊldə] Schulter I
shout [ʃaʊt] schreien, rufen I • **shout at sb.** jn. anschreien I
show [ʃəʊ] Show, Vorstellung I
show [ʃəʊ], **showed, shown** zeigen I • **show sb. around** jn. (in der Stadt/im Museum/... herumführen) III
show off [ˌʃəʊ ˈɒf], **showed off, shown off** angeben, prahlen IV
shower [ˈʃaʊə] Dusche I • **have a shower** (sich) duschen I
shown [ʃəʊn] siehe **show**
shut up [ˌʃʌt ˈʌp], **shut, shut** den Mund halten II
shy [ʃaɪ] schüchtern, scheu II
sick [sɪk] krank IV • **I feel sick.** Mir ist schlecht. IV
side [saɪd] Seite II • **side door** Seitentür IV
sidetrack [ˈsaɪdtræk]: **get sidetracked** abgelenkt werden V 2 (34)
sidewalk [ˈsaɪdwɔːk] (AE) Gehweg, Bürgersteig IV
sight [saɪt]: **Get out of my sight.** Geh mir aus den Augen. IV
sights (pl) [saɪts] Sehenswürdigkeiten II
sightseeing [ˈsaɪtˌsiːɪŋ] Sightseeing; das Anschauen von Sehenswürdigkeiten IV
sign [saɪn] unterschreiben III
sign [saɪn] Schild; Zeichen III

silent letter [ˌsaɪlənt ˈletə] „stummer" Buchstabe *(nicht gesprochener Buchstabe)* II
silly [ˈsɪli] albern, dumm II
°**similar** [ˈsɪmələ] ähnlich
since September [sɪns] seit September III
Sincerely (yours) [sɪnˈsɪəli] *(AE)* mit freundlichen Grüßen IV
°**Sindhi** [ˈsɪndi] *Bewohner/in der pakistanischen Provinz Sindh*
sing [sɪŋ]**, sang, sung** singen I
singer [ˈsɪŋə] Sänger/in II
°**singer-songwriter** [ˌsɪŋəˈsɒŋraɪtə] Liedermacher
single [ˈsɪŋgl] ledig, alleinstehend I **single bed** Einzelbett V 3 (64) • **a single parent** ein(e) Alleinerziehende(r) II
sink [sɪŋk] Spüle, Spülbecken I
sink [sɪŋk]**, sank, sunk** sinken V 1 (16)
sir [sɜː] Sir *(höfliche Anrede, z. B. für Kunden, Vorgesetzte oder Lehrer)* IV • **Dear Sir or Madam ...** Sehr geehrte Damen und Herren IV
sister [ˈsɪstə] Schwester I
sister city [ˈsɪstə ˌsɪti] *(AE)* Partnerstadt IV
sit (-tt-) [sɪt]**, sat, sat** sitzen; sich setzen I • **sit down** sich hinsetzen II • **sit up** sich aufsetzen II **Sit with me.** Setz dich zu mir. / Setzt euch zu mir. I
site [saɪt] *siehe* **website**
situation [ˌsɪtjuˈeɪʃn] Situation IV
sixth [sɪksθ] Sechstel V 3 (62)
size [saɪz] Größe I
skate [skeɪt] Inliner/Skateboard fahren I
skateboard [ˈskeɪtbɔːd] Skateboard I
skates *(pl)* [skeɪts] Inliner I
sketch [sketʃ] Sketch I
ski [skiː] Ski III • **ski slope** Skipiste III
ski [skiː] Ski laufen/fahren III • **go skiing** [skiːɪŋ] Ski laufen/fahren III
skiing instructor Skilehrer/in V 1 (6/168)
skiing: go skiing [skiːɪŋ] Ski laufen/fahren III
skill [skɪl] Fähigkeit, Fertigkeit IV
skills file [ˈskɪlz faɪl] Anhang mit Lern- und Arbeitstechniken I
skim a text (-mm-) [skɪm] einen Text überfliegen *(um den Inhalt grob zu erfassen)* III
skin [skɪn] Haut IV
skirt [skɜːt] Rock II
sky [skaɪ] Himmel II • **in the sky** am Himmel II

°**skydiving** [ˈskaɪˌdaɪvɪŋ] Fallschirmspringen, Skydiving
skyline [ˈskaɪˌlaɪn] Horizont, Skyline IV
skyscraper [ˈskaɪskreɪpə] Wolkenkratzer IV
°**slap on a hat** [ˌslæp ˈɒn] einen Hut aufsetzen
slave [sleɪv] Sklave, Sklavin II
slavery [ˈsleɪvəri] Sklaverei IV
sledge [sledʒ] Schlitten III
sleep [sliːp]**, slept, slept** schlafen I
sleep [sliːp] Schlaf I
sleepover [ˈsliːpəʊvə] Schlafparty III
slept [slept] *siehe* **sleep**
°**slid** [slɪd] *siehe* **slide**
slide [slaɪd] Folie *(bei Präsentationsprogrammen)* V 2 (45)
°**slide** [slaɪd]**, slid, slid** rutschen **slide on some sunglasses** eine Sonnenbrille aufsetzen
°**slip (-pp-)** [ˌslɪp]**: slip on some clothing** Kleidung überziehen
slogan [ˈsləʊgən] Slogan, Losung IV
°**slop (-pp-)** [ˌslɒp]**: slop on some sunscreen** Sonnenschutzmittel auftragen
slope: ski slope Skipiste III
slow [sləʊ] langsam II
slum [slʌm] Slum, Elendsviertel V 3 (50)
small [smɔːl] klein II • **small letters** Kleinbuchstaben III
smart [smɑːt] schlau IV
smell [smel] riechen II
smell [smel] Geruch II
smile [smaɪl] lächeln I • **smile at sb.** jn. anlächeln II
smile [smaɪl] Lächeln II • **give (sb.) a smile** lächeln, jn. anlächeln IV
smoke [sməʊk] rauchen IV
smoke [sməʊk] Rauch IV • **There's no smoke without fire.** Wo Rauch ist, ist auch Feuer. IV
smoothie [ˈsmuːði] *dickflüssiger Fruchtshake mit Milch, Joghurt oder Eiscreme* II
smuggle [ˈsmʌgl] schmuggeln IV
snack [snæk] Snack, Imbiss II
snake [sneɪk] Schlange I
°**snorkel** *(BE:* **-ll-**)* [ˈsnɔːkl] schnorcheln
snow [snəʊ] Schnee II
snowball [ˈsnəʊbɔːl] Schneeball IV
so [səʊ]
1. also; deshalb, daher I • **So? Und? / Na und?** II • **So what?** [səʊ ˈwɒt] Und? / Na und? II
2. **so sweet** so süß I • **so far** bis jetzt, bis hierher III • **so (that)** sodass, damit III

3. **I hope so.** Ich hoffe es. II **I think so.** Ich glaube (ja). I **I don't think so.** Das finde/glaube ich nicht. I • **Do you really think so?** Meinst du wirklich? / Glaubst du das wirklich? II
4. **so has crime** die Kriminalität auch V 3 (56)
▶ S.186 English 'so' = German 'auch'
soap [səʊp] Seife I
soap (opera) [ˈsəʊp ˌɒprə] Seifenoper IV
so-called [ˌsəʊˈkɔːld] so genannt V 4 (87)
social [ˈsəʊʃl] sozial, Sozial-, gesellschaftlich V 4 (84) • **social services** Sozialeinrichtungen V 4 (89)
°**social networking site** [ˌsəʊʃl ˈnetwɜːkɪŋ] *eine Website zur Bildung und Unterhaltung sozialer Netzwerke*
Social Studies [ˌsəʊʃl ˈstʌdiz] Gemeinschaftskunde, Politische Bildung, Sozialkunde IV
sock [sɒk] Socke, Strumpf I
soda [ˈsəʊdə] *(AE)* Limonade IV
sofa [ˈsəʊfə] Sofa I
soft [sɒft] weich, sanft III • **soft drink** alkoholfreies Getränk IV
software [ˈsɒftweə] Software II
soil [sɔɪl] *(Erdreich)* Erde IV
sold [səʊld]
1. *siehe* **sell**
2. **sold out** [ˌsəʊld ˈaʊt] be sold out ausverkauft/vergriffen sein III
soldier [ˈsəʊldʒə] Soldat/in IV
solve [sɒlv] lösen IV
some [səm, sʌm] einige, ein paar I **some cheese/juice/money/English** etwas Käse/Saft/Geld/Englisch I
somebody [ˈsʌmbədi] jemand I **Find/Ask somebody who ...** Finde/Frage jemanden, der ... II
somehow [ˈsʌmhaʊ] irgendwie IV
someone [ˈsʌmwʌn] jemand III
something [ˈsʌmθɪŋ] etwas I
sometimes [ˈsʌmtaɪmz] manchmal I
somewhere [ˈsʌmweə] irgendwo(hin) II
son [sʌn] Sohn I
song [sɒŋ] Lied, Song I
soon [suːn] bald I • **as soon as** sobald, sowie II
sore [sɔː]**: be sore** wund sein, wehtun II • **have a sore throat** Halsschmerzen haben II
sorry [ˈsɒri]**: (I'm) sorry.** Entschuldigung. / Tut mir leid. I • **Sorry, I'm late.** Entschuldigung, dass ich zu spät bin/komme. I • **Sorry?** Wie bitte? I • **say sorry** sich entschuldigen II

sort [sɔːt] einteilen; sortieren IV
sort (of) [sɔːt] Art, Sorte II
°**SOS** [ˌes_əʊ_ˈes] SOS(-Ruf) *(Notsignal)*
sought [sɔːt] *siehe* **seek**
soul [səʊl] Soul(musik) III
sound [saʊnd] klingen, sich (gut usw.) anhören I
sound [saʊnd] Laut; Klang I
sound file [ˈsaʊnd faɪl] Tondatei, Soundfile III
soup [suːp] Suppe II
sour [saʊə] sauer III
source [sɔːs] Quelle *(Informationsquelle, Textquelle)* IV
south [saʊθ] Süden; nach Süden; südlich II • **southbound** [ˈsaʊθbaʊnd] Richtung Süden III
south-east [ˌsaʊθˈiːst] Südosten; nach Südosten; südöstlich II
southern [ˈsʌðən] südlich, Süd- III • **south-west** [ˌsaʊθˈwest] Südwesten; nach Südwesten; südwestlich II
souvenir [ˌsuːvəˈnɪə] Andenken, Souvenir III
space [speɪs]
1. Weltraum II
2. Move back one space. Geh ein Feld zurück. II • Move on one space. Geh ein Feld vor. II
spaghetti [spəˈɡeti] Spaghetti II
spark [spɑːk] Funke II
speak (to) [spiːk], **spoke, spoken** sprechen (mit), reden (mit) II
special [ˈspeʃl] besondere(r, s) II
Did you do anything special? Habt ihr irgendetwas Besonderes gemacht? I
species [ˈspiːʃiːz] Art *(biologisch)*, Spezies V 1 (9)
specific [spəˈsɪfɪk] bestimmte(r, s), spezifische(r, s) IV
spectacular [spekˈtækjələ] spektakulär IV
speech [spiːtʃ] Rede IV • **make/give a speech** eine Rede halten IV
°**speech bubble** [ˈspiːtʃ ˌbʌbl] Sprechblase
speed [spiːd] rasen, schnell fliegen III
speed [spiːd] Geschwindigkeit III
°**full speed ahead** volle Kraft voraus • **speed limit** Geschwindigkeitsbegrenzung, -beschränkung III
spell [spel] buchstabieren I
spelling [ˈspelɪŋ] Rechtschreibung V 2 (39)
spend [spend], **spent, spent**:
spend money (on) Geld ausgeben (für) II • **spend time (on)** Zeit verbringen (mit) II
spent [spent] *siehe* **spend**
spice [spaɪs] Gewürz III
spicy [ˈspaɪsi] würzig, scharf gewürzt III
spill [spɪl] verschütten IV
spit (at sb.) (-tt-) [spɪt], **spat, spat** (jn. an)spucken IV
splash [splæʃ] spritzen IV
°**split** (-tt-) [splɪt], **split, split** spalten III
spoke [spəʊk] *siehe* **speak**
spoken [ˈspəʊkən]
1. *siehe* **speak**
2. mündlich V 2 (38)
spoon [spuːn] Löffel III
sport [spɔːt] Sport; Sportart I • **do sport** Sport treiben I
sports gear *(no pl)* [ˈspɔːts ɡɪə] Sportausrüstung, Sportsachen II
sports hall [ˈspɔːts hɔːl] Sporthalle III
spot (-tt-) [spɒt] entdecken III
spray [spreɪ] spritzen, (be)sprühen, sprayen IV
spray can [ˈspreɪ ˌkæn] Spraydose V 4 (84)
spread [spred], **spread, spread** (sich) ausbreiten, (sich) verbreiten IV
spring [sprɪŋ]
1. Frühling I
2. Quelle *(Wasser)* IV
spy [spaɪ] Spion/in I
square [skweə] Platz *(in der Stadt)* II
square km (sq km) [skweə] Quadratkilometer III
square brackets [ˌskweə ˈbrækɪts] eckige Klammern IV
squash [skwɒʃ], *pl* **squash** Kürbis IV
squatter [ˈskwɒtə] Haus-, Landbesetzer/in V 3 (63)
squeeze [skwiːz] drücken; (aus)pressen III
squirrel [ˈskwɪrəl] Eichhörnchen II
stadium [ˈsteɪdiəm] Stadion III
staff [stɑːf] Personal, Belegschaft; Lehrerkollegium IV • **member of staff** *(BE)* Mitarbeiter/in IV • **staff member** *(AE)* Mitarbeiter/in IV
▶ S.182 Collective nouns
stage [steɪdʒ] Bühne I
stairs *(pl)* [steəz] Treppe; Treppenstufen II
stamp [stæmp] Briefmarke I
stand [stænd], **stood, stood**
1. stehen; sich (hin)stellen II
2. ertragen, aushalten, ausstehen II • I can't stand it. Ich kann es nicht ertragen/aushalten/ausstehen. II

standard of living [ˈstændəd] Lebensstandard V 3 (56)
star [stɑː]
1. Stern II
2. (Film-, Pop-)Star I
stare (at sb./sth.) [steə] (jn./etwas an)starren V 3 (65)
°**starfish** [ˈstɑːfɪʃ]: **crown-of-thorns starfish** [ˌkraʊn_əv ˈθɔːnz] Dornenkronenseestern
start [stɑːt] starten, anfangen, beginnen (mit) I • **start a business** ein Unternehmen gründen V 2 (46)
start [stɑːt] Anfang V 2 (46)
°**from the start** von vorn
state [steɪt] Staat III; die öffentliche Hand V 4 (89)
static (electricity) [ˈstætɪk, ˌstætɪk_ɪˌlekˈtrɪsəti] elektrische Aufladung IV
station [ˈsteɪʃn]
1. Bahnhof I • **at the station** am Bahnhof I
2. (radio/pop) station (Radio-/Pop-)Sender III
statistics *(pl)* [stəˈtɪstɪks] Statistik V 1 (10)
statue [ˈstætʃuː] Statue II
status [ˈsteɪtəs] Status, Stand V 4 (80)
stay [steɪ] bleiben; wohnen, übernachten II • **stay out** nicht nach Hause kommen, draußenbleiben III
steady [ˈstedi] stetig V 3 (62)
steak [steɪk] (Rinder-)Steak IV
steal [stiːl], **stole, stolen** stehlen II
steel [stiːl] Stahl III
steel drum [ˌstiːl ˈdrʌm] Steeldrum III
steer [stɪə] lenken, steuern III
step [step]
1. Schritt I • **take steps** Schritte machen/unternehmen III • **take sth. a step at a time** etwas eins nach dem anderen tun; etwas Schritt für Schritt tun IV
2. Stufe IV
stereo [ˈsteriəʊ] Stereoanlage III
stew [stjuː] Eintopf(gericht) III
stick (on) [ˌstɪk_ˈɒn], **stuck, stuck** (auf)kleben I • °**stick close to sb.** *(infml)* an jm. kleben
stick: **(drum-)stick** [stɪk] Trommelstock III
stick out of sth. [stɪk], **stuck, stuck** aus etwas herausragen, herausstehen III
still [stɪl]
1. (immer) noch I
2. trotzdem, dennoch II
still [stɪl] still *(bewegungslos)* IV
stole [stəʊl] *siehe* **steal**

stolen ['stəʊlən] *siehe* **steal**
stomach ['stʌmək] Magen II
 stomach ache Magenschmerzen, Bauchweh II
stone [stəʊn] Stein II
stood [stʊd] *siehe* **stand**
stop (-pp-) [stɒp]
 1. aufhören I
 2. anhalten I
 ▶ S.181 Same verb, different meaning
 Stop that! Hör auf damit! / Lass das! I • °**stop a danger** einer Gefahr Einhalt gebieten
stop [stɒp] Halt, Anhalten IV
store *(AE)* [stɔː] Laden V 4 (88)
°**store** [stɔː]: **hold in store** bereithalten
storm [stɔːm] Sturm; Gewitter II
stormy ['stɔːmi] stürmisch II
story ['stɔːri] Geschichte, Erzählung I • **crime story** Krimi IV
straight [streɪt] direkt IV
straight on [streɪt ˈɒn] geradeaus weiter II
straightaway [ˌstreɪtə'weɪ] sofort, gleich III
straighten sth. up [ˌstreɪtn ˈʌp] etwas aufräumen, etwas in Ordnung bringen V 4 (84)
strange [streɪndʒ]
 1. seltsam, sonderbar I
 2. fremd V 2 (34)
stranger ['streɪndʒə] Unbekannte(r), Fremde(r) V 2 (34)
strawberry ['strɔːbəri] Erdbeere II
street [striːt] Straße I • **at 7 Park Street** in der Parkstraße 7 I
street performer [pə'fɔːmə] Straßenkünstler/in III
strength [streŋθ] Kraft, Stärke V 1 (23)
stress ['stres] Betonung III
stress [stres] betonen V 3 (61)
stressful ['stresfl] anstrengend, stressig V 2 (47)
stretch [stretʃ] sich (er)strecken IV
strict [strɪkt] streng III
strike [straɪk] Streik II • **be on strike** streiken, sich im Streik befinden III • **go on strike** streiken, in den Streik treten III
string [strɪŋ] Saite III
strong [strɒŋ] stark II
structure ['strʌktʃə] strukturieren, aufbauen II
structure ['strʌktʃə] Struktur; Gliederung III
stuck [stʌk] *siehe* **stick**
student ['stjuːdənt] Schüler/in; Student/in I • **exchange student** Austauschschüler/in III
studio ['stjuːdiəʊ] Studio I

study ['stʌdi] lernen; studieren III
study hall ['stʌdi hɔːl] *Zeit zum selbstständigen Lernen in der Schule* IV
study skills *(pl)* ['stʌdi skɪlz] Lern- und Arbeitstechniken I
stuff [stʌf] Zeug, Kram I
stupid ['stjuːpɪd] blöd, dämlich V 1 (25)
style [staɪl] Stil III • **military-style fashion** Mode im Militärstil V 4 (85/192)
sub-heading ['sʌbˌhedɪŋ] Zwischenüberschrift IV
subject ['sʌbdʒɪkt]
 1. Subjekt I
 2. Schulfach I
 3. Thema IV
 4. Untertan/in; Staatsangehörige(r) *(in einer Monarchie)* IV
subjective [səb'dʒektɪv] subjektiv V 3 (60)
subscribe (to sth.) [səb'skraɪb] etwas abonnieren; etwas abonniert haben V 1 (6)
suburb ['sʌbɜːb] Vorort V 3 (55)
subway ['sʌbweɪ]: **the subway** *(AE)* die U-Bahn II
succeed (in sth.) [sək'siːd] Erfolg haben, erfolgreich sein (mit etwas, bei etwas) III
success [sək'ses] Erfolg III
successful [sək'sesfəl] erfolgreich V 2 (39)
such [sʌtʃ]: **such a nice person** so ein netter Mensch III • **such good books** so gute Bücher III • **such as** wie zum Beispiel III
°**suck** [sʌk]: **That sucks!** Das ist Mist!
sudden ['sʌdn] plötzlich IV
suddenly ['sʌdnli] plötzlich, auf einmal I
suffer (from) ['sʌfə] leiden (an) IV
suffix ['sʌfɪks] Suffix, Nachsilbe IV
sugar ['ʃʊgə] Zucker II
suitable ['suːtəbl] geeignet, passend V 2 (39)
sum (sth.) up (-mm-) [ˌsʌm ˈʌp] (etwas) zusammenfassen V 4 (82) **To sum up, …** Resümee: …; Zusammenfassend: … V 4 (82/191)
summarize ['sʌməraɪz] zusammenfassen V 3 (61)
summary ['sʌməri] Zusammenfassung IV
summer ['sʌmə] Sommer I
sun [sʌn] Sonne II
Sunday ['sʌndeɪ, 'sʌndi] Sonntag I
sung [sʌŋ] *siehe* **sing**
sunglasses *(pl)* ['sʌnglɑːsɪz] (eine) Sonnenbrille I
sunk [sʌŋk] *siehe* **sink**

sunny ['sʌni] sonnig II
sunrise ['sʌnraɪz] Sonnenaufgang IV
sunscreen ['sʌnskriːn] Sonnenschutzmittel V 1 (9)
sunset ['sʌnset] Sonnenuntergang IV
sunshine ['sʌnʃaɪn] Sonnenschein IV
°**sunsmart** ['sʌnˌsmɑːt]: **Be sunsmart.** *etwa:* Schütze dich intelligent gegen die Sonne.
suntan ['sʌntæn] Sonnenbräune V 1 (9) • **have a suntan** sonnengebräunt sein III
supermarket ['suːpəmɑːkɪt] Supermarkt I
°**superstar** ['suːpəstɑː] Superstar
supper ['sʌpə] Abendessen, Abendbrot IV
support [sə'pɔːt] unterstützen, befürworten V 3 (52) • **support a team** eine Mannschaft unterstützen; Fan einer Mannschaft sein III
support [sə'pɔːt] Unterstützung IV
supporter [sə'pɔːtə] Anhänger/in, Fan III
suppose [sə'pəʊz] annehmen, vermuten I
sure [ʃʊə, ʃɔː] sicher I • **make sure** sich vergewissern IV
surf [sɜːf] surfen V 1 (6) • **go surfing** wellenreiten gehen, surfen gehen II • **surf the internet** im Internet surfen II • **surf instructor** Surflehrer/in V 1 (6)
surfboard ['sɜːfbɔːd] Surfbrett II
surprise (for/to) [sə'praɪz] Überraschung (für) III
surprise sb. [sə'praɪz] jn. überraschen III
surprised (at sth.) [sə'praɪzd] überrascht (über etwas) III
surprising [sə'praɪzɪŋ] überraschend V 1 (15)
surround [sə'raʊnd]: **be surrounded** umgeben sein IV
survey (on) ['sɜːveɪ] Umfrage, Untersuchung (über) II
survival [sə'vaɪvl] Überleben II
survive [sə'vaɪv] überleben II
suspense [sə'spens] Spannung V 4 (95)
swam [swæm] *siehe* **swim**
swap (-pp-) [swɒp] tauschen I **swap sth. (for sth.)** etwas (ein)tauschen (für/gegen etwas) IV
sweat [swet] schwitzen IV
sweat [swet] Schweiß IV
sweatshirt ['swetʃɜːt] Sweatshirt I
sweep [swiːp], **swept**, **swept** fegen, kehren IV

sweet [swiːt] süß I
sweetheart ['swiːthɑːt] Liebling, Schatz II
sweets (pl) Süßigkeiten I
swept [swept] siehe sweep
swim (-mm-) [swɪm], swam, swum schwimmen I
swimmer ['swɪmə] Schwimmer/in II
swimming ['swɪmɪŋ] Schwimmen I • go swimming schwimmen gehen I • swimming instructor Schwimmlehrer/in V 1 (6/168)
swimming pool ['swɪmɪŋ puːl] Schwimmbad, -becken II
swimming trunks [trʌŋks] Badehose III
swimsuit ['swɪmsuːt] Badeanzug III
swum [swʌm] siehe swim
syllable ['sɪləbl] Silbe I
synagogue ['sɪnəgɒg] Synagoge III
▶ S.185 Religions
synonym ['sɪnənɪm] Synonym (Wort mit gleicher oder sehr ähnlicher Bedeutung) IV
system ['sɪstəm] System IV

T

table ['teɪbl]
1. Tisch I • table tennis Tischtennis I • table tennis bat Tischtennisschläger III
2. Tabelle V 1 (10) • table of contents Inhaltsverzeichnis V 2 (43)
tablecloth ['teɪblklɒθ] Tischdecke IV
take [teɪk], took, taken
1. nehmen I
2. (weg-, hin)bringen I
3. dauern, (Zeit) brauchen III
I can take it. Ich halt's aus. / Ich kann's aushalten. IV • take a break eine Pause machen III • take a left/right (AE) nach links/rechts abbiegen IV • take a trip (AE) einen Ausflug/eine Reise machen IV Take another turn. (beim Spielen) Würfel noch einmal. II • take care of sth./sb. sich um etwas/jn. kümmern III • take notes sich Notizen machen I • take sth. off etwas ausziehen (Kleidung); etwas absetzen (Hut, Helm) II • take 10 c off 10 Cent abziehen I • take sth. out etwas herausnehmen I take sth. over etwas übernehmen; etwas in seine Macht bringen IV take part in sth. teilnehmen an etwas III • take photos Fotos machen, fotografieren I • take place stattfinden II • take responsibility (for) Verantwortung (für) übernehmen V 2 (39) • take a ride eine Spritztour/Fahrt machen III take sth. a step at a time etwas eins nach dem anderen tun; etwas Schritt für Schritt tun IV • take steps Schritte machen/unternehmen IV • take turns to do sth. sich abwechseln, etwas zu tun IV I'll take it. (beim Einkaufen) Ich werde es (ihn, sie) nehmen. / Ich nehme es (ihn, sie). I
takeaway ['teɪkəweɪ] Restaurant, das auch Essen zum Mitnehmen verkauft; Essen zum Mitnehmen III
taken ['teɪkən] siehe take
talent ['tælənt] Talent, Begabung III
talk [tɔːk]: talk (about) reden (über), sich unterhalten (über) I
talk (to) reden (mit), sich unterhalten (mit) I
talk [tɔːk] Rede, Gespräch; Vortrag, Referat IV
talk show ['tɔːk ʃəʊ] Talkshow V 2 (32)
tall [tɔːl]
1. groß (Person) III
2. hoch (Gebäude, Baum) IV
°Tamil ['tæməl] Tamile/Tamilin (Bewohner/in des indischen Bundesstaats Tamil Nadu)
Taoism ['taʊɪzm] Taoismus V 3 (52/185)
Taoist ['taʊɪst] Taoist/in, taoistisch V 3 (52/185)
▶ S.185 Religions
tap [tæp] Wasserhahn V 3 (59)
taste [teɪst] schmecken; kosten, probieren IV
taste [teɪst] Geschmack IV • be in good/bad taste geschmackvoll/geschmacklos sein IV
taught [tɔːt] siehe teach
tavern ['tævən] Schenke, Gastwirtschaft IV
taxi ['tæksi] Taxi III
tea [tiː] Tee; (auch:) leichte Nachmittags- oder Abendmahlzeit I
tea bag Teebeutel IV
teach [tiːtʃ], taught, taught unterrichten, lehren I
teacher ['tiːtʃə] Lehrer/in I • head teacher Schulleiter/in III
team [tiːm] Team, Mannschaft I
▶ S.182 Collective nouns
tear [teə], tore, torn (zer)reißen IV
tear [tɪə] Träne II
tease [tiːz] necken, auf den Arm nehmen III
teaspoon ['tiːspuːn] Teelöffel III

technique [tek'niːk] (Arbeits-)Verfahren, Technik, Methode IV
technology [tek'nɒlədʒi] Technologie V 2 (35)
teddy bear ['tedi beə] Teddybär III
teen (bes. AE) [tiːn]
1. Teenager- III
2. Teenager/in V 4 (84)
teenage ['tiːneɪdʒ] Teenage- V 2 (46)
teenager ['tiːneɪdʒə] Teenager, Jugendliche(r) II
teeth [tiːθ] Plural von „tooth" I
telephone ['telɪfəʊn] Telefon I
telephone number Telefonnummer I
television ['telɪvɪʒn] Fernsehen I
tell (about) [tel], told, told erzählen (von), berichten (über) I • Tell me your names. Sagt mir eure Namen. I • tell sb. the way jm. den Weg beschreiben II
temperature ['temprətʃə] Temperatur II • have a temperature Fieber haben II
temple ['templ] Tempel V 3 (52/185)
▶ S.185 Religions
tennis ['tenɪs] Tennis I
tense [tens] (grammatische) Zeit, Tempus III
tent [tent] Zelt IV
term [tɜːm] Trimester II
terrible ['terəbl] schrecklich, furchtbar I
terrified ['terɪfaɪd]: be terrified (of) schreckliche Angst haben (vor) IV
terrorism ['terərɪzm] Terrorismus IV
°terrorist ['terərɪst] terroristisch
test [test] Klassenarbeit, Test, Prüfung II
text [tekst] Text I
text (message) ['tekst ˌmesɪdʒ] SMS II
text sb. [tekst] jm. eine SMS schicken II
°textiles (pl) ['tekstaɪlz] die Textilindustrie
than [ðæn, ðən] als II • more than me mehr als ich II
thank [θæŋk]: Thank God. Gott sei Dank. IV • Thank you. Danke (schön). I • Thanks. Danke. I Thanks a lot! Vielen Dank! I Thanks very much! Danke sehr! / Vielen Dank! II • give thanks danken, feierlich danksagen IV
that [ðət, ðæt]
1. das (dort) I
2. jene(r, s) I • that day an jenem Tag III • That's me. Das bin ich. I That's right. Das ist richtig. / Das stimmt. I • That's up to you. Das liegt bei dir. / Das kannst/musst du

Dictionary

(selbst) entscheiden. III • **that's why** deshalb, darum I
that [ðət, ðæt] dass I
that [ðət, ðæt] der, die, das; die (Relativpronomen) III
the [ðə, ði] der, die, das; die I
theatre [ˈθɪətə] Theater II
their [ðeə]
1. ihr, ihre (Plural) I
2. sein oder ihr (= **his or her**) IV
theirs [ðeəz] ihrer, ihre, ihrs II
them [ðəm, ðem]
1. sie; ihnen I • **the two of them** die beiden; alle beide II
2. ihn oder sie (= **him or her**) IV
theme park [ˈθiːm pɑːk] Themenpark II
themselves [ðəmˈselvz]
1. sich III
2. selbst IV
then [ðen]
1. dann, danach I
2. damals II
Then what? Was dann? II • **just then** genau in dem Moment; gerade dann II
theocracy [θiˈɒkrəsi] Theokratie V 3 (59/187)
▶ S.187 Different forms of government
there [ðeə]
1. da, dort I
2. dahin, dorthin I
down there (nach) dort unten II • **in there** dort drinnen I • **over there** da drüben, dort drüben I • **up there** dort oben III • **there are** es sind (vorhanden); es gibt I • **there's** es ist (vorhanden); es gibt I • **there isn't a ...** es ist kein/e ...; es gibt kein/e ... I
thermometer [θəˈmɒmɪtə] Thermometer II
these [ðiːz] diese, die (hier) I
they [ðeɪ]
1. sie (Plural) I • **They say ...** Man sagt, ... III
2. er oder sie (= **he or she**) IV
thief [θiːf], pl **thieves** [θiːvz] Dieb/in II
thing [θɪŋ] Ding, Sache I • **What was the best thing about ...?** Was war das Beste an ...? II
think [θɪŋk], **thought, thought** glauben, meinen, denken I • **Do you really think so?** Meinst du wirklich? / Glaubst du das wirklich? II • **I think so.** Ich glaube (ja). I • **I don't think so.** Das finde/glaube ich nicht. I • **think about** 1. nachdenken über II;
2. denken über, halten von II
think of 1. denken über, halten

von II 2. denken an; sich ausdenken II
third [θɜːd]
1. dritte(r, s) I
°2. Drittel
thirsty [ˈθɜːsti] durstig I • **be thirsty** Durst haben, durstig sein I
this [ðɪs]
1. dies (hier) I
2. diese(r, s) I
This is Isabel. Hier spricht Isabel. / Hier ist Isabel. (am Telefon) II
this morning/afternoon/evening heute Morgen/Nachmittag/Abend I • **this way** hier entlang, in diese Richtung II
those [ðəʊz] die (da), jene (dort) I
thought [θɔːt]
1. siehe **think**
2. Gedanke IV
thousand [ˈθaʊznd] tausend, Tausend I
threw [θruː] siehe **throw**
throat Hals, Kehle II • **have a sore throat** [sɔː ˈθrəʊt] Halsschmerzen haben II
through [θruː] durch II
throughout October [θruːˈaʊt] den ganzen Oktober hindurch IV
throw [θrəʊ], **threw, thrown** werfen I • **throw the dice** würfeln II
throw up sich übergeben IV
thrown [θrəʊn] siehe **throw**
thunderstorm [ˈθʌndəstɔːm] Gewitter V 3 (57)
Thursday [ˈθɜːzdeɪ, ˈθɜːzdi] Donnerstag I
°**tick** [tɪk] ankreuzen, ein Häkchen machen
ticket [ˈtɪkɪt]
1. Eintrittskarte I
2. Fahrkarte III
ticket machine [ˈtɪkɪt məˌʃiːn] Fahrkartenautomat III
ticket office [ˈtɪkɪt ˌɒfɪs] Kasse (für den Verkauf von Eintrittskarten); Fahrkartenschalter IV
tide [taɪd] Gezeiten, Ebbe und Flut II • **the tide is in** es ist Flut II • **the tide is out** es ist Ebbe II
tidy [ˈtaɪdi] aufräumen I
tidy [ˈtaɪdi] ordentlich, aufgeräumt II
tie (-ing form: **tying**) [taɪ] (fest)binden IV
°**tie** [taɪ] Schlips, Krawatte
tiger [ˈtaɪɡə] Tiger II
tight [taɪt] eng; fest IV
tights (pl) [taɪts] Strumpfhose III
till [tɪl] bis (zeitlich) I

time [taɪm] Zeit; Uhrzeit I • **in time** rechtzeitig II • **What's the time?** Wie spät ist es? I • **a long time** lange III • **a short time** kurz IV • **time zone** Zeitzone IV
time(s) [taɪmz] Mal(e); -mal II **for the first time** zum ersten Mal II
timeline [ˈtaɪmlaɪn] Zeitstrahl, Zeitleiste IV
timetable [ˈtaɪmteɪbl] Stundenplan I
timing [ˈtaɪmɪŋ]: **bad timing** schlechtes Timing, schlechte Wahl des Zeitpunkts III
tin [tɪn] Dose V 1 (21)
tip [tɪp]
1. Tipp III
2. Spitze IV
tired [ˈtaɪəd] müde I • **be tired of sth.** genug von etwas haben, etwas satt haben IV • **get tired of sth.** einer Sache überdrüssig werden, die Lust an etwas verlieren IV
title [ˈtaɪtl] Titel, Überschrift I
to [tə, tu]
1. zu, nach I • **an e-mail to** eine E-Mail an I • **to Jenny's** zu Jenny I • **to the doctor's** zum Arzt III • **to the front** nach vorn I • **I've never been to Bath.** Ich bin noch nie in Bath gewesen. II • **write to** schreiben an I
2. **quarter to 12** Viertel vor 12 (11.45 / 23.45) I • **from Monday to Friday** von Montag bis Freitag III
3. **try to do** versuchen, zu tun I
4. um zu I
toast [təʊst] Toast(brot) I
today [təˈdeɪ] heute I
toe [təʊ] Zeh I
together [təˈɡeðə] zusammen I
toilet [ˈtɔɪlət] Toilette I • °**toilet blocks** Toiletten • **toilet paper** Toilettenpapier V 3 (63)
told [təʊld] siehe **tell**
tomato [təˈmɑːtəʊ], pl **tomatoes** Tomate II
tomorrow [təˈmɒrəʊ] morgen I
tone of voice [təʊn] Ton(fall) V 3 (61)
tonight [təˈnaɪt] heute Nacht, heute Abend I
too [tuː]: **from Bristol too** auch aus Bristol I • **Me too.** Ich auch. I
too much/big/... [tuː] zu viel/ groß/... I
took [tʊk] siehe **take**
tool [tuːl] Werkzeug IV
tooth [tuːθ], pl **teeth** [tiːθ] Zahn I
toothache [ˈtuːθeɪk] Zahnschmerzen II

top [tɒp]
1. Spitze, oberes Ende I • **at the top (of)** oben, am oberen Ende, an der Spitze (von) I • °**on top** oben drauf
2. Top, Oberteil I
top [tɒp] (adj) Spitzen-, oberste(r, s) III
topic ['tɒpɪk] Thema, Themenbereich I • **topic sentence** Satz, der in das Thema eines Absatzes einführt II
tore [tɔː] siehe **tear**
torn [tɔːn] siehe **tear**
tortoise ['tɔːtəs] Schildkröte I
touch [tʌtʃ] berühren, anfassen I
touch [tʌtʃ]: **keep in touch** in Verbindung bleiben, Kontakt halten III
tough [tʌf] tough, selbstsicher, zäh III; schwierig, hart IV
tour (of the house) [tʊə] Rundgang, Tour (durch das Haus) I
tourist ['tʊərɪst] Tourist/in II
tourist information Fremdenverkehrsamt II
toward [tə'wɔːd] (AE) siehe **towards**
towards Mr Green [tə'wɔːdz] auf Mr Green zu, in Mr Greens Richtung I
towel ['taʊəl] Handtuch II
tower ['taʊə] Turm I
town [taʊn] Stadt I • **the centre of town** die Mitte der Stadt III • **in town** in der Stadt III • **into town** in die Stadt III
°**town hall** [ˌtaʊn 'hɔːl] Rathaus
°**township** ['taʊnʃɪp] Township (während der Apartheid für die nicht weiße Bevölkerung eingerichtete Wohngegend)
track [træk]
1. Stück, Titel, Track (auf einer CD) III
2. Spur, Fährte; Pfad, Weg V 1 (16)
°3. Gleis
trade [treɪd] Handel II
trade [treɪd] Handel treiben V 3 (52)
tradition [trə'dɪʃn] Tradition IV
traditional [trə'dɪʃənl] traditionell III
traffic ['træfɪk] Verkehr II
trail [treɪl] (Lehr-)Pfad IV
train [treɪn] Zug I • **on the train** im Zug I • **mule train** Maultierkarawane IV
train [treɪn]
1. trainieren III
2. **train as ...** eine Ausbildung machen zu ... V 4 (84)
trained [treɪnd] ausgebildet V 4 (88)
trainers (pl) ['treɪnəz] Turnschuhe II
training session ['seʃn] Trainingsstunde, -einheit III
tram [træm] Straßenbahn III

translate (from ... into) [træns'leɪt] übersetzen (aus ... in) III
translation [træns'leɪʃn] Übersetzung III
transparency [træns'pærənsi] Folie V 2 (45)
transport (no pl) ['trænspɔːt] Transport(wesen) III • **public transport** öffentlicher Verkehr IV
trap [træp] Falle II
trap (-pp-) [træp] (mit einer Falle) fangen II
trash [træʃ] (AE) Abfall, Müll V 4 (88)
travel (-ll-) ['trævl] reisen II
°**travel agent** ['trævl ˌeɪdʒənt] Reisebüro
Travelcard ['trævlkɑːd] Tages-/Wochen-/Monatsfahrkarte (der Londoner Verkehrsbetriebe) III
travel guide ['trævl ˌɡaɪd] Reiseführer (Buch) V 3 (67)
treason ['triːzn] Hochverrat IV
treat [triːt] behandeln V 3 (57)
tree [triː] Baum I • **Christmas tree** Christ-, Weihnachtsbaum V 2 (34/176) **palm tree** Palme V 3 (64)
trend [trend] Trend V 3 (60) • °**set a trend** einen Trend bestimmen/auslösen
trendy ['trendi] modisch, schick III
tribal ['traɪbl] Stammes- IV
tribe [traɪb] (Volks-)Stamm IV
trick [trɪk]
1. (Zauber-)Kunststück, Trick I • **do tricks** (Zauber-)Kunststücke machen I
2. Streich II • **play a trick on sb.** jm. einen Streich spielen II
trick sb. [trɪk] jn. austricksen, reinlegen V 1 (17)
trick sb. into doing sth. [trɪk] jn. mit einer List / einem Trick dazu bringen, etwas zu tun V 1 (17)
tricky ['trɪki] verzwickt, heikel V 1 (15)
trillion ['trɪliən] Billion V 3 (62)
trip [trɪp] Reise; Ausflug I • **go on a trip** einen Ausflug/eine Reise machen II • **take a trip** (AE) einen Ausflug/eine Reise machen IV
trombone [trɒm'bəʊn] Posaune III
trouble ['trʌbl] Schwierigkeiten, Ärger II • **be in trouble** in Schwierigkeiten sein; Ärger kriegen II
troublemaker ['trʌblˌmeɪkə] Unruhestifter/in V 4 (84)
trousers (pl) ['traʊzəz] Hose II
truck [trʌk] Lastwagen, LKW V 1 (17)
true [truː] wahr II • **come true** wahr werden II
truly ['truːli]: **Yours truly** (AE) mit freundlichen Grüßen IV

trumpet ['trʌmpɪt] Trompete III
trust [trʌst] trauen, vertrauen V 2 (47)
try [traɪ]
1. versuchen I
2. probieren, kosten I
try and do sth. / try to do sth. versuchen, etwas zu tun I • **try sth. on** etwas anprobieren (Kleidung) I
▶ S.181 Same verb, different meaning
tsunami [tsuːˈnɑːmi] Tsunami III
T-shirt ['tiːʃɜːt] T-Shirt I
tube [tjuːb]: **the Tube** (no pl) (BE) die Londoner U-Bahn III
Tuesday ['tjuːzdeɪ, -di] Dienstag I
tuition [tjuːˈɪʃn] (Nachhilfe-)Unterricht V 3 (54)
tune [tjuːn]: **tune a radio to a station** ein Radio auf einen Sender einstellen IV • **You're tuned to Radio Bristol.** Sie hören gerade Radio Bristol. IV
tune [tjuːn] Melodie III
tunnel ['tʌnl] Tunnel II
turkey ['tɜːki] Pute, Truthahn IV
turn [tɜːn]
1. sich umdrehen II • **turn around** sich umdrehen IV • **turn left/right** (nach) links/rechts abbiegen II **turn to sb.** sich jm. zuwenden; sich an jn. wenden V
2. **turn sth. off/on** etwas aus-/einschalten I • **turn sth. down/up** etwas leiser/lauter stellen III
turn [tɜːn]: **(It's) my turn.** Ich bin dran / an der Reihe. I • **Miss a turn.** Einmal aussetzen. II • **Take another turn.** (beim Spielen) Würfel noch einmal. II • **take turns to do sth.** sich abwechseln IV
turtle ['tɜːtl] Wasserschildkröte V 4 (88)
TV [tiːˈviː] Fernsehen I • **on TV** im Fernsehen I • **watch TV** fernsehen I
twice [twaɪs] zweimal III
twin [twɪn]: **twin brother** Zwillingsbruder I • **twins** (pl) Zwillinge I **twin town** Partnerstadt I
°**type** [taɪp] Typ
typical (of) ['tɪpɪkl] typisch (für) V 2 (40)

U

ugly ['ʌɡli] hässlich V 4 (92)
ultimate ['ʌltɪmət] ultimativ, perfekt IV
ultraviolet rays (UV rays) (pl) [ˌʌltrəˌvaɪələt 'reɪz] ultraviolette Strahlen V 1 (9)

unable [ʌnˈeɪbl]: **be unable to do sth.** etwas nicht können V 2 (37/178)
unafraid [ˌʌnəˈfreɪd]: **be unafraid** keine Angst haben V 2 (37/178)
unanswered [ʌnˈɑːnsəd] unbeantwortet IV
unavailable [ˌʌnəˈveɪləbl] nicht erhältlich, nicht vorrätig V 2 (37/178)
uncle [ˈʌŋkl] Onkel I
unclear [ˌʌnˈklɪə] unklar, undeutlich II
uncomfortable [ʌnˈkʌmftəbl] unbequem II
unconscious [ʌnˈkɒnʃəs] bewusstlos II
uncool [ˌʌnˈkuːl] (infml) uncool III
under [ˈʌndə] unter I
under age [ˌʌndər ˈeɪdʒ] minderjährig V 4 (84)
under control [kənˈtrəʊl] unter Kontrolle IV
underground [ˈʌndəɡraʊnd]: **the underground** die U-Bahn II
underground [ˌʌndəˈɡraʊnd] unterirdisch IV
°**underline** [ˌʌndəˈlaɪn] unterstreichen
understand [ˌʌndəˈstænd], **understood, understood** verstehen, begreifen I
understanding [ˌʌndəˈstændɪŋ] verständnisvoll IV
understood [ˌʌndəˈstʊd] siehe **understand**
underwear (no pl) [ˈʌndəweə] Unterwäsche V 3 (63)
unequal [ʌnˈiːkwəl] ungleich V 2 (37/178)
unexpected [ˌʌnɪkˈspektɪd] unerwartet, überraschend V 4 (95)
unfair [ˌʌnˈfeə] unfair, ungerecht II
unfriendly [ʌnˈfrendli] unfreundlich II
unhappy [ʌnˈhæpi] unglücklich II
unhealthy [ʌnˈhelθi] ungesund III
uniform [ˈjuːnɪfɔːm] Uniform I
unimportant [ˌʌnɪmˈpɔːtnt] unwichtig III
uninteresting [ʌnˈɪntrəstɪŋ] uninteressant II
unique [juˈniːk] einzigartig, einmalig V 1 (9)
unit [ˈjuːnɪt] Kapitel, Lektion I
unite (with sb./sth.) [juˈnaɪt] sich (mit jm./etwas) vereinigen, vereinen V 3 (56) • **the United Kingdom (UK)** [juːˌnaɪtɪd ˈkɪŋdəm], [ˌjuː ˈkeɪ] das Vereinigte Königreich (Großbritannien und Nordirland) III • **the United States (US)** [juːˌnaɪtɪd ˈsteɪts], [ˌjuːˈes] die Vereinigten Staaten (von Amerika) III

university [ˌjuːnɪˈvɜːsəti] Universität, Hochschule V 2 (32) • **go to university** mit dem Studium anfangen V 2 (43)
unknown [ʌnˈnəʊn] unbekannt IV
unless [ənˈles] es sei denn, außer (wenn) V 4 (86)
unlike [ˌʌnˈlaɪk] im Gegensatz zu III
unload [ʌnˈləʊd] entladen III
unlucky [ʌnˈlʌki]: **be unlucky** Pech haben V 2 (37/178)
unpopular [ʌnˈpɒpjələ] unpopulär, unbeliebt V 2 (37/178)
unreal [ˌʌnˈrɪəl] unwirklich V 2 (37/178)
unrealistic [ˌʌnrɪəˈlɪstɪk] unrealistisch V 2 (37/178)
unreliable [ˌʌnrɪˈlaɪəbl] unzuverlässig V 2 (37/178)
unsafe [ʌnˈseɪf] nicht sicher, gefährlich III
unsure [ˌʌnˈʃʊə, ˌʌnˈʃɔː] unsicher II
untidy [ʌnˈtaɪdi] unordentlich III
until [ənˈtɪl] bis III
unwanted [ˌʌnˈwɒntɪd] unerwünscht, ungewollt V 4 (80)
▶ S.178 Negative prefixes
up [ʌp] hinauf, herauf, nach oben I
up the hill den Hügel hinauf II
up there dort oben III • **That's up to you.** Das liegt bei dir. / Das kannst/musst du (selbst) entscheiden. III • **What's up?** Was ist los? IV
upper-class [ˌʌpə ˈklɑːs] der Oberschicht zugehörig, vornehm, edel V 3 (63)
uprising [ˈʌpraɪzɪŋ] Aufstand V 3 (56)
upset (about) [ˌʌpˈset] aufgebracht, gekränkt, mitgenommen (wegen) III
upset sb. (-tt-) [ʌpˈset], **upset, upset** jn. ärgern, kränken, aus der Fassung bringen III
upstairs [ˌʌpˈsteəz] oben; nach oben I
urban [ˈɜːbən] städtisch, Stadt- V 3 (50)
us [əs, ʌs] uns I
US [ˌjuːˈes] US-amerikanische(r, s) IV
use [juːz] benutzen, verwenden I
use force Gewalt anwenden V 4 (87)
use [juːs] Gebrauch III
used [juːst]: **get used to sth./sb.** sich gewöhnen an jn./etwas IV
I used to be Früher war ich (immer) ... V 1 (6/168)
▶ S.168 ... used to be/do ...
useful [ˈjuːsfl] nützlich V 1 (10)
useless [ˈjuːsləs] nutzlos, unfähig IV

usual [ˈjuːʒuəl] gewöhnlich, üblich IV
usually [ˈjuːʒuəli] meistens, gewöhnlich, normalerweise I

V

vacation [vəˈkeɪʃn, AE: veɪˈkeɪʃn] (AE) Urlaub, Ferien III
valley [ˈvæli] Tal II • **valley floor** Talboden II
valuable [ˈvæljuəbl] wertvoll, nützlich V 2 (38)
value [ˈvæljuː] Wert IV
vandalism [ˈvændəlɪzəm] Vandalismus, Zerstörungswut V 4 (84)
vandalize [ˈvændəlaɪz] mutwillig beschädigen, mutwillig zerstören V 4 (84)
vegetable [ˈvedʒtəbl] (ein) Gemüse III
verse [vɜːs] Vers (von der Bibel); Strophe IV
version [ˈvɜːʃn] Fassung IV
original version Originalfassung IV
°**versus** [ˈvɜːsəs] gegen; gegenüber
very [ˈveri] sehr I • **like/love sth. very much** etwas sehr mögen/lieben II • **Thanks very much!** Danke sehr! / Vielen Dank! II
°**vibe** [vaɪb] (infml) Stimmung
victim [ˈvɪktɪm] Opfer III
victory [ˈvɪktəri] Sieg IV
video [ˈvɪdiəʊ] Video III • **video projector** Videoprojektor, Beamer V 2 (45)
view (of) [vjuː]
1. Aussicht, Blick (auf) II
2. Ansicht, Meinung III
in my view meiner Ansicht nach III • **point of view** [ˌpɔɪnt əv ˈvjuː] Standpunkt II • **from my point of view** aus meiner Sicht; von meinem Standpunkt aus gesehen II
°**view** [vjuː] betrachten, sehen; im Fernsehen/Kino anschauen
villa [ˈvɪlə] Ferienhaus; Villa II
village [ˈvɪlɪdʒ] Dorf I
vineyard [ˈvɪnjəd] Weinberg IV
violence [ˈvaɪələns] Gewalt, Gewalttätigkeit IV
violent [ˈvaɪələnt] gewalttätig, gewaltsam IV
violin [ˌvaɪəˈlɪn] Violine, Geige III
play the violin Geige spielen III
visibility [ˌvɪzəˈbɪləti] Sicht(weite) IV
visit [ˈvɪzɪt] besuchen, aufsuchen II
visit [ˈvɪzɪt] Besuch II
visitor [ˈvɪzɪtə] Besucher/in, Gast I

visual aids *(pl)* [ˌvɪʒuəl_ˈeɪdz] Anschauungsmaterialien V 2 (45)
vocabulary [vəˈkæbjələri] Vokabelverzeichnis, Wörterverzeichnis I
voice [vɔɪs] Stimme I • **tone of voice** Ton(fall) V 3 (61)
volleyball [ˈvɒlibɔːl] Volleyball I
volunteer [ˌvɒlənˈtɪə] sich freiwillig melden, sich bereit erklären IV; ehrenamtliche Arbeit leisten für/bei V 4 (84)
volunteer work [ˌvɒlənˈtɪə] Arbeit als Freiwillige(r) III
vote [vəʊt]
1. (for/against sb./sth.) für/gegen jn./etwas stimmen IV
2. zur Wahl gehen, wählen V 2 (46)
vote [vəʊt] (die) Stimme(n); Stimmrecht III
vowel sound [ˈvaʊəl saʊnd] Vokallaut II

W

wait (for) [ˈweɪt fɔː] warten (auf) I **I can't wait to see …** ich kann es kaum erwarten, … zu sehen I **Wait a minute.** Warte mal! / Moment mal! II • **Wait and see!** Wart's ab! III • °**wait in line (for sth.)** sich (nach etwas) anstellen
wake [weɪk], **woke, woken**
1. wake sb. (up) jn. (auf)wecken III
2. wake up aufwachen III
walk [wɔːk] (zu Fuß) gehen, laufen I; spazieren gehen III • **walk on** weiterlaufen III • **walk around** herumlaufen III • **walk the dog** den Hund ausführen V 4 (90)
walk [wɔːk] Spaziergang II • **go for a walk** spazieren gehen, einen Spaziergang machen II
wall [wɔːl] Wand; Mauer I
wander [ˈwɒndə] schlendern, herumirren IV
want [wɒnt] (haben) wollen I **want to do** tun wollen I • **They want me to say something.** Sie möchten, dass ich etwas sage IV
war [wɔː] Krieg III • °**fight a war** einen Krieg führen
wardrobe [ˈwɔːdrəʊb] Kleiderschrank I
warm [wɔːm] warm II
warming [ˈgləʊbl]: **global warming** Erwärmung der Erdatmosphäre V 3 (52/184)
warn sb. (about/of sth.) [wɔːn] jn. vor etwas warnen IV
warning [ˈwɔːnɪŋ] Warnung IV
was [wəz, wɒz] *siehe* **be**

wash [wɒʃ] waschen I • **I wash my hands.** Ich wasche mir die Hände. I
washing machine [ˈwɒʃɪŋ məˌʃiːn] Waschmaschine II
waste sth. (on) [weɪst] etwas verschwenden, vergeuden (für) III
waste [weɪst]
1. Verschwendung IV
2. Abfall V 3 (50) • °**waste disposal** Abfallbeseitigung, Abfallentsorgung
watch [wɒtʃ] beobachten, sich etwas ansehen; zusehen I **watch TV** fernsehen I
watch [wɒtʃ] Armbanduhr I
water [ˈwɔːtə] Wasser I • °**drinking water** Trinkwasser
waterproof [ˈwɔːtəpruːf] wasserdicht, -fest V 1 (17/173)
°**water buffalo** [ˈwɔːtə ˌbʌfələʊ] Wasserbüffel
waterfall [ˈwɔːtəfɔːl] Wasserfall III
wave [weɪv] winken II • **wave at sb.** jm. zuwinken V 4 (92)
wave [weɪv] Welle IV
way [weɪ]
1. Weg; Strecke II • **a long way (from)** weit entfernt (von) I • **ask sb. the way** jn. nach dem Weg fragen II • **on the way (to)** auf dem Weg (zu/nach) I • **tell sb. the way** jm. den Weg beschreiben II • **What's the best way to get there?** Wie komme ich am besten dahin? III • **I'm on my way.** Ich bin (schon) unterwegs. IV
2. Richtung II • **the other way round** anders herum II • **the wrong way** in die falsche Richtung II • **this way** hier entlang, in diese Richtung II • **which way?** in welche Richtung? / wohin? II
3. No way! [ˌnəʊ ˈweɪ] Auf keinen Fall! / Kommt nicht in Frage! II; Was du nicht sagst! / Das kann nicht dein Ernst sein! III
4. by the way übrigens, nebenbei (bemerkt) III
5. Art und Weise • **way of life** Lebensart III • **the way you** … so wie du …, auf dieselbe Weise wie du … I
▶ S.180 German „Möglichkeit"
we [wiː] wir I
weak [wiːk] schwach II
weakness [ˈwiːknəs] Schwäche, Schwachpunkt V 2 (44)
wealth [welθ] Reichtum IV
wealthy [ˈwelθi] reich IV
wear [weə], **wore, worn** tragen, anhaben (Kleidung) I

weather [ˈweðə] Wetter II
weatherproof [ˈweðəpruːf] wetterbeständig, -fest V 1 (17/173)
webcam [ˈwebkæm] Webcam, Internetkamera II
web design [ˈwebdɪˌzaɪn] Webgestaltung V 2 (38)
website [ˈwebsaɪt] Website II
Wednesday [ˈwenzdeɪ, ˈwenzdi] Mittwoch I
week [wiːk] Woche I • **days of the week** Wochentage I • **a three-week holiday** ein dreiwöchiger Urlaub III • **once a week** einmal pro Woche III
weekend [ˌwiːkˈend] Wochenende I • **at the weekend** am Wochenende I • **on the weekend** *(AE)* am Wochenende IV
weigh [weɪ] wiegen III
weight [weɪt] Gewicht IV
weird [wɪəd] seltsam III
welcome [ˈwelkəm]
1. Welcome (to Bristol). Willkommen (in Bristol). I
2. You're welcome. Gern geschehen. / Nichts zu danken. I
welcome sb. (to) [ˈwelkəm] jn. begrüßen, willkommen heißen (in) I **They welcome you to …** Sie heißen dich in … willkommen I
welcoming [ˈwelkəmɪŋ] gastfreundlich, einladend (place) V 3 (57)
well [wel] *(gesundheitlich)* gut; gesund, wohlauf I
well [wel] gut II • **go well** gut (ver)laufen, gutgehen II • **You looked after them well.** Du hast dich gut um sie gekümmert. II **Oh well …** Na ja … / Na gut … I **Well, …** Nun, … / Also, … I • **well-structured** gut aufgebaut, gut strukturiert V 2 (45)
Welsh [welʃ] walisisch; Walisisch II
went [went] *siehe* **go**
were [wə, wɜː]: **(we/you/they) were** *siehe* **be**
west [west] Westen; nach Westen; westlich II • **westbound** [ˈwestbaʊnd] Richtung Westen III
western [ˈwestən] westlich, West- III
wet [wet] feucht, nass II
wetsuit [ˈwetsuːt] Nassanzug *(Tauch- oder Surfanzug)* V 1 (15)
whale [weɪl] Wal V 1 (9)
what [wɒt]
1. was I
2. welche(r, s) I
like what? wie zum Beispiel? IV
So what? [ˌsəʊ ˈwɒt] Und? / Na und? II • **Then what?** Was dann?

Dictionary

II • **they didn't know what to do** sie wussten nicht, was sie tun sollten; sie wussten nicht, was zu tun war III • °**What a ...!** Was für ein(e) ...! • **What a bummer!** *(infml)* So ein Mist! / Wie schade! III • **What about ...? 1.** Was ist mit ...? / Und ...? I; **2.** Wie wär's mit ...? I • **What are you talking about?** Wovon redest du? I • **What can I get you?** Was kann/darf ich euch/Ihnen bringen? II • **What colour is ...?** Welche Farbe hat ...? I • **What for?** [ˌwɒt ˈfɔː] Wofür? II • **What have we got next?** Was haben wir als Nächstes? I • **What kind of car ...?** Was für ein Auto ...? III • **What page are we on?** Auf welcher Seite sind wir? I • **What's for homework?** Was haben wir als Hausaufgabe auf? I • **What's the best way to get there?** Wie komme ich am besten dahin? III • **What's the point?** Was soll das? III • **What's the time?** Wie spät ist es? I • **What's the matter?** Was ist los? / Was ist denn? II • **What's up?** Was ist los? IV • **What's wrong with you?** Was fehlt dir? II • **What's your name?** Wie heißt du? I • **What was the weather like?** Wie war das Wetter? II
whatever [ˌwɒtˈevə] egal; wie dem auch sei; was (auch) immer IV • **whatever the movie** egal, in welchem Film IV
wheel [wiːl] Rad III • **big wheel** Riesenrad III
wheelchair [ˈwiːltʃeə] Rollstuhl I
when [wen] wann I • **When's your birthday?** Wann hast du Geburtstag? I
when [wen]
1. wenn I
2. als I
whenever [ˌwenˈevə] wann (auch) immer; egal, wann IV
where [weə]
1. wo I
2. wohin I
Where are you from? Wo kommst du her? I • **He had no idea where to go.** Er hatte keine Ahnung, wo er gehen sollte. IV
wherever [ˌwerˈevə] wo(hin) (auch) immer; egal, wo(hin) IV
whether [ˈweðə] ob IV
which [wɪtʃ] welche(r, s) I • **Which picture ...?** Welches Bild ...? I
which way? in welche Richtung? / wohin? II

which [wɪtʃ] der, die, das; die (Relativpronomen) III
while [waɪl]
1. *(conj)* während III
2. *(n)* **(for) a while** eine Weile, einige Zeit IV
whisper [ˈwɪspə] flüstern I
whistle [ˈwɪsl] pfeifen II
whistle [ˈwɪsl] Pfiff; (Triller-)Pfeife II
white [waɪt] weiß I
who [huː]
1. wer I
2. wen / wem II
Who did she talk to? Mit wem hat sie geredet? II • **He had no idea who to ask.** Er hatte keine Ahnung, wen er fragen sollte. IV
who [huː] der, die, das; die (Relativpronomen) III
whoever [ˌhuːˈevə] wer/wen/wem (auch) immer; egal, wer/wen/wem IV
whole [həʊl] ganze(r, s), gesamte(r, s) II • **the whole of 2006** das ganze Jahr 2006 II • °**on the whole** im Großen und Ganzen IV
whom [huːm]: **To whom it may concern** (bes. AE) Sehr geehrte Damen und Herren IV
whose [huːz] wessen II • **Whose are these?** Wem gehören diese? II
whose [huːz]: **the man whose statue ...** der Mann, dessen Statue ... II
why [waɪ] warum I • **Why me?** Warum ich? I • **that's why** deshalb, darum I
wide [waɪd] weit, breit III • **far and wide** weit und breit IV
wife [waɪf], *pl* **wives** [waɪvz] Ehefrau II
wild [waɪld] wild II
wildfire [ˈwaɪldfaɪə] Waldbrand, Buschbrand IV
wildlife [ˈwaɪldlaɪf] Tierwelt, frei lebende Tiere IV
will [wɪl]: **you'll be cold (= you will be cold)** du wirst frieren; ihr werdet frieren II • **you'll have travelled** du wirst gereist sein III
win (-nn-) [wɪn], **won, won** gewinnen I • °**an Oscar-winning film** ein mit einem Oscar ausgezeichneter Film
win [wɪn] Sieg III
wind [wɪnd] Wind I
windproof [ˈwɪndpruːf] winddicht V 1 (17/173)
window [ˈwɪndəʊ] Fenster I
windy [ˈwɪndi] windig I
wine [waɪn] Wein IV

winemaker [ˈwaɪnmeɪkə] Winzer/in IV
winemaking [ˈwaɪnmeɪkɪŋ] Weinherstellung IV
wing [wɪŋ] Flügel IV
winner [ˈwɪnə] Gewinner/in, Sieger/in II
winter [ˈwɪntə] Winter I
°**winter's day** Wintertag
wipe [waɪp] (ab)wischen IV
wish [wɪʃ] sich etwas wünschen III • **You wish!** *etwa:* Das hättest du wohl gerne! IV
wish [wɪʃ]: **Best wishes** Viele Grüße IV
with [wɪð]
1. mit I
2. bei I
Sit with me. Setz dich zu mir. / Setzt euch zu mir. I • **be with sb.** mit jm. zusammen sein IV
within [wɪˈðɪn] innerhalb (von) V 2 (46)
without [wɪˈðaʊt] ohne I
witness (to sth.) [ˈwɪtnəs] Zeuge, Zeugin (für/von etwas) V 3 (60)
wives [waɪvz] *pl von* „**wife**" II
woke [wəʊk] *siehe* **wake**
woken [ˈwəʊkn] *siehe* **wake**
wolf [wʊlf], *pl* **wolves** [wʊlvz] Wolf II
woman [ˈwʊmən], *pl* **women** [ˈwɪmɪn] Frau II
won [wʌn] *siehe* **win**
wonder [ˈwʌndə] sich fragen, gern wissen wollen II
wonderful [ˈwʌndəfəl] wunderbar II
won't [wəʊnt]: **you won't be cold (= you will not be cold)** du wirst nicht frieren; ihr werdet nicht frieren II
wood [wʊd] Holz II • **woods** *(pl)* Wald, Wälder II
woodpecker [ˈwʊdpekə] Specht II
woods *(pl)* [wʊdz] Wald, Wälder II
word [wɜːd] Wort I • **word building** Wortbildung II • **word field** Wortfeld III
wore [wɔː] *siehe* **wear**
work [wɜːk]
1. arbeiten I • **work hard** hart arbeiten II • **work on sb./sth.** an jn./etwas arbeiten I • **work out** klappen, gutgehen IV • **work sth. out** etwas herausfinden, etwas herausarbeiten IV
2. funktionieren III
work [wɜːk] Arbeit I • **at work** bei der Arbeit / am Arbeitsplatz I • **be in a line of work** einen Beruf ausüben IV • **volunteer work**

Arbeit als Freiwillige(r) III • **work experience** (no pl) Arbeits-, Praxiserfahrung(en) V 2 (38)
worker ['wɜːkə] Arbeiter/in II
work(place) ['wɜːkpleɪs] Arbeitsplatz (Ort) IV
worksheet ['wɜːkʃiːt] Arbeitsblatt I
workshop ['wɜːkʃɒp] Workshop, Lehrgang III
world [wɜːld] Welt I • **all over the world** auf der ganzen Welt III **from all over the world** aus der ganzen Welt II • **in the world** auf der Welt II • °**the New World** die Neue Welt (Amerika) • **world music** Weltmusik III • °**world war** Weltkrieg
°**world-class** [ˌwɜːld ˈklɑːs] (adj) von Weltklasse
world-famous [ˌwɜːld ˈfeɪməs] weltberühmt II
worldwide [ˌwɜːldˈwaɪd] weltweit IV
worn [wɔːn] siehe **wear**
worried ['wʌrid]: **be worried (about)** beunruhigt sein, besorgt sein (wegen) I
worry ['wʌri] Sorge, Kummer II **No worries!** (bes. Australisches E) Kein Problem! V 1 (6)
worry (about) ['wʌri] sich Sorgen machen (wegen, um) I • **Don't worry.** Mach dir keine Sorgen. I
worse (than) [wɜːs] schlechter, schlimmer (als) II
worst [wɜːst]: **(the) worst** am schlechtesten, schlimmsten; der/die/das schlechteste, schlimmste ... II
worth [wɜːθ]: **it is worth doing sth.** es lohnt sich, etwas zu tun IV **It's worth it.** Es lohnt sich. IV **It isn't worth it.** Es lohnt sich nicht. IV
would [wəd, wʊd] würde, würdest, würden II • **I'd like ... (= I would like ...)** Ich hätte gern ... / Ich möchte gern ... I • **Would you like ...?** Möchtest du ...? / Möchten

Sie ...? I • **I'd like to go (= I would like to go)** Ich würde gern gehen / Ich möchte gehen I • **I wouldn't like to go** ich würde nicht gern gehen / ich möchte nicht gehen I
wrist [rɪst] Handgelenk IV
write [raɪt], **wrote, written** schreiben I • **write down** aufschreiben I • **write to** schreiben an I
writer ['raɪtə] Schreiber/in; Schriftsteller/in II
written ['rɪtn]
1. siehe **write**
2. schriftlich V 2 (38)
wrong [rɒŋ] falsch, verkehrt I °**do sth. wrong** etwas Verbotenes tun • **get sth. wrong** etwas falsch machen III • **the wrong way** in die falsche Richtung II • **What's wrong with you?** Was fehlt dir? II
wrote [rəʊt] siehe **write**

Y

yard [jɑːd]
1. Hof II • **in the yard** auf dem Hof II
2. Yard (Längenmaß, 0,91 m) IV
yawn [jɔːn] gähnen II
°**Yay!** [jeɪ] ja
year [jɪə]
1. Jahr I • **a 70-year-old teacher** ein 70-jähriger Lehrer III
2. Jahrgangsstufe I
yellow ['jeləʊ] gelb I
yes [jes] ja I
yesterday ['jestədeɪ, 'jestədi] gestern I • **the day before yesterday** vorgestern II • **yesterday morning/afternoon/evening** gestern Morgen/Nachmittag/Abend I
yet [jet]: **not (...) yet** noch nicht II **yet?** schon? II
°**YMCA** [ˌwaɪ em siː ˈeɪ] (Young Men's Christian Association) dem CVJM (Christlicher Verein Junger Menschen) vergleichbare Organisation

yoga ['jəʊɡə] Yoga I
yogurt ['jɒɡət] Jogurt III
you [juː]
1. du; Sie I
2. ihr I
3. dir; dich; euch I
4. man III
How are you? Wie geht es dir/Ihnen/euch? II • **You're welcome.** Gern geschehen. / Nichts zu danken. I • **you two** ihr zwei I • **You wish!** etwa: Das hättest du wohl gerne! II
young [jʌŋ] jung I
your [jɔː]:
1. dein/e I
2. Ihr I
3. euer/eure I
yours [jɔːz]
1. deiner, deine, deins II
2. eurer, eure, eures II
Yours faithfully mit freundlichen Grüßen IV • **Yours sincerely** (BE) mit freundlichen Grüßen IV **Yours truly** (AE) mit freundlichen Grüßen IV
yourself [jəˈself, jɔːˈself]
1. dir/dich III • **about yourself** über dich selbst III
2. selbst IV
yourselves [jəˈselvz, jɔːˈselvz]
1. euch/sich IV
2. selbst IV
youth [juːθ] Jugend III
youth group ['juːθ ˌɡruːp] Jugendgruppe III
youth hostel ['juːθ ˌhɒstəl] Jugendherberge III
yummy ['jʌmi] (infml) lecker III

Z

zebra ['zebrə] Zebra II
zero ['zɪərəʊ] null I
zone [zəʊn] Zone, Bereich III **time zone** Zeitzone IV
zoo [zuː] Zoo, Tierpark I

Countries and continents

Country/Continent	Adjective	Person	People
Africa ['æfrɪkə] *Afrika*	African ['æfrɪkən]	an African	the Africans
America [ə'merɪkə] *Amerika*	American [ə'merɪkən]	an American	the Americans
Asia ['eɪʃə, 'eɪʒə] *Asien*	Asian ['eɪʃn, 'eɪʒn]	an Asian	the Asians
Australia [ɒ'streɪliə] *Australien*	Australian [ɒ'streɪliən]	an Australian	the Australians
Austria ['ɒstriə] *Österreich*	Austrian ['ɒstriən]	an Austrian	the Austrians
Belgium ['beldʒəm] *Belgien*	Belgian ['beldʒən]	a Belgian	the Belgians
Canada ['kænədə] *Kanada*	Canadian [kə'neɪdiən]	a Canadian	the Canadians
China ['tʃaɪnə] *China*	Chinese [,tʃaɪ'niːz]	a Chinese	the Chinese
Croatia [krəʊ'eɪʃə] *Kroatien*	Croatian [krəʊ'eɪʃn]	a Croatian	the Croatians
Cuba ['kjuːbə] *Kuba*	Cuban ['kjuːbən]	a Cuban	the Cubans
the Czech Republic [,tʃek rɪ'pʌblɪk] *Tschechien, die Tschechische Republik*	Czech [tʃek]	a Czech	the Czechs
Denmark ['denmɑːk] *Dänemark*	Danish ['deɪnɪʃ]	a Dane [deɪn]	the Danes
England ['ɪŋglənd] *England*	English ['ɪŋglɪʃ]	an Englishman/-woman	the English
Europe ['jʊərəp] *Europa*	European [,jʊərə'piːən]	a European	the Europeans
Finland ['fɪnlənd] *Finnland*	Finnish ['fɪnɪʃ]	a Finn [fɪn]	the Finns
France [frɑːns] *Frankreich*	French [frentʃ]	a Frenchman/-woman	the French
Germany ['dʒɜːməni] *Deutschland*	German ['dʒɜːmən]	a German	the Germans
(Great) Britain ['brɪtn] *Großbritannien*	British ['brɪtɪʃ]	a Briton ['brɪtn]	the British
Greece [griːs] *Griechenland*	Greek [griːk]	a Greek	the Greeks
Holland ['hɒlənd] *Holland, die Niederlande*	Dutch [dʌtʃ]	a Dutchman/-woman	the Dutch
Hungary ['hʌŋgəri] *Ungarn*	Hungarian [hʌŋ'geəriən]	a Hungarian	the Hungarians
India ['ɪndiə] *Indien*	Indian ['ɪndiən]	an Indian	the Indians
Iraq [ɪ'rɑːk] *Irak*	Iraqi [ɪ'rɑːki]	an Iraqi	the Iraqis
Ireland ['aɪələnd] *Irland*	Irish ['aɪrɪʃ]	an Irishman/-woman	the Irish
Italy ['ɪtəli] *Italien*	Italian [ɪ'tæliən]	an Italian	the Italians
Japan [dʒə'pæn] *Japan*	Japanese [,dʒæpə'niːz]	a Japanese	the Japanese
Mexico ['meksɪkəʊ] *Mexiko*	Mexican [kə'riən]	a Mexican	the Mexicans
the Netherlands ['neðələndz] *die Niederlande, Holland*	Dutch [dʌtʃ]	a Dutchman/-woman	the Dutch
New Zealand [,njuː 'ziːlənd] *Neuseeland*	New Zealand [,njuː 'ziːlənd]	a New Zealander	the New Zealanders
Norway ['nɔːweɪ] *Norwegen*	Norwegian [nɔː'wiːdʒən]	a Norwegian	the Norwegians
Pakistan [,pækɪ'stæn, ,pɑːkɪ'stɑːn] *Pakistan*	Pakistani [,pækɪ'stæni, ,pɑːkɪ'stɑːni]	a Pakistani	the Pakistanis
the Philippines ['fɪlɪpiːnz] *die Philippinen*	Philippine ['fɪlɪpiːn]	a Filipino [,fɪlɪ'piːnəʊ]/ Filipina [,fɪlɪ'piːnə]	the Filipinos/ Filipinas
Poland ['pəʊlənd] *Polen*	Polish ['pəʊlɪʃ]	a Pole [pəʊl]	the Poles
Portugal ['pɔːtʃʊgl] *Portugal*	Portuguese [,pɔːtʃu'giːz]	a Portuguese	the Portuguese
Russia ['rʌʃə] *Russland*	Russian ['rʌʃn]	a Russian	the Russians
Scotland ['skɒtlənd] *Schottland*	Scottish ['skɒtɪʃ]	a Scotsman/-woman, a Scot [skɒt]	the Scots, the Scottish
Slovakia [sləʊ'vɑːkiə, sləʊ'vækiə] *die Slowakei*	Slovak ['sləʊvæk]	a Slovak	the Slovaks
Slovenia [sləʊ'viːniə] *Slowenien*	Slovenian [sləʊ'viːniən], Slovene ['sləʊviːn]	a Slovene, a Slovenian	the Slovenes, the Slovenians
Spain [speɪn] *Spanien*	Spanish ['spænɪʃ]	a Spaniard ['spænɪəd]	the Spaniards
Sweden ['swiːdn] *Schweden*	Swedish ['swiːdɪʃ]	a Swede [swiːd]	the Swedes
Switzerland ['swɪtsələnd] *die Schweiz*	Swiss [swɪs]	a Swiss	the Swiss
Turkey ['tɜːki] *die Türkei*	Turkish ['tɜːkɪʃ]	a Turk [tɜːk]	the Turks
the United Kingdom (the UK) [juˌnaɪtɪd 'kɪŋdəm, ˌjuː'keɪ] *das Vereinigte Königreich (Großbritannien und Nordirland)*	British ['brɪtɪʃ]	a Briton ['brɪtn]	the British
the United States of America (the USA) [juˌnaɪtɪd ˌsteɪts_əv_ə'merɪkə, ˌjuː_es_'eɪ] *die Vereinigten Staaten von Amerika*	American [ə'merɪkən]	an American	the Americans
Wales [weɪlz] *Wales*	Welsh [welʃ]	a Welshman/-woman	the Welsh

First names
(Vornamen)

Aggie ['ægi]
Albert ['ælbət]
Ali ['æli]
Alonzo [əˈlɒnzəʊ]
Anna ['ænə]
Arthur ['ɑːθə]
Asad [æˈsæd]
Ashley ['æʃli]
Bill [bɪl]
Brian ['braɪən]
Britney ['brɪtni]
Candice ['kændɪs]
Cath [kæθ]
Charlie ['tʃɑːli]
Chiraj [tʃɪˈrɑːdʒ]
Chris [krɪs]
Colm [kɒlm, 'kɒləm]
Damaria [ˌdɑməˈriə]
Darren ['dærən]
Dave [deɪv]
David ['deɪvɪd]
Delaney [dɪˈleɪni]
Ella ['elə]
Gavin ['gævɪn]
Gerard ['dʒerɑːd, dʒəˈrɑːd]
Heather ['heðə]
Ishmael ['ɪʃmeɪl]
Jacob ['dʒeɪkəb]
James [dʒeɪmz]
Jeannie ['dʒiːni]
Jeeta ['dʒiːtɑ]
Jemma ['dʒemə]
Jenny ['dʒeni]
Jeremy ['dʒerəmi]
Jess [dʒes]
Jessica ['dʒesɪkə]
Jill [dʒɪl]
Johnny ['dʒɒni]
Jon [dʒɒn]
Jude [dʒuːd]
Judith ['dʒuːdɪθ]
Julia ['dʒuːliə]
Kashmira [kæʃˈmɪərə]
Kelly ['keli]
Kevin ['kevɪn]
Kirsty ['kɜːsti]
Kwok Leong [gɒgˈlɜŋ]
Langston ['læŋstən]
Laurie ['lɒri]
Lea ['liɑ]
Lee [liː]
Leo [liəʊ]
Lindsay ['lɪnzi]
Lucy ['luːsi]
Luke [luːk]
Mani ['mæni]
Marcel [mɑːˈsel]
Margaret ['mɑːgrət]
Maria [məˈriə]
Martin ['mɑːtɪn]
Matt [mæt]
Michael ['maɪkl]
Missy ['mɪsi]
Mohini [məˈhɪniː]
Natasha [nəˈtæʃə]
Nelson ['nelsən]
Nimita [nɪˈmiːtə]
Noelle [ˌnəʊˈel]
Orazio [ɔːˈræziəʊ]
Paris ['pærɪs]
Phil [fɪl]
Presley ['prezli, 'presli]
Razz [ræz]
Reece [riːs]
Richard ['rɪtʃəd]
Riley ['raɪli]
Rita ['riːtə]
Rob [rɒb]
Robert ['rɒbət]
Sally ['sæli]
Sarina [səˈriːnɑ]
Scobie ['skəʊbi]
Shane [ʃeɪn]
Sheth [ʃet]
Simon ['saɪmən]
Sipho ['siːpɔː]
Stella ['stelə]
Suketu [sʊˈkeɪtu]
Terence ['terənts]
Tsotsi ['tsɒtsi]
Victoria [vɪkˈtɔːriɑ]
Vivek ['vɪvek]
Wallace ['wɒlɪs]
Yates [jeɪts]
Zita [ziːtə]

Family names
(Familiennamen)

Anderson ['ændəsən]
Armstrong ['ɑːmstrɒŋ]
Aylen ['eɪlən]
Bauer [baʊə]
Bin Saif [bɪn 'sɑiːf]
Bird [bɜːd]
Brown [braʊn]
Chweneyagae [ˌtʃweneɪjɑˈxaɪ]
Clegg [kleg]
Cook [kʊk]
de Klerk [də ˈkleək]
Dube ['duːbeɪ]
Faulkner ['fɔːlknə]
Ford [fɔːd]
Gandhi ['gændi]
Gubbins ['gʌbɪnz]
Halse [hæls]
Hilton ['hɪltn]
Hood [hʊd]
Hughes [hjuːz]
Lee [liː]
Le Gallienne [ləˌgæliˈen]
Leseur [ləˈzɜː]
Mackintosh ['mækɪntɒʃ]
Mandela [mænˈdelə]
Mchunu [mˈkuːnu]
McQueen [məˈkwiːn]
Mehta ['metə]
Mourning ['mɔːnɪŋ]
Murray ['mʌri]
Mzila [mˈziːlə]
Nalick ['nælɪk]
Neuwirth ['njuːwɛːθ]
Newton ['njuːtən]
Ng [ŋ]
Preston ['prestən]
Qualls [kwɒlz, kwɔːlz]
Row [rəʊ]
Rudd [rʌd]
San Souci [ˌsæn səˈsi]
Saunders ['sɔːndəz]
Senne ['seneɪ]
Sheen [ʃiːn]
Smith [smɪθ]
Spears [spɪəz]
Tang [tæŋ]
Thomas ['tɒməs]
Wallace ['wɒlɪs]
Walters ['wɔːltəz]
White [waɪt]
Wilson ['wɪlsn]
Wright [waɪt]
Zorzotto [zɔːˈzɒtəʊ]

Place names
(Ortsnamen)

Adelaide ['ædəleɪd]
Alexandria [ˌælɪgsˈɑndriə]
Alice Springs [ˌælɪs 'sprɪŋz]
the **Antarctic** [ænˈtɑːktɪk]
Atlanta [ətˈlæntə]
Bangor ['bæŋgə]
Berlin [bɜːˈlɪn]
Bombay [ˌbɒmˈbeɪ]
Bristol ['brɪstl]
Buenos Aires [ˌbweɪnɒs ˈaɪriːz]
Cairns [keənz, kænz]
Canberra ['kænbərə]
Causeway Bay [ˌkɔːzweɪ 'beɪ]
Ceduna [səˈduːnə]
Chicago [ʃɪˈkɑːgəʊ]
Chowpatty Beach [ˌtʃaʊˈpæti]
Cologne [kəˈləʊn], *Köln*
Colorado [ˌkɒləˈrɑːdəʊ]
Darlington ['dɑːlɪŋtən]
Darwin ['dɑːwɪn]
Detroit [dɪˈtrɔɪt]
El Paso [el ˈpæsəʊ]
Fountain Valley [ˌfaʊntn ˈvæli]
Frankfurt ['fræŋkfɜːt]
the **Great Barrier Reef** [ˌgreɪt ˈbæriə riːf]
the **Great Victoria Desert** [ˌgreɪt vɪkˌtɔːriə ˈdezət]
Hamburg ['hæmbɜːg]
Heathrow [hiːθˈrəʊ]
Hickory ['hɪkəri]
Hillbrow ['hɪlbrəʊ]
Hobart ['həʊbɑːt]
Hong Kong [ˌhɒŋ ˈkɒŋ]
Istanbul [ɪstænˈbʊl]
Jinxu ['dʒɪŋksu]
Jogeshwari [ˌdʒɒgeʃˈvɑːri]
Johannesburg, Joburg, Jozi [dʒəʊˈhænɪsbɜːg], [ˈdʒəʊbɜːg], [ˈdʒəʊzi]
Katherine ['kæθrɪn]
Kowloon [ˌkaʊˈluːn]
Lagos ['leɪgɒs]
Lantau Island [ˌlænˈtaʊ]
Lincoln Park [ˌlɪŋkən ˈpɑːk]
London ['lʌndən]
Los Angeles [lɒs ændʒəliːz]
Maharashtra [ˌmæhəˈræʃtrə]
Marine Drive [məˈriːn]
Melbourne ['melbən, 'melbɔːn]
Mexico City [ˌmeksɪkəʊ ˈsɪti]
Miami [maɪˈæmi]
Moscow ['mɒskəʊ]
Mumbai ['mʊmbaɪ]
Munich ['mjuːnɪk], *München*
Nashville ['næʃvɪl]
New Delhi [ˌnjuː ˈdeli]
New Orleans [ˌnjuː ˈɔːlɪənz, ˌnjuː ɔːˈliːnz]
New York [ˌnjuː ˈjɔːk]
Onslow ['ɒnzləʊ]
Paris ['pærɪs]
Provincetown ['prɒvɪnstaʊn]
Queensland ['kwiːnzlænd]
Rio De Janeiro [ˌriːəʊ də ʒəˈnɪərəʊ]
Rome [rəʊm]
Sandton ['sændtən]
San Francisco [ˌsæn frənˈsɪskəʊ]
Sanjay Gandhi Nagar [ˌsændʒeɪ ˌgændi naˈgɑːr]
São Paulo [saʊm ˈpaʊləʊ]
Soweto [səˈwetəʊ]
Sydney ['sɪdni]
Tampa ['tæmpə]
Tara Downs [ˌtɑːrə ˈdaʊnz]
Tasmania [ˌtæzˈmeɪniə]
Tokyo ['təʊkiəʊ]
Toronto [təˈrɒntəʊ]
Uluru [ˌuːləˈruː, ˈuːləruː]
Uluru-Kata Tjuta [ˌuːləruː ˌkætə ˈtjuːtə]
Ur [ɜː]
Uruk ['uːrʊk]
Venice ['venɪs]
Victoria [vɪkˈtɔːriə]
Victoria Peak [vɪkˌtɔːriə ˈpiːk]
Weeki Wachee Springs [ˌwiːki ˌwɑːtʃi ˈsprɪŋz]
Wellington ['welɪŋtən]
Worita [wəˈriːtə]
Yarra ['jærə]

Other names
(Andere Namen)

the **African National Congress** [ˌæfrɪkən ˌnæʃnəl ˈkɒŋgres]
Alice in Wonderland ['ælɪs], ['wʌndələænd]
Ashmead's Kernel [ˌæʃmiːdz ˈkɜːnəl]

List of names

Batman [ˈbætmæn]
Big Buddha [ˌbɪg ˈbʊdə]
Bollywood [ˈbɒlɪwʊd]
the **Champions League** [ˈtʃæmpɪənz liːg]
Charles Ross [ˌtʃɑːlz ˈrɒs]
Cupid [ˈkjuːpɪd]
Discovery [dɪsˈkʌvəri]
Disneyland [ˈdɪznɪlænd]
the **East India Company** [ˌiːst_ˈɪndɪə ˌkʌmpəni]
Excalibur [ekˈskælɪbə]
the **Excelsior Hotel** [ekˈselsɪə]
Ffordd Deiniol [ˌfɔːð ˈdeɪnɪɒl]
Gascoyne's Scarlet [ˌgæskɔɪnz ˈskɑːlət]
Gateway School [ˈgeɪtweɪ]
Gold Reef City [ˌgəʊld riːf ˈsɪti]
Hogwarts [ˈhɒgwɔːts]
Ida Red [ˌaɪdə ˈred]
Jaguar [ˈdʒægjʊə]
Jonathan [ˈdʒɒnəθən]
Juluka [dʒʊˈluːkə]
Love Parade [ˈlʌv pəˌreɪd]
Mahatma („Große Seele") [məˈhɑːtmə]
Majiraj [ˌmædʒɪˈrɑːdʒ]
McIntosh [ˈmækɪntɒʃ]
Moorfield High School [ˈmʊəfiːld]
Motown [ˈməʊtaʊn]
the **Nobel Peace Prize** [nəʊˈbel]
Northern Spy [ˌnɔːðən ˈspaɪ]
Orange Pippin [ˌɒrɪndʒ ˈpɪpɪn]
Oz [ɒz]
Russett [ˈrʌsɪt]
Rusty [ˈrʌsti]
Savuka [səˈvuːkə]
Tasmanian Devil [tæzˌmeɪnɪən ˈdevəl]
Tatji [ˈtætʃi]
Tin Annie [ˌtɪn ˈæni]
Universal Men [ˌjuːnɪˌvɜːsəl ˈmen]
Wandies [ˈwɒndiːz]
Worcester [ˈwʊstə]
Zulu [ˈzuːluː]

English sounds (Englische Laute)

Die Lautschrift in den eckigen Klammern zeigt dir, wie ein Wort ausgesprochen wird.
In der folgenden Übersicht findest du alle Lautzeichen.

Vokale (Selbstlaute)

[iː]	green	[ʊ]	book	[ɪə]	here	
[i]	happy	[ʌ]	mum	[eə]	where	
[ɪ]	in	[ɜː]	T-shirt	[ʊə]	tour	
[e]	yes	[ə]	a partner			
[æ]	black	[eɪ]	skate			
[ɑː]	park	[aɪ]	time			
[ɒ]	song	[ɔɪ]	boy			
[ɔː]	morning	[əʊ]	old			
[uː]	blue	[aʊ]	now			

Konsonanten (Mitlaute)

[b]	box	[l]	hello	[ʒ]	television
[p]	play	[r]	red	[tʃ]	teacher
[d]	dad	[w]	we	[dʒ]	Germany
[t]	ten	[j]	you	[θ]	thanks
[g]	good	[f]	full	[ð]	this
[k]	cat	[v]	very	[h]	he
[m]	mum	[s]	sister	[x]	loch
[n]	no	[z]	please		
[ŋ]	sing	[ʃ]	shop		

The English alphabet (Das englische Alphabet)

a [eɪ]
b [biː]
c [siː]
d [diː]
e [iː]
f [ef]
g [dʒiː]
h [eɪtʃ]
i [aɪ]
j [dʒeɪ]
k [keɪ]
l [el]
m [em]
n [en]
o [əʊ]
p [piː]
q [kjuː]
r [ɑː]
s [es]
t [tiː]
u [juː]
v [viː]
w [ˈdʌbljuː]
x [eks]
y [waɪ]
z [zed]

Irregular verbs

Infinitive	Simple past form	Past participle	
(to) be	was/were	been	sein
(to) beat	beat	beaten	schlagen; besiegen
(to) become	became	become	werden
(to) begin	began	begun	beginnen, anfangen (mit)
(to) bleed [iː]	bled [e]	bled [e]	bluten
(to) blow	blew	blown	wehen, blasen, pusten
(to) break	broke	broken	zerbrechen, kaputt machen
(to) bring	brought	brought	(mit-, her)bringen
(to) broadcast	broadcast	broadcast	ausstrahlen; senden
(to) build	built	built	bauen
(to) buy	bought	bought	kaufen
(to) catch	caught	caught	fangen; erwischen
(to) choose [uː]	chose [əʊ]	chosen [əʊ]	(aus)wählen; (sich) aussuchen
(to) come	came	come	kommen
(to) cut	cut	cut	schneiden
(to) deal with [iː]	dealt [e]	dealt [e]	sich beschäftigen mit
(to) do	did	done [ʌ]	tun, machen
(to) draw	drew	drawn	zeichnen
(to) drink	drank	drunk	trinken
(to) drive [aɪ]	drove	driven [ɪ]	(ein Auto) fahren
(to) eat	ate [et, eɪt]	eaten	essen
(to) fall	fell	fallen	(hin)fallen, stürzen
(to) feed	fed	fed	füttern
(to) feel	felt	felt	(sich) fühlen; sich anfühlen
(to) fight	fought	fought	kämpfen
(to) find	found	found	finden
(to) fly	flew	flown	fliegen
(to) forget	forgot	forgotten	vergessen
(to) forgive	forgave	forgiven	vergeben, verzeihen
(to) get	got	got	bekommen; holen; werden; (hin)kommen
(to) give	gave	given	geben
(to) go	went	gone [ɒ]	gehen, fahren
(to) grow	grew	grown	wachsen; anbauen, anpflanzen
(to) hang	hung	hung	(etwas) aufhängen
(to) have (have got)	had	had	haben, besitzen
(to) hear [ɪə]	heard [ɜː]	heard [ɜː]	hören
(to) hide [aɪ]	hid [ɪ]	hidden [ɪ]	(sich) verstecken
(to) hit	hit	hit	treffen; schlagen
(to) hold	held	held	halten
(to) hurt	hurt	hurt	wehtun; verletzen
(to) keep	kept	kept	(be)halten; aufbewahren
(to) kneel [niːl]	knelt [nelt]	knelt	sich hinknien
(to) know [nəʊ]	knew [njuː]	known [nəʊn]	wissen; kennen
(to) lay the table	laid	laid	den Tisch decken
(to) lead [iː]	led [e]	led [e]	führen
(to) leave	left	left	(weg)gehen; abfahren; verlassen; zurücklassen
(to) lend	lent	lent	leihen
(to) let	let	let	lassen

Irregular verbs

Infinitive	Simple past form	Past participle	
(to) lie	lay	lain	liegen
(to) lose [uː]	lost [ɒ]	lost [ɒ]	verlieren
(to) make	made	made	machen; bauen; bilden
(to) mean [iː]	meant [e]	meant [e]	bedeuten; meinen
(to) meet	met	met	(sich) treffen
(to) pay	paid	paid	bezahlen
(to) put	put	put	legen, stellen, *(wohin)* tun
(to) read [iː]	read [e]	read [e]	lesen
(to) ride [aɪ]	rode	ridden [ɪ]	reiten; *(Rad)* fahren
(to) ring	rang	rung	klingeln, läuten
(to) rise [aɪ]	rose	risen [ɪ]	(auf)steigen
(to) run	ran	run	rennen, (ver)laufen
(to) say [eɪ]	said [e]	said [e]	sagen
(to) see	saw	seen	sehen; besuchen, aufsuchen
(to) seek [iː]	sought [ɔː]	sought	suchen
(to) sell	sold	sold	verkaufen
(to) send	sent	sent	schicken, senden
(to) set a trap	set	set	eine Falle stellen
(to) sew	sewed	sewn	(an)nähen
(to) shake	shook	shaken	schütteln
(to) shine	shone [ɒ, *AE* əʊ]	shone [ɒ]	scheinen *(Sonne)*
(to) shoot [uː]	shot [ɒ]	shot [ɒ]	(er)schießen
(to) show	showed	shown	zeigen
(to) shut up	shut	shut	den Mund halten
(to) sing	sang	sung	singen
(to) sink	sank	sunk	sinken
(to) sit	sat	sat	sitzen; sich setzen
(to) sleep	slept	slept	schlafen
(to) speak	spoke	spoken	sprechen
(to) spend	spent	spent	*(Zeit)* verbringen; *(Geld)* ausgeben
(to) spit	spat	spat	spucken
(to) spread [e]	spread [e]	spread [e]	(sich) ausbreiten, (sich) verbreiten
(to) stand	stood	stood	stehen; sich (hin)stellen
(to) steal	stole	stolen	stehlen
(to) stick	stuck	stuck	herausragen, herausstehen; (auf)kleben
(to) sweep [iː]	swept [e]	swept [e]	fegen, kehren
(to) swim	swam	swum	schwimmen
(to) take	took	taken	nehmen; (weg-, hin)bringen; dauern, *(Zeit)* brauchen
(to) teach	taught	taught	unterrichten, lehren
(to) tear [eə]	tore [ɔː]	torn [ɔː]	(zer)reißen
(to) tell	told	told	erzählen, berichten
(to) think	thought	thought	denken, glauben, meinen
(to) throw	threw	thrown	werfen
(to) understand	understood	understood	verstehen
(to) upset	upset	upset	ärgern, kränken, aus der Fassung bringen
(to) wake up	woke	woken	aufwachen; wecken
(to) wear [eə]	wore [ɔː]	worn [ɔː]	tragen *(Kleidung)*
(to) win	won [ʌ]	won [ʌ]	gewinnen
(to) write	wrote	written	schreiben

Was DU im Klassenzimmer sagen kannst

Du brauchst Hilfe
Tut mir leid, ich habe das nicht verstanden.
Können Sie/Kannst du das bitte noch einmal sagen?
Können Sie/Kannst du bitte lauter sprechen?
Kann ich eine Frage stellen?
Können Sie/Kannst du mir bitte helfen?
Was bedeutet …?
Ich habe … – ist das auch richtig?
Können Sie … bitte buchstabieren?
Wie spricht man das erste Wort in Zeile 2 aus?
Können Sie es bitte an die Tafel schreiben?
Tut mir leid, ich finde es nicht. Auf welcher Seite sind wir?
Was haben wir (als Hausaufgabe) auf?

Du hast ein Problem
Entschuldigung, dass ich zu spät komme/meine Hausaufgaben nicht gemacht habe, Herr …/Frau …
Tut mir leid, dass ich mein Schulheft vergessen habe.
Ich bin noch nicht fertig.
Entschuldigung, ich habe nicht zugehört/ das weiß ich nicht.
Ich kann Nummer 3 nicht lösen.

Über Texte reden
Die Geschichte/Das Theaterstück/Das Gedicht/ Das Lied/ Der Film handelt von …
Die Handlung spielt während/in …
In Zeile 15–20 steht, dass …
Die Hauptfigur ist …
Der Mann/Die Frau/… scheint sehr einsam/zornig/ traurig/… zu sein.
Die Beziehung zwischen … und … ist sonderbar/…
Es war lustig/unheimlich/langweilig/…, als …
Ich fand es gut/nicht gut, als …,
Ich fand den Schluss überraschend/blöd/… , weil …
Ich finde die Geschichte ist lustig/aufregend/…, weil …
Die Geschichte hat mich glücklich/wütend/… gemacht.

In einer Diskussion
Meiner Meinung nach …
Ich will dir ein Beispiel geben: …
Erstens … / Zweitens … / Und schließlich …
Ich stimme (…) zu/nicht zu, weil …
Ja, du hast Recht. / Genau!
Was Tim sagt, ist richtig/falsch.
Du sagst …, aber …
Was genau meinst du?
Du könntest Recht haben, aber …
Ich bin mir nicht sicher. Vielleicht …
Was meinst du (zu …)?

Bei der Partner- oder Gruppenarbeit
Kann ich mit … arbeiten?

What YOU can say in the classroom

You need help
Sorry, I don't understand.
Can you say that again, please?
Can you speak louder, please?
Can I ask a question, please?
Can you help me, please?
What does … mean?
I've got … – is that right too?
Can you spell …, please?
How do you say the first word in line 2?
Can you write that on the board, please?
Sorry, I can't find it. What page are we on?
What's for homework?

You're in trouble
Sorry, I'm late/ I haven't done my homework, Mr/Mrs/Ms/Miss …
Sorry, I've forgotten my exercise book.
I haven't finished yet.
Sorry, I wasn't listening / I don't know.
I can't do number 3.

Talking about texts
The story/play/poem/ song/ film is about …
The action takes place during/in …
In lines 15–20 it says that …
The main character is …
The man/woman/… seems to be very lonely/ angry/ sad/…
The relationship between … and … is strange/…
It was funny/scary/boring/… when …
I liked it/didn't like it when …
I found the ending surprising/stupid/… because …
I think the story is funny/exciting/…because …
The story made me (feel) happy/angry/…

In a discussion
In my opinion …
Let me give you an example: …
First … / Second … / And finally …
I agree/disagree with … because …
Yes, you're right. / Exactly!
What Tim says is right/wrong.
You say …, but …
What do you mean exactly?
You may be right, but …
I'm not so sure. Maybe/Perhaps …
What do you think (about …)?

Working with a partner or in a group
Can I work with …?

Classroom English

Was machen wir als Erstes?	What are we going to do first?
Lass/Lasst uns die Aufgabe noch einmal lesen.	Let's read the task again.
Wer ist dran? – Ich bin/Du bist dran, das zu schreiben/die Fragen zu stellen.	Whose turn is it? – It's my/your turn to write/ask questions.
Ich finde, wir sollten/könnten …	I think we should/could …
Hast du eine Idee/einen Vorschlag?	Have you got any ideas?
Mir gefällt deine Idee sehr gut. / Das klingt gut.	I really like your idea. / That sounds good.
Wo können wir etwas zu … finden?	Where can we find out about …?
Was hast du im Internet gefunden?	What did you find on the internet?
Was hältst du von meinem Text/Bild/…?	What do you think of my text/picture/…?
Ich verstehe nicht, was du meinst. / Ich bin mir da nicht sicher.	I don't understand what you mean./I'm not sure about that.
Lass/Lasst uns … auf unser Poster schreiben.	Let's write … on our poster.
Lass/Lasst uns das Bild hier hinsetzen/-kleben.	Let's put the picture here.
Wie viel Zeit haben wir (noch)?	How much (more) time do we have?
Wir haben nur noch … Minuten Zeit.	We've only got … minutes left.
Lass/Lasst uns … schnell machen und dann mit … fortfahren.	Let's do … quickly and then go on to …
Vielleicht sollten wir … weglassen / etwas zu … sagen.	Maybe we should leave out … / say something about …
Wir sind fast fertig. Ich denke, wir sollten … weglassen.	We've nearly finished. I think we should leave out …

Bei einer Präsentation / Giving a talk / presentation

Das Thema meines Vortrags ist …	The topic of my talk/presentation is …
Ich werde meinen Vortrag in … Teile gliedern.	I'm going to divide my talk into … parts.
Erstens/Als nächstes/… würde ich gern …	First/Next/… I would like to …
Zum Schluss werde ich etwas über … erzählen.	Finally, I'll tell you something about …
Auf der ersten Folie links/rechts könnt ihr sehen …	On the first slide on the left/right you can see …
Zusammenfassend möchte ich sagen, …	To sum things up I'd like to say …
Gibt es/Habt ihr Fragen oder Kommentare dazu?	Are there any questions or comments?

What YOUR TEACHER says / Was DEIN/E LEHRER/IN sagt

Copy/Fill in the chart/form.	Kopiert/Füllt die Tabelle/das Formular aus.
Correct the mistakes.	Verbessert die Fehler.
Don't forget to check your spelling.	Vergesst nicht die Rechtschreibung zu überprüfen.
Be careful with the word order.	Achtet auf die Satzstellung.
Write it on the board, please.	Schreibe es bitte an die Tafel.
Compare your sentences/answers/… with your partner.	Vergleiche deine Sätze/Antworten/… mit deinem Partner/deiner Partnerin.
Discuss … with your partner/in your group.	Diskutiert … mit einem Partner/einer Partnerin/in der Gruppe.
Practise/Act out the dialogue with a partner, please.	Bitte übe/spiele den Dialog mit deinem Partner/deiner Partnerin.
Walk around the class and ask other students.	Geht durch die Klasse und fragt andere Schüler/innen.
Take notes.	Macht euch Notizen.
Imagine you are …	Stellt euch vor, ihr seid …
What do you think of …?	Was haltet ihr von …?
Have you got any other ideas?	Habt ihr andere/sonstige Ideen?
Give three reasons.	Nenne drei Gründe.
Have you finished?	Seid ihr/Bist du fertig?
Present your talk/poster/… to the class.	Präsentiere dein Referat/Poster/… vor der Klasse.
Do exercise 3 for homework, please.	Macht bitte Übung 3 als Hausaufgabe.

Illustrationen

Silke Bachmann, Hamburg (S. 14; 25; 99 2. v. unten (u. 115); 99 unten (u. 121); 120 unten); **Christian Bartz**, Berlin (S. 79 oben); **Roland Beier**, Berlin (S. 9 oben; 67; 87; 106 (u. 99 5. v. oben); 123–126; 129–193); **Carlos Borrell**, Berlin (vordere und hintere Umschlaginnenseite; S. 9 unten; 10; 11 unten re.; 100/101 Hintergrund); **Dylan Gibson**, Pitlochry (S. 36; 42; 90); **Christian Görke**, Berlin (S. 51 (u. Inhaltsverz.); 103; 120 oben; 127 oben); **Graham-Cameron Illustration**, UK: **Eoin Coveney** (S. 93–94); **Alfred Schüssler**, Frankfurt/Main (S. 91 oben re.; 102 Vignetten (M))

Bildquellen

A1PIX, Taufkirchen (S. 53 unten Mitte: JTB); Your_Photo_Today/Gerolf Nießner (S. 33 Mitte); **Action Press**: Rex Features (S. 17 re. un.), Om Shanti Om (movie title), from left: Deepika Padukone, Shahrukh Khan (actors), 2007. © Eros International/ Courtesy: Everett Collection (S. 62 un. re.); Frank Bienewald (S. 66 Mitte un. re.); **Alamy**, Abingdon (S. 12 Bild B (u. 126): photocay; S. 13 Mitte li.: Buzz Pictures; S. 16 un. re.: © Cindy Hopkins, S. 19 unten: Susanna Bennett; S. 30 unten re.: Brownstock Inc. (RF); S. 32 unten li.: BlueMoon Stock (RF), unten 2. v. re.: Rob Walls; S. 37: SHOUT; S. 56 oben re.: AfriPics.com; S. 57 unten: PCL; © Prisma Bildagentur AG (S. 75 Mitte); S. 78 Bild A: Photofusion Picture Library, Bild D: Steve Skjold; S. 79 Bild G: JJ pixs (RF); S. 88 tin (M): FB-StockPhoto; S. 89 unten li.: Jim West, unten Mitte: Bubbles Photolibrary, unten re.: PhotoAlto (RF); S. 104 Bild 3: David Page, unten: Alex Maddox; S. 111 unten re.: Bill Brooks; S. 139 „Kit's Wilderness" teenagers: BananaStock (RF), „The Australian Connection" man: StockImage/Pixland (RF)); **Associated Press**, Frankfurt/Main (S. 33 unten 2. v. li.; S. 101 unten re.; S. 112 unten: Gurinder Osan); Australia Post (S. 139 „From Prison to Prosperity" stamp); **BBC Motion Gallery**, London, UK (S. 53 oben); **Chuck Braverman. Art and Design** © 2004 **New Video Group, Inc.** (S. 85 film still taken from "High school boot camp"); **CartoonStock**, Bath (S. 39: Ralph Hagen; S. 82: Dave Carpenter; S. 83 unten (u. 98): W. B. Park; S. 121 unten: KES); **Cinetext**, Frankfurt/Main (S. 61 re.: Kinowelt); **Corbis**, Düsseldorf: S. 6 Bild 1: Dennis Degnan; S. 7 Bild 2: Aurora Open/Lars Schneider (RF); S. 12 Bild C: © 2/Sean Murphy/Ocean; S. 16 oben re.: Charles & Josette Lenars; S. 32 unten re.: Lawrence Manning; S. 50 oben: Nik Wheeler; S. 57 2. v. oben: Jon Hicks; S. 78 Bild B: © Wavebreak Media LTD/LightWave; S. 80 (und Inhaltsv.): © Georgia Kuhn; S. 84 (ob. re.): © Alejandro Almaraz; S. 86 un.: © Nancy Honey; S. 110 unten re.: Araldo de Luca); **Corel Library** (S. 41; S. 139 „Kit's Wilderness" landscape, „Pick a Poem" scrabble tiles, LOVE sign, „The Australian Connection" fish, „From Prison to Prosperity" sea); **Cornelsen Verlag**, Berlin (S. 44 oben; S. 45 oben: Michael Weihrauch; S. 89 (Mitte): Clair Cunningham); **ECHO BRIDGE ENTERTAINMENT LLC**, Needham, USA (S. 49); **Gareth Evans**, Berlin (S. 40); **Fotofinder**: jfmueller (S. 64 un.); **Fotosearch**, Waukesha (Inhaltsverz. 2. v. li. (u. 32 Mitte re.): WestEnd61 (RF)); **F1online**, J.W.Alker/Imagebroker (S. 8 li.ob.); **Fountain Valley School of Colorado**, Colorado Springs (S. 89 oben website, logo (M)); **Getty Images**, München (Inhaltsverz. oben re. (u. 78): Rubberball (RF); Inhaltsverz. 2. v. re. (u. 53 re.): Manfred Gottschalk; S. 6/7 Uluru: Ted Mead; S. 7 Bild 3: Bec Parsons, Bild 6: Doug Armand; S. 9: Jeff Hunter; S. 12 oben girl (M): Jack Hollingsworth (RF); S. 13 oben: Anthony Ong (RF), unten li.: James Knowler, unten re.: Tony Lewis; S. 16 oben li.: AFP; S. 22: Ian Waldie; S. 28 Bild 5: UpperCut Images (RF); S. 29 oben: Annie Griffiths Belt; S. 32 unten 2. v. li.: Sean Ellis; S. 33 oben li.: Daly & Newton, unten li.: Image Source (RF), unten re.: John Kelly; S. 52 oben re.: AFP; S. 53 Mitte li.; S. 53 (Mi. li.): Mark Dadswell; S. 60: AFP; S. 63 re.: AFP; S. 66 unten (u. 99 u. 112): AFP; S. 68 oben, unten: Allan Danahar (RF); S. 99 2. v. oben (u. 103), 5. v. unten (u. 109): Redferns); **Bonnie Glänzer**, Berlin (S. 46 unten); **Guardian News & Media Ltd 2008** (S. 17 oben: Barbara McMahon); **Marcus Hansson**, Göteborg (S. 53 unten li.); **The Hickory Daily Record**, Hickory (S. 88 unten website, logo, unten li.: Robert Reed); **Inkcinct Cartoons**, Soldiers Hill (S. 11 unten li.); **iStockphoto**, Calgary (Inhaltsverz. unten (u. 33 oben re.): LajosRepasi; S. 6 oben: Renee Lee; S. 12 Bild A: John Simmons; S. 20 re.: Timothy Ball; S. 26 unten li.: Gene Chutka, re.: Jeffrey Smith; S. 27 (u. 101): susan flashman; S. 29 unten: Chuck Babbitt; S. 30 oben: Pali Rao, unten li. monitor (M): zak, question mark (M): Zeffss1; S. 32 oben li.: Lisa Klumpp; S. 33 unten 2. v. re.: Rich Legg; S. 44 unten: dawn liljenquist; S. 55: Kuzma; S. 61 oben li.: Chris Schmidt; S. 62 (u. 64) Hintergrund pattern: Niels Laan; S. 70 unten re.: Diane White Rosier; S. 71: Chris Schmidt; S. 74 li.: Søren Sielemann, 2. v. li.: Rich Legg, Mitte: Chris Schmidt; 2. v. re.: ronen, re.: Suzanne Tucker; S. 79 Bild I lipstick kiss (M): konstantin32; S. 99 3. v. oben (u. 104): James Bowyer; S. 100 Mitte: KJA; S. 102 lake (M): Paul Morton; S. 104 Bild 1: Linda & Colin McKie, Bild 4 u. Bild 5: david franklin; S. 111 unten li.: Nell Redmond; S. 137 unten: james steidl);

Acknowledgments

Lonely Planet Images, London (S. 57 2. v. unten: Richard I'Anson); **http://manateens.blogspot.com** (S. 88 oben website, background, logo (M): used with permission of Volunteer ManaTEE. Volunteer Services of Manatee County, Inc. (Stand 15.06.2009)); **mauritius images**, Juergen & Christine Sohn (S. 7 un.li); Mittenwald (S. 89 Mitte: Cultura Images Ltd. (RF)); © **Ewa Nogiec/iamprovincetown.com** (S. 91 oben li.); **Okapia**, Frankfurt/Main: (S. 23: Hans Reinhard); **Onslow College**, Johnsonville (S. 97 logo, students: James Gilberd); **Photofusion Picture Library**, London (Inhaltsverz. unten (u. 79 Bild H): Ulrike Preuss); **Photolibrary**, London (S. 62 oben re.: Imagestate/Christophe Bluntzer; S. 78 Bild E (u. 79 background): Cultura/Britt Erlanson; S. 108: age fotostock/Herve Donnezan; S. 111 oben re.: imagebroker.net/White Star/M Hernandez); Photoshot: World Pictures (S. 50 un. re.); **Picture - Alliance**, Frankfurt/Main (S. 13 Mitte re.: dpa – Report; S. 28 Bild 3: dpa-Report/ZB/Martin Schutt; S. 32 Mitte li.: dpa – Fotoreport; S. 53 unten re.: Bildagentur Huber; S. 56 unten: Sven Simon; S. 59: dpa; S. 63 li.: GODONG/Philippe Lissac; S. 65 re.: dpa; S. 72: empics; S. 99 4. v. unten (u. 110): dpa – Report; S. 100 unten: KPA; S. 101 oben: NHPA/photoshot, unten li.: dpa-Report; S. 110 oben Mitte: Bildagentur Huber, unten li.: akg-images; S. 111 oben li.: Berlin Picture Gate); **The Picture Desk**, London (S. 73 li. u. re.: Film 4/Celador Films/Pathe International/The Kobal Collection; S. 76 Mitte li.: EON/DANJAQ/SONY/The Kobal Collection, Mitte re.: New Line Cinema/The Kobal Collection, unten li.: LUCASFILM/20TH CENTURY FOX/The Kobal Collection, unten Mitte: 20TH CENTURY FOX/The Kobal Collection, unten re.: 20TH CENTURY FOX/The Kobal Collection); **Damaria Senne/http://damariasenne.blogspot.com**, Johannesburg (S. 57 oben); **Shooting Jozi, a project of Global Studio 2007 and the individuals who participated** (S. 58 (u. 128)); **Shutterstock**, New York (Inhaltsverz. oben li. (u. 21): ILYA GENKIN; S. 7 Bild 4: Sharyn Young; S. 8 re.: Andrei Marincas; S. 11 oben: Susan Law Cain; S. 12 oben trees (M): aliciahh; S. 19 oben: Carsten Reisinger; S. 20 li.: Ashley Whitworth; S. 21 oben: aliciahh; S. 26 oben: Rob Wilson; S. 28 Bild 1: Rob Wilson, Bild 2: Gregory Gerber; S. 32/33 Hintergrund: javarman; S. 32 oben re.: Shmeliova Natalia; S. 45 2. v. unten: Tracy Whiteside, unten: Jeff Banke; S. 52 background pattern: fotohunter, li. (u. 56 u. 62): Chris P.; S. 54 unten: KONG; S. 56 Hintergrund: Ferin; S. 61 unten li.: Monkey Business Images; S. 65 background pattern: claus+mutschler; S. 70 oben li.: Robert Ranson, oben re.: Rick Becker-Leckrone, unten li.: Amy Myers; S. 76 oben li.: Marina Krasnorutskaya, oben re.: Valeria73; S. 79 Bild I mobile (M): Tatiana Popova; S. 83 oben li.: Jaimie Duplass, oben re.: Carme Balcells; S. 89 unten li.: Ronald Sumners; S. 91 unten: Andresr; S. 95: Alex Staroseltsev; S. 99 oben: Patsy A. Jacks, 4. v. oben (u. 105): Serg64, 6. v. oben (u. 107): Pinkcandy; S. 100 oben: oksana.perkins; S. 135: Holger Mette; S. 137 oben: Tatiana Popova); **Superbild Bildagentur**, Taufkirchen (S. 101 Mitte li.: JTB); **ullstein bild**, Berlin (S. 65 Berlin emblem: Probst, li.: Keute); **vario-images**, Bonn (S. 88 oben snorkeling (M)); **Vector-Image**s, Bradenton (S. 64 Mumbai emblem); Fotoagentur VISUM, Hamburg (S. 28 Bild 4: Wildlight); **voicephotography**, HoChiMinh City (S. 110 oben re.: Nicole Vooijs); **Martynka Wawrzyniak**, New York (S. 46 oben; S. 47); **Wellington High School**, Wellington (S. 43)

Titelbild

Plainpicture, Hamburg (jeans with map (M): Sina Preikschat); **Alamy**, Abingdon (Sydney Opera (M): Iconotec (RF)); **Corel Library** (flag background (M))

Textquellen

S. 17 Children were stolen for a racist ideal. Now a nation says sorry. Adapted from "Snatched from home for a racist ideal. Now a nation says sorry" by Barbara McMahon, 11.2.2008, http://www.guardian.co.uk/world/2008/feb/11/australia. Copyright Guardian News & Media Ltd 2008; **S. 20–24** (u. 138) In the outback. Abridged and adapted from „Children of the Wind - A Prayer for Blue Delaney" by Kirsty Murray. Allen & Unwin, Crows Nest, Australia, 2005 (www.allenandunwin.com); **S. 43** Wellington High School article printed with permission; **S. 49** Job Day from SPEAK by Laurie Halse Anderson. Copyright © 1999 by Laurie Halse Anderson. Reprinted by permission of Farrar, Straus and Giroux, LLC; **S. 50** A world of cities? Adapted from "The Endless City: The Urban Age Project" by the London School of Economics and Deutsche Bank's Alfred Herrhausen Society, ed. Burdett & Sudjic, Phaidon. London, 2007; **S. 53** Hong Kong by Brian Ng Kwok Leong; **S. 57** Five reasons why I love Johannesburg. Adapted from "10 Reasons I Love Johannesburg – Part 1" http://ezinearticles.com/?10-Reasons-I-Love-Johannesburg---Part-1&id=856855 and "10 Reasons I Love Johannesburg – Part 2" http://ezinearticles.com/?10-Reasons-I-Love-Johannesburg--Part-2&id=856895 by Damaria Senne (http://damariasenne.blogspot.com); **S. 63** Mumbai slums. Abridged and adapted from „Shadow Cities: A Billion

Squatters, A New Urban World" by Robert Neuwirth. Routledge, New York, 2004. Reprinted by permission of Dunow, Carlson & Lerner Literary Agency. Copyright 2004, Robert Neuwirth. First appeared in Shadow Cities; **S. 64–65** Mumbai homes. Abridged and adapted from KOYAL DARK, MANGO SWEET by Kashmira Sheth. Copyright © 2006. Used with permission of the author. All Rights Reserved; **S. 68** Etiquette, Getting around, Emergencies, Precautions. Reproduced with permission from Best of Mumbai © 2006 Lonely Planet Publications Pty Ltd; **S. 69** Slumdog Millionaire: changing film-making in India. Abridged and adapted from "How Slumdog Millionaire is changing film-making in India" by Paul MacInnes, Mumbai, 4 June 2009, http://www.guardian.co.uk/film/2009/jun/04/slumdog-millionaire-india (Stand 29.07.2009). Copyright Guardian News & Media Ltd 2009; **S. 81** 14: a txt msg pom. Taken from "The message is the medium" by Victor Keegan, 3.5.2001, http://www.guardian.co.uk/technology/2001/may/03/internet.poetry Poem © Julia Bird, 2001/www.juliabird.wordpress.com; **S. 84** 'ASBO has helped me'. Adapted from "ASBO made me give up life as a yob". http://www.mirror.co.uk/news/top-stories/2007/11/13/asbo-made-me-give-up-life-as-a-yob-115875-20099323/ by Jeremy Armstrong, 13.11.2007. Mirror Syndication International, London; **S. 88** Springs Clean-up. Text adapted from http://manateens.blogspot.com/ (Stand 15.06.2009) used with permission of Volunteer ManaTEE. Volunteer Services of Manatee County, Inc, Hickory Soup Kitchen. Adapted from "Students soup up kitchen" by Sarah Newell Williamson, 6.8.2008, http://www2.hickoryrecord.com/content/2008/aug/06/students-soup-kitchen/. Used with permission of The Hickory Daily Record, Hickory; **S. 89** Community Service. Adapted from http://www.fvs.edu/podium/default.aspx?t=39763. Used with permission of Fountain Valley School of Colorado, Colorado Springs; **S. 91** Ein Beitrag für sich und die Gesellschaft. Auszug aus der Informationsbroschüre "Für mich und für andere" http://www.bmfsfj.de/bmfsfj/generator/RedaktionBMFSFJ/Broschuerenstelle/Pdf-Anlagen/Fuer-mich-und-fuer-andere-FSJ-FOEJ-GFD,property=pdf,bereich=bmfsfj,sprache=de,rwb=true.pdf. Herausgegeben vom Bundesministerium für Familie, Senioren, Frauen und Jugend. Berlin, 2008; **S. 92–94** The caller by Robert D. San Souci. Reprinted by permission of Carus Publishing Company, from DARE TO BE SCARED: THIRTEEN STORIES TO CHILL AND THRILL by Daniel D. San Souci, text © 2003 by Robert D. San Souci; **S. 97** Onslow. Used by permission of Onslow College, Wellington, NZ; **S. 105** Somewhere in the sky. Copyright © Leo Aylen. First published in "Rhymoceros: poems by Leo Aylen" (Macmillan London 1989) subsequently published as title poem in "Somewhere in the Sky" (Nelson 1996) and also in four other anthologies. It was selected as one of the poems to be performed in the 2008 Hong Kong Festival of Speech, Dreams (u. 138) by Langston Hughes. Copyright © 1994 by the Estate of Langston Hughes. Abdruck mit Genehmigung der Liepman AG, Zürich; **S. 107–108** Mr. Wah goes to Hong Kong. Abridged and adapted from "The Ferry". Taken from "The train to Lo Wu", a collection of short stories by Jess Row. The Dial Press. New York, 2005; **S. 112** A lover's embrace. Abridged and adapted from "Mumbai" by Suketu Mehta. Copyright © 1997 by Suketu Mehta. Originally published by Granta Books. Reprinted by permission of William Morris Endeavor Entertainment, LLC on behalf of the Author; **S. 113–114** Luuurve debate. From "Don't Call Me Ishmael" by Michael Gerard Bauer. Text copyright © Michael Gerard Bauer, 2006. Cover and text illustrations © Joe Bauer, 2006. First published by Omnibus Books, a division of Scholastic Australia Pty Ltd, 2006. Published in Germany by Carl Hanser Verlag München, 2008. Reproduced by permission of Scholastic Australia Pty Limited; **S. 115–119** Who's guilty? Abridged and adapted from "Just", taken from a collection of plays: Shell Connections 2005, New plays for young people, Faber & Faber, 2005. JUST © 2004, Ali Smith. All rights reserved; **S. 120–122** Bus attack Part 1, Bus attack Part 2. Abridged and adapted from case study 4, taken from http://www.restorativejustice.org.uk/Media/pdf/Case%20Study%20-%20Bus%20Co.pdf (30.06.2009). Used by permission of Restorative Justice Consortium, London; **S. 124** Auszug v. S. 516 aus „English G 2000 Wörterbuch – Das Wörterbuch zum Lehrwerk". Herausgegeben von der Langenscheidt-Redaktion Wörterbücher und der Cornelsen-Redaktion Englisch. © 2002 Cornelsen Verlag GmbH & Co. OHG, Berlin und Langenscheidt KG, Berlin und München.

Liedquellen

S. 105 *Breathe*. Words and Music by Anna Christine Nalick. © 2004 Annibonna Music/Shapiro Bernstein & Co Limited. Reproduced by permission of Faber Music Ltd. All Rights Reserved. [Lyrics only]; **S. 109** Journey's End. Musik & Text: Jonathan Paul Clegg © H.R. Music B.V. Alle Rechte für Deutschland, Österreich und Schweiz bei SMPG Publishing (Germany) GmbH.

Getting ready for a test 1

1 LISTENING Travelling to Australia

1 (Gate) 17
2 pasta (with tomato sauce); fruit juice, water, cola
3 passport office
4 2.50; 52.50
5 227; 7 (o'clock)/10:30 (a.m.)

2 LISTENING Shark attack!

Part 1: *1* C ; *2* A ; *3* B ; *4* D
Part 2: *1* C , *2* D , *3* C , *4* B , *5* C

3 LISTENING Young Australians and the internet

Student 1: E
Student 2: C
Student 3: A
Student 4: F
Student 5: G
Student 6: D

Getting ready for a test 2

1 READING Dev Patel

1 C ; *2* C ; *3* D ; *4* A ; *5* B ; *6* D ; *7* C ; *8* A

2 READING Choosing a book

Student A : 7
Student B : 5
Student C : 1
Student D : 4
Student E : 3

English-speaking countries

Country	Area (km²)	Population (2008 estimate)	Pop./km²	English as first language (est.)*	English as additional language (est.)**
Australia	7,691,951	20,951,000	3	15,581,329	2,591,660
Bahamas	13,878	335,000	24	260,000	28,000
Barbados	416	295,000	709	262,000	13,000
Belize	22,965	294,000	13	190,000	56,000
Bermuda	50	65,000	1294	63,000	***
Botswana	581,730	1,906,000	3	***	630,000
Cameroon	475,650	18,920,000	40	***	7,700,000
Canada	9,984,670	33,170,000	3	17,694,830	7,551,390
Dominica	751	67,000	89	3,000	60,000
Fiji Islands	18,333	844,000	46	4,930	14,900
Gambia	10,689	1,754,000	164	***	40,000
Ghana	238,537	24,947,000	100	***	1,400,000
Guyana	214,970	736,000	3	650,000	30,000
India	3,287,263	1,186,186,000	361	320,000	90,000,000
Ireland	70,273	4,380,000	62	4,123,000	257,000
Jamaica	10,991	2,728,000	248	2,600,000	50,00
Kenya	582,646	38,550,000	66	***	2,700,000
Lesotho	30,355	2,020,000	67	***	500,000
Liberia	97,754	3,942,000	40	600,000	2,500,000
Madagascar	587,295	20,215,000	34	***	***
Malawi	118,500	14,288,000	121	209	540,000
Malta	316	408,000	1292	2,400	370,000
Marshall Islands	181	61,000	335	***	60,000
Mauritius	2040	1,272,000	623	2,000	200,000
Micronesia	700	112,000	159	3,540	***
Namibia	824,268	2,102,000	3	14,000	300,000
Nauru	21	10,000	485	800	9,200
New Zealand	268,680	4,215,000	16	3,700,000	***
Nigeria	923,768	151,478,000	164	4,000,000	75,000,000
Pakistan	796,095	166,961,000	210	***	17,000,000
Palau	490	20,000	42	500	18,000
Papua New Guinea	462,840	6,458,000	14	150,000	3,000,000
Philippines	300,016	89,651,000	299	3,427,000	45,373,000
Puerto Rico	8,870	4,012,000	452	100,000	1,840,000
Rwanda	26,340	10,009,000	380	***	20,000
Seychelles	455	87,000	191	3,000	30,000
Sierra Leone	71,740	5,969,000	83	500,000	4,400,000
Singapore	704	4,490,000	6378	665,087	1,128,158
Solomon Islands	28,896	536,000	19	10,000	165,000
South Africa	1,219,090	48,832,000	40	3,673,203	10,000,000
Swaziland	17,363	1,148,000	66	***	50,000
Tanzania	883,749	41,464,000	47	***	4,000,000
Trinidad and Tobago	5,128	1,338,000	261	1,145,000	***
Uganda	241,548	31,903,000	132	***	2,500,000
United Kingdom	242,495	61,019,000	253	58,100,000	1,500,000
United States of America	9,826,675	308,798,000	31	215,423,557	35,964,744
Vanuatu	12,190	232,000	19	60,000	120,000
Zambia	752,612	12,154,000	16	110,000	1,800,000
Zimbabwe	390,757	13,481,000	35	250,000	5,300,000

* People who learned English as a child and prefer English in a multi-lingual environment
** People whose first language is not English but who may have to regularly use English in daily life
*** No reliable data
(Population and area: Statistisches Bundesamt, Statistisches Jahrbuch 2008; English as first or additional language: various sources)